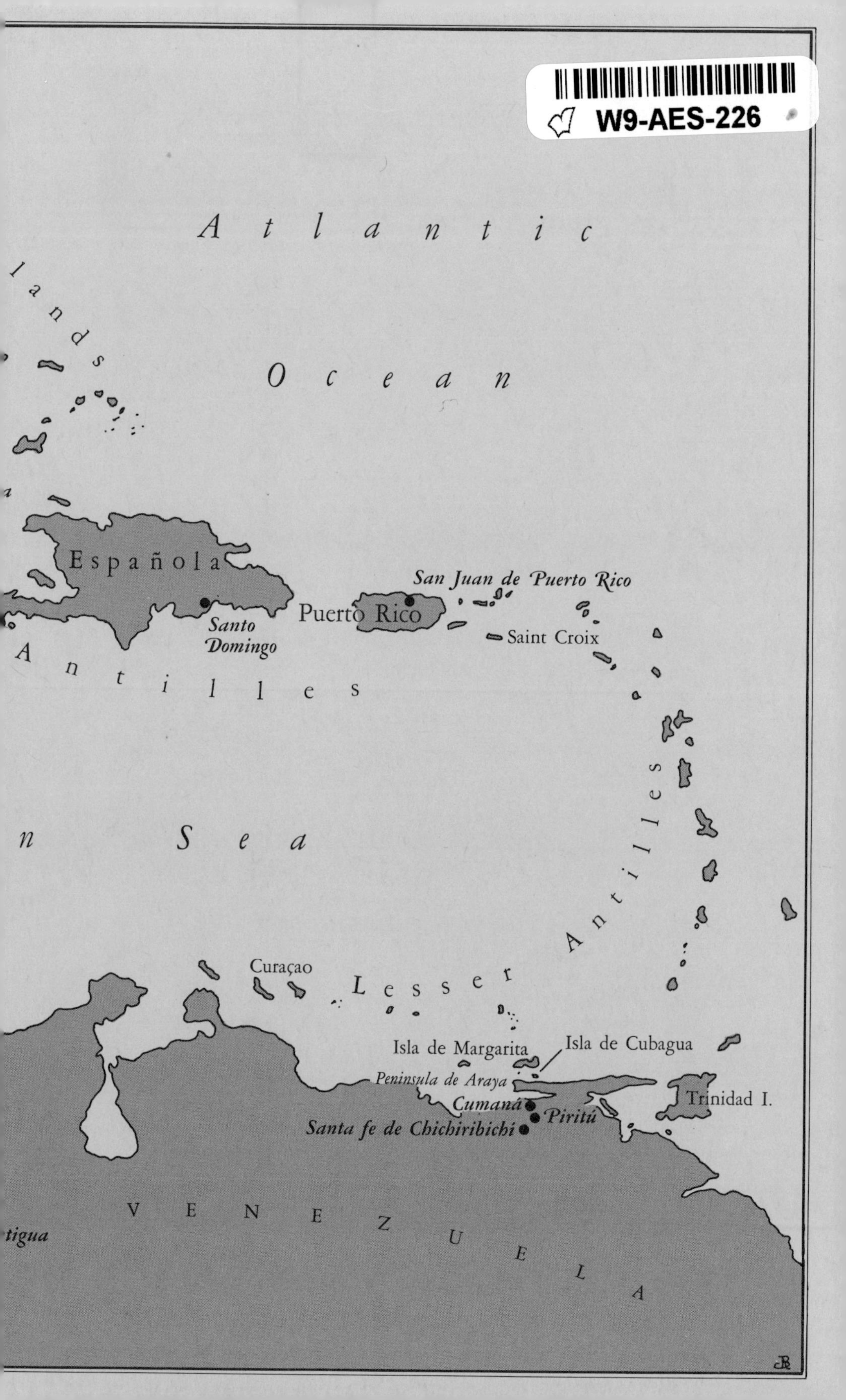
W9-AES-226
Atlantic
Ocean
Española
Santo Domingo
Puerto Rico
San Juan de Puerto Rico
Saint Croix
Antilles
Sea
Curaçao
Lesser Antilles
Isla de Margarita
Isla de Cubagua
Peninsula de Araya
Cumaná
Piritú
Santa fe de Chichiribichi
Trinidad I.
VENEZUELA

The Columbus Dynasty in the Caribbean, 1492-1526

The Columbus Dynasty in the Caribbean 1492-1526

Troy S. Floyd

UNIVERSITY OF NEW MEXICO PRESS
Albuquerque

Manufactured in the United States of America
Library of Congress Catalog Card No. 73-77918
International Standard Book No. 0-8263-0283-1
First edition

Contents

PREFACE vii

ABBREVIATIONS xi

INTRODUCTION 1

CHAPTER ONE Columbus and Española (1429–1500) 9

CHAPTER TWO Española During the Gold Rush (1500–1508) 48

CHAPTER THREE Ferdinand V and Caribbean Expansion (1508–1515) 89

CHAPTER FOUR Diego Colón and Española (1509–1515) 123

CHAPTER FIVE Reform and Readjustment (1515–1520) 159

CHAPTER SIX The Restoration of Diego Colón (1520–1523) 194

CHAPTER SEVEN Church, State, and Society by 1526 217

NOTES 234

APPENDIX I Governors of the Caribbean Islands (1492–1526) 273

APPENDIX II Royal Fifth of Gold Sent to Spain 274

APPENDIX III Royal Fifth of Pearls Sent to Spain from Cubagua and Environs 276

BIBLIOGRAPHY 277

INDEX 285

Preface

It is understandable that the historiography of the early Caribbean should often have been written according to the Romantic tradition. Biography is the belles lettres of history and Christopher Columbus has attracted a number of biographers. The inspiring social reformer, Bartolomé de las Casas, may have attracted almost as many, for his career—from one point of view—seems to be that of a fictional hero persistently battling the forces of evil and social tyranny. These two outstanding men alone have provided the focus for the beginnings of many a general history or survey course on Latin America. From Las Casas it is usual to move on to Cortés, which suggests that early Caribbean history is like a wide river, murky and forbidding with all its whirlpools and concealed eddies; across it the historian leaps thankfully, without getting his feet overly wet, on the biographical rocks of these three figures, with Cortés affording a hasty exit to the more familiar grounds of Mexico.

History can do much worse than provide inspiration through the lives of great men. Yet if the subject chosen is the history of the early Caribbean comprising, among other matters, the careers of the first colonizers, the Romantic tradition scarcely penetrates this period's maze of events, though it comes closest to doing so during Columbus's rule of Española to 1500. Because of Las Casas's late emergence, his influence on history begins only after 1515. Contrasted with his early attempts at reform in the Caribbean, this influence is more remarkable for its long-term results and its implications for liberty and equality generally than for any immediate effects it might have had. Romanticism, whether expressed in the nineteenth century by Washington Irving or in our own time by Giménez Fernández (who combines the view, to be sure, with indefatigable research), various *indigenistas,* and Falangists, has done little to advance historical knowledge. The individual heroes and villains of early Romanticism have been today displaced by heroic ethnic blocs and utopian ideologies pitted against villainous cultures and economic systems, seen alike in the past or the present. The Romantic view has proved persistent, to offer a few examples, with respect to Columbus and Ferdinand V. An essential part of Romanticism was the assumption that vice or virtue in human character was reflected in history. Columbus had long been viewed as a poor judge of men for selecting Roldán as his *alcalde mayor,* though Friar Cipriano de Utrera proved some years ago in a little known article that, upon the first vacancy, Roldán had already been designated to succeed to the position without Columbus's specific approval—and even before the latter's departure from Spain on the second voyage. Ferdinand V has been most often considered as being covetous of gold and callous to the deaths of the Indians, but José M. Doussinague has recently shown that the king's foreign policy, not his character, lay behind his incessant need for funds. The first apostolic vicar to the New World, Friar Boyl, has for years been considered quarrelsome, but Andrés Martín has shown that the friar longed to return to the meditative life—one of the principal activities of the Iberian religious orders since the early Renaissance.

Two other tendencies in the writing of history have helped close the great gaps left by the biographical approach. Institutional history has provided accounts of the government, the fiscal system, the *encomienda,* or the Church, as for instance by Clarence Haring, Silvio Zavala, or the Jesuit fathers, Lopétegui and Zubillaga. Since such topics are, however, better illustrated on the American mainland than in the Caribbean, the institutional approach tends to draw only isolated examples from early history and furnishes little sense of continuity or the historical situation that gave rise to or thwarted establishment of the institutions. Finally, nationalism has provided a matrix into which much more detail has been poured making possible, in turn, a better grasp of the Greater Antilles as a whole, even though the histories of individual islands fragment a single geographic region.

Still, all the works taken together do not provide an adequate account of the various political, economic, and social changes taking place in the Caribbean. General works, whether dealing with the whole region or all of Latin America, must necessarily gloss over little known subperiods of early history and are obliged by vagueness to commit numerous errors of fact. The identity of the governors of Española and Puerto Rico is scarcely known after 1509, when Professor Lamb ended her study of Ovando. Ponce de León's career was rather mystifying until Murga Sanz gathered much data about him. Most writers still presume that only the Dominicans were sensitive to the need for social reform (other than Las Casas), though Giménez Fernández proved otherwise; most suppose that the Indians were gathered into villages as a result of the Law of 1503 and the Laws of Burgos but this is at best a half truth. A much used text on Latin America established the first town on Puerto Rico too late and with the wrong name and founded Santiago de Cuba four years too early. A general standard history established Santo Domingo on August 5, 1494; soon after its publication, Friar Utera showed that both the date and the year were wrong. It would be pointless to name these works, for they are typical of the largest part of early Caribbean historiography, which contains many small errors of fact owing mainly to the small basis of sources on which they rest.

My purpose is to provide a fairly detailed and connected account of events and processes on the four islands from the beginnings until 1526, when most of the principal figures are dead. I have attempted to relate these events to others in Spain where the interconnection seemed especially close. Explorations along the Spanish Main and the mainland itself have been generally excluded, except as the Pearl Coast relates to the economies of Española and Puerto Rico. Since the period opens with the discovery by Columbus and ends with the death of his son Diego, signifying the end of the politically entangling Columbian viceroyalty, the periodization on political grounds alone seems justifiable. The importance of the terminal date has been suggested some years ago by Guillermo Céspedes.

I wish to express my gratitude to the Research Allocations Committee of the University of New Mexico for its generous financial aid, and to Professor Edwin Lieuwen for his valuable assistance in finding funds for the purchase of microfilm. I especially wish to thank Professor Emeritus France V. Scholes for enabling me to procure microfilm from the Archivo General de Indias and for lending me the typescript of an important document. Sra. Angelina López of the AGI provided excellent assistance as did Dorothy Wansmos of the University of New Mexico Library. To my wife, Dorothy, I shall be forever obligated for her inestimable aid.

University of New Mexico

Troy S. Floyd

Abbreviations

AA *Anthológica annua* (Rome)
AAHC *Anales de la academia de la historia* (Havana)
AEA *Anuario de estudios americanos* (Seville)
AGI Archivo general de Indias (Seville)
AHR *American Historical Review* (London and Lancaster, Pa.)
AIA *Archivo ibero-americano* (Madrid)
AUH *Anales de la universidad hispalense* (Seville)
BAGNSD *Boletín del archivo general de la nación* (Santa Domingo)
BHPR *Boletín histórico de Puerto Rico* (San Juan, P.R.)
BRAH *Boletín de la real academia de la historia* (Madrid)
CDAHC *Colección de documentos. Academia de la historia de Cuba.* (Havana)
CDIA *Colección de documentos inéditos relativos al descubrimiento, conquista y organización de . . . América y Oceania. . . .* (Madrid)
CDIE *Colección de documentos inéditos para la historia de España* (Madrid)
CDIHA *Colección de documentos inéditos para la historia de Hispano-America* (Madrid)
CDIU *Colección de documentos inéditos de Ultramar* (Madrid)
CHR *Catholic Historical Review* (Washington, D.C.)
CQJ *Caribbean Quarterly* (Mona, Jamaica)
EHR *The English Historical Review* (London)
HAHR *Hispanic American Historical Review* (Durham, N.C.)
KCDH Konetzke, ed., *Colección de documentos para la historia de la formación social de Hispano-América, 1493–1810* (Madrid)
MH *Missionalia hispánica* (Madrid)
MHDPR Vicente Murga Sanz, ed., *Historia documental de Puerto Rico* (Río Piedras)
MRAE *Memorias de la academia española* (Madrid)
RAEC *Revista de arqueología y etnología* (Havana)
RBC *Revista Bimestre Cubana* (Havana)
RBNC *Revista de la biblioteca nacional* (Havana)
RCHG *Revista chilena de historia y geografía* (Santiago de Chile)
Recop. *Recopilación de leyes de los reynos de las Indias* (Madrid)
REHNY *Revista de estudios hispánicos* (New York)
RI *Revista de Indias* (Madrid)

Introduction

The leitmotiv of Spanish history in Spain and the Caribbean during the first generation—from Columbus's discovery until 1526 when most of the important figures were in their graves—is a fear of divisiveness and civil war. The specter haunted Ferdinand V[1] all his adult life, though he met it astutely with cautious and circumspect policies, and it undergirded the policies of his successor, the great Cardinal Jiménez de Cisneros, who tempered his sympathy for the Indians with a concern for political unity. Both Ferdinand and Jiménez were born in a peninsula wracked by civil wars among rival forces that had supported and opposed the lax monarch, Henry IV. The bloody War of Succession (1474–80) confirmed the accession of Isabel, and her Aragonese husband Ferdinand to the throne of Castile. When he inherited the throne in 1517, Charles was too young and inexperienced, having been born and raised in Flanders, to appreciate the need for caution, but the Comunero Revolt of 1520–22 imbued him with it and he rapidly completed the unification of Spain on the base laid down by his grandparents.

The monarchy of the Catholic kings was thus inaugurated during a civil conflict that made painfully real all the weaknesses inherent in feudalism and, in what had become for the Christian kingdoms of Spain by the late Middle Ages, a destructive religious plurality of Christians, Jews, and Moslems. The conflict understandably made a deep impression on Ferdinand. Certain bishops, possessors of great temporal *señoríos* (fiefs) had personally led armies against the Catholic kings, and a goodly number of the grandees and lesser nobles had added their contingents to the armies that had fought on the side of the rival contender, Alfonso V, king of Portugal.[2] The Catholic kings' abiding concern to acquire full patronage over the Church was, as a result, as much motivated by the desire to prevent a recurrence of civil war as it was to recover episcopal income that often went to foreign, absentee bishops. For these reasons—not because of covetousness as is so often alleged in the literary tradition—Ferdinand was almost hypersensitively concerned with acquiring royal patronage over the Spanish Church and, above all, in the New World; his concern inadvertently contributed to the long delay in establishing American bishoprics. Though these institutions were first projected in 1504 they were not effectively established before 1520, in spite of a brief start between 1512 and 1515; since the fully established bishoprics follow the discovery of America by twenty-eight years, and the initial formal establishment by sixteen years, the importance of Ferdinand's caution can hardly be overstated. Other matters, especially his expensive and ambitious Mediterranean policy, contributed to the prolonged inchoateness of the bishoprics in the Caribbean islands.

At the same time, he exercised great care to prevent the creation of hereditary fiefs in the islands by denying to the *vecinos* (principal settlers) the retention of *encomiendas,* or entrustments of a certain number of Indians, for more than the life of the present holder, though a two-life tenure was granted in a few cases. The rather rapid decrease of the Indian population, of course, made such precautions unnecessary, though Ferdinand failed to appreciate this fact until shortly before his death.

The Catholic kings have long been recognized as the architects of modern Spain, bringing order out of chaos, supplanting feudal institutions with a national army, treasury, bureaucracy, and law code; and imposing religious unity by obliging Jews and Moslems to conform to the faith or leave the country. By finally defeating the Granadan Moors in 1492 and the separatist Navarrese with their French supporters in 1512, they rounded out Spain's natural borders and, at the Cortes of Toledo in 1480, they gave the *letrados,* (lawyers) a much more important role in such political institutions as the Council of Castile and the law courts or *audiencias,* which were now multiplied. The nobility was placated by privileges without power and by diversion, whether more frivolously to the monarchs' court or more seriously as protagonists of the royal foreign policy. The privileges or *fueros* of the towns were reaffirmed and amplified, and they were afforded a greater measure of autonomy through the *Santa Hermandades,* or local police forces, nuclei of the city militia. The monarchs also assumed administration of the main military orders, giving them access to much income, though they did not incorporate the orders into the Crown. Moreover, the *comendadores* of such orders, whom they appointed, were among their most reliable political officials. In all this, a certain social solidarity was achieved; the feeling was shared by all classes and especially by the middle and lower segments, with whom the warm and pious Isabel was especially popular. The ambulatory court gave thousands of Spaniards the opportunity to see their king and queen and to enjoy a sense of community in royal festivities.

The Catholic kings nurtured a similar unity in the Caribbean islands, though with less success. Here there were no powerful ducal houses with armies rivaling the royal forces, but a potentially dangerous divisiveness assumed several forms. A movement rose on Española to oppose Columbus, which resulted in his removal as governor partly because he could not restore order (he had actually imposed peace by the time he was removed), and partly because Queen Isabel felt that his sending of Indian slaves to Spain was morally wrong. The monarchs turned to the letrado class as a source for recruiting governors of the island; they first named Bobadilla, and then went on to the model governor Nicolás de Ovando, the Comendador of Alcántara, whose seven-year tenure (1502–09) bridged the troubled times between the death of the queen in 1504 and the resumption of power by

Ferdinand, after a disturbed hiatus, three years later. By 1503, however, Española was well tied to the monarchy, a process completed in Spain with the establishment that year of the Casa de Contratación, also staffed by letrados, to control a quickening commerce based on gold from the island. Later threatened strife took the form of factionalism over encomiendas, intensified after 1509 by the arrival of Diego Colón, Columbus's son and heir, whose struggle to uphold and enhance the rights and privileges of the Columbus family constitute the main political thread of early Caribbean history. But the threat that reformers might succeed in abolishing the encomienda helped keep potential factionalism within bounds and assured Ferdinand and his immediate successors that both civil strife and Colón could be safely circumscribed.

With the death of the queen, Ferdinand's popularity rapidly dissipated in Castile where he was viewed as a foreigner by the nobles, some of them losers in the war that established the monarchy. He no longer was titled king, though he continued to direct the government as regent until the arrival in 1506 of Philip the Handsome and Juana; that summer Ferdinand left Spain for Naples, where he reigned as Ferdinand II of Aragón. He was recalled as regent and governor when Philip died after a few months' rule, to enter upon the most ambitious and hectic years of his life. He was more purely Aragonese now, both in the eyes of Castilians who disliked him, and in his own outlook, for he was mainly concerned with the Mediterranean. Since his boyhood he had nourished the great ambition of recovering Jerusalem from the Turks (a pious hope voiced by many Christians including Columbus), which would culminate his policy of steadily rolling back the infidel from the periphery of the Mediterranean. Such aims were strongly supported by certain of the Castilian nobility, but the towns were reluctant to finance the enterprise; thus Ferdinand perforce fell back upon the Aragonese for subsidies supplemented by gold from Española, which he exempted from the tithe in 1510. In so doing, he made it virtually impossible for the bishoprics to be established until a sufficiently broad agricultural base had been created. His high ambition in one part of the world thus refuted his professed aim of founding episcopacies in the Indies, as he pursued an expensive foreign policy on a precarious and small economic base. Yet he was circumspect enough to avoid pressing the Castilian towns for money and avoided the revolt that his grandson would unwisely precipitate. This is not to say that the New World bishops invariably resented this reduction of the tithe; the bishops of Puerto Rico and Concepción on Española complained, for they were the only two to take possession of their sees in 1512–13, but others were so habituated to absenteeism, a long prevailing custom, that they seemed content to collect whatever their distant sees furnished.

The unacceptability of Ferdinand to certain Castilian nobles on his return to Spain in 1507 placed him in a weak position for a time; he had to rally support wherever he might find it, and was obliged to forcibly put down the intractable nobles by a series of military actions.[3] Among Ferdinand's leading supporters was the Duke of Alba whose relatives and *criados* included Diego Colón, a nephew by marriage and heir to the titles and privileges of the Discoverer. Though it is impossible to know what arguments the Duke put forward in behalf of Colón's claims, it is this writer's opinion that the king named him governor in 1508 to keep peace with the Duke, a bulwark for his contested rule. It is true that the Royal Council confirmed the royal appointment in 1511 and attempted to clarify and justify Colón's powers and privileges, but the decision could hardly have taken the king by surprise and he may even have consented in advance to the decision. Though Colón was even then troublesome, Ferdinand was confronted with a crisis in Italy[4] by 1511 and needed more than ever to obviate potential conflicts in the Indies and Spain. The importunate and rash Diego had laid his impassioned claims before the king since the death of Columbus; they vastly exceeded what the king wished to yield, including one-tenth of the royal income from the New World, part of which the king was as certain Columbus had not discovered as Diego was that the had. It cannot be imagined then that Ferdinand viewed Diego as anything but a necessary liability, a belated feudal lord intruding into the New World on the basis of the loosely worded capitulations of 1492. Had Ferdinand commanded more wealth, or more kingdoms as Charles V[5] did, he might have diverted the headstrong Colón to other pursuits. As it was, he had to compromise in the Indies to shore up his weak position in Spain; Colón's first governorship finally proved so divisive that the king angrily recalled him in 1515 to avert a civil conflict in the islands over the issue of control of the Indians.

Until Ferdinand's death even the conquest of the New World and its attendant evangelism—those linked dual purposes of the Spanish advance in America—were at best inharmonious. Though the Spanish clergy, and later the Franciscans and Dominicans, had carried the gospel to the heretics and the Moors in Spain and North Africa during the Middle Ages, the predominant mood by the early sixteenth century was introspective among part of the religious body, and decidedly secular among the remainder. Since the fifteenth century many Spanish Franciscans had been repulsed by crass secularism and turned to a simple, austere life, persevering "in prayer, tears and the exercise of virtue."[6] The inward life, the saving of one's own soul, and mystical contemplation took precedence over the outward-looking, street evangelism of early Franciscanism, with all its risks for salvation. Many Franciscans and members of other orders in Spain thus rejected the world; in France, however, the Franciscans in Burgundy and Picardy were apparently unaffected by the retreat to monasticism, and they would be almost as numerous as the Spanish Franciscans when evangelism on Española was slowly beginning.

There the Franciscans ultimately chose a semi-monastic style of evangelism, educating a few cacique's sons within the monastery walls rather than preaching on the *estancias* and in the mines. The Dominicans, soon joined by certain Franciscans, were on the other hand critically observant of the bad living conditions of those Indians subjected to forced labor, and their energies were initially concentrated on criticizing the existing social situation rather than on evangelism.

Only when Cardinal Jiménez de Cisneros became regent in 1516 was evangelism significantly advanced, for his encouragement coincided with the awakening of Franciscans and Dominicans to the opportunities in Venezuela, and to the impasse reached on the islands. This impasse was partly due to Jiménez himself, whose policy of upholding unity among the encomenderos at the expense of blunting further reforms in behalf of the Indians was in harmony with the views of the Jeronymites who longed to return to their monasteries.

Though the coming of Charles V was hailed as the inauguration of a new era, neither state nor Church was notable for energetic direction during his early reign. The remaining Indians on Española and Puerto Rico were finally freed in 1520—a few at once, most on the death of their present holder—but government in the Indies was characterized by weak royal power, divided command, prolonged and incomplete investigations, confusion, and smuggling. The Church languished, acephalous and impoverished. Governors in the islands obeyed only the orders they agreed with; in Spain the Castilian towns boiled over in rage against repeated, arbitrary requests for subsidies from a spendthrift court replete with Flemings and Aragonese, and protested against the king's choosing, without consulting them, to become Holy Roman Emperor.

Like his grandfather Ferdinand, Charles was a foreigner in an increasingly hostile Castile. In 1520 traveling toward Galicia from Catalonia, he hardly resembled a king as he draggled through the soaking rain from Burgos to escape a violent mob. He, too, restored Diego Colón to the governorship in 1520 in order to mend his fences at home, though there was no reason to think Colón was likely to govern any more effectively than he had five years before. Lured by the most coveted political title of Europe, Charles left in his wake a Spain rent by bloody civil war of such critical proportions that Adrian, one of his governors, just managed to escape the enemy after being held prisoner for several weeks. Meanwhile Diego Colón enjoyed a final fling as the unchallenged viceroy of the New World, unmolested by the curb of royal power.

When the dismayed and sobered Emperor Charles eventually returned in 1522 he began to institute unifying measures that built upon the foundations laid down by the Catholic kings. Possessing a vastly more wealthy empire than Ferdinand, Charles was able to relax economic pressure on the Caribbean islands while at the same time putting Church and state on the firmest basis yet attained in both Spain and the Indies. Only then was the long parenthesis of discontent and disunity that had begun after the death of Queen Isabel and had affected both Spain and the Indies finally ended.

1

Columbus and Española (1492-1500)

The story of Columbus and his greatness as a man of immense faith, courage, and navigational skill has been told so often and so convincingly that we tend to overlook the fact that he was a rather average man in certain respects. He was typical of the Genoese and certain other Italians of his time who had moved with the tides of commerce throughout the Mediterranean, out into the Atlantic, and up to northern Europe reaching—as Columbus did—Iceland, as well as southward with the Portuguese to the hump of Africa and beyond. The typical Italians, whether naturalized or merely resident in Seville or Jerez, aspired, as Ruth Pike shows,[1] to use the quickening commerce as a stepping stone to aristocracy, that their sons might be priests or lawyers or acquire titles of lower nobility. The contract of 1492 with the Catholic kings, divested of its great implications for world history, was a mercantile venture by which Columbus hoped to rise from his status as merchant-sailor on the basis of one-tenth of the wealth he would find, probably barter for, in the fabled lands of Cipangu, Marco Polo's name for Japan. He would establish, if the conditions were favorable, a *factoría* like the Portuguese trading forts on the African coast, a partnership operation held exclusively by himself and the Crown. On the basis of this wealth, as his capitulations stipulated, he would hold the titles of admiral and viceroy, to be passed on to his heirs, and the Columbuses would be addressed as "dons" and "doñas" signifying their rise into the *hidalgo* class.

The contract was obviously drawn up in haste and the terms were in some respects vague, if only because its drafters and the Queen accepted Columbus's insistence on these high sounding titles with perhaps only half a mind that the whole matter would come to anything. If Columbus was indeed to establish a trading post in Asia the title of viceroy could only be honorific, and that of admiral would give him powers of government over the post itself and jurisdiction in trade disputes. The document was so worded as to imply that all such powers were hereditary, rather than simply the titles alone which past kings had always prodigally distributed; perhaps this point was overlooked because of the improbability that anything important would ever come of the venture.[2] Later when Columbus's discoveries led to the discovery of much wealth, he used part of it to hire an attorney who made a strong case for the document's literal wording; the king, for by this time, Isabel had died and Ferdinand had to fight the battle alone, found himself tied up in litigation that was still unresolved at his death. The conflict he thus waged had overtones of the feudalism he was otherwise careful to restrain; as for the Columbuses, the contract was the financial means by which they became the foremost *hidalgo* clan in the New World prior to the rich mainland conquests.

In 1492, however, when Ferdinand had just brought the Granadan war to a conclusion, such difficulties were still many years away. As Columbus's small expedition disappeared over the horizon and ventured into the uncharted sea, it doubtlessly also disappeared from Ferdinand's thoughts as he looked east to problems connected with his Italian kingdoms. Columbus sailed from Palos on August 3 with three ships and about one hundred men[3] after the Crown invested a fair sum borrowed from the treasury of the Santa Hermandad,[4] and Columbus secured some backing from Italian merchants[5] and Martín Alonso Pinzón, Palos pilot and fairly wealthy merchant-shipowner. Pinzón not only contributed an important amount but figured prominently in the famous voyage. Except for its due westward route by which Co-

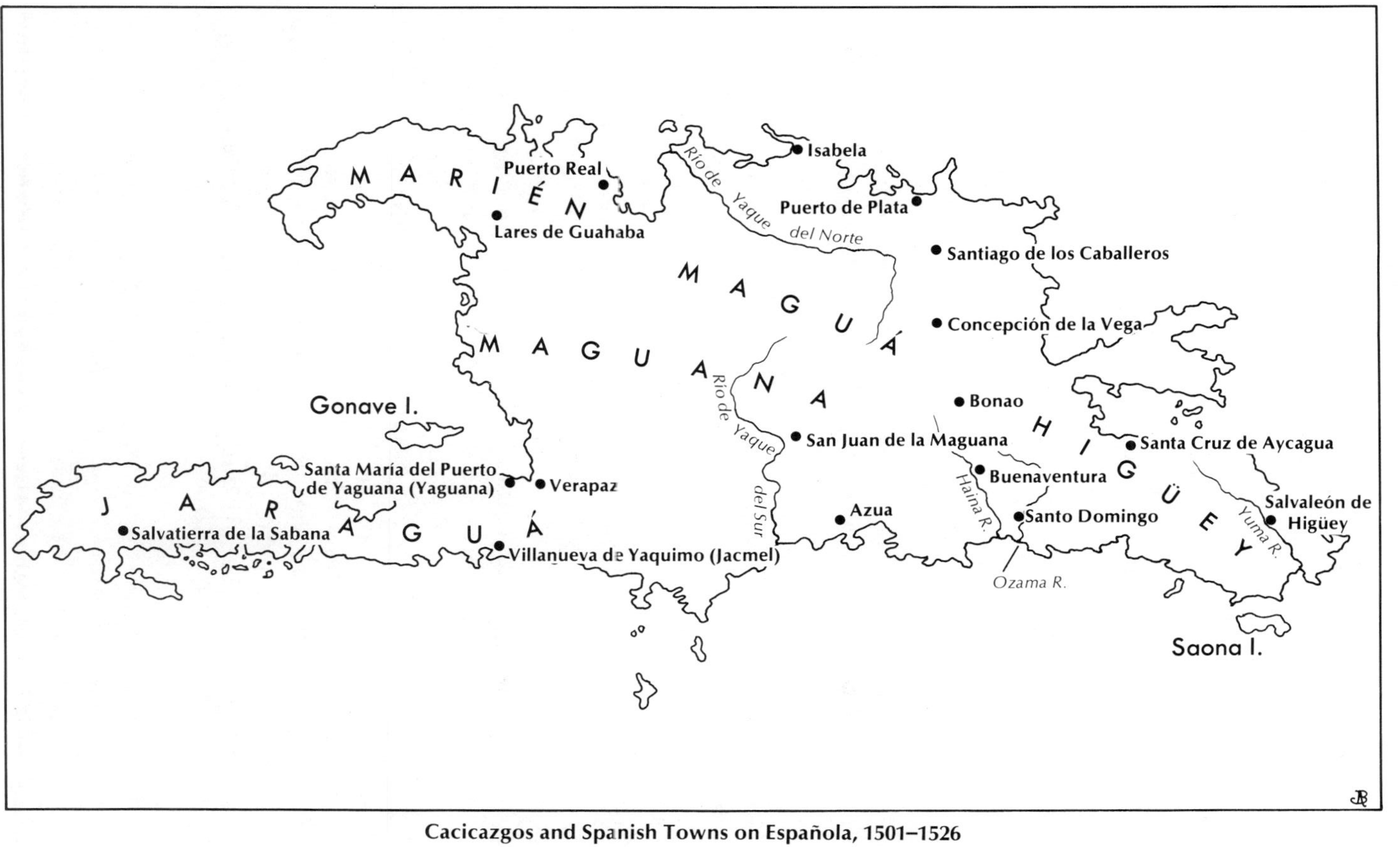

Cacicazgos and Spanish Towns on Española, 1501–1526

lumbus braved the unknown with his faith, and the later significance of his discoveries, the expedition was not untypical of many others that had gone southward along the African coast for years, with or without Portuguese permission; most of the crew were veteran sailors and barterers with the Arabs and Negroes.[6] Hardly any of the expeditionaries would be prominent in later Caribbean history, though some became explorers and pearl barterers along the Venezuelan coast. The pilot Bartolomé Roldán was exceptional because he would reside on Española until his death in or after 1512.[7] The purpose of the expedition, as Columbus saw it, was solely for exploration and barter somewhere in Asia with the question of settlement left for the future. Even the setting up of a trading fort was the result of accidental circumstances.

When the expedition reached the Bahamas on October 12 after the now well-known struggle between doubt and persistence, Columbus had entered the northern fringe of the islands then inhabited mainly by Arawaks, or Taínos, to use a word derived from their own term for the upper class—the *nitainos.* In the twelfth and thirteenth centuries, the Taínos had been migrating along the great arc of islands comprising the Lesser Antilles, and by the fifteenth century they had occupied the Greater Antilles and the Bahamas. Their migration had proceeded westward only as far as the modern Oriente province of Cuba, which was otherwise occupied by earlier arrivals, the Siboneys; at the far western end lived a more primitive tribe of still earlier origins—the Guanahatebeys. Close behind the Taínos, raiding and looting came the Caribs, also from the South American continent, who by this time were settled in various places along the Orinoco river and adjacent parts of the Venezuelan coast. They also held the Lesser Antilles from which they were in both hostile and friendly contact with the Taínos of Puerto Rico.

The population of the islands, especially that of the Greater Antilles which the Spaniards would occupy, has been a subject of considerable speculation for which any firm basis is necessarily lacking in the absence of written records such as tribute rolls. Las Casas's figures of 1,100,000 for Española, and comparably high estimates for the other islands, meant little more than that the islands were populous. The more modest estimates of Rosenblatt of 100,000 for Española and lesser figures for the other three main islands, have been generally accepted by modern scholars.[8] Assuming these figures to be approximately correct, the decline in Indian population was to be neither so drastic nor so rapid as is often stated. In 1526 there were still many Indians living in Cuba and a fair number still remained on the other three islands, not all of whom were under Spanish control. The causes for the disappearance or death of the Taínos are best assessed in conjunction with later developments.

Columbus was chiefly interested—to emphasize his concern for barter rather than any curiosity about this exotic world—with the signs of gold in the Bahamas, such as the ornaments worn by the Taínos which had been obtained by barter from Cuba or Española. The Indians had long washed out gold or merely picked it up from the streams of the Greater Antilles and cold hammered it into various figurines and ornaments; the metal was often impure containing a high amount of copper, and the alloyed objects made from this the Spaniards would call *guanines.* Taking on board one or more interpreters, one of whom was subsequently baptized and named Diego Colón,[9] Columbus sailed southward toward Cuba assured that gold came from there. He explored the northern and eastern coasts of Cuba during November and December, made contact with the Taínos, and was directed eastward toward what he thought was Cipangu but what the Indians actually said was Cibao. This referred to the central mountain range of Española and toward that island Columbus sailed in early December.

Off the northern coast of present-day Haiti just east of Cap Haïtien, the Spaniards saw an unusually large number of Indians near the shore. They landed there, making friendly overtures by offering to barter beads and other goods and assuring, through their interpreter, that they meant no harm. Columbus eventually met the main *ca-*

cique, Guacanagarí, and learned from him that the main source of gold lay farther east, the Cibao being the domain of another cacique named Caonabó. The islands of the Greater Antilles were, in fact, subdivided into ill-defined tribal divisions called *cacicazgos*, ruled by caciques who exercised absolute authority over their immediate tribe but whose authority over their entire cacicazgo depended more on the individual cacique's power to instill fear and enforce obedience.[10] The society was vertically structured with the *nitainos*, a directing class, ruling beneath the cacique level (although many of these nitainos either assumed the title cacique later, or were given it by the Spaniards for purposes of labor control). The *naborias*, men and women who performed the common labor, occupied the lowest position. The Spaniards were to adopt all of these terms and would preserve the class structure, although the cacicazgos would soon collapse as recognizable units due to Indian revolts and tribal relocations connected with the mining industry.

As always the barter system minimized potential cultural clash, and Columbus and the Spaniards got along wonderfully with Guacanagarí and his nitainos; there were no recorded instances of mistreatment of the Indians. Columbus planned to continue eastward toward the Cibao in further explorations. However the Santa María was wrecked owing to negligence at the watch, obliging Columbus to leave part of the men with Guacanagarí. Thus he had erected, partly out of salvaged ship timber, a rude fort called La Navidad and left there thirty-nine men,[11] along with goods for barter and European foods and seeds. He then sailed eastward, by now having been joined by Martín Alonso Pinzón commanding the Pinta; after further explorations along the north coast during which Columbus took on water at the mouth of the Yaque del Norte where gold grains lodged in the barrel hoops,[12] the two vessels sailed for Spain. Inland from Monte Cristi Bay, Pinzón had also bartered for a substantial amount of gold and had, as a result, made contact with the Cibao region.

Columbus departed for Spain in a mood of high elation; the island, which he named Española, seemed a paradise with its great prospects for gold and its kindly, peaceful Indians who had furnished him with cassava, yams, and peppers for his homeward voyage. He was overly sanguine on both accounts: the gold would prove uncommonly hard to find in quantity, and he had made a hasty if understandable judgment about the Indians. Columbus had come upon only the most peaceful tribes and under the best conditions—with a few men desiring only to barter. Neither the Cuban Taínos (at this time) nor Guacanagarí, the cacique of Marién, were bellicose, but he was apparently the most docile of the Española caciques. Elsewhere, caciques were much more hostile, probably because of recent contact with Caribs, if indeed some caciques were not actually of that tribe.[13] They would offer considerable, though in the long run futile, resistance to the Spanish advance. A corrective would seem to be needed against the impression, so pointedly made by Las Casas, that the docile Indians could do little else than offer their bare bellies to the Spanish swords. They had two weapons that they put to good use in conjunction with stealth and deception: fire, and the pliable *bejuco* cane used as a cord for strangulation.[14] Unfortunately, the Spaniards were their equals at deception and had far superior weapons.

Columbus publicized his great discovery with its untold possibilities for wealth and conversion of the natives by a letter written in the Azores, enroute back to Palos.[15] Martín Alonso Pinzón was blown north off his course so as to arrive in Bayona, Galicia at about the same time. The Catholic kings were at Barcelona where Ferdinand had just negotiated the Treaty of Narbonne with Louis VIII, a tactic by which he retained control of his small trans-Pyrenean kingdoms and forestalled encroachments into Naples. He received Columbus there sometime in April, and the King showed his elation by renewing the navigator's contract; Ferdinand urged his minister for the Indies, Bishop Juan Rodríguez de Fonseca, and certain other officials at Jerez and Cádiz, to arrange for the outfitting of a second and much larger expedition. Meanwhile, the king secured possession to the newly found lands from Pope Alexander VI by the well-known bull of May 3, 1493, three times restated and modified between then and September.

Recruiting for the expedition was of two sorts: a more or less informal convergence of peasants and hidalgos on Seville, and the king's selection of a friar to head the first missionary movement to the New World. Both the monarchs and the Pope were agreed that conversion was the prime motive for settling the islands, and the Alexandrine bull implied that the right of possession and duty of conversion were inseparable. Ferdinand selected as his vicar, with papal approval, Friar Bernardo Boyl who had been until recently a Benedictine, as Las Casas called him, but who had by this time joined the order of Minim friars. He was caught up in the mainstream of monastic reform and passionately desired the dedicated, disciplined monastic life—the turning inward from worldly affairs, and the devout pursuing of the semi-mystical way toward purity of soul and communion with God.[16] Still Ferdinand could hardly have appreciated this; he had counted on the friar in earlier times as his special emissary in diplomatic matters in Sicily and France[17] and he naturally assumed, since Friar Boyl was too obedient to refuse duty, that one who had served him well in the past would do so again. One may only suppose, however, that the Friar sailed to Española with great reluctance, and since circumstances there would prove difficult for even the most zealous churchman, he was all too inclined to throw up his hands and return to Spain upon the slightest pretext. Thus, from the very beginning the monastic movement adversely cut across the path of duty in America. Fortunately the recruiting or volunteering of certain other friars was more promising. The Catalan Ramón Pane, although a Benedictine and a monastic, looked outward toward the challenge of the New World. Two lay friars from Burgundy, Juan de la Deule and Juan Tisín, who heard of the unprecedented opportunity from brothers then attending a chapter meeting at Florenzac, France, received permission to join Fr. Boyl.[18] The remainder of the friars and secular priests—there were to be about 13 in all[19]—made no recorded mark on Española.

While Ferdinand initiated the first missionary force for America, lay persons of the restless hidalgo or peasant classes were trooping to Seville to sign the fleet register administered by Bishop Rodríguez de Fonseca. We may surmise from the places from which a number of them came that the Aragonese learned of it in or around Barcelona, that others viewed Pinzón's landing in Galicia, that still others were eye-witnesses to Columbus's journey from Palos to Barcelona by way of Seville and his return journey to Seville by way of the Shrine of Guadalupe in Extremadura. To reside in or near Seville was of course the most advantageous position of all.

By September, 1493, following a summer of hectic preparations, a fleet of seventeen ships and an expeditionary force of some fifteen hundred men had been assembled and was ready to sail. This was in the greatest contrast with the inconspicuous little venture of the year before. The multifarious and numerous adventurers were virtually a microcosm of Spain: sailors, hidalgos, artisans, peasants, and priests. Though such diverse participants were united in support of Spain's great aims of conquest and conversion, they would soon factionalize and quarrel over gold and Indians. They expected the rewards of an hidalgo, not the meager salary paid them by a profit-minded Genoese. This great migration has often been called the first colonizing expedition to the New World, which is true in certain respects. Seeds, livestock, and building materials were taken along, and a fair number of the expeditionaries would live out their lives in the islands. Yet colonizing implies the migration of families and there were no women aboard. The majority of the men were single; moreover many of them apparently never sent for their wives. Colonization resulted from the expedition, but the second voyage was actually a seaborne gold rush of lone males

Columbus intended it to be a *factoría* expedition, such as the Portuguese had made from Lisbon to establish São

Jorge da Mina under the African hump.[20] Most of the men sailed as salaried employees of the Crown, with Columbus as the royal agent and co-partner. The seeds and livestock were to be converted into provisions for the employees for Columbus knew, after seeing the Portuguese fort, that Europeans fared poorly if at all on native food. The enterprise departed only from this character to the extent that mining operations were to supplement barter as a means of getting gold. Columbus, in theory at least, exercised complete control as the royal governor (aside from titles of Viceroy and Admiral), and could, by the officials he appointed such as an *alcalde mayor* and *contador,* enforce strict control over commerce and barter.

One may at once perceive a striking anomaly: a few officials intended to control fifteen hundred men who had no desire to labor as salaried employees aiding a Genoan to become rich. Yet Columbus made no effort to limit so large an expedition, and if the nearly insoluble problem of control occurred to him, he must have subordinated it to his generally sanguine outlook.

The inner conflict was, however, more than mere numbers. There was a certain harmony of purpose about the first voyage for the sailors of the Tinto-Odiel, the region including Palos and Moguer, were used to the mercantile institution of the factoría, which was the institutional framework within which Caribbean history begins. But a great number of men on the second expedition had taken the oath of obedience to the factor Columbus as a mere gesture.[21] Many of them were of the potential hidalgo class, criados of dukes and archbishops and other prominent men; since their ambitions were blocked in Spain, they looked to new opportunities overseas for which gold was but a means to achieving hidalgo status and to enjoying seignorial life. They were, in sum, potential feudal lords whose ambition was to rule over serfs, to acquire and display the fineries of their time, to own land, and if great deeds made it possible, to win a title. Their upward aspirations were thus a factor from the outset and Columbus's troubles could easily be predicted.

The potential conflict was not between adventurers and authority, but between factions. The path upward lay in attaching oneself to a master, an overlord, who would provide the means, with luck and ability, of reaching the desired goal. The potential hidalgo class would thus fragment along these lines and although we cannot know precisely how early such alignments were formed, it is certain they began during or soon after the second voyage. Columbus was of course in the ascendant and with the coat of arms he acquired while in Barcelona, and the title of "don" for his brothers Bartolomé (who would not sail until the spring of 1494), and Diego , he was the foremost social leader, whose favor was essential to success. Some of the most prominent Spaniards of the next three decades accompanied Columbus and were loyal adherents, with rare exception, of the Discoverer and his son Diego, the second Viceroy. Supporting the Columbus family often determined success or failure in the islands, for the Columbuses ruled actively seventeen years out of the thirty-five from 1492 to 1526, and were otherwise influential even when not in power. Diego Velázquez, the *conquistador* and first governor of Cuba, was a follower of Columbus and later a criado of Bartolomé, Columbus's brother.[22] Francisco de Garay, the effective early governor though not the initial conqueror of Jamaica, was Columbus's brother-in-law and always his supporter,[23] and Miguel Díaz, co-founder with Garay of Santo Domingo and founder of San Germán, Puerto Rico, was long favored by the Columbus family. These criados, whose success was due in part to their own abilities, supported Columbus in the trying years ahead and profited later by positions and advantages granted them by Diego Colón. They were among the main founders of Spanish civilization in the Caribbean.

Other prominent members of the second voyage included Juan Ponce de León, a criado of Don Pedro Núñez de Guzmán, comendador mayor of Calatrava[24]; Alonso de Ojeda, known personally to Bishop Rodríguez de Fonseca; and Francisco Roldán, recommended by the Archbishop of Toledo, Pedro González de Mendoza.[25] None of these men were followers of Columbus; Ponce was not known to be antagonistic but he preferred loyalty to the Crown; Ojeda soon broke with Columbus to compete in explorations and discovery, and Roldán, who sailed with a patent for the position of alcalde mayor to be filled on the first vacancy, would prove to be Columbus's nemesis.[26]

Factionalism was to prove characteristic of Spanish society in the Caribbean and its outlines were adumbrated on the second voyage by the tendency to support or remain aloof from the Columbuses. Underlying factionalism was the almost constant disparity between great expectations and dismal reality, between rumors of rich gold mines and the actuality of limited gold veins and evanescent placers. Thousands rushed to the islands and a few score realized substantial wealth. Immigration followed an erratic rhythm now and throughout the Caribbean's early history; the king and the authorities tried to cope with either an excess or a paucity of immigrants depending on which way the winds of rumored fortune were blowing. Divisiveness during Columbus's governorship would be especially acute because he, considered a covetous Genoese by the have-nots, tried to impose a monopoly on barter, mining, and land holding or, as Pérez Tudela saw it, Columbus placed the capitalistic factoría system in conflict with the older *Reconquista* tradition in which would-be *caballeros* won wealth and fame by their own efforts.[27]

Columbus's second expedition left Cádiz on September 23, 1493, and after a stopover on the Canaries to take on livestock and other supplies, the navigator directed the voyage somewhat farther south, entering the Lesser Antilles at the Dominica Passage. By November, the fleet was moving northward through the inside passage of Guadaloupe and other islands, and coming upon signs of cannibalism among the Caribs. Off St. Croix on November 14 a Basque sailor was fatally wounded by a Carib arrow and died about a week later, the only casualty of the expedition. After stopping in the Bay of Añasco on the eastern shore of Puerto Rico, the expedition headed for the north coast of Española.

As the vessels coasted off the mouth of the Río Yaque del Norte, passengers saw the first evidence that all had not gone well for the men left at La Navidad. The corpses of two Spaniards were floating in the estuary, their arms bound tightly with bejuco cords; they had been either drowned or garroted. One observer saw that their eyes had been removed. The Taínos had none of the European's certainty about the dividing line between death and life, and did not distinguish between material objects and corpses. As animists, although tending toward anthropomorphism with their *cemis*,[28] they believed these images of cotton or wood or stone had souls, that trees and rocks were animate, and that human beings were probably still alive while their eyes were in their heads.[29] They were not at all certain, at first, just what was required to kill these strange new men: Taínos on Puerto Rico once drowned a Spanish youth but waited several days with the body before they were certain he was really dead.[30] Spanish friars did not have to oppose materialism in the Taínos but to reduce their conception of immortality to human beings only.

When the expedition reached La Navidad on November 27, the Spaniards realized that a calamity had overtaken the men left there. The fort had been burned to the ground—by Caonabó, so relatives of Guacanagarí told Columbus. A day or so later Columbus and a few of his men came upon the cacique Guacanagarí in one of his villages farther east. The cacique confirmed the account, pointing to his bandaged leg as proof of his efforts to defend the fort against the chieftain of the Cibao. Dr. Chanca[31] found that there was no wound under the bandage and although Friar Boyl demanded that the cacique and any others found guilty should be summarily executed, Columbus thought it unwise to punish Guacanagarí who still showed signs of loyalty and who may not have been directly responsible. He learned later that several Spaniards had killed Jácome, the Genoese cabin boy, indicating that quarreling among themselves accounted for part of the trouble, and Indians also said that the Spaniards had taken three or four women each as concubines.

Columbus was probably wise not to punish Guacanagarí, for he would desperately need him to furnish food in the bleak months ahead. He was more concerned with finding gold that was rumored to lie in the Cibao, and should Caonabó prove as hostile as the Marién tribe claimed he would need allies. That Indians of the Marién cacicazgo probably did kill the Spaniards, or most of them, seems fairly certain for the cacicazgo extended to the lower Yaque river where the first two bodies were found. Moreover when the Spaniards later crossed the Yaque into the Cibao the Indians there showed no signs of ever having seen Europeans before. This would have made it quite improbable that Caonabó had led an expedition to La Navidad, for some of these Indians would certainly have accompanied the cacique.

Since Columbus had no reason to relocate at La Navidad, which was far from the gold fields of the Cibao, he sent out reconnaissance ships east and west before deciding to move the fleet in early January 1494, eastward to an open harbor on the north coast, near Monte Cristi. A more thorough reconnaissance, impossible because of sickness among both human passengers and horses, might have turned up better harbors. As it was, the site for Isabela, as Columbus christened his first factoría and town, had some promise. The site had a nearby water supply in the Bajabónico River, good stones for buildings, an adjacent Indian village, and fertile if rather limited ground for cultivation.[32] Here the passengers gradually debarked; the first Mass was celebrated on January 6 and Columbus laid out a town of about 200 thatch huts around a plaza on which Columbus's house fronted. His house, which was to double as an arsenal, and his supply warehouse were both made of stone for security reasons. The immediate problem was scarcity of food, which contributed to widespread illness and death. The seeds of vegetables, fruits, and grains, sprouted readily and grew rapidly, as Dr. Chanca and Columbus both reported, but this optimism was based on limited experience. On the whole, wheat headed out poorly and vineyards matured slowly; most Spaniards apparently could not work or even stay healthy without wheat and wine. Hurricanes and droughts also caused serious setbacks to crops, and reliance on Indians to provide yams and cassava proved an unreliable source of supplies. The food shortage, however, was not absolute. Certain Spaniards were much more resilient than others. They managed to stomach cassava and yams, to mix with and live among the Indians rather than to cower, starving, within the forts; in short, to become wholly acculturated. These men survived while others died. The significance of such acculturation has perhaps been most fully appreciated by Pérez de Tudela who had in mind the followers of Roldán who settled a few years later in southwestern Española.[33] But such mixing actually began within a few weeks or months after the founding of Isabela in the north, and the result there and elsewhere was the rise of a *mestizo* population, born within and outside of marriage. At this time, they were counted as whites and were specifically excluded from the subsequent forced labor system.[34]

While some Spaniards laid out the new town, Columbus sent exploring parties inland in January 1494, guided by local Indians. The two parties of fifteen to twenty men each were led by Francisco Gorbalán, soon to return to Spain, and by Alonso de Ojeda, restless, ambitious, and intrepid, who would spend the next twenty years on the islands and the Spanish Main in an almost continuous pursuit of wealth, fame, hardship, and danger. These parties crossed the nearby *cordillera septentrional,* (northern range) debouched onto the immense Vega, crossed the Yaque del Norte and passed up one of its tributaries that drained the opposite mountain range, the *cordillera central* (central range). The Taínos, who lived in populous towns along the banks of the Yaque, greeted them hospitably and without fear.

Both parties bartered for grains of gold and small nuggets. Neither they—nor for that matter, other Spaniards during the next five or six years—knew how to trace down the gold-bearing weathered rock from which these grains had come. This technological failure would give to Española a reputation for fool's gold which it only overcame after 1500, too late for Columbus to enjoy directly the gold-rich factoría he presently hoped to establish. However, barter brought in a satisfying amount of gold and there were other encouraging signs, such as peaceful Indians and fast growing crops. When the two parties returned from the goldfields in late January, bearing gold worth 30,000 ducats[35] (25,000 *pesos de oro*), an elated Columbus hastily dispatched this treasure for Spain with his trusted ship captain, Antonio de Torres. Columbus apologized to Ferdinand, naively as it turned out, for not finding more than he had. In fact, he had already found more gold than would be discovered in any of the next six years. "There is more gold here than iron in the Biscay," he estimated, quickly adding that food and medicines were desperately needed. According to Martyr, Torres returned with three hundred Spaniards who, tired of the hardships, would have gladly traded all the nuggets, real or fancied, on Española, just to reach Spain alive.[36]

Columbus now looked confidently to ths future. Pending the return of Torres he would see to the gathering of a great amount amount of gold in the Cibao, for which a second fort would be necessary farther inland, both for the security of the gold and the factoría employees. As Columbus prepared for an expedition inland which he himself would lead, the vision of the garroted Spaniards, deceived by the Taíno's seeming naiveté and obsequiousness, still haunted him. He could well believe Ojeda's recent report that Caonabó was a dangerous foe—evil and ignorant was the way Columbus characterized him. When he marched inland on March 14, he took several hundred troops to thwart any attack Caonabó might make, and should mere numbers of armed men prove too subtle for his Taíno mentality, Columbus had drums beaten and muskets fired for better deterrent effect.

In the vicinity where Ojeda had earlier been, they put up a stockade, near the present village of Jánico, and christened it Santo Tomás. The Taínos were still eager to barter and even during the few days Columbus remained, a fair amount of gold was collected. Columbus, experienced in the perils of loose administration of factorías, exacted harsh penalties for concealment of gold. As his fellow Genoan and companion Michele de Cuneo said: "Some had their ears split, and some their nose, which was pitiful to see."[37] Still Columbus did not find the gold mines he sought; gold was thinly dispersed among the sands of innumerable streams. Barter would soon furnish diminishing returns, provoking one skeptic to remark that the Indians gave us gold heirlooms accumulated over centuries.[38] With that treasure in their hands, the Spaniards could expect to find little else.

Leaving an Aragonese veteran of the Granadan wars, Pedro Margarit, as fort captain with full powers, Columbus departed for Isabela with all but fifty two of the men. He would seem to have imitated the proverbial king who marched his men up the hill and down again for reasons kept secret in the royal breast. Columbus probably brought such a large number of men into the interior as a security precaution; he may also have expected to find two or more rich gold-bearing areas, which would have required the establishment of several forts. Since such areas were not found—even on the return journey where he took a different, exploratory route—the bulk of the men probably were withdrawn because of the lack of further discoveries.

However that may be, he found on reaching Isabela that food supplies there had seriously dwindled, owing partly to spoilage, and that the number of sick had greatly increased. While pondering this desperate situation, Columbus learned from a messenger that Caonabó planned an attack upon the small garrison at Santo Tomás. In a sudden reversal of plans, Columbus dispatched 400 men to the fort—a timely move that probably saved many of them from starving to death.

Columbus now elaborated on his barter system writing out orders for Margarit and entrusting them to Ojeda, whom he named *alcaide* (castellan) and charged with escorting the troops on the return journey. Fifty men were to remain in the fort while Margarit was to send out three squads of fifty men each. Each unit would be commanded by a captain, who would have strict orders to barter only in the presence of an official, assigned to keep careful records of the transactions. He named Luis de Arriaga his contador, who would presumably receive and record all barter as it was brought into the fort. This method was expected not only to increase the amount of gold but to solve the food supply, since barter goods were to be exchanged partly for food. Undoubtedly many men had come to realize that they would have to overcome initial dislike of native fare if they were to survive.

There was something bizarre, however, about expecting men to consider themselves on regular salary in the wilderness, to roam about the Vega and be content with cassava and yams for payment. Discipline under such circumstances was impossible, which explains why Margarit resigned in disgust the following summer and returned to Spain. Arriaga, whether on his own decision or by orders of Columbus, deemed it expedient to establish a second fort on the Yaque which he called La Magdalena. It was a way station between Isabela and Santo Tomás, which would not only enhance security but would lessen the need for such a large amount of food at the first interior fort. Probably not more than one hundred men—or fifty each—ever stayed in the two forts. What the others, who were on bartering expeditions in the Vega, did is a matter of conjecture; we do know that some sought refuge with the friendly cacique of Marién, doubtless driven there more by need of food than any prospect of gold.[39] Still others must have found hospitality among the villages along the Yaque del Norte and its tributaries—that is, worked out their own solutions to the problems of security and threatened starvation. The evidence is necessarily indirect and inferential, for neither Margarit nor Ojeda wrote about such matters. Not many years later, a few Spaniards were fluent in one or another of the Taíno dialects (whereas most knew scarcely a word), and a minor cacique in the Vega soon appeared named Diego Márques, meaning he had changed names with Columbus's *veedor*.[40] A few years later it is evident that a considerable number of Spaniards lived with their various concubines among the tribes, or married *cacicas* and, to the great consternation of later governors, claimed hegemony over whole tribes and even cacicazgos as a result. A small, nascent, and suppressible native feudalism was the political outcome; culturally, Spaniards learned to adjust, which in all respects was a subtle breakaway from Columbus's factoría system long before he recognized it. In short, they scattered along the Yaque and into the Marién in the northwest where they reappear but rarely in public documents or *probanzas*.

Columbus, meanwhile, believing he had done enough to secure his bartering system on Española, fitted out three caravels and sailed westward on April 14, 1494, to explore the southern coast of Cuba and discover the north coast of Jamaica. His voyage was not otherwise of immediate consequence, though he saw the south coast of Española on the return voyage and found rich stands of brazilwood on the southwestern littoral at the present site of Jacmel.[41] This was the first sign of wealth on the south coast, which, together with the discovery of gold on the Haina, would lead to the founding of Santo Domingo in a few years.

When Columbus reached Isabela on September 29, 1494, he found that Bartolomé had arrived (probably the previous June), and that Friar Boyl, Margarit, and a few others had returned to Spain on the same fleet of three ships which had brought his brother. All problems were now compounded: a meager food supply, fewer Indians coming to Isabela to barter, and fewer Indians bringing in gold or food to the interior forts. The Discoverer was at a dismal impasse. Soon Ferdinand would be hearing from Friar Boyl and others about the terrible conditions and pessimistic prospects for the enterprise; the king would be told about the disciplined labor and parceling out of rations, the high death rate, and the poor site that had been selected for the first town. The whole undertaking, the grandiose plan for which Columbus had already risked so much and spent so many years hung in the balance, for the next ships from Spain might bring orders for his recall.

Other than gold, which he still hoped to find in quantity, all that the islands offered as a valued commodity in Spain was slaves which for Columbus, who had spent his formative years among the slave marts of the Mediterranean, were an acceptable alternative when barter failed to produce gold. While off eastern Española on his return voyage he had considered capturing Caribs on St. Croix, whom he knew were cannibals, but a severe illness drove him to Isabela empty-handed. As he lay ill in the small coastal village, and presumably between the time that Antonio Torres arrived with four ships in October and departed in the following February for Spain, Columbus decided that Caonabó and his tribe, whom he believed were responsible for killing the Spaniards at La Navidad, could be justifiably attacked and his people enslaved.

Meanwhile the Indians revolted on the Vega, affording Columbus even better prospects for taking slaves. Apparently the revolts were caused by pressure on the Taínos' food supplies, and by misunderstandings stemming from different languages and customs, which had led to violence and counterviolence. Columbus now sent five hundred men into the Vega, ostensibly to find provisions for Isabela, but more likely to take slaves. This invasion of the Vega led to further bloodshed, and to revenge carried out by Guatiguaná, a cacique of the western Vega (or *Macorix de abajo*), who ambushed and killed ten Spaniards and set fire to a thatch hut in which forty others lay ill, presumably burning them alive. This, in turn, led to the capture of some fifteen hundred Indians in this area, of whom five hundred were sent back to Spain on Torres's ships in February 1495.

A Taíno reprisal soon followed, as various caciques mustered forces and marched on La Magdalena, laying siege to the fort from which Arriaga sent a message for aid. Columbus himself led the counterattack and met the Indians near the fort in what has been described and mythologized as the Battle of the Vega, an "Armageddon" between the hosts of paganism and Christianity.[52] There are no eye-witness reports of the battle, details of which have sifted down through Las Casas's memory from hearing participants discuss it. Though the battle has been regarded as a decisive struggle for possession of the great valley, with the victors aided by divine intervention, the few facts do not support a battle of this scope. The battle apparently made but slight impression on Columbus, since he did not mention it as being decisive when reporting on his partial conquest of the island; moreover, tribes of the populous Concepción de la Vega or San Juan de la Maguana regions were not involved. The battle seems rather to have been a sound defeat for the particular Taíno tribes engaged, who felt for the first time the rude impact of Spanish arms, cavalry, and dogs. Most survivors were enslaved. It put such fear in caciques living nearby that they agreed to whatever terms Columbus decided to impose.

Columbus's first assumption that gold could be obtained by barter was now destroyed. Instead, he initiated a tribute system which he imposed upon caciques in the Vega and the Cibao over the next ten months. Through his interpreters he instructed that all males between the ages of 14 and 70 would deliver to one of the three forts, every three months, gold in grain or ornament worth 25 ducats. Columbus held to the opinion that the Indians could easily pan out the tribute from an inexhaustible supply of surface gold, and that he had replaced the voluntary barter system with an involuntary regularized tribute.

The tribute system was imposed over a much wider area than the barter system had encompassed. Columbus, probably after Ojeda captured Caonabó by a ruse, crossed the cordillera central, apparently marching up the Yaque del Norte and southward down its couterpart, the Yaque del Sur, to the site of Caonabó's town (where San Juan de la Maguana would be later established). At this site another chieftain, Beehechio, whose village, Jaraguá, lay southwest along the south shore of Lake Enriquillo, came forward to offer tribute without waiting for the Spaniards to approach him. This system continued until sometime after Columbus returned to Spain in the spring of 1496, and fell off unevenly owing to Indian revolts encouraged by dissident Spaniards, and to the impressment of Indians into direct mine labor.

During these ten months Columbus also expanded his

system of blockhouses to facilitate the collection of tribute and to secure the conquered region. To the line of forts beginning with Isabela and extending to La Magdalena and Santo Tomás, Columbus added a fourth, between the last two, called Santa Catarina. Southwestward up the Vega, Columbus established additional forts spaced at about a day's journey—at Esperanza, Santiago (near the later town Santiago de los Caballeros), and Concepción de la Vega. No fort was put up at San Juan de la Maguana, probably because of communications difficulties and lack of manpower.

Columbus was now in a much more favorable position than he had been on his return from Cuba. He had successfully established a factoría complex and had conquered a good part of the island. He had decapitated, in the case of Caonabó and the cacique near Magdalena, the reportedly most powerful cacicazgos and had secured the obedience of Guarionex and Beehechio. The rank and file were not prone to offer armed resistance, and the more plastic processes of acculturation could continue with less need for watchful security. In a confident mood, Columbus could meet Ferdinand's investigating official, Juan de Aguado, without undue apology. Aguado had arrived at Isabela in October, 1495, with three caravels, bringing supplies and about ninety settlers. Columbus could now assure him that all the complaints poured into the ear of Ferdinand by Margarit and Friar Boyl were taken care of: rations were not withheld for minor infringements of his authority; gold was carefully received and recorded, not hoarded by himself and his aides; and relations with the Indians had now been put on a firm basis.

The Discoverer believed that the factoría was now solidly enough established so that he might return to Spain to further assure the king of the good prospects for the future and to renegotiate his contract. But his return to Spain was delayed when a hurricane struck in October, destroying all ships in the harbor. By March, 1496, two ships had been repaired making it possible for Columbus and Aguado to depart for Spain.

Once back in Spain he was to wait an unexpectedly long time before starting back to Española in June, 1498. In the meantime, however, he could envision a bright future as yet undarkened by the frustration and despair that awaited him. His powers were reaffirmed in 1497, although the issue of their exact scope and legality was left conveniently vague; the grant of a *mayorazgo,* or inalienable estate, to Columbus gave the family permanence on Española, and Bartolomé was given the title of *adelantado*—the first such title in the New World. Columbus's dreams of impending wealth were written into his will in 1498. He bestowed millions of *maravedís* upon his son Diego; handsome incomes were to be provided for his two brothers, Bartolomé and Diego, and his illegitimate son, Fernando. His will included needy relatives and the burdened taxpayers of Genoa, and in a peroration of piety, he counseled Diego to always support the Catholic kings in their efforts to recover Jerusalem and the Pope, unless he should be a heretic.[43] Columbus's mood was one of profound gratitude and hope. Even the decree of 1495 that infringed upon his original contract and his exploration rights in the New World had not yet been acted upon, partly owing to the usual delay in fitting out expeditions, which would not sail until the following year. As viceroy of the king, he could feel that the New World, momentarily and precariously, was still his alone. The social ascendancy of the Columbus family, and by extension those loyal to them, was thus further assured.

Columbus's delay of two years in Spain was due primarily to a lack of organization in the preparation of a new fleet for the Indies. Ships and supplies had thus far been raised by Bishop Rodríguez de Fonseca who drew upon shipowners of the Tinto-Odiel or Seville. This improvised method could easily fail when various additional demands on shipping and funds happened to coincide with the preparations for Columbus's new fleets, as happened between 1496 and 1498. Ferdinand had at first alloted six million maravedís to fit out eight ships for Columbus. However, upon being told that Peralonso

Niño would soon be returning from Española with great amounts of gold, Ferdinand spent the anticipated funds on defense for the small trans-Pyrenean kingdoms in southeastern France. When, as it turned out, Niño brought little or no gold—only Indian slaves—the king was obliged to raise part of the funds by selling wheat to Genoa; the remainder apparently came from private sources—presumably Genoese merchants. Shipping was also in short supply as a large and expensive armada was organized in 1496 to convoy Princess Juana to Flanders in the style suitable for a royal marriage. The monarchs were otherwise preoccupied with marrying off their son, Prince Juan, the following year, and the widowed Princess Isabel to Manuel I of Portugal. These royal preoccupations were further complicated by the deaths of both Juan and his bride the same year, and by Ferdinand's apparent suspension of Rodríguez de Fonseca while the monarch dallied with appointing Antonio de Torres as quartermaster for the Indies expeditions, Columbus fretted and fumed at the delay but could do little to hasten preparations for his return voyage.

Columbus's long absence from Española—he would not return until August, 1498—virtually left the small settlements isolated and forgotten. In 1497 for the first year since the discovery, not a single ship sailed between Spain and the island. No wonder that some of the settlers assumed that the Columbuses were no longer a power to be reckoned with. Meanwhile, however, under the energetic direction of Bartolomé Colón, Spaniards explored southward from the Vega.

Miguel Diaz and Francisco de Garay, working their way down the Haina river, discovered rich deposits of gold in the river sands perhaps twenty-five miles from the coast. Whether this discovery was made, as Oviedo recounted, while Díaz was in temporary withdrawal from Bartolomé as the result of a quarrel with a Spaniard whom he fatally stabbed, or whether it resulted from explorations ordered by Bartolomé with the aim of finding a better, hurricane-sheltered port, cannot be determined.[44] The discovery must have occurred between

March and July, 1496, for by the latter month three caravels under the command of Peralonso Niño, who left Cádiz soon after the arrival of Columbus, had reached Isabela. Bartolomé loaded them with Indian slaves and sent back the good news that the long sought gold had at last been found in quantity. The news, as it turned out, was potentially true, though great amounts seem not to have been found as quickly as the discoverers anticipated. In Spain, where Niño held up his report to the king for some months, the news had the indirect effect of further delaying Columbus's return and discrediting his enterprise which so often seemed on the verge of producing great amounts of gold but so far never had. Ferdinand and others heard the confused rumor that Niño brought much gold—not just news about its discovery. Involved in a war with Louis XII of France, who pressed him simultaneously in Naples and on the borders of his hard-to-defend kingdoms of Narbonne and Roussillon in southeastern France, Ferdinand expended the funds he had set aside for Columbus on the grounds that the gold from Española would easily defray the next expedition. When this proved false, raising the funds a second time proved difficult and required more than a year.

Niño had brought Bartolomé much-needed provisions and, after the pilot's departure, the adelantado organized an expedition for the purpose of building a fort within the region of the newly found gold deposits. It may be taken for granted that Bartolomé took with him not only miners and their tools and Indians for carriers, but also those men he believed were most loyal. This doubtless included Díaz and Garay, unless they had remained on the Haina. Many who stayed behind resented, then or soon after, being left out, and the prospects were good for rebellion against the Columbus faction. Always mindful of the need for provisions, Bartolomé arranged for the caciques of the Vega to produce and deliver still greater amounts of cassava and yams as tribute. This would supply the new mining operation while continuing to provide tribute to Isabela and the northern forts. Such caciques as Guarionex resented having to furnish the additional tribute so far to the south, and their resentment was soon fanned by the Spaniards left out of what they envisioned as a gold rush enjoyed by the Columbus clan. A revolt was latent, and it only needed a bold leader to take command.

The itinerary of Bartolomé Colón over the next year can only be put together by inference; so far as is known, he wrote nothing of his activities. The chroniclers do not lay out a clear path—Las Casas because of his repetitive fallacy, and Martyr and Fernando Colón because of their striving for literary effect often at the expense of logic or even what was physically possible. Once on the Haina at a site presumed to be well situated within the gold region, Bartolomé had a fort built, which he named San Cristóbal. The food supply soon dwindled down and starvation once more threatened, one survivor recalling years later that he stayed alive on a diet of crabs.[45] A few of the men, perhaps ten or twenty, were left at the fort while Bartolomé and the main party turned west. He sought to obtain food and other provisions from Beehechio, the cacique at Jaraguá, who had pledged obedience to Columbus a year earlier. Another purpose that motivated Bartolomé was cutting the dyewood that Columbus had seen at Jacmel in 1494. Still it is unlikely that Bartolomé's expedition greatly relieved the men at San Cristóbal. What actually occurred there can only be surmised in the light of what is known to have happened by 1498; soon after Bartolomé's departure, a second fort had been put up on the Ozama, to the southeast, where the estuary teemed with fish and where Indians raised cassava and yams in nearby *conucos*.[46] What probably occurred was that Miguel Díaz, or someone for him, procured food by contacting the cacique of Higüey, who resided on the Yuma river to the southeast. It is not clear whether he also agreed to transfer some of his people to the Ozama, where Indians subsequently were very populous. These inferences suggest that Miguel Díaz and his followers were, in effect, the de facto founders of the fort in 1496, which two years later became the town of Santo Domingo.[47]

During the remainder of 1496 and early 1497, Bartolomé divided his time between a sojourn at Jaraguá, where he was entertained by Beehechio and his sister, Anacaona, widow of Caonabó; a return to Fort San Cristóbal; and suppression of an incipient revolt led by the cacique Guarionex near Concepción, presumably over increased tribute and personal services. According to Las Casas, Bartolomé made a second journey to Jaraguá. This must have occurred in late 1496, after he received word that large amounts of tribute were ready to be picked up. Bartolomé sent word to Diego Colón in Isabela that a caravel be sent to the bay near the Indian village (bay of Port-au-Prince) while he, Bartolomé, went by land. After the cassava and cotton were loaded, and the dyewood which had been cut and stacked at Jacmel was picked up, the caravel followed the coast to Isabela. Bartolomé and his men then returned overland to San Cristóbal and the fort on the Ozama, probably with Indians carrying provisions for the new settlement.

Meanwhile in Isabela, where Diego Colón had been left in command, a general discontent was fanned to rebellion by rumors that the Columbus faction was striking it rich to the south. This coincided with a promising situation for wresting political control from the hated Genoese and their followers. The possibilities rested partly with Indian discontent on the Vega, and even more, if unrecognized at the time, in the ties of concubinage, *guatiao*,[48] and mutual understanding that furthered this potential interracial alliance. The time could not be more opportune, for the long silence from Spain harbingered apparent ignominy for Columbus. The discontent found a leader in the bold and energetic Francisco Roldán, who had recently become alcalde mayor but was by sympathy aligned with the disfavored Spaniards and—in their view at least—persecuted by the Columbuses among whom the stern Bartolomé was the most hated.

Roldán has been traditionally viewed as a main contributor to the turbulence that would lead to Columbus's removal in 1500, and Columbus has, on the other hand, been regarded as a poor judge of men for selecting such a contentious person for his alcalde mayor. The tradition remains roughly accurate in the first respect, but not in the second. As Ballesteros partly perceived, and Cipriano Utrera saw more clearly,[49] Columbus never trusted Roldán, even when he left the island in March, 1496. Before departing from Spain on the second voyage, Columbus had been permitted by the king to name Gil García as his alcalde mayor, though the capitulations called for nomination by the so-called ternary system: Columbus would nominate three candidates for official positions, and the king would select one. But because of the need for the second expedition's prompt dispatch the king had waived his rights. Yet as Utrera convincingly argues, Roldán must have sailed with the proviso that he would succeed to the position should it become vacant. Roldán's native town lay within the direct influence of the archbishop of Toledo, considered the most influential figure in Spain next to the king. Who actually recommended Roldán is not known, but it seems certain that he was begrudgingly accepted by Columbus, especially since the Discoverer asked for his removal soon after he reached Spain—months before rebellion broke out on the island.

Roldán's plans were to take over Fort Concepción, the strongest fort on the island next to Isabela. This would permit him to hold the region on which the Columbuses depended for provisions, and to join forces with Guarionex, whom Roldán had befriended. He covertly began the rebellion apparently in May, 1497, by marching from Isabela to Fort Concepción, announcing that his purpose was to quell an Indian rising. At the fort, the Catalan Miguel Ballester, a supporter of the Columbuses, got word of Roldán's intent and sent a messenger to Bartolomé Colón, who would have been either at Fort San Cristóbal or the Ozama fort.

Roldán, finding it impossible to take the fort with such forces as he had, returned rapidly to Isabela to force the arsenal, while the timid Diego Colón took refuge in the stone warehouse. Roldán then countermarched to the

Vega with additional men, livestock, horses, and arms. Other Spaniards and some caciques joined him, especially at La Magdalena, and he possibly had the great majority of the Indians ready to fight at his bidding for he promised to free them of tribute. But he still could not take the fort, probably for want of artillery, and retired to Guarionex's village a few miles away. During the next ten months or so, until March, 1498, several interchanges took place between Bartolomé and Roldán, but to no effect other than to rekindle a mutual hatred. Bartolomé's actions during this time are obscure; the chroniclers simply state that he remained in the fort under siege by Roldán. If so, some of the Indians must have remained friendly, or the defenders could not have survived for want of food. On the part of Roldán and his followers, relations with many of the Indians reached the point that Roldán viewed them as his people. He would later take several hundred with him to Jaraguá, and would demand that Columbus release five hundred of them enslaved as rebels.

The deadlock on the Vega was broken in March, 1498, when word came to Barolomé from the south that two caravels had arrived under the command of Pedro Hernández Coronel, Columbus's *alguacil mayor* (law enforcement officer). Barolomé marched southward to learn what news this first voyage to the south coast had brought; he was followed, presumably at a discreet distance, by Roldán and his men. The thin assumptions on which Roldán based his original actions now collapsed, as he learned that Columbus's capitulation had been confirmed, that he would soon be returning to resume the governorship, and that his hated antagonist Bartolomé had been rewarded with the title of adelantado. Although Bartolomé offered, with what sincerity one may question, to negotiate peace with Roldán, the latter decided to withdraw to Jaraguá, probably to avoid possible capture from forces that might well have been increased by the recent expedition.

Meanwhile a few missionaries were making converts among the Taínos in northern Española. The Indians who came to Isabela almost daily to barter yams,cassava, and peppers, were attracted by the novelty of these strange men with their colored beads and bright cloth, which could be obtained by barter. They marvelled at the brass bell that "talked," calling the Spaniards to mass. "They are good prospects for the Christian faith," Dr. Chanca, the physician, wrote to the king. "they already imitate us as we pray, even without instruction."[50] Columbus also had written the king of the natural piety of the Indians and their apparent desire to accept the Christian faith.

Not many of the friars, it seems, ventured forth from Isabela to win souls on the Vega. Here, where Indian relations soon deteriorated as Spaniards pressed on the native food supply, cut off ears for theft, or seized native women, the prospects would be less promising. Friar Boyl remained in the coastal fort, as did most of the others, but Ramón Pane and Juan de Deule were already at Fort Magdalena soon after it was erected and Pane, at least, was an eye-witness to the burning of the fort that year. After the Battle of the Vega, which opened up the valley as far as Concepción, Pane situated himself at the latter place and began missionary work among the tribe led by Guarionex, who had agreed to furnish tribute to Columbus.

Friar Pane is the actual inaugurator of evangelization on Española.[51] Although of monastic training, like most of the others, he sensed and responded to the unique challenge of winning converts of a culture greatly different from his own. He was unlike Friar Boyl, who wrote the king that nothing could be done without Indian interpreters, and who sent a few Indians back to Spain with Antonio de Torres in February, 1494. Pane proceeded patiently to learn the language, to see beyond the veneer of nakedness and occasional repulsive custom to the precious humanity embodied in a kind act or the Indians' simple wonder. As Boyl and an unknown number of other friars returned to Spain in the late summer of 1494, Pane, sometimes accompanied by Friar Deule, began making converts over a period of about two years—to 1498. His first convert was Juan Mateo who was baptized on September 21, 1496. Friar Pane then converted an entire family of seventeen, and made some progress with Guarionex, the main cacique at Concepción. During these years he also compiled a record of Taíno customs and legends. This was to be the best source on the Arawaks, whose population was to be greatly depleted, and the first major anthropological document of the New World.[52]

But this notable effort by a single man, or at best two if one counts Friar Deule, was to be ruined as a result of the conflict initiated by Roldán. When the rebel leader incited Guarionex to revolt, the first word Pane had of its effect was that Indian followers of the cacique had attacked and killed his converts. After killing the Indian Christians, who had been left by the friar in a thatch *oratorio*, Guarionex's men removed and buried the sacred Christian images. Pane learned from an Indian, that Mateo had died crying "*Dios naboria Daca*" (I am a servant of God).[53] Friar Pane stayed on for a time—Columbus mentions him in autumn, 1498—but he is not heard from again. Whether he returned to Spain, overcome by great discouragement, or was killed by Indians, is not known.

As Roldán and his men, who numbered about seventy-five, crossed the Haina and the Yaque del Sur to the Jaraguá basin, their movement was in one sense a ploy in an uncertain game that had momentarily gone against them. With their Indian followers and families, they would take up residence among the lake basin tribes, to infiltrate the native cacicazgos, to unite their own purposes with the Indians' aim of rejecting the more onerous demands of the foreigners. In another sense, it was the advance of Spaniards into the Indian culture of southwestern Española, an assimilation without force, but as much an occupation of the land as the conquest of the Vega or the expedition to the lower Haina and Ozama rivers. Casas, who was in certain respects sympathetic to Columbus, saw the *roldanistas* as the epitomy of lust and brutality; Pérez de Tudela's contemporary view is that the Spaniards adapted easily, even enthusiastically, to the polygamous society, whose women were considered the most attractive on the island, while exacting light labor from the Indians.[54] His *roldanistas* seem forerunners of the Spaniards who later entered the Guaraní society of Paraguay. In the long run, the roldanistas could only be separated from their Indian allies by the surgery of violence, an excision performed six years later by Governor Ovando. Meanwhile, Roldán bided his time and was kept informed of events at Santo Domingo by friends still resident on the Vega or at Bonao, a small fort thrown up to link San Cristóbal and Concepción.

Around Concepción, Guarionex, who feared punishment for complicity with the Roldán revolt, fled to the cordillera septentrional and took refuge among the bellicose Ciguayos, a subtribe. Bartolomé waged a hard three-months' campaign through the mountains before a few of his men, disguised as Indians, captured the hapless cacique. It was his last revolt. Put in chains and held in the stockade at Concepción, he and Roldán would find a common ocean grave in the great shipwreck of 1502. Roldán, meanwhile waiting for the Admiral's arrival—whom he found easier to get along with—was further emboldened when three vessels, sent out by Columbus with supplies, missed the mouth of the Ozama and put ashore near Jacmel.[55] Although the vessels were commanded by such faithful supporters of the Admiral as Alonso Sánchez de Carvajal, and Columbus's relative, Giovanni Colombo, the rank and file were of the Spanish peasantry, with a small sprinkling of criminals. Roldán or his men persuaded forty of these to desert to their Edenic valley and avoid the hard-handed treatment they could expect from the Genoese tyrants. To the protests of Carvajal, Roldán replied with mock humor that he had an order of observants here and piously declined to refuse admittance to just anyone.

The three ships finally beat their way back against countervailing winds to Santo Domingo, to find that Columbus had just arrived from his explorations off the Pearl Coast of Venezuela. The Navigator had docked on August 31, broken in health, but sanguine in spirit, carrying perhaps 170 pearls, and planning to send Bartolomé to establish a factoría there at the earliest opportunity. At Santo Domingo, Indians had planted a conuco of 80,000 hills of yuca, thatch huts were sprouting along the Ozama, and the mines along the Haina were showing better results.[56] He might have been on the verge of enjoying the fruits of six years of anguish and hardship, if it were not for the news that his alcalde mayor had disowned his authority and was entrenched like a rebel kinglet in the southwest. It might be supposed that Columbus could have brought Roldán forcibly to justice, for the rebel had, by this time, only about 115 men and his Indian allies would not be decisive in a contest with Spanish arms. But this choice was not open to Columbus. The vast majority of the perhaps four hundred men on the island had no desire to support the Genoese in warfare against a Spaniard; Spanish nativism and anti-Genoese feeling were deeply rooted, for the Genoese were enviably prosperous in Seville and shared with the Jews a reputation, warranted or not, for greed and sharp bargaining. Columbus's alcaide, Miguel Ballester, warned him that he could scarcely count on seventy men for active support. Nor was the choice of simply ignoring Roldán in his self-imposed exile an alternative. King Ferdinand might understand that great amounts of gold could not be produced overnight; he could never countenance failure to maintain control, for weak royal government bred disaster. Columbus knew he must do everything possible to eliminate the rebellion for pearls alone would not keep him in the position of viceroy.

Conscious of his weak position, he opened negotiations with Roldán who had come to the Bonao to join his friends there.[57] The rebel was likewise soon sentient of his strength and planned to make the most of it. Through Ballester and subsequently through Carvajal, whom the rebels found especially congenial, Columbus offered free passage to Castile for Roldán, his men, and their Indian families; in addition they would receive full payment of back salary, and the Admiral's personal recommendation to the king that they had served well and should be rewarded. The negotiations continued through the autumn of 1498, and were for a time forestalled as Roldán insisted on the return of five hundred Indians that Bartolomé had enslaved during his earlier campaign, and who were presently in the holds of five caravels about to depart for Spain. But Columbus would not yield on this point, and Roldán finally agreed to the terms proffered at Concepción on November 17, 1498. Columbus was to send two ships to the bay of Jaraguá within fifty days, provisioned for the voyage to Spain.

Thus Columbus gave up his planned expedition of Bartolomé to Venezuela, for he had to use two of his three remaining vessels to deal with the more critical matter of Roldán. The two vessels were dispatched in January, 1499, but were partly wrecked by a storm and had to put in at the site of Azua for repairs. Columbus had gone to the Vega in an effort to detach the caciques from the anti-Columbus Spaniards by suspending tribute for a certain time. He returned to Santo Domingo in May to learn that Roldán had informed Carvajal, who had proceeded overland to Jaraguá from Azua, that the agreement was broken since Columbus had failed to furnish the ships in fifty days. Roldán's men had added that the condition of the ships suggested that Columbus hoped they would embark on the open sea in two floating coffins.

With the first agreement broken off, Columbus could only hope to offer even more gratifying terms with which to win the Roldanistas back to his nominal authority. Considering the known circumstances of the rebel group, many of them deserters from the king's payroll, criminals who would not be given a second chance, it seems unlikely that more than a minority ever wanted to return to Spain. This was confirmed when Columbus reopened negotiations in the summer of 1499 with Roldán, who was quite willing to continue discussions. A second agreement was arranged at Azua in August, between Carvajal and Roldán, in which fifteen men were to be provided free passage to Spain; all others were to be given land and Indians to serve them (in most cases, a mere legal confirmation of what they already had) and payment of back salaries. Roldán was to be restored to his former position as alcalde mayor, which Bartolomé had divested him of in 1498. Columbus thus won over Roldán, however superficially, to his authority. Had it not been for other complications—the time lag in communications with Spain, the awakened concern of Queen Isabel about Indian slavery, and finally, the particular interpretation Francisco de Bobadilla made of his instruction—Columbus might well have continued as viceroy, as anti-Genoese feeling subsided in proportion with each new discovery of gold.

Even the agreement with Roldán did not end all strife on the island, although the conflicts that continued were personal, of limited dimension, and were not of themselves more than an unweighable contributing cause for Columbus's removal. Roldán ably defended his cacicazgo later in 1499, when Alonso de Ojeda who, with Vespucci, had quickly followed up Columbus's voyage to the Pearl Coast with his own, came to Jacmel on his return voyage to load up with dyewood and Indian slaves.[58] Ojeda had first-hand knowledge that the monarchs planned to send an investigator who would, temporarily at least, remove Columbus, and he tried to incite Roldán's men to overthrow the Navigator. But Roldán had already pressed his luck far enough; he rejected the offer and forestalled Ojeda's attempts to subvert the roldanistas. After this, Roldán fell to quarreling with various of his followers, notably Hernán Guevara, who wanted to marry a daughter of Anacaona whom Roldán already considered one of his concubines. Roldán finally arrested Guevara and sent him as a prisoner to Santo Domingo, but the latter's cousin, Andrés de Mújica, resumed the feud from Concepción. At the time of their removal, the Columbuses were jailing and hanging Spaniards who had been sent to them by Roldán, in a belated and unfortunate display of force after the main threat to their authority had already passed.

Just as Columbus's days were numbered as governor of Española, the great gold strikes, the main objective since

1494, were finally being made. Certainly the discovery of large nuggets by Miguel Díaz and Francisco de Garay in 1496 on the lower Haina had furnished a clue to where rich deposits might lie, and had led to the founding of Santo Domingo two years later. These nuggets had been found in a six-mile area pockmarked by ancient pits, but still bearing important deposits, and the field came to be known as the San Cristóbal (later Minas Viejas) mines. However, no miners then present apparently knew how to read the geological structure with a practiced eye.

Certain miners who arrived in the 1498 voyages were more knowledgeable, and they made the first major discovery of gold in 1499 on the northern slope of the cordillera central, where Columbus and his men had been in 1494.[59] As later geological knowledge showed, wherever mountain spurs bearing quartz diorite appeared, surface gold had worked its way up from the parent rock.[60] This structure traced out the two main mining regions of the next twenty years: San Cristóbal–Buenaventura on the southern spur of the cordillera central, and the La Vega-Cotuy-Bonao triangle to the north, generally called the Cibao. These discoveries would lead to pit mining and were to constitute the core of the mining zone. By centering the population in that area until the post-1515 decline, Isabela was depopulated by 1500, and perhaps hundreds of placers would be rather quickly washed out. A mining boom was in the offing, supplemented by discovery of new mines in the years ahead within the same zone.

Worn down by years of disappointment and embittered by the revolts against him, Columbus could only philosophize on learning of the great news:

> I was on the verge of letting it all go and escaping from life if I could, when Our Lord consoled me miraculously, saying; be bold, do not dismay do not fear; I will see that all is provided. The seven years of the golden age have not passed.[61]

Faced with countless demands for mine labor, Columbus now gave out squads of Indians in varying numbers to work for short periods of time. Thus, his last step in trying to develop the island was to adopt forced labor. In the pandemonium that ensued many men, especially recent arrivals, did not receive Indians. At Santo Domingo the enterprise was viewed as one more example of Genoese cupidity, with Columbus's favorites getting the richer deposits and first access to labor.

Meanwhile Queen Isabel had received complaints about Columbus, his tyranny, and his executions of rebels. The message had probably been smuggled aboard the five-ship fleet that left Santo Domingo in October, 1498. Isabel was probably more incensed with Columbus's sending five hundred slaves to Spain, than with his punishment of rebels. She ordered that the Indians be held pending their return to Española with an investigator who would inquire into the justice of Columbus's rule. She chose Francisco de Bobadilla, a comendador of the order of Calatrava, who was typical of the officials relied upon by the kings. His exact identity has been apparently confused—until the corrective research of Incháustegui Cabral in 1964—with the corregidor of Calatrava,[62] who was genuinely pious and even tempered, a conciliator well suited to bring peace. The comendador, on the other hand, had a long record of forthright action that stirred up numerous lawsuits against him by towns, and in one instance he had narrowly excaped assassination. He was presumably selected for loyalty and vigor, but he was not instructed, so far as documents show, to depose the Columbuses.

The Comendador Bobadilla sailed for Santo Domingo in June, 1500, with a small group of immigrants and six Franciscan friars; as a body they bore the anti-Genoese prejudices of their time, always deeper among the popular element, which Bobadilla represented, than among the upper class. Their expectations about Genoese tyranny seemed well supported as they saw corpses swinging from gallows along the Ozama, although they had been executed for rebelling against Roldán. Bobadilla took immediate action: he arrested Diego Colón and sent a party out after the two brothers who were in the interior.

Meanwhile, possibly carried away by the popularity of his actions, Bobadilla declared that mining would be virtually free. He announced that miners would pay only one-eleventh to the Crown and, in effect, abolished the share of one-tenth to Columbus and the royal share of one half. On what authority he acted has never been made clear, but it is evident that his short rule would have been even shorter if it had not been for the slowness of communications and the time needed to find a successor. Columbus naturally opposed abolition of his contract, an attitude Bobadilla and others interpreted as rebellious. Columbus nonetheless submitted peacefully to Bobadilla as an agent of the king, and all three Columbuses were sent back to Spain.

"The island has been liberated from King Pharaoh," Friar Trasierra, one of the newly arrived Franciscans, wrote to Jíménez de Cisneros, "for the covetous Genoese have been hurled from the island before they could completely ruin it. Beseech the king that they never return."[63] Their comment seemed to support Columbus's wry opinion, later expressed, that he could do nothing right on Española, for "if I built a church they would call it a cave for thieves."[64]

During the Discoverer's eight-year governorship, much of western and central Española had been occupied, a chain of forts linked the northern and southern coasts, and gold had at last been discovered in quantity. By a sequence of trial and error, Columbus had moved from barter to tribute to forced labor, thus demonstrating that the factoría system was ill suited to a land where the natives had low acquisitive power and the Spaniards expected to enjoy a proportionate share in whatever wealth might be found. Though the Catholic kings had removed Columbus primarily to avert what they saw as potential civil strife, the island was still not under royal control. The Roldanistas remained in Jaraguá like feudal lords, controlling thousands of Indians. The church had barely begun its missionary task, partly for want of friars, but significantly too because it lacked motivation. Since Friar Boyl's hasty return to Spain, the few Franciscans on

Española preferred to work quietly within their thatch convents to convert a few caciques' sons. Spanish civilization thus rooted itself slowly in Española and in ways not always planned by the Spaniards themselves.

2

Española During the Gold Rush (1500-1508)

Expansion and Control

Ever since 1493 when hordes of gold-seekers had enthusiastically joined Columbus's second voyage only to find disillusionment or death, or at best a thatched hut and a Taíno harem, Española had been acquiring a reputation as a tropical graveyard for the gullible and a dumping ground for convicts. In the following years while a few score settlers immigrated to Española on the several small chartered expeditions, hundreds decided to return to Spain. This irregular ebb and flow of immigration was typical of early Caribbean history and indeed of the whole sixteenth century in America. Conquests or mining strikes precipitated rushes disproportionate to the gains to be shared; after a brief heyday, those who lost out either returned to Spain or pursued a new rumor of wealth in unsettled lands. The Crown was interested in permanent occupation of the land and in economic development that would outlast the evanescent gold placers; but there were almost always either too many people or too few. The later gold rushes to Puerto Rico, Cuba, and Panama, and the frantic rush to Mexico in 1520, illustrate the erratic rhythm of migrations. Just before 1500, when the first important gold strikes on Española were made, the island was about to be written off as a small provisioning station useful only for supporting more fortuitous ventures.

Certainly Columbus's venture had been profitless to

Ferdinand, who had invested much and received little in return.[1] The finding of gold nuggets was about as rare as the saving of Taíno souls. But he had not given up on Columbus for he renewed the capitulation in 1497 and encouraged him to make a third voyage of exploration. However, when even the bruited wealth on the Haina did not at once materialize, the king felt that other explorers should have the chance to try their luck, provided they remained outside the areas—vague with regard to the Venezuelan coast—that Columbus had discovered.

In the fall of 1498 Columbus had sent back enough pearls to whet the appetites of the king and explorers alike. Attracted by these pearls from the Venezuelan coast, for which a map drawn on Columbus's voyage was an adequate guide, pearl barterers left the ports of Cádiz, Palos, and Moguer in considerable numbers. There were a half dozen voyages between 1499 and 1500, a cycle inaugurated by Alonso de Ojeda and Amerigo Vespucci and concluding with the voyage of Rodrigo de Bastidas to the gulf of Urabá in 1500–01. A few other unsuccessful voyages followed, but shipwrecks, Carib poisoned arrows, and the great gold strikes on Española diverted attention from the Pearl Coast for a few years. In spite of such setbacks, the discovery of pearls placed the New World in a more promising aura. This coincided with the news of important gold discoveries which were reported to the monarchs while they were in Granada in the autumn of 1500 (Ferdinand was much more interested in such matters than the queen). The king was there anxiously awaiting word on Gonzalo de Córdoba's progress in Naples; Ferdinand was also keeping an eye on the restless Moors, who sensed liberation with each Turkish advance in the eastern Mediterranean. The great news of the gold strike was brought to him by Friar Francisco de Ruiz.[2] The king was subsequently informed of the gold strikes by Columbus himself, who had been invited to come to Granada in December. The Navigator warned him that the gold was slipping through their fingers, that it was being smelted privately in crucibles and shipped secretly to merchants in Spain. Nor were the pearls usually finding their way to the royal treasury, as the king learned later. Peralonso Niño and Cristóbal Guerra, whose voyage (1499–1500) was one of the most lucrative, put in at Bayona, Galicia, where many of the pearls were reported stolen.[3] The Voyagers had paid the royal fifth, at least on the remainder, but the great irregularities and the need for control were all too clear. In addition, the pearl ships carried Indians whose enslavement was hardly justifiable, even on traditional grounds. Dyewood was also brought in and was peculated by the two merchants authorized to handle its purchase and sale for the king.[4] Columbus assured him that there was serious need for an efficient and trustworthy contador and treasurer on the island. Till now there had been so little income and so much turbulence that the performance of minor public servants had been overlooked. In sum, the Indies conjured fantastic visions of wealth, and the king now moved forthrightly to control it in all ways possible; the wealth was furthermore linked with Ferdinand's ambitions to assume the leadership of Christendom against the Islamic foe and he may even now have been forming the great plans he would execute after the death of the queen. These were years of thrilling expectancy. In 1501, the king learned of another gold strike on the upper Haina, where Columbus's cousin, Giovanni Colombo, had found rich deposits in the fields—later called Minas Nuevas—near Buenaventura, up the river from San Cristóbal.[5]

Ferdinand's primary aim was henceforth to bring the island and its wealth under the control of the crown, while meeting the obligations of the bull of 1493 by putting the nascent mission church on a firmer footing. In the latter respect he took a decisive step by instructing his ambassador to the Holy See to request a bull from the Pope allowing royal collection of the tithes, an important preliminary in securing control of the Church. His motive was not, as has so often been charged, that he simply desired absolute power. The king had learned bitter lessons from trying to coexist with a quasi-independent Church, especially when he faced powerful warrior bishops in the civil war that secured the throne for himself and his queen. Though he now had loyal appointees, confirmed by the Pope, in the key positions of the Church hierarchy, the Church was by no means exclusively under his patronage. He and the queen had been waging a running conflict with the Pope for twenty years over papal appointment of bishops and the sending of episcopal revenues to the papacy.[6] The prelates appointed by the Popes, moreover, were often foreigners and absentees, a practice that ran countergrain to the renascent Spanish nativism the monarchs had so successfully nurtured. Thus Ferdinand's acquisition of the bull of 1501, granting him the right to collect the tithes in the Indies, was motivated primarily by experience, not political theory, and the alert Aragonese monarch moved swiftly to exact from a Pope who needed his support against France what he had so long been denied in the past. Ferdinand would not obtain royal patronage, however, until 1508, a delay caused by the failure of the 1504 bulls to specifically award it and by the exigencies attendant to the interregnum after the queen's death. But the first bishop to the New World would not arrive until the end of 1512, as territorial expansion made the 1508 bull obsolete and further delayed the establishment of the episcopacies.

It was equally important for the king to gain control over the weak island government, as Columbus had been obliged to placate rather than rule the settlers, now enjoying the early gold boom with a low tax on gold decreed by Bobadilla, and evading even that by smuggling. The selection of a firm and loyal governor and the establishment of a reliable treasury that would assure the crown's one-third were paramount matters. After some deliberation, the king chose Nicolás de Ovando of the Order of Alcántara (later Comendador de Lares of that order) to serve for two years. Ovando, a native of Extremadura, whose father had supported the Catholic kings in the civil war, had served loyally and capably in the lands administered by that order; he had himself witnessed as a youth the civil wars there, and thus shared the king's concern with preventing the resurrection of rebellious feudalism.[7] Moreover, he was devout in his personal life and a faithful Catholic, which made him an equally good choice to further establishment of the church. Ovando was instructed in 1501 to conduct Bobadilla's *residencia* (an investigation into an outgoing official's conduct while in office), to look into the causes for the Roldán revolt and its ensuing civil strife, and to see that Columbus's newly assigned one-tenth was collected and his properties restored. The royal treasury was to include not only a contador and treasurer, but also a royal factor who, in addition to handling the sale of such monopolized commodities as dyewood and salt, was to be the only seller of European goods to the colonists. The king justified this last measure on the grounds that the crown had borne great expenses for eight years during the search for gold, and had a right to reap all possible profits now that the long-awaited bonanza had arrived. Finally, a veedor was to supervise the mining operations in the interests of general efficiency, productiveness, and the honest return of metals to the royal foundries.

Greater supervision in America would of course be pointless without equally close control at some port in Castile, where ships engaging in the Indies trade might be cleared on departure or return. Until 1501–1502 when Governor Ovando was fitting out what would be the largest expedition thus far to sail for America, fleets had sailed from Cádiz or adjacent ports with the logistics chiefly being arranged by Bishop Juan Rodríguez de Fonseca, a cleric with great administrative ability, and on whom Ferdinand had relied since Columbus's return from his first voyage. Rodríguez de Fonseca, in turn, depended on various assistants, including the *corregidor* of Jerez (near Cadiz), and while this informal means of fitting out worked well for small expeditions, the great delay involved in dispatching Ovando was alone sufficient evidence that better organization was needed. Moreover, many other conditions argued for such a body, such as the smuggling of gold and pearls, and the simultaneous demand for ships, supplies, men, and arms for the Canaries, the Barbary Coast, and Italy. Then, too, such an organization could handle the sale of crown goods, which Ferdinand had now decided to monopolize.

For all these reasons, the Casa de Contratación, as the organization was called, came to be established in Seville in January, 1503. Its first officials were a treasurer, Dr. Sancho de Matienzo, a contador, Jimeno de Bribiesca, and a factor, Francisco Pinelo. It served as a model for the similar though smaller organization established at about the same time by Governor Ovando at Santo Domingo. The Casa de Contratación assumed other duties in the next few years: supervising the economic development of Española, recruiting and fitting out expeditions, and training pilots to prevent ships returning to such wayward places as France, Portugal or Galicia, as they did on occasion, the pilots claiming that they had miscalculated their directions on the return voyage.[8] About the time that Governor Ovando sailed, then, the king had with characteristic energy created the instruments of royal control over the government, fisc, and commerce of Española, and had taken initial steps to establish the Church in America. Taken together, the unifying measures represented the crest of control and order carried out by the Catholic kings, measures that would be supplemented on Española by Governor Ovando and upheld by him until 1509, five years after he wished to return. His relatively long governorship of seven years retained order in the Indies while disorder, after the death of the queen in 1504, threatened at times to engulf Spain.

Meanwhile the great Ovandine fleet had been slowly fitted out at San Lúcar de Barrameda. Perhaps owing to the long time required for these preparations, word of the gold boom on Española circulated widely, attracting the some twenty five hundred expeditionaries who looked forward to making their fortunes. Among these were *hidalgos* from Andalusia like Diego de Nicuesa from Baeza, and Lúcas Vázquez de Ayllón from Toledo, later to be prominent as a letrado, judge, and explorer. Like Columbus, who had many more men than could be cared for in

1493, Ovando also had a great surplus, whose numbers would soon be diminished by starvation and disease and whose desires for economic gain he would partly satisfy by completely occupying the island. The expedition was the second and last large movement of people to Española and would inaugurate the period of maximum early prosperity on the island lasting until approximately the end of Ovando's governorship. There was more intrinsic harmony in this expedition than in the one of 1493. Ovando and the hidalgo class understood each other; not a few of them followed the governor from Extremadura where the Reconquest mentality—the desire for land, wealth, and serfs won in warfare—was deeply rooted.[9] The military character of the occupation was adumbrated in these aspirations.

The mission church still seemed reluctant to accept the challenge of converting an untold number of heathen Indians. Friar Ruiz had prevailed upon Jiménez de Cisneros, Archbishop of Toledo, to recruit thirteen Franciscans; the contingent was headed by Friar Alonso de Espinar as prior.[10] But the size of this contingent of friars was insignificant in light of the enormous number of fortune-seekers, for it meant that only about twenty-five friars were resident on the island at the outset of Ovando's governorship. Even without the great obstacle of a gold rush economy and forced labor for the Indians, the progress would necessarily have been limited.

The great armada finally cleared the harbor at San Lúcar in February, 1502, and after a single mishap—a ship was lost near the Canaries—reached Santo Domingo in April in two separate flotillas.

Governor Ovando's initial duty was to conduct the *residencia* of Frey Bobadilla, his predecessor, and of Francisco Roldán, the alcalde mayor. Roldán was at best in an untenable position with respect to his past actions toward the Columbuses, who represented, after all, royal authority on the island. The charges were presumably written up against both men by July, when they and an unknown number of Roldán's followers were put aboard the return fleet for Spain. Nothing is known of Ovando's recommendations for their possible punishment, because the thirty-ship fleet was all but completely destroyed in the Mona passage by a hurricane. The two men were drowned along with most of the passengers and few vessels, one of them bearing Rodrigo de Bastidas whose own ships had been destroyed off western Española earlier when he returned from Panama, ever reached Spain. The disaster badly disrupted communications with Spain, for the queen still had no word of what had happened to the ships a year later, although the chronicler Bernáldez understood that several vessels made their way to different parts of Spain. The whole matter, the residencias and the shipwreck, remain obscure, and though Ovando must have surely commented on both matters later, his letters have never been found.[11]

The same hurricane had swept across the southern part of the island, flattening Santo Domingo except for its few stone houses, lessening an already scanty food supply, which contributed to the deaths of up to a thousand Spaniards, many of whom had returned or were returning from unsuccessful, amateurish prospecting excursions into the interior gold fields. The town was now rebuilt on the right bank of the Ozama where it would remain, although the vecinos still held conucos across the river and the town was linked to the left bank by barges operated by the city council. The governor might well have been subjected to criticism for dispatching the fleet, for Columbus had been off Santo Domingo outbound on his fourth voyage and had sent warning of an imminent storm. However that may be, the monarchs doubtless felt that Ovando's otherwise fine qualities for governing and developing the island offset his mistake in this respect.

Having dealt with the matter of misrule prior to his arrival, however accidental the outcome, Ovando faced the far more formidable task of expanding and bringing the mining industry under control, and usefully deploying the hundreds of men across the island, who might otherwise become a serious obstacle to orderly rule. The fundamental matter to be dealt with was to assure a labor force of a size commensurate with maximum production, and to look to the provisioning of the mines with adequate amounts of equipment from both local resources and Spain, and to provide a sufficient amount of foodstuffs—cassava, yams, *ají,* (pepper) and meat. The island was essentially divided, as the Spaniards soon realized, into two main zones: the mining region that encompassed the cordillera central with its southern spur, and the food zone, the highlands or valleys where crops could be raised. The more mines in operation, the more food was needed, and since mining was moving toward full stride soon after Ovando arrived, it was necessary to provide food from conucos other than those adjacent to the mines. This might well have meant a peaceful occupation of the eastern and western parts of the islands, an establishment of Spanish towns among tribes who would agree to furnish foodstuffs, for agricultural labor was not onerous. Circumstances were nonetheless to bring Spaniards and Indians into conflict, owing to earlier occurrences in the Higüey and at Jaraguá.

When Ovando arrived in Santo Domingo, he learned that the Taínos had risen in the eastern part of the island, the cacicazgo of Higüey, and had killed eight of nine Spaniards in a fort emplaced there to assure a regular supply of cassava to the mines. One Spaniard managed to escape the disaster, and according to Las Casas, who is the principal source for information about the conquest of Higüey, the vecinos were overjoyed at the chance to take slaves. It may be supposed that Miguel Diaz or Francisco de Garay had made friends with the cacique of Higüey, Cotubanamá, a year or two earlier, as they were the earliest settlers at the proximate site of Santo Domingo and were, consequently, instrumental in keeping the nascent colony of 1496–1498 alive with foods brought in by tribes situated near Santo Domingo. A legend repeated about Diaz's liaison with an Indian woman there is probably apocryphal but is suggestive of his good relations with the Indians; perhaps she later induced Cotubanamá to supply food from the Yuma valley, in the far eastern part of the cacicazgo. This area was well suited for the cultivation of cassava; though the northern part, bounded by the Yuna river, was largely mountainous, the littoral on the south coast of Samaná bay, the Yuna and Yuma valleys, and many fertile basins among the hills, produced excellent cassava, as did the offshore island of Saona. This small fertile island had by 1500 become a chief supplier of cassava to Santo Domingo, the Spaniards calling there in brigantines to pick up the harvest. But good relations with the Taínos on Saona were rudely broken when a Spanish dog attacked and disemboweled a local cacique on the island, after his master had playfully but stupidly urged the animal to attack. A peace-making expedition was subsequently dispatched, possibly led by Juan de Esquivel, which succeeded in making a new arrangement for the supply of cassava; to assure the source, the men erected a fort on the Yuma where the nine men were garrisoned. Presumably the attack whose repercussions enlivened Santo Domingo on Ovando's arrival, occurred about March, 1502.

The one and only campaign to subdue the Higüey, in this writer's interpretation, occurred during the summer and fall of 1502. Las Casas, our only source, tells of two campaigns, one in 1502, and another in 1504; if so, they are unlikely to have occurred in the manner in which he relates them. Both campaigns, he reports, were caused because of an Indian attack in which one man escaped, both required three hundred men, and both expeditions were led by Juan de Esquivel. In the last detail at least, this is surely a repetitive fallacy. Esquivel was in Spain as procurador of the island at approximately the time of the second campaign, which casts further doubt on the actuality of two wars.[12]

Although Governor Ovando might have restricted himself to sending a punitive expedition against the cacicazgo of Higüey, he evidently decided that, following its submission, Spaniards should be settled in the region's towns. Thus he had in mind a common solution that would rid the mining zones of surplus Spaniards and that would firmly occupy agricultural lands in the eastern part of the island. He called for levies from the newly established mining towns of Santiago de los Caballeros, Concepción, and Bonao, entrusting the expedition to Diego de Escobar, a pardoned Roldanista residing at Concepción. Among the soldiers were Juan Ponce de León, Juan de Esquivel, and Bartolomé de las Casas, the latter indistinguishable in these years from the average wealth-seeking Spaniards. Accompanied by a large contingent of Taínos from that region, the expeditionaries marched down the Yuna valley to launch campaigns that were to last several months, and which were preceded by scouting, tracking, and watching for signs of smoke. Las Casas, the only eyewitness known to have written about the campaign, depicted it as an orgy of atrocities—severing hands, impaling babies on swords, and roasting caciques alive. Although he does not report how many Spaniards were killed, from his account of a hand-to-hand combat between a Spaniard and an Indian, one may suppose that the Indians gave a good account of themselves in the rough terrain where horses were of no advantage.

The cacique Cotubanamá had meanwhile taken refuge on Saona island, where Juan de Esquivel was determined to capture him. He sent for a caravel from Santo Domingo and transported his men across the narrow channel separating the mainland from the island. One of the patrols came upon the chieftain, who was badly wounded in a struggle that nearly cost the life of the Spaniard who first discovered him on one of the island's paths. Captured and sent to Santo Domingo, Cotubanamá was hanged on Ovando's orders. A number of other Indians were enslaved during the campaign and sold at Santo Domingo.

The expeditionaries then established two towns, Salvaleón de Higüey on the lower Yuma, and Santa Cruz de Aycagua near the south shore of the Bay of Samaná.[13] Ponce de León settled in the former town where he remained until his expedition to Puerto Rico; Casas and his relatives were also resident there for some time, and all vecinos were granted *repartimientos* (essentially encomiendas) by the governor. The Taínos did not attempt another rising, as far as is known; one cannot know whether the campaign was as bloody as Las Casas depicted it, for he gives no estimate of the number slain, if indeed this could be known. Judging from the vecinos holding encomiendas there as late as 1514, at a time when population was declining in peripheral regions, the Higüey must have been populous when the Spaniards first settled there.[14]

The occupation of the eastern cacicazgo helped to resolve the food supply problem in two ways: by assuring that the subjugated Taínos would furnish provisions, and by dispersing some of the Spaniards from Santo Domingo and the mines where the food shortage was chronic. Still Ovando faced an acute problem in furnishing Indian labor for the many Spaniards who now wished to exploit the gold placers. It seems unrealistic to assume that the cédula of March, 1503, by which Queen Isabel ordered that the Indians be treated as free, voluntary workers, was an actual problem for him. Surely the gold rush, then fully underway, was not halted while Ovando set the Indians free and wrote the queen that they would not work voluntarily. Mining must have continued as before; a literal interpretation of the royal provision would have provoked, if not a revolt, a prompt dispatch of complaining procuradores.

Rather, the problem derived from a very different situation. Since the Spaniards had first debouched onto the Vega in 1494, gradually to find lodging among the Taíno tribes and to acquire concubines, there was the distinct possibility that they would claim title to the cacicazgo (or in actuality a subtribe of it) on the grounds of marriage to a *cacica*. Such marriages were performed by priests who had come out on Columbus's second voyage and who were probably untroubled by the implications. Not all such marriages were, to be sure, inspired by economic advantages, for, as we know, by the Repartimiento of 1514, many Spaniards were married to Taíno women who were not cacicas; a genuine affection must surely have bound together marriages where the Spanish husband even took his Indian wife to Castile for a sojourn. But claims to control populous tribes by reason of marriage now and again plagued Ovando in the mining zone and he dealt with them individually. If honored, such claims would have given the Spanish cacique control of hundreds of Indians while other Spaniards possessed few or none—a sure source of discontent and trouble. The king, moreover, who supported Ovando constantly on this matter, probably saw in it potential fiefs. Ovando obliged the claimants to settle for retention in his household of only his wife's immediate relatives; uncooperative Spaniards were sent back to Spain.[15] While these claims in the mining zones could be dealt with individually, such claimants in the cacicazgo of Jaraguá constituted a veritable phalanx. Here there were surely at least one hundred Spaniards, the nucleus consisting of the men who had followed Roldán to Beehechio's village—the cacique who before 1504 was to be succeeded by his sister, Anacaona. To the original band of Roldanistas were joined deserters from the ships that accidently arrived there, such as the advance fleet of Columbus's third voyage, which had been paid six months' advance salary by the crown, but chose to risk the penalties of desertion for the pleasures of Roldán's paradise. Still other deserters came from Ojeda's ships in 1499.

The region of Jaraguá, consisting of the lowlands along the south shore of Lake Enriquillo and extending into the cul-de-sac around today's Port-au-Prince, was the basis for the highest Taíno culture. Here crops were irrigated by water from the Camu river and unusually fine cotton mantas were woven; the Taínos also carved out and burnished bowls and benches (*duhos*) out of black wood obtained from trees on the adjacent island of Guabo (modern Gonave).[16] Ever since the first contact of Spaniards with this tribe, when Bartolomé Colón submitted them peacefully to tribute, they were considered the most physically attractive and intelligent of the Taínos. Martyr's lyrical pen limned an alluring account of how the nude Taíno women, dancing and singing and waving palm fronds,[17] customarily received visitors. The women were so desirable that Roldán and a rival quarreled over one of Anacaona's daughters, with Roldán emerging the victor. The Spaniards, most of whom were humble peasants, had indeed discovered a Muslim paradise. Some married into the tribes, and others simply took concubines. From Roldán they received title to lands on which their tribes lived, by which they could claim, if they desired, a double right to this native feud: by official title and by marriage.[18] But many of them had broken the law in one way or another and could expect summary justice if they fell into official hands—that was probably decisive in keeping them ensconced, in spite of the gold rush, in their *caciquils*. They shared a common fear and presented a common front. Governor Ovando thus faced a native feudalism of possibly serious proportions for if the lords were few, their retainers were many.

Taking the *residencia* of Roldán had nothing to do with the cacicazgo of Jaraguá. Roldán had long since detached himself from that region and his followers to occupy land on the Vega; indeed, during his revolt he would have come to terms sooner with Columbus had his men not feared justice would descend upon them. They preferred refuge among the Taínos of the southwest.

Ovando can be reasonably expected to have been in communication with the cacicazgo of Jaraguá long before he departed westward about July, 1503, with an expedition of three hundred men and perhaps several hundred Indians. He must have earlier found that his requests for more provisions and more Indians for mining repartimientos were evaded. The size of his expedition, and his personal leadership, meant that he was prepared for trouble should it arise; but the slow and deliberate pace he took overland, sending an exploring party to the highest peak of the southern range, suggested that he wished to find out what the land and its villages were like, and what the possibilities were for new mining enterprises. He either stopped by, or sent some men to Jacmel, the main dyewood port, for when Diego Méndez reached there from his harrowing canoe expedition from Jamaica, where Columbus was marooned, he learned from the comendador, Gallego, that Ovando was in Jaraguá dealing with a revolt.[19] His purposes were thus broader than merely visiting Jaraguá, for he wished to occupy the western part of the island wherever there were profitable economic commodities.

Exactly what happened at Jaraguá will presumably

never be known, though Las Casas may have and Martyr certainly talked about it to one or more participants. These writers understood that Ovando was well received, but that the ceremonious hospitality was in this instance a ruse, for the village was bristling with caciques who had come in from the mountain villages apparently prepared to offer resistance when they thought the time opportune. Ovando is alleged to have outdeceived the deceivers, and to have enticed them into a *batey* (large hut) to witness a tournament by Spaniards; when he touched his pectoral cross—a prearranged signal—Spaniards seized and bound the caciques, while others fell on the Indians milling about outside. Some eighty caciques were supposed to have been burned alive, while an unknown number of other Indians were slaughtered. Martyr relates the curious fact that mounted Spaniards tried to save children by carrying them off on their horses, but other Spaniards attacked and killed both the rescuers and the rescued.[20]

The obscurity of this information certainly invites reservations about exactly what occurred. First, the fragmentary accounts make it appear to be wholly a war of Spaniards against Indians, which is extremely improbable since Spaniards had lived and intermarried among these Indians for about six years. The children cut down as they rode behind persons trying to evacuate them could only mean mestizo children—the offspring of Spaniards who were making a last stand in their native caciquils. Finally, some fifty Spaniards were said to have lost their lives, which is an excessively high figure if the struggle pitted only Spaniards against Indians.

It can be further argued that there is at least reason to doubt whether Ovando resorted to burning caciques alive, even though Peter Martyr and Las Casas heard that this was what happened. That the caciques of Jaraguá, among the most intelligent and astute on the island, would permit themselves to be lured into a batey, when they themselves were planning an attack on the Spaniards does strain credulity. Moreover, that Ovando, with a large armed force, including horsemen with swords and lances, would find it necessary to use this stratagem, seems also unlikely. Finally, would the Spaniards married into the cacicazgo be so naive as to permit the caciques to be duped, even granting they were this gullible? The whole event is thus fraught with ambiguity and obscurity; Ovando took statements from participants to justify his attack on the cacicazgo, but such statements have never been found. What seems certain is that the Indians and their allies were badly defeated and Anacaona was hanged. Certain caciques fled to Cuba where they would face Diego Velázquez in 1511. The native feuds were broken, and Ovando gave out lands and Indians to the soldiers who accompanied him.

Having broken this pocket of resistance to his occupation of the western part of the island, the governor directed various of his lieutenants to submit the tribes to Spanish authority and establish towns in the more populous regions. Jaraguá became the *villa* of Verapaz, on or near the same site as Anacaona's village. Diego Velázquez led forces to the southwest to establish Salvatierra de la Sabana on the south shore of the peninsula of Guacayarima, a floodplain rich in soils and fisheries. Other forces, led by Rodrigo Mejía Trillo, established San Juan de la Maguana where Caonabó formerly resided, and then worked their way northwestward to establish Puerto Real on the north coast and Lares de Guahava, the latter village named after Ovando in his capacity as Comendador de Lares. Lares was inland from Puerto Real where copper was discovered at about this same time. Still other groups established Azua and earlier, Jacmel.

Thus, the conquest resulted in the founding of three inland towns and four ports; the lands brought under Spanish control represented important new sources of labor and provisions for the mining industry. Many of the three hundred men with Ovando settled down, for the time being, in these western villages to form mining partnerships with persons living in the mining zone. Ovando returned to Santo Domingo, apparently about March, 1504, where he would reside until his long-delayed return to Castile some five years later.

By the time Ovando returned to Santo Domingo, a

full-fledged mining system was in operation which would bring the island to the apex of its prosperity within a few years. There were no more Indian revolts, and Ovando was politic enough to discourage and obviate factionalism. His duties henceforth were to see that the system ran smoothly, that the king received his due share of profits, and that his subordinate officials were efficient and honest.

The mining industry was based on the Taínos' forced labor, supplemented in these years by a few Negro slaves; laborers were assigned to Spaniards by tribes or squads, numbering anywhere from a few Indians to several hundred. These allotments disrupted the main cacicazgos and eventually resituated and depleted the many small clans comprising them; to be sure, these processes were in part also attributable to the Indians' death rates and migration to other islands. As mentioned above, the natives were usually allotted to Spaniards by tribes consisting of a cacique and his extended family, although the great number of caciques listed in the documents suggests that the title was extended indiscriminately to many Indians who were formerly nitainos. The essence of the labor system was the encomienda, established by the cédula of December, 1503, which required that those Spaniards who had been entrusted with Indians had to see that their charges were given sufficient food and clothing and were instructed in the faith; in return for fulfilling these obligations, *encomenderos* could reap the benefits of the Indians' labor in mines and conucos. The tendency was toward a universal encomienda during these years, for nearly all Spaniards, no matter how humble, held at least a few Indians.[21] This represented a general victory for petty hidalgo ideals, but as the number of Indians declined, and courtiers in Spain (especially after 1514) acquired encomiendas as a source of revenue, the Spaniards left without Indians steadily increased. A *visitador*, or inspector, was assigned to each of the fifteen towns on the island to see that the encomendero's obligations were fulfilled, but as the visitador also depended on an encomienda for his income, he was unlikely to see anything wrong with the system as a whole. Indians who fled from their encomenderos were pursued and sometimes captured by *alguaciles de campo* who returned them, for a fee, to their encomendero. Such control was extremely loose, however, for many Indians drifted from one town or one encomendero to another, and after about 1509, Spaniards deserted their encomiendas about as often as Indians fled from them. This is to suggest that a picture of chained Indians, marching methodically to the mines and death, is an exaggeration, for as gold placers played out, which was often very rapidly, some encomenderos held on to their Indians without much working them even though Ferdinand repeatedly warned that anyone who did not keep one third of his Indians at work in the mines would lose them.[22]

With a labor system established, the seasons set a regular rhythm to mining operations. The Indians worked during the dry season, a variable period of six to nine months that began in January; during the wet season in the fall, called the *demora*, the Indians were permitted to return to their villages. During this time, gold was brought to the foundries for smelting, stamping, and payment of taxes and debts, while the miners and their families surrounded the event with a festive air, like the trade fairs of Spain, by holding jousting tournaments and other festivities.[23] The shipmasters from Seville gradually learned to accommodate themselves to this rhythm so as to arrive with a not overly long layover. Thus, a regular maritime trade was established soon after the gold discoveries, although we only have records of the ships calling after 1506. They brought over picks and shovels, wheat flour, salted fish, Dutch velvets and English camlets, livestock and seeds, and returned with gold bullion, dyewood, cotton, and hides.[24] The ships also brought immigrants, so many that by 1508 there were reported to be some twelve thousand Spaniards on the island, vastly more than the economy could support at its best, and it was by that time in decline.[25]

The heart of activity was concentrated in the general

center of the island—the mining region. Commerce from Spain was funneled through Santo Domingo, although the main port on the northern coast, Puerto Plata, also received a few ships from Spain. The main mining towns were Buenaventura, Bonao, Concepción de la Vega, and Santiago de los Caballeros. But during these years, the towns to the east and west in the purely agrarian zones also enjoyed a prosperity owing to their economic ties with the mining zone. These towns—Santa Cruz de Aycagua and Salvaleón de Higüey in the east, Sabana de Salvatierra, Verapaz, and San Juan de la Maguana in the west—were all important sources of provisions for the mines. Santa Cruz was especially productive of cassava, and Verapaz probably supplied bateas,[26] which were in constant demand in the placers. Azua had salt mines,[27] and all port towns could supply fish. These agrarian towns looked inward upon the mining zone, and the Spaniards who had taken up residence there were for a time reasonably content. Although there are no descriptions of this island trade, it is likely to have been primarily cabotage rather than overland, for we know that port towns were the chosen residence of sailors from Columbus's fourth voyage, who elected to remain on the island.[28] We also know from Chaunu's records that a high percentage of the ships coming out from Spain did not return, though ships were on occasion also built at Santo Domingo.[29] Thus, it is reasonable to suppose that provisions were transported by water to Santo Domingo or Puerto Plata and then carried inland by Indians or pack animals. The Spaniards engaged in supplying provisions to the miners were typically their partners and, as Las Casas observed, the farmer usually became rich, while the miner was left without a shirt on his back. This was perhaps typical though not invariable. Indians were unlikely to have been sent to the mines from the agrarian zone during Ovando's governorship, at least not in any great numbers, for the evidence suggests that a pronounced decline in the native population did not begin until about 1508,[30] and there would have been less need for them up to that time. After that, the periphery's depopulation process began, owing to both centripetal and centrifugal forces—that is, to a demand for labor in the mines and to explorations which took many Indians off the island.

Governor Ovando had brought with him the royal officials who were to administer the king's regalia, his share of the gold, and his monopolies on commerce, dyewood, salt, firearms, and horses. Since up to now gold had been smelted in crucibles and smuggled out by devious ways, Ovando must necessarily control gold production at the source. He had brought with him Rodrigo de Alcázar, the first official founder, and he established smelters at Concepción and Buenaventura to handle the output from the Cibao and Haina mines. Alcázar came equipped with bellows and was assigned an encomienda of Indians; henceforth the gold was smelted into ingots, the king's one-third laid aside, and the whole stamped with the weight, value, and the yoke and arrows—official insignia of the Catholic kings.[31] Further control was exercised by a system of licensing miners at a few *tomines* (the tomin was worth two reales) per license, the primary purpose being to have a record of miners in the event anyone failed to turn in gold ore during the demoras.

Control at the mines was matched by control at Santo Domingo, the island's main port. Here what was at first called the Casa de Contratación was established, a replica of its counterpart in Seville, with a treasurer, contador, and factor. The treasurer looked to the payment of salaries, and the collection of Crown income, the contador kept records on such receipts and disbursements, and the factor was to handle the sale of European goods and items monopolized by the Crown. The factor, however, was to decline in importance over the years and one of his duties—the handling of European trade—was already essentially removed by 1504. Though the king wished to recover his losses as rapidly as possible and had thus exercised his right to monopolize trade, the *vecinos* soon objected to high prices and scarce goods, and as the Spanish population was increasing, the king relinquished this right and opened the island to free trade in 1504.[32] The king was willing to compromise differences with the hidalgo class, on whom he depended for the island's conquest, but he astutely found some compensation by instituting the *almojarifazgo* tax on trade in 1508, an import tax of 7½ percent on European goods.[33] Ferdinand showed the same flexibility with respect to the royal share in the mines. He had at first exacted one-half of all gold produced, but on Ovando's advice had reduced this to one-third in 1502.[34] Subsequently, as procuradores of the island asked for a further reduction to one-fifth, he allowed the *quinto* in 1504.[35] At the same time, however, Ovando established the royal mines with their adjunctive conucos, thus placing the king directly in the mining business. The king became as a result the largest miner and encomendero on Española, as he would be on the other islands until the reforms under Charles V. Ovando henceforth kept one thousand Indians in the royal mines, and although this practice was almost as restrictive of hidalgo economic interests as the royal taxes formerly had been, the hidalgos apparently considered the King's economic activities for a time as beyond complaint.

Ferdinand had made the right choice in his selection of Nicolás de Ovando to implement royal control over the island that Columbus had discovered but was unable to govern. He had established fifteen towns, and stimulated and controlled the mines that possibly produced as much as 450,000 *pesos* a year.[36] On this base, the island was prosperous and European trade reached a peak of forty-five ships annually by 1508.[37] He had subdued factionalism and had faithfully seen to collection of Columbus's one-tenth; neither had he discriminated against the followers of Columbus still resident on the island.[38] The vecinos were reasonably satisfied with their share of the wealth, owing to the king's compromises and to the judicial officials named by Ovando—an alcalde mayor at Santo Domingo and another at Concepción. The latter was Lucas Vázquez de Ayllón who would spend the rest of his life as an encomendero, official, and explorer in the Caribbean.

The Hidalgo-Letrado Class and the Church

The hidalgos, the peasants who aspired to become hidalgos, and the few letrados, were the essential explorers, conquerors, and populators of Española. The movement was not dissimilar to the Reconquest of Spain, especially in Old Castile where plebians pushed back the Moors, established towns, and acquired privileges from the king. A similar populist movement on Española provides the underlying current of historical continuity below the more evanescent and protean surface of conspicuous facts—Columbus's factoría system, Ovando's bureaucracy, and later, the confusion and factionalism especially noticeable after 1514. The islanders aspired to the seignorial status much admired in Spain; they desired a life surrounded by *criados* and serfs and slaves, the display of mansions and lands, and of silk and velvet. Though the Roldanistas in their Indian harems seemed almost to pervert these traditional social aims, no few vecinos of the mining zone realized them—however briefly—during the Ovandine era of prosperity.

During Ovando's time there was considerable solidarity of interest among the vecinos, for the gold and the Indians were plentiful. They expressed this solidarity through their procuradores to the court, as their *Reconquista* forebears had done, with the aim of ennobling their towns, increasing their economic opportunities, and limiting the retention of encomiendas to married conquerors or original settlers while seeking to exclude latecomers and absentees.[39] As the number of Indians gradually decreased they would request that still others—bishops and finally resident officials—be excluded. They were in a strong bargaining position with the king, for they could threaten to return to Spain if he insisted on too great a share of the wealth for himself or his courtiers. They—or the Roldanistas for them—had broken the factoría monopoly by revolt, and the vecinos subsequently reduced the king's and Columbus's share—for these were tied together—from a half to a third, and finally by 1504 to a fifth. In this way Ferdinand retained the loyalty of the towns and thereby minimized the number who looked to Columbus and, after 1508, to his son Diego, as the fount of privileges and opportunities.

After Ovando's time, there were too many Spaniards for the Indian population, considering that two hundred Indians were held necessary for a reasonably profitable mining operation, and hence a decently supported seignorial existence. Solidarity was broken among the vecinos and factionalism was chronic, a situation that divided the society between those supporting the local bureaucracy and those following the Columbuses, though the lines of factionalism were not hard and fast. After 1508, the vecinos would dispute more and more over less and less till by 1520 there were few encomiendas to vie for. During Ovando's governorship, however, many vecinos had reason to believe their fondest seignorial dreams would be realized on Española.

The survivors of the second expedition had settled the Vega and the mining towns linked the north with Santo Domingo, and they provided the experienced leadership for the conquest of the eastern and western parts of the island. Together with others who had come with Ovando they settled the ports and the agricultural villages and assumed the town council positions of *alcaldes, regidores,* and *alguaciles.* Though these officials were appointed by Columbus and later Ovando, by 1508–1509 the towns received a *merced,* or favor, from the king to elect their own alcaldes who, in turn, would appoint the alguaciles. But it would be overly sentimental, as well as historically inaccurate, to suggest that the vecinos consistently aspired to town autonomy and constantly opposed the centralizing tendencies of the crown or, after 1508, of Diego Colón, the semi-feudal viceroy. They tended to support whatever was economically advantageous or socially desirable; they held no deep convictions about representative town government, sometimes arguing for it and at other times accepting lifetime appointments as regidores from the king. For the same reasons, some supported a hereditary governor for the island, while others believed that a royal governor of limited tenure would best serve their interests. In the long run, of course, supporting the king was most advantageous for the majority, so that the feudal aims of the Columbuses were foredoomed from the start; the hardiness of feudalism was due to the hiatus in effective royal power manifest in Spain after 1504—a hiatus that would be apparent on Española after Ovando's departure.

Like the hidalgos of the Reconquest, the islanders appealed to the king to enhance their economic and social positions on the grounds of securing the royal domain; the gold-mining era was hardly underway before the towns sent two procuradores, Juan de Esquivel of Concepción and Francisco Velázquez of Santo Domingo (representing the northern and southern regions) to ask for a larger share of the gold produced and for more plentiful and cheaper imports. It would have been impolitic for the monarch to deny them, for the success of both the economic enterprise and the religious aims depended on the maintenance of peace and the mining industry. The king agreed in 1504 that his share of one-third could be reduced to a fifth, and that the monopoly on commerce he had imposed in 1501 could now be relinquished, especially since the market for Spanish goods exceeded the means of a single royal factor to supply it adequately. The Aragonese king was sufficiently business-minded to find other ways of sustaining royal income. He ordered Governor Ovando to reserve certain of the best mines for the crown and to keep one thousand Indians employed in them under the supervision of salaried miners. Ovando, aided by veedores who exercised direct supervision, thus kept the crown directly in the mining industry, while allowing private miners to exploit the rest of the mines by paying the quinto. What these royal mines yielded cannot be known, for the reports of gold sent to the king usually lump together all sources of royal income, but they must have furnished an important part of the king's revenue. Ovando was thereby both a governor and a majordomo for royal economic interests, besides owning various conucos and *estancias* operated by his private managers.[40] Later, on the other islands, the king would directly enter the mining or farming industries by means of partnerships with the leading officials. On Española he further offset the loss of income attendant to retracting the royal monopoly on commerce by imposing a $7^1/_2$ percent almojarifazgo on European goods, and by instructing his royal factor to introduce goods for sale now and again whenever the local market seemed to warrant it. In these ways, supplemented by the monopolies on dyewood and salt, the king continued to count heavily upon Española (and later the other islands and mainland coasts) to provide him a margin of income making it unnecessary to press the Castilian towns very frequently for subsidies. Ferdinand has been often called greedy and covetous, but his aims were actually far more grandiose: he aspired to liberate Jerusalem from the Turks, which involved an expensive foreign policy for the impecunious monarch of "little Spain," and the few overseas islands the crown then possessed. But presumably no courtier admonished him, as one did the young Charles with his great empire, that a grand monarch should not be involved in such petty things as business enterprises in the New World.

The letrado-hidalgo class enjoyed a considerable prosperity during Ovando's governorship. The Indians were still numerous and it was an unlucky immigrant who did not hold at least a half dozen for mining or for household service. The more prominent settlers held multiple encomiendas in several towns—how many we do not know. During these years gold mining reached its peak, and for that matter its breadth; the majority of miners washed out the placers of innumerable tributaries in the Cibao and along the Haina; others, including the crown, worked the more permanent pit mines of the main spurs.[41] Still other encomenderos living in the peripheral towns or the central valleys, raised livestock and *yuca*, and typically were partners in a two-man company, the other partner supervising the mining operation. Finally, others of the letrado-hidalgo class, while putting Indians into the mines (probably renting them out), were officials at Santo Domingo or navigator-merchants engaged in the trade with

Spain. Mining was the one great industry, the lodestar of hidalgo hopes, the partial sump for Indian labor, and the economic margin which kept Ferdinand's government from becoming unbearable to the Castilian towns.

Success was typically demonstrated in two ways: by the number of criados one lodged in his *posada* and fed at his table;[42] and by the imported silk shirts, velvet caps, and passementerie one wore to the main towns during the demora and at the occasional festivals. Only a few vecinos built stone houses, except at Santo Domingo, where Ovando, for the benefit of his order of Alcántara rather than for himself, put up fifteen; Francisco de Garay also built a stone posada, large enough to accommodate many guests; and the navigator-merchant Bartolomé Roldán added to his wealth by building and renting out a number of such houses.[43] Outside Santo Domingo only Juan Ponce de León is known to have built a stone house—at Salvaleón de Higüey—which was typical of his usual prudence, according to one of his biographers.[44]

Gold was typically if not invariably spent before it was mined, and so much European cloth was bought on credit that the king, some years later, had to declare sumptuary laws limiting what could be worn.[45] The merchant and royal treasurer at Santo Domingo, Cristóbal Santa Clara, held a banquet for Ovando, and was said to have dramatized the current prosperity by filling the salt cellars with gold dust. Though this might simply be Casas's repetition of a current *malicia*, certainly Santa Clara typified the easy-come, easy-go mentality of the gold rush, for he not only spent his own funds but 80,000 pesos from the royal fisc.[46] Toward the end of Ovando's governorship the complaints of debtors were numerous, for the scope of mining operations was already contracting, and the governor was obliged to limit how much a creditor could collect at any one demora.

The height of seignorial ambition was to attain a title and coat of arms attesting to military prowess; but on Española during this time, none was acquired or possibly even asked for, owing to the apparently easy victories over the Taínos. Only Bartolomé Colón was named an adelantado, a title made famous during the reconquest. The letrado-hidalgo class as a whole contented themselves with acquiring coats of arms for their towns in 1508 to commemorate their settlement of the land and, in the case of Verapaz, their victory over the Indians.[47] The coats of arms thus became community surrogates for individual vecinos, whose general inclination was toward living out their lives on the island as small, feudal lords. To that end they asked the king to grant them hereditary rights to their encomiendas for two or three generations, or failing that, for the life of the present holder. This request touched on the fears of the king concerning feudalism, and he refused any such commitment. But even had he done so, feuds based on Indians would prove of ephemeral worth owing to the gradual depopulation. Moreover, factionalism characterized the allotment of encomiendas, especially after Ovando departed, and only the most astute, favored, or lucky, held on to their encomiendas.

The decline of the Indians has been most often attributed to harshness of mine labor, on the circumstantial evidence that Indians dying at or near the mines must have been literally worked to death. Whatever the reasons—which are many—for the decline in Indian population, it is unlikely that mine labor was more than a contributing factor. Placer mining involved a digging, carrying, and washing operation in gold-bearing sand and gravel that was only moderately onerous; in the few pit mines on Española, Negroes were employed increasingly after 1505 for the hard pick and bar work. Actually when details of many documents are pulled together, rather than relying solely on Las Casas's account, the picture of the Taínos in Spanish society is considerably toned down from one depicting them as whipped, beaten, and starved to death. In 1514 many Taínos too old to work were still living, which suggests that they survived the gold-rush years of 1500–08.[48] Hundreds if not thousands of Taínos never worked in the mines, but were employed raising yuca, herding livestock, or working as household servants. Scores of others were helpers to artisans in the town, worked as fishermen, and later served aboard brigantines and caravels in the inter-island trade. The Taínos rather easily fled harsh masters and found better ones, if only because their labor became more valuable as it became scarcer. A good many Spaniards married Taíno women even though the marriage itself may have brought them few Indians. Las Casas's descriptions of callousness toward dying Indians fails to take into account that widowed Indian women were at once taken into Spanish households to be cared for thereafter.[49] A Taíno who begged on the streets of Santo Domingo to keep a blind Spaniard alive suggests a relationship that transcends the stereotyped picture of harsh exploitation of the conquered by the conquerors.[50] Nor did the Taínos always remain meek lambs. In one instance—the example is drawn from Puerto Rico—an Indian escaped the stocks by having an accomplice grease his arms and legs, and revenged himself by killing six Spaniards after making good on his escape.[51] Small rebellions and flights to the mountains were chronic on Española, years before the legendary Enriquillo revolt of 1519.

Among the several thousand Spaniards who resided on the island at this time, only a few acquired much wealth; hence a small number would remain on Española, or for that matter, on the adjacent islands. But these few were the actual founding fathers of Spanish civilization in the Caribbean. Some of these settlers came with Columbus on his second voyage; others came with Ovando or on some obscure intermediate voyage between these times or after, or on one of the many vessels carrying the Indies trade. In what was collectively a flotsam and jetsam population, whose members were as quick to return to Spain as they were to migrate to new islands and lands, certain groups or clans nonetheless remained permanently on Española or the adjacent islands.

An official position was of utmost advantage in acquiring wealth, though it was possible to do so on the basis of entrepreneurship or good mercantile connections in Seville. The Spanish monarchy only gradually attained to that vision of disinterested, salaried professional bureaucrats, prohibited even to unite themselves or their families by marriage to local inhabitants. If Ferdinand was engaged in business on Española, his officials could have no qualms about private enterprise compromising their positions. Consequently, Ovando and his officials were at the same time encomenderos, farmers, miners, and merchants, if only indirectly in some enterprises. Ovando was surely the largest landholder on the island during his governorship, excepting only the king. His conucos and hog farms were heavily concentrated in the vicinity of Santo Domingo, though he held others around Buenaventura and Concepción de la Vega. His conucos, measured in hills of yuca, were worth thousands of pesos, and the value of his hog farms was enhanced by *bohíos* (crude huts) for hog herders, tools for cultivation, watchdogs, and herds of small livestock.[52] They were retained by the order of Alcántara for some years after Ovando's departure, but eventually were liquidated along with most state and absentee enterprises; the properties were sold to private vecinos. Ovando was also engaged in the importation and sale of European goods, for which he employed a factor, Pedro Gutiérrez de Alcántara in Seville, and was granted a merced from the king to import sixty tons of goods a year without payment of taxes.[53] Ovando was not personally concerned with amassing wealth. Probably part of his profits went indirectly to the king who was Grand Master of the order of Alcántara.

Less is known of the officials supervised by Ovando, but there is no reason to doubt that they all held encomiendas to supplement their small salaries. The propensity to splurge of the treasurer, Cristóbal Santa Clara, has already been mentioned, which in turn raises the question why Ovando, otherwise so stern and scrupulous in such matters, tolerated such looseness in handling the king's funds. One explanation may be that their relationship was not simply that of a governor and his treasurer, for Cristóbal and his brother Bernardino were merchants linked commercially with Ovando's factor in Seville, thus blurring the distinction between state and private enterprise.[54]

However much wealth the Crown and Ovando held in the short run, the major Caribbean family was undoubtedly the Columbuses; they eventually had the most wealth, attained the highest social prestige, and boasted the greatest number of *criados*. The Columbus influence would subsequently be extended throughout Española and, later, to the other three major islands and the Venezuelan coast. The growth of this family could hardly be foreseen during the governorship of Ovando, although its basis had been established. Columbus had already declared his holdings on the island to constitute a mayorazgo. This included the establishment of an estancia in the Vega, which he placed under the supervision of his loyal erstwhile alcaide, Miguel Ballester;[55] his one-tenth of the gross income had been restored, although one may seriously doubt that this tenth was the main basis for family wealth. The reason is that when the king reduced his share from one-third to a fifth, Columbus's income fell off accordingly; moreover, the king excluded the tithes, his own royal mines and farms (which he considered private), and certain other monopolized items from this figure. Nonetheless the tenth was important and was guaranteed, unlike the precarious income of miners depending solely on encomiendas that could vanish as their Indians died or as they lost favor with the *repartidores de indios*, who assigned encomiendas.

A more important reason for the influence and permanence of the Columbus family on Española was its connection with the main capitalists in Spain—the Genoese and Florentine communities of Seville. Since 1492, Columbus had been closely associated with these merchants who had partly financed his first voyage; on his second voyage he brought the first Genoese factor to the New World, Rafael Cattaneo, whom he left in charge of his interests in 1500.[56] A little later, Cattaneo was joined by his brother, Juan, and the two merchants remained as factors for their mercantile house in Seville, after the liberalized commercial decree of 1504 made such operations possible. The Columbuses retained these valuable connections, which were mutually profitable; both the Navigator and his son Diego owned small debts to certain Genoese, unpaid during their lifetime;[57] but the Genoese merchants were granted mercantile privileges, especially later during Diego Colón's governorships, that more than offset these unpaid obligations.

But it was not to be expected that Columbus's followers would fare especially well during Ovando's governorship, though he included them in the distribution of encomiendas and was a model of rectitude in minimizing factionalism caused by playing favorites; indeed his caution in this respect has been judged excessive, since he would not permit Columbus to land on the island in 1502, and permitted him only a short sojourn there on his return to Spain two years later. Even so, one expects that Ovando's expropriation of the gold mines operated by Miguel Diaz and Francisco de Garay, presumably about 1504, may not have been entirely welcome by those criados of the Columbuses, though they are not known to have complained.[58] They had been the de facto founders of Santo Domingo as criados of Bartolomé Colón, and they subsequently had found and exploited rich placers on the Haina till their expropriation. Unlike less versatile miners, they rented out their encomiendas and shifted into maritime commerce to supplement their income. By 1509, they were joint owners of a *nao*, piloted by Las Casas's nemesis, Juan Bono de Quejo, and had made several voyages to Spain for merchandise, which was partly advanced on credit by the Genoese in Seville.[59] Although supported by their connection with the Columbus family, they were still unusual men in their own right. Diaz would be second only to Ponce de León as a settler of Puerto Rico, and Garay, brother-in-law of Columbus, would be the main settler, though not the founder, of Spanish civilization on Jamaica. Their lives ran along an almost fictional parallel course: they were the discoverers of gold on Española, and they would end their lives in a fruitless venture to settle a vaguely defined grant on the Mexican mainland extending from Pánuco to Florida. Concerning other adherents of Columbus and later, of his son, we know less in these early years. Juan Mosquera, later wealthy, had taken up residence at Santo Domingo; Juan de Villoria, a former criado of king Ferdinand, and Juan de Esquivel, founder of the first Spanish settlement on Jamaica, were vecinos at Concepción, presumably engaged in mining. Villoria later was engaged in commerce with the commercial houses of Grimaldo and Centurión in Seville.[60]

Santo Domingo would prove in the long run to be the preferred place for residence on the island: its advantages being that it provided easy access to the governor and his officials, it was the main port of call for ships from Spain, and the best site for the permanent retention of encomiendas if only because Indians were resituated there as needed. Finally, the area contained the most suitable land for the cultivation of sugar cane, a necessary economic shift when the mines began to decline.

Second as an urban center to Santo Domingo during the Ovando period was the great Vega, adjacent to the Cibao mines and comprising a complex of three towns: Santiago de los Caballeros, Concepción de la Vega, and Puerto Plata—the port on the north shore which succeeded in attracting some ships from Spain when the mines were at the height of their productivity. If the Columbus family was the potentially most prominent at Santo Domingo, the Manzorro-Becerra clan tended to dominate the north. Rodrigo Manzorro was perhaps the earliest member of this family to immigrate to Española; he may have come with Columbus in 1493, and was certainly in Santo Domingo by 1498.[61] With the advent of the gold rush, he resituated himself at Santiago de los Caballeros and was subseqently, during Ovando's time, joined by a brother, Licentiate Fernando Becerra and another relative, Bachelor Juan Becerra. A cousin, Bartolomé Becerra, had meanwhile taken up residence in Sabana de Salvatierra. Other Becerras, who are probably members of the same family, included Bernardino at Jacmel, another Bartolomé at Puerto Real, Francisco at Lares de Guahava, and Miguel at Puerto Real.[62] Their linkage with Concepción is suggested by the marriage, at an unknown date but probably between 1506 and 1509, of the alcade mayor of Concepción, Lucas Vázquez de Ayllón, with Juan Becerra's daughter;[63] their ties with Puerto Plata are better seen in their later Indian slaving expeditions to the Bahamas. The most prominent criado of the Becerra clan was Francisco de Barrionuevo, son-in-law of Rodrigo Manzorro, whose later economic activities would extend to Puerto Rico and Venezuela. Still later he was governor of Panama.[64]

Equally successful and prominent at Concepción was Diego de Nicuesa, a virtual paradigm of the hidalgo class. He had been a criado of Ferdinand's uncle, Enrique Enríquez, and after arriving at Santo Domingo with Governor Ovando, had moved to the Cibao. Polite and talented, a viola player, and a skilled horseman, Nicuesa must have contributed greatly to the cavalier tone of the mining society, while he, with an unknown partner, earned a considerable fortune during these years.[65] The lure of new wealth at Panama would subsequently cost him his encomiendas and his life.

Residence in the mining zone, while not a guarantee of permanent wealth, was considerably more secure than residence on the periphery. Here were the purely agricultural towns, where decline would set in first and where the expansionist urge would be most in evidence. This could not have been foreseen at the time the Spaniards settled in these towns, and for a time a good income was made selling cassava and renting out Indians to the mines. The western area was much more populous and hence profitable than the eastern region, and it was here that Diego Velázquez had taken his numerous following who carried out the conquest of Jaraguá, and subsequently spread out to the likely town sites in the west.

Velázquez was an hidalgo of Cuéllar who became a criado of Bartolomé Colón. But he was of such expansive geniality and great energy that he overcame what would have been a handicap after 1500, when the Columbuses were out of power. Ovando named him his chief lieutenant in the west, probably because he was recommended by the contador, Cristóbal de Cuéllar, whom Velázquez had surely known in Spain.[66] He subsequently became a favorite of Bishop Juan Rodríguez de Fonseca, the untitled minister of the Indies whose influence counted for a great deal. Thus Velázquez had his fences mended well all around. His subsequent career is unique among island governors in that he alone served (except for a short suspension) as *teniente de gobernador* of Cuba from 1511, when he initiated occupation of the island, until his death in 1524, thirteen years later. When it is considered that he survived two governorships of Diego Colón, who was hostile toward him the second time, and three interim commands on Española in between these governorships, it can be appreciated that his long tenure was a measure of his loyalty to the Crown, his affability toward all, and his tact and shrewdness. Bishop Rodríguez de Fonseca helped but he was not always in a position to save Velázquez from a possible deposition.

When he settled at Verapaz after the conquest, he was unquestionably head of a superclan, which more or less blanketed the western region. Velázquez himself, reportedly wealthy in island terms by 1511, held encomiendas at Verapaz, Salvatierra de la Sabana, and Santiago de Caballeros, where he was in partnership with an unidentified encomendero in mining enterprises;[67] one may well suppose that his encomienda at Salvatierra produced cassava and other foodstuffs that were shipped north to the mining zone. The Velázquezes were numerous. They included two brothers of Diego, Antonio and Francisco, two nephews, Antonio and Diego, and two brothers-in-law, both named Juan Velázquez. Other Velazquezes of unknown relationship to Diego included Bernardino at Verapaz, and Gonzalo at San Juan de la Maguana. Still others of the clan, not bearing the name of Velázquez but bound to them by affection and economic interest, included the brothers-in-law, Pedro Núñez de Guzmán and Pedro de Paz, who were partners holding encomiendas and conucos at San Juan de la Maguana, and Pánfilo de Narváez, of Verapaz.[68] Many of this clan would move with Diego to Cuba in 1511; Narváez would arrive later by way of Jamaica, and a few others came after 1515.

Eastern Española, the cacicazgo of Higüey, was less

attractive than Jaraguá; here there were no Indians of higher culture such as surrounded Anacaona's court in the west, and they were if anything more bellicose and ready to desert their conucos for the mountains should a smoke signal be sent aloft by a rebellious cacique. The land held only modest promise. It produced yuca in the environs of Salvaleón de Higüey and Santa Cruz de Aycagua, its only two towns. One cannot know how Juan Ponce de León came to the attention of Ovando as a likely lieutenant for the eastern zone. He had taken part in the campaigns of 1502 but other soldiers, such as Juan de Esquivel, were even more prominent. His early service in Spain may furnish a clue: he had been a page of Pedro Núñez de Guzmán, comendador mayor of Calatrava, which may have been reassuring to Ovando, who as the comendador of Lares doubtless put great faith in the military orders and in those who had served in them. Furthermore, Ponce was a cousin of the marchioness of Zahara, Doña Francisca Ponce de León, which meant he was an hidalgo like other *tenientes* of the governor.[69]

Little is known of Ponce's life at Salvaleón de Higüey. He became owner of a ship during these years and there is reason to believe that he engaged in transporting cassava to Santo Domingo for sale.[70] Since he married a young woman who worked in an inn there, named Leonor (she assumed her husband's name, which would indicate her own family in Spain was of humble circumstances), one may imagine that they met during his sojourns there.[71]

Ponce probably made a modest living at Salvaleón de Higüey, where encomiendas were not sizable or numerous. He had some loyal friends, but his income was not such as to undergird a clan or extended family. It was only later, after Ponce had settled in Puerto Rico, that his relatives from the little town of Santervás de Campos in the province of Valladolid come to join him.[72] It is understandable that the first migration from Española would be drawn from the eastern part of the island where the basis for a seignorial life was less promising than in any of the other main zones.

Ferdinand V had succeeded rather well in supporting this letrado-hidalgo class on Española: the most fortunate had acquired wealth and advanced their social position; the king had found the point of compromise between their interests and his own. But what of another aim of the king and of Spanish Catholic civilization—the conversion of the Indians and the establishment of the Church? Had that aim been served as well, or was it subordinated to other considerations, declarations of intent notwithstanding? The great limiting force for evangelism in the New World was, at the outset, the dualism within Franciscanism that had run through the fifteenth century and continued into the sixteenth. On the one hand, conventual Franciscans tended toward a relaxed, secular life, without desire for hazardous, sacrificial missions; on the other, the broadening reform movement opposed to secularism, the turning to the inner life of piety and prayer and to rejection of the world, turned Observant Franciscans away from evangelism. Given this not untypical division within the religious orders, few Franciscans in Spain—other orders were scarcely in touch with the court at this time—were at work in the secular world.

As we have seen, a bare handful of Franciscans, accompanied by a few lay clerics and members of other orders came to Española during Columbus's governorship. Even this many might not have come without the urging and recruiting of Archbishop Jiménez de Cisneros the great reformer of the Franciscan order,[73] who strongly believed in and helped carry out the difficult and unpopular reform of the Franciscan convents.[74] But at the same time he did not reject the world; he was sensitive if eclectic toward the currents of Renaissance thought, encouraged studies at the university he founded in Alcalá de Henares, and laid on the conscience of the Franciscans that it was not enough just to reform themselves. They must also advance the faith in the New World lest so great an opportunity be lost and the king's conscience be thereby burdened. It was Jiménez de Cisneros, too, who helped recruit the friars for Bodadilla's expedition (six friars, including the two French lay friars who had come in 1493), and who continued to use his influence to enlist the thirteen Franciscans who sailed with Ovando in 1502 under the prior, Alonso de Espinar. This last contingent increased the number of religions on Española to a total of about twenty-five.

The Franciscans who had come with Bobadilla began their work at Santo Domingo in 1500 in a euphoric mood: Friar Ruiz (whose illness obliged him to return to Spain in a few months) was said to have baptized the greatest part of two to three thousand Indians in that short time.[75] It is likely that he worked among the populous tribe of the cacica Inés de Cayacoa who resided on or near the Ozama. Although we do not have statements from Espinar and other friars, it may be presumed that they followed the same method: mass baptisms by tribes as the friars followed the conquest and established themselves in the main towns. They apparently interpreted the Taínos' mimicry of liturgical response, as Dr. Chanca had at Isabela, as signs of a desire to embrace the faith. They felt that they were accomplishing the initial and crucial task, for baptism meant salvation.

In this way, a very few friars apparently baptized many Taínos. Word of this rich harvest must have reached the queen, for Isabel in early 1503 visualized the establishment of Indian pueblos organized into parishes, each pueblo with its cleric and lands and its tithe-paying Indians who worked voluntarily for the Spaniards.[76] She shared with Ferdinand the faith that Christianization and the adoption of Spanish ways did not depend solely on the few friars, but would come about as a result of daily contacts with lay Spaniards—what Friar Borges has called the capillary method whereby parishioners, like hundreds of rivulets, comprise a great stream leading to full conversion of Indians to the new faith and its culture.[77] The assumption has always been supported by partial evidence; all men have some good in them, and even bad men do some good. On Española nearly all Spaniards had a few *naborias de casa* (as distinguished from *naborias de servicio*), whom they treated as members of their own household, cared for in old age, and took along on voyages to and from Spain. How strange that these Indians sickened and died perhaps even more rapidly than did those in the mines. Household intimacy was an unconscious kiss of death, transcending the usual categories of human innocence or guilt. Here Indians were apt to be in frequent contact with Negro slaves from the earliest years, which is of great significance for their rapid demise. The death rate in the mines for encomienda Indians, who were but slightly in contact with their masters, was also rapid because after 1505 Negro slaves were used with growing frequency for the hard pick and bar labor.

After the initial wave of baptisms, the Franciscans settled down in convents. The first friary was built at Santo Domingo in 1503, a thatch structure which was partly converted to stone by 1508. Within a few years after the first friary was built, convents were established at Buenaventura, Bonao, Concepción de la Vega, and Verapaz in the other populous regions. In 1505, Friar Espinar requested that the Franciscan chapter at Laval, France, approve establishment of a Franciscan province, the Province of the Holy Cross, first in the New World, that he might supervise from Santo Domingo these outlying friaries.[78] The Franciscans had been authorized by the Pope since 1493—the bull was restated in 1503—to perform the sacraments and other priestly functions proper to the secular Church.[79] Thus, Queen Isabel's vision of Indian parishes, the free communities which Las Casas later projected in great detail and strongly urged, would seem to be a distinct possibility. The vision was nonetheless far from reality. Had the parish organization been carried out, one would have expected Friar Espinar to have dispatched friars to all fifteen towns, where they could regularly visit the Indian villages near them. There is reason to believe this was not done, for there is no evidence of a resident friar in most of the peripheral towns such as Azua, Jacmel, Puerto Real, Lares de Guahava, Puerto Real, Santa Cruz de Aycagua and Salvaleón de Higüey. Additional evidence may be seen in the vecinos' complaint that Governor Ovando required their attendance in church at a town so far from their estancias they had to buy expensive horses to make the journey.[80] The conclusion seems to be that the plan for Indian parishes failed, just as the free Indian communities, with which it was related, were not established until much later.

Franciscanism on Española during Ovando's governorship was not equal to the great challenge it faced. The weight of the past was yet too heavy—the latent desire to retreat into monasticism and the equally strong impulse toward accommodation with existing society. The partial retreat to monasticism is seen in the decision to restrict evangelism to educating cacique's sons within the monastery walls that they might serve later to teach the faith to their tribe. Under more stable conditions this "vertical approach" worked well, but on Española it was too limited and too slow. The secular impulse is probably reflected in the acceptance of encomiendas, managed by majordomos, to supplement the annual stipend from the Crown of 100 *pesos de oro* for each friar.[81] Most Franciscans at this time lacked the patience of Friar Pane to learn the Taíno tongue, to penetrate the natives' way of thought and thereby create unprecedented ways of conversion, to teach the faith no matter what the odds in the mines, on the estancias, and among the dispersed Indian villages. Franciscanism would a few years later begin to awaken to the challenge, only partly by the inspiration of Dominicanism.

During Ovando's time others were more closely associated with the Indians' daily lives. Perhaps the first advocate of abolishing the encomienda was an obscure Spaniard with a facility for learning a strange language: Cristóbal Rodríguez, often called Cristóbal La Lengua, because of his ability as an interpreter; he had come out with Columbus in 1493. His knowledge of the Taíno tongue may have made him unusually sensitive to the changes wrought in tribal life by forced labor. He was exiled to Spain by Governor Ovando for arranging the marriage of Juan Garcés to a cacica, probably with the intent of removing her tribe from the encomienda system. In Spain, he urged the king to re-establish tribute; the king was then receptive, but nothing came of the proposal for Ferdinand had too many troubles at home and too much need for funds from Española to consider seriously altering the established labor system.[82] Rodríguez, it should be observed, did not aim to free the Indian of labor; he assumed, as Las Casas did much later, that Indians would work the mines voluntarily, and he anticipated that this structural change would save the lives of the Indians, as most persons have assumed since that time.

If the missional Church seems small and less vigorous than it might have been, the cathedrals were not even begun in spite of the tithes having been collected since 1501. The postponement was due to many causes during and after Ovando's time. Though Ferdinand V possessed authority from the Pope to collect tithes, the bulls he received in 1504 to erect an archbishopric and two bishoprics on Española failed to grant him the patronage;[83] this omission went countergrain to his conviction born of painful experience, and his determination to secure patronage, complicated by the interregnum after 1504, delayed the matter until 1508. For these reasons the episcopacies lacked whatever direction capable bishops might have given, while the potential economic base began slowly to erode with the decline of mining,

But the failure to lay even the foundations of cathedrals was due to the priorities of the letrado-hidalgo class taking precedence over tithe-paying, just as Ferdinand's priorities would, a little later, contribute to the unlikelihood that cathedrals would be soon built. The vecinos' support of the Church revealed that they were only average Christians, for they were rising in wealth but were indebted for personal gauderies. They utilized Indian labor to erect only thatch churches, which repeatedly burned to the ground. In 1508 they complained of this to the king, asking for master masons to build stone churches, but this was after the greatest wealth had already been acquired and spent. Their priorities in this respect were all too clear, and they thus contributed to the somewhat haphazard Catholicism that prevailed on the island. Friars could not place valuable ornaments and vestments, still less the Sacred Host—the essence of Christ's body—in a church that might be destroyed within minutes.[84] A few members of the letrado-hidalgo class built their own houses of stone at Santo Domingo, by which one may see that their priorities emphasized their own newly acquired social status or, as with Governor Ovando, the furtherance of the order of Alcántara.

Toward the end of Ovando's governorship, the Church, both missional and secular, consisted nominally of fifteen parish churches but actually of only five thatched convents. Fidel Fita called it the "orphan church" and though Professor Lamb has pointed out that Ovando did all he could to support it and urge its expansion,[85] Ferdinand's problems and the islanders' overriding personal priorities combined to make Fita's appraisal a fairly accurate one.

3

Ferdinand V and Caribbean Expansion (1508-1515)

While Governor Ovando was establishing Española's mining colony and organizing its gold production to the temporary satisfaction of Ferdinand and the encomenderos, the King urged other hidalgos and explorers to unveil the mysteries of lands yet unknown. He was the driving force behind Aragonese expansion into the familiar Mediterranean and Castilian conquests in the exotic Caribbean. In 1504 he contracted with Vicente Yáñez Pinzón to settle Puerto Rico, and he supported the voyage of Juan de la Cosa to Urabá, a follow-up expedition to Bastidas's three years earlier.[1] Ferdinand urged Governor Ovando to establish a fort on the Pearl Coast, which was not accomplished, but pearl bartering was resumed.[2] None of the early explorations, however, had any immediate material results; though they were not necessarily disrupted by the death of Queen Isabel in 1504, soon thereafter the king sensed his power crumbling as his Aragonese profile appeared conspicuous in Castile without the queen. Discontent also mounted among the grandees and in Flanders, where Philip the Handsome contemplated assuming the Castilian throne with his wife and heir, Juana. Among these contingencies, and in this potential hiatus of royal power, expansion was delayed till Ferdinand could resolve these pending questions of royal succession.

Ferdinand was not averse to the accession of Philip and Juana to the throne for their assumption accorded with Castilian tradition, but his deep fear of feudalism prompted him to suggest a joint reign to the young Philip, inexperienced in the ways of the proud and sensitive Castilian nobility.[3] Philip felt, however, that the sharing of power was patronizing, and he went so far as to jail Ferdinand's diplomatic representative to his court, Lope de Conchillos, who was accused of trying to influence him through Queen Juana. Philip's representatives at Ferdinand's court intrigued with the anti-Aragonese grandees, and other Flemish diplomats easily persuaded Louis XII of France to press his claims in Italy as a means of rendering Ferdinand's position additionally untenable.[4] The Aragonese king unraveled part of this network of intrigue against him by negotiating the Treaty of Blois in 1505 with the French king whereby he promised friendship and support for Louis's claims in Italy, a promise he further bolstered by agreeing to marry Germana of Foix, young niece of the French monarch.[5] Seeing his position weaker now, Philip agreed to come to Castile for a joint rule; Ferdinand had successfully met his first obstacle.

Even so, certain of the Castilian grandees, the powerful Duke of Medina Sidonia and the Count of Ureña among others, still worked against Ferdinand; they as well as Philip saw the Aragonese monarch's marriage as divisive for it was not their intention that the union of Castile and Aragón should be terminated, which it well might be if Ferdinand's marriage to the young Germana produced an heir for the Aragonese throne.[6] Their discontent, at the bottom of which often lay resentment over forts and lands taken in the aftermath of the civil war on the succession of the Catholic kings, was made more manifest when Philip and Juana arrived in April, 1506. Although Ferdinand and Philip signed an accord at Villafáfila in June, Ferdinand decided it would be in the interests of peace if he withdrew to Italy, at least for a time.[7] He departed with his bride soon after his meeting with Philip and would remain in his eastern kingdoms for approximately a year.

Ferdinand had hardly been absent from Castile two months before the weakness in royal power, with its inevitable turbulence among the grandees, became apparent; the young Philip died in September and Juana was plunged deep into a melancholia that rendered her unfit to rule. Cardinal Jiménez de Cisneros tried to keep some vestige of order while Juana moodily procrastinated, then finally called her father to the throne;[8] meanwhile the Duke of Medina Sidonia attempted to recapture forts near San Lúcar de Barrameda, once part of his duchy, amid a wave of small defiances and disloyal acts that swept across Castile.[9] Ferdinand delayed his return from Italy until July,1507, mainly, it may be supposed, to see what support he could count on, and to make further arrangements for closer ties with the Pope, to their mutual advantage. It was at this time that he secured a cardinalate for Jiménez de Cisneros, perhaps hoping to assure the loyalty of that doughty reformer.[10] Certainly he could rely on the continued support of Bishop Rodríguez de Fonseca, who had been his chief official for the Indies since 1493, and on Lope de Conchillos who had by this time been released from prison; although the bad conditions there had left him permanently bald, his loyalty was not lessened one whit for the king who had sent him on the unfortunate mission to Philip.[11] Still more important, he could count on the powerful Duke of Alba and several other Castilian nobles who felt Ferdinand's hand was necessary for peace and order.[12] Less important, as he supposed at the outset, was the overly eager support of Diego Colón, the young spendthrift son of the recently deceased Columbus, married to a niece of the Duke of Alba. The debonair Colón, raised in the king's court, rushed with his large retinue to meet Ferdinand almost before the king had set foot on Spanish soil in Valencia.[13]

With this support, Ferdinand was able to consolidate his power. When his invitation to marry the young son of the Duke of Urbina to his granddaughter was rejected on the grounds that Duke Enrique was already pledged to marry into another powerful feudal family—exactly what the king was trying to prevent—he sent forces into the fief of Urbina to neutralize this potential threat to his power. When a favorite of Philip the Handsome retained, through his supporters, the main fort at Burgos, Ferdinand threatened to take it by storm and hang all survivors. The fort was delivered in the face of armed invasion.[14] As a result of these and other similar actions, the king solidified his position as Regent of Castile; he still faced intrigue from Emperor Maximilian, grandfather of the heir Charles, now a minor, but Ferdinand was able to resolve that matter by the Pact of Blois of 1509, by which Ferdinand was to rule until Charles reached age 20.[15] The arrangement proved more than adequate, as Ferdinand's death in 1516 occurred four years prior to Charles's planned accession to the throne of Castile.

In achieving this victory over dissident nobles, Ferdinand accrued a great political debt that he could only meet by extensive patronage. What he had to bestow was in the New World, for he did not care to disturb the seignorial status quo in Castile, and what the New World had chiefly to offer was Indian labor. Ferdinand consequently initiated the absentee encomienda, bestowing two hundred or more Indians on Juan Rodríguez de Fonseca, Lope de Conchillos, and other members of his royal council; where patronage exceeded the safe limits of absentee encomienda grants, he could allot small stipends such as the dross from foundries, the right to issue licenses to mine, or to act as public notaries. These went to the widow and sons of his former secretary Gaspar Gricio or as additional emoluments to his ambitious secretary Lope de Conchillos.[16] The effect of the absentee encomienda grants was to dispossess various vecinos on Española who were consequently ready to occupy other islands. In handing down these perquisites, the Regent Ferdinand was essentially acting in the patrimonial tradition and in ways that had the merit, from his point of view, of spurring the expansionism of which he could again be chief director. Yet it may not be supposed that such patronage was dispensed by a financially secure monarch wishing to be generous.

Ferdinand was still in a weak position and would rarely be in any other as Aragonese ruler of Castile. Had he not been, he is unlikely to have agreed with the powerful

Duke of Alba that Diego Colón should succeed Ovando on Española, where he was expected to refurbish the declining mines and to occupy a pivotal position in the expansion that Ferdinand was just now able to continue. A less promising candidate than the young Diego could hardly have been found among the more irresponsible and impractical nobles of Castile. His lavish life style and his constant indebtedness did not augur well for Española's royal treasury, thousands of miles overseas; worse, his well-known passion, passed on to him by his father, for the pretentious hereditary title of viceroy conjured a nightmare of litigation stemming from that hastily and vaguely written document of 1492. What arguments the Regent raised against the appointment are not known, but he did not issue it until August, 1508,[17] which was doubtless many months after the matter had been pressed upon him. He named Diego governor only, leaving the issue of the exact extent of his powers to chance, and the issue of hereditary rights to a suit that was soon placed in litigation in his royal court. Diego would require almost a year to prepare what he fancied would be a splendid royal court overseas, and would sail with a large coterie of followers in May, 1509, to arrive at Santo Domingo three months later.[18] Nothing so reveals the relatively weak position of Ferdinand than the appointment of Diego, the incarnation of the feudalism Ferdinand so detested and feared. The impulsive Diego would cause the Regent endless irritation until he felt obliged to recall him to Spain in 1515.

Still if he must compromise at the prestigious level of a governorship, he need not do so in the area of administration, for the Castilian monarchs had exercised an unchallenged right to appoint their own treasurers and other administrators since the early Middle Ages. Ferdinand needed a reliable administrator to control the capricious Diego. His choice fell upon Miguel de Pasamonte, formerly secretary of Queen Isabel and more lately dispatcher of the royal mail for Lope de Conchillos. Pasamonte, like Conchillos, was a native of the province of Calatayud in Aragón and was recommended as being efficient and completely reliable.[19] He was indeed a rare find. Ferdinand named him treasurer general of the Indies in April, 1508,[20] thus showing that his delay in naming Diego Colón governor rested partly on his finding a suitable official to control the strings of real power—the treasury. Pasamonte's importance for royal government in the Caribbean can hardly be exaggerated. He reached Santo Domingo in November, 1508,[21] and would serve in his post uninterruptedly until his death seventeen years later. In charge of royal funds, absolutely loyal to the king, circumspect in his dealings with others, a bachelor without the entanglements of numerous relatives, he was the epitomy of the loyal bureaucrat on which the otherwise wavering royal power so largely depended. Other positions in the Española treasury Ferdinand would fill to his satisfaction somewhat later. The key man, Pasamonte, had been found, and expansion beyond Española and more intensive development of the mines on the island could now be expected.

Having attended, as best he could, to the appointment of his officials on Española, Ferdinand next turned to improving the Casa de Contratación, which had operated rather laxly in his absence. Too much gold from Española still failed to reach the Casa, and too many ships put in somewhere on the coasts of France, Galicia, or Portugal claiming, sometimes truthfully, that their pilots had been deflected from the true route by a storm or navigational errors.[22] To correct this, Ferdinand was instrumental in establishing a pilot's school as an adjunct of the Casa, to be headed by a *piloto mayor.* The famous Amerigo Vespucci was the first incumbent. The Regent filled the vacancy of the Casa's contador,[23] following the death of Jimeno de Bribiesca, with Juan López de Recalde, young and energetic though not especially scrupulous, and named as factor Ochoa de Isásaga. Isásaga, a Basque who had served ably as diplomatic representative to Lisbon in a dispute over El Peñón, proved especially valuable, for at the request of Ferdinand he rewrote in 1510 the Casa's ordinances which put that body on a more efficient operating basis for many years.[24] With these reforms, Ferdinand was prepared to resume encouragement of expansion with the expectation that he had the administrative machinery to control the anticipated wealth whether in the Indies or Spain.

Within the next few years, Ferdinand urged on the expansion so long delayed: he signed a contract with Diego de Nicuesa and Alonso de Ojeda in 1508 to settle adjacent grants at Veragua and Urabá where gold had already been obtained on earlier voyages; he ordered Diego Colón in 1509 to explore Cuba as "we have an idea there is gold on the island," and he approved in 1508 Ovando's sending of Juan Ponce de León to Puerto Rico to follow up rumors of gold.[25]

His expansionist aims had strong support on Española, where the Indian population had begun to decline especially in 1507–1508, owing in all likelihood to the transmission to the Indies of the epidemic then raging in southern Spain. Since European diseases invariably affected the Indians more severely than the Spaniards, a considerable number of the Taínos, probably in the mines and at Santo Domingo where contact would be at its greatest, must have perished. Ovando, concentrating on mining production, noticed this only in an indirect way: food supply for the mines, which came especially from the peripheral towns, was running short. As the king told Ovando, it was not simply a matter of sending more Indians to the mines but of increasing the production of cassava as well.[26] The general demographic shift was toward the mines where the death rate was highest (though the cause may not be due to mine labor as such). Mine labor repartimientos were replenished with Indians from the peripheral towns, thinning out the population in these areas.[27] Spaniards in the peripheral towns were the first to lose out, for the mines had the priority on Indian labor. The situation, then, was one in which food supplies and Indian labor had to be quickly found on an island other than Española, or the Spaniards would have to migrate to find gold mines elsewhere. This situation also buttressed Ferdinand's expansionist program.

Ponce de León had probably visited Puerto Rico several times before 1508 to barter for foodstuffs. According to documents published by Aurelio Tío, he attempted a settlement in 1506 in the Bay of Aguado, but abandoned the effort the following year, owing to settlement's destruction by a hurricane.[28] The documents consist of probanzas sworn to by two participants, both of whom declared the settlement to have been founded in that year: but what renders the matter uncertain, aside from the fact that both men swore to the truth of something that had occurred thirty years before, is that Ponce did not visit the site in 1508–09, though many Indians lived there and could have helped supply him with much needed food. The issue of the 1506 settlement thus remains less than certain. What seems clear is that Ponce already had knowledge of gold on the island prior to the summer of 1508 when he made his first official expedition, and that he seems to have been on familiar terms with a cacique living near the southern coast.[29]

By June, 1508, Ponce had broached Governor Ovando about beginning explorations for gold on Puerto Rico and in that month signed a contract which gave the explorer one-third and the king two-thirds of the gold discovered.[30] Both Ovando and Ponce had an interest in keeping this expedition secret—Ovando, because the island fell within the claims of Diego Colón—and Ponce, partly perhaps for reasons of profit since fewer men meant larger shares. But Ponce was one of the first to be concerned with mistreatment of the Indians and he wanted to prevent the breaking up of tribes, leading to revolt and bloodshed, which had accompanied the Española gold rush.[31] When he left Santo Domingo on July 12, 1508, he had only about fifty men aboard the ship he jointly owned with Alonso Sarmiento. With him were fellow vecinos from Salvaleón including Diego Gómez, a sailor who had remained on Española from Columbus's fourth voyage; Luis de Añasco, who would give his name to a main river and a pueblo in western Puerto Rico; a free Negro, Juan Garrido; and Juan González, a miner.[32]

The expedition was anything but a conquest. To prevent annoying the Indians by asking for an unusually large amount of cassava, Ponce arranged with Indians he already knew on the fertile island of Mona to supply him on the voyage out and thereafter in the future. Sailing to the south coast, he stopped near Guánica and went inland to greet the main cacique of that part of the island, Agueybana. They exchanged names, and the cacique agreed to accompany Ponce around the island to the north coast where he knew there was gold in the stream beds.[33]

The Taínos of Puerto Rico lived mainly toward the west and the north, along the rivers flowing north off the cordillera central such as the Loíza, Bayamón, Toa, and Cebuco, and along the Rio Grande de Añasco and tributaries of the Culebrinas that flowed westward off the same range.[34] Their population has been estimated at anywhere from 30,000 to 100,000. They were in most respects no different from the Taínos on Española: ruled by about a dozen caciques, they fought with the same weapons and had the same religious beliefs including the blurred division between life and death common to animism.[35] The demographic concentration in the northwest was probably not accidental. Caribs occupied the islands to the south and east of Puerto Rico. Their attitude toward the Taínos was ambivalent: on some occasions they captured and ate them; on others, as after the arrival of the Spaniards, they stirred certain caciques to resistance and helped deplete the island's population by a forced or voluntary withdrawal of many Indians to the Lesser Antilles. The Caribs constituted a formidable wall beyond which neither Taínos nor Spaniards would effectively penetrate. The boundaries of Taíno civilization approximated the later line of Spanish settlement.

As Ponce sailed eastward around the north coast, he continued to move with the same slowness and respect for Indian customs as he had in his relations with Agueybana. That cacique put him in friendly contact with the five main caciques along the northern rivers. Ponce explored along the coast for a month to six weeks, trying first one site for a town, then another, before settling in a valley enclosed by hills several miles inland; there, on an

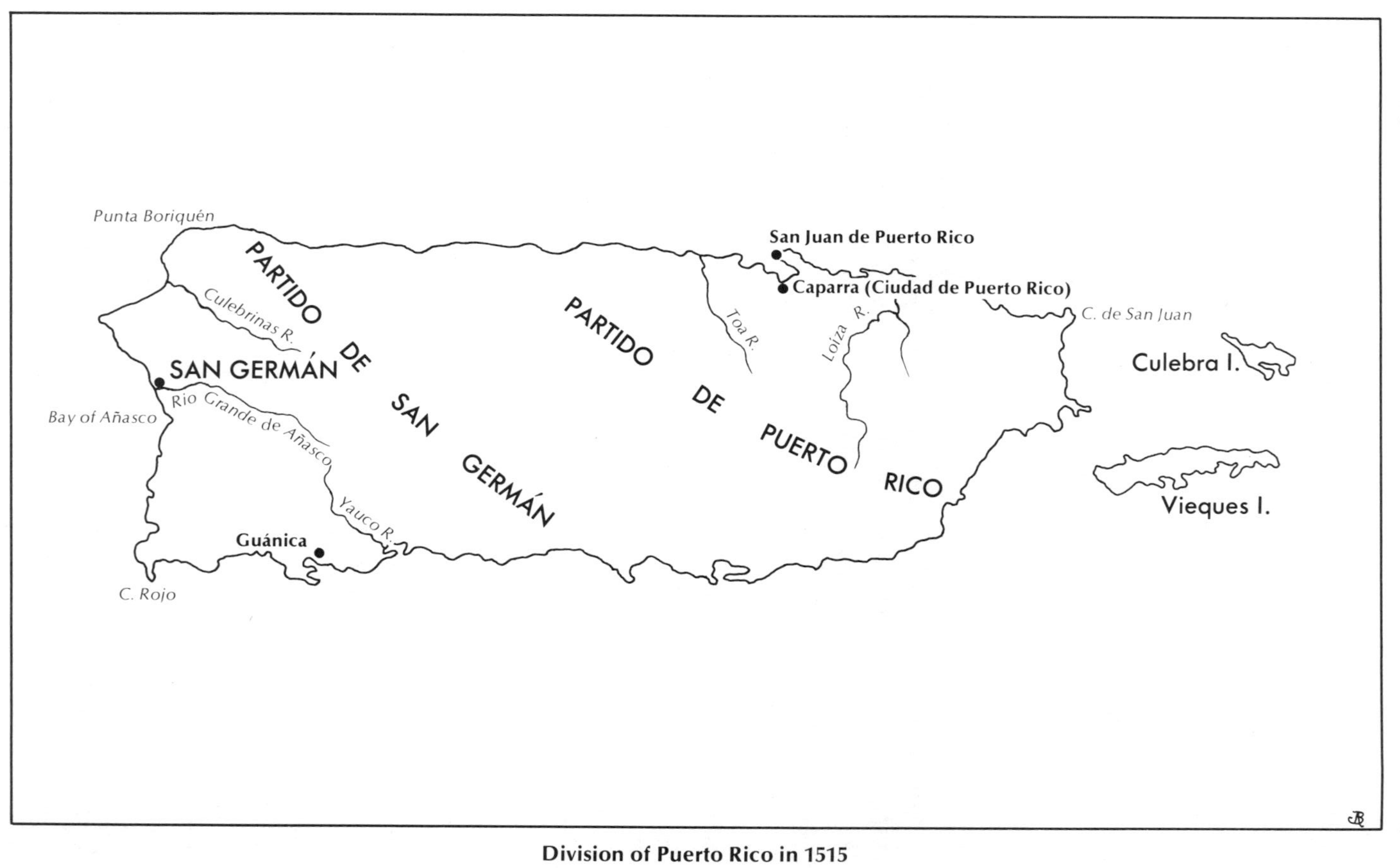

Division of Puerto Rico in 1515

arm of the Bayamón River, he established the first Spanish town on Puerto Rico. Ovando named it Caparra, and thus it may have been called by the early settlers, but the king called it Ciudad de Puerto Rico, and Caparra is not mentioned in official documents. Here thatch huts were put up, a small group went prospecting for gold, and the *caravelón* twice sailed, during the summer and fall, to Mona for provisions.[36]

The placer gold in the river beds was promising but not startling. Up to April, 1509, a period of about nine months, Ponce's few miners sifted out gold in the value of 836 pesos. Ponce was convinced that a permanent settlement was worth making, and many if not all of his followers were of like mind. In April, Ponce sailed for Santo Domingo with a few men to renegotiate his contract on more favorable terms, and to bring over his family and those of several of his followers. Ovando agreed that henceforth Ponce might enjoy half the net profits, and by July, 1509, he was prepared to return to the small settlement he had so quietly begun without causing conflict with the Indians.[37] The beginning of Spanish civilization on Puerto Rico, was, it would seem, almost idyllically peaceful.

In Spain, Ferdinand was sanguine that a new gold boom was in the offing on Puerto Rico, and fearing that Diego Colón might gain too great control of the enterprise, he urged various loyal hidalgos to emigrate there with their criados so that he could be assured the island would be occupied by men loyal to himself. One of these was Cristóbal de Sotomayor, a former secretary to Queen Juana and a member of a Galician noble family, who set sail with a few followers at the same time, or soon after, Diego Colón departed. They arrived about the time that Ponce left for Puerto Rico on his return voyage.[38]

Colón was incensed at what he saw as the king's trickery; while still in Spain, he had already protested Ponce's[39] occupation of the island. Now he sought out two loyal followers of his father and uncle, Miguel Diaz and Juan Cerón, whom he named alguacil mayor and alcalde mayor respectively, and sent to the island. When they left, along with Sotomayor, in October, 1509, they were accompanied by several hundred migrants eager to get at the rich gold placers of which they had now heard; some had come with Colón and still others were part oc the restless, surplus population of Española. What Ponce had tried to forestall, and had succeeded in doing for more than a year, now descended upon him.

The coming of the Cerón expedition (Diaz came separately, a little later) not only destroyed Ponce's plans for a small controlled mining operation that would not be oppressive to the Indians, but it also created factionalism on the island. Ponce did not at first oppose Cerón's assumption of authority, and the latter made the first repartimiento of Indians in November, giving out fifty-five hundred Indians to forty-eight encomenderos.[40] These included the absentee officials in Spain such as Lope de Conchillos as well as Pasamonte, the treasurer at Santo Domingo. The number of Indians allotted varied from three hundred for officials and other important persons, such as Sotomayor, to fifty for the ordinary expeditionary. Ponce also received two hundred for himself, but his contract with the king was made inoperable, even though Cerón assigned five hundred Indians to the Crown. He tried to work out an arrangement, but resigned from the royal partnership in disgust in May, 1510.[41]

Many of the newcomers fanned out across the northwest, thus widening the area of occupation. In the general region around Caparra, settlers occupied the rivers from the Loíza in the east to the Toa in the west, pressing the caciques for Indians to wash the gold-bearing sands. Sotomayor at first settled down at Guaymá, a pueblo near Guánica where Ponce had met Agueybana, who was dead by this time. The hidalgo's three hundred Indians were of the same tribe, under the successor cacique Güaybana. He had made arrangements to supply the northern mines with cassava, and hoped to discover gold placers in the streams flowing southward from the central range.[42]

Meanwhile, the king issued a cédula appointing Ponce governor of the island; the document reached Caparra in May, 1510, placed secretly aboard a vessel from Santo

Domingo by Pasamonte, without Colón's being aware of it.[43] Waiting for his best opportunity, and supported by Sotomayor, who was at that time in Caparra having brought provisions from his encomienda, Ponce showed Cerón his cédula, and when the latter refused to acknowledge Ponce's authority, he was arrested. A few days later Ponce also arrested Miguel Diaz and a third official. The three were returned to Spain in July aboard a vessel piloted by Juan Bono de Quejo, who also represented Caparra as its first procurador before the king. The island was now—and would be for about two years—under Ponce as governor for the Crown. On hearing of this affront to his authority, Colón notified his procurador in Spain to protest this violation of his rights, while contenting himself for the nonce with embargoing Ponce's property at Salvaleón de Higüey, and ejecting Pedro Moreno, Ovando's former secretary, from Ponce's stone manse in that town. Moreno then migrated to Caparra.[44]

Ponce was now in a position to direct the island's development and tend to his own affairs, and although he could not abolish the repartimiento, he proceeded to see that miners were sold cassava from the royal conucos. These he had had the Indians plant earlier so that the food they raised for their own use would not be appropriated. Though he had formally withdrawn from the royal company in May, even before the arrest of Colón's officials, he continued to act as majordomo, but not partner, for the king's interests. At Caparra, he had a stone house and fort put up for his residence and as an arsenal, the stone having been brought from the small island where San Juan de Puerto Rico would later be established; arranged around a plaza, where a thatch foundry had also been set up, were twenty or thirty huts on four streets.[45]

Mining now went forward under various partnerships. The most profitable were those including actual miners, rather than amateur prospectors directing Indian labor; the proceeds of the smelting of October, 1510, show that the most profit was made by Ponce, Miguel Díaz (then an absentee), and Cristóbal Sotomayor (who probably furnished either cassava or Indians or both from the south coast). The smelting evidently produced over 10,000 *pesos de oro,* for the royal fifth, paid by 176 persons, produced 2,645 *pesos de oro.*[46] Not everyone was fortunate, however, and no few persons produced less gold than the cost of the cassava sold them. The king remained an unpaid creditor, and hence suspicious if not of Ponce, at least of his royal officials who were soon to take charge; he viewed the whole industry as mismanaged until he put together a combination of competent officals within the last two years of his reign.

Meanwhile the western end of the island moved toward revolt, which would erupt in January or February of 1511. The reasons for a rebellion there, and not in the more intensive mining district along the Bayamón and Toa, are not readily apparent. Cristóbal de Sotomayor, with his nephew, Diego, and certain others, had established a village near Guaynilla, which he called Guaymá; Sotomayor had taken as his concubine the cacique's sister, although there is no reason to suppose this was a source of conflict; indeed, such relations tended to assure harmony with the native clans. The southern slope was apparently disappointing for gold. Oviedo relates that Spaniards combed the southern rivers in their search; Sotomayor finally sent Diego de Salazar northwestward, where he founded a town named after his overlord, Sotomayor, on a tributary of the Culebrinas; at about the same time, Luis de Añasco had established himself on the river bearing his name, just to the south, where he formed another small village, having been assigned an encomienda of one hundred Indians by Juan Cerón.[47]

The causes for Indian revolts are usually difficult to determine. It may well be that the Indians were treated worse in this area far from Ponce's influence, whereas he may have been able to exercise some restraint by way of advice and counsel in the northern goldfields. Even more probable as a general cause is that the cacique at Guaynilla must have been in touch with Caribs on Santa Cruz (St. Croix) island, if not elsewhere; the revolt broke out almost simultaneously in two different areas, on the Yauco at Guaynilla, and in the northwest, at Sotomayor and Añasco. Sotomayor, his nephew, and three others, twice warned of a pending revolt, finally decided to make a seemingly casual excursion toward Caparra (their route was apparently up the Yauco). The Indians in this area had recently drowned a Spanish boy merely to see whether he would actually die, and they now threatened to revolt because they feared punishment. The Sotomayor party hoped to escape by pretending that nothing had happened. Before they had gone far they were overtaken and killed; their interpreter, Juan González, managed to persuade the Indians that he sided with them, and subsequently escaped across the cordillera and to the conucos on the Toa where he gave the alarm. At about the same time in the northwest, Guarionex attacked the village of Sotomayor and burned it, killing an unknown number of Spaniards; Diego de Salazar led the survivors along the northern skirt of the cordillera to Caparra. The number killed cannot be known, owing to a paucity of records for expeditions to the island and ignorance of the locations of encomiendas granted in 1509. The estimate by Oviedo of eighty Spaniards killed is possible, but certainly open to doubt, especially since there is no evidence that gold in quantity had as yet been found toward the west, making it unlikely that such a large number of Spaniards had settled there.[48]

Ponce chose to attack first at Guánica bay and the mouth of the Arauco, perhaps because he wished to interdict any possible reinforcements of Caribs; he fitted out an expedition under himself and García Cansino, and sailed for the Yauco by way of the Pasaje de Vieques. As he told the king later, "I twice required them to submit, then attacked;" Ponce captured sixty-seven Indians, Cansino only nine. These were duly branded with an "F" (for Ferdinand) on the cheek and sold to the highest bidder. Since the auction was held in February, 1511, one may surmise that Ponce's counterattack had been very prompt following news of the revolt. In another foray at about the same time, Captain Sancho de Arango captured eighty-two Indians. Nonetheless, 158 Indians is a very small number compared with the hundreds or even thousands which were more or less involved in the rebellion. After returning to Caparra, Ponce with three captains, went overland to the northwest and in a number of raids captured eighty-two Indians. Oviedo related that 150 Indians were killed in a battle in which the Spaniards lost none; so phenomenal a victory is not mentioned by Ponce in his correspondence with the king. It seems suspect as a literary device. On the termination of this first Indian revolt, Ponce wrote the king in June, 1511, that the island was for the present pacified, and that he had enslaved rather than killed wherever possible.[49]

Ponce was seemingly now at the peak of his career as governor; he had been the real founder of Caparra, the first, and allowing for change of site, the most important settlement. He had survived the royal-feudal conflict with a minimum of strife, had tolerated a repartimiento system that went against his advice and wishes, and, with a minimum of bloodshed, had now put down the revolt he could well have predicted. His wise Indian policy was vindicated as the Indians along the Bayamón and Toa did not join the revolt; thus placer mining could continue and in the second smelting on the island from May to June, 1511, gold in the amount of ten thousand pesos was produced for the king.[50] On receipt of this, Ferdinand thought that Puerto Rico was his richest possession, and he was probably responsible for using the term, Ciudad de Puerto Rico rather than Caparra.

But unlike Diego Velázquez, his contemporary on Cuba, Ponce was not to enjoy a lifetime governorship of the island where he had initiated Spanish civilization. Ferdinand had perforce to return the island to Diego Colón's control, at least in judicial affairs, as the result of a decision handed down by the Royal Council, May 5, 1511, which he confirmed on June 17.[51] Ferdinand, always sensitive to the intricate web of feudal privileges, legal precedents, and volatile factions in Spain, accepted the decision and at once set Cerón and Díaz free, with orders to return to their offices. He notified Ponce to return power to them on their arrival and to keep peace and harmony. Ever the consummate politician within whatever fabric of adverse circumstances, Ferdinand now set to work to put his new kingdoms together another way, to mould loyalty and stability by devious means, leaving Colón with little more than the pomp and circumstance of a powerless feudal lord; he would build a populist base, create an efficient treasury, and establish a loyal court. Just now, however, in the seemingly magnanimous gesture of a king obeying the law, he permitted and enabled the Colón restoration on Puerto Rico. Ponce, faithful royal servant, quietly complied.

Cerón and Díaz reached Santo Domingo in October, 1511, where they undoubtedly conferred with Diego Colón about the general government and development of the newly occupied island. Colón favored a more intensive development of mining. Armed with a decree from the king who accepted at face value the colonists' statements about the severity of the Carib menace, Diego likewise favored a vigorous prosecution of the war both on and near the island to drive the Caribs away from the surrounding islands, detach them permanently from alliance with the Taínos, and in general to pacify many more Indians and utilize their labor. It was also decided, if not at this meeting then somewhat later, to establish a town on a firmer basis on or near the site of the burned Sotomayor. Colón also visualized making this new town the main settlement on the island in order to minimize the influence of Ponce, whom he suspected would tend to indirectly reinforce royal as against feudal power, Cerón proceeded directly to Caparra where he arrived later in October, taking power peaceably from Ponce; Miguel Diaz apparently sailed later, perhaps in early 1512, and laid the foundations for the town of San Germán on the Rio Grande de Añasco, presumably named for the patron saint of Ferdinand's young queen, Germana.[52] Ponce's disappointment was slightly allayed by the king's urging him to undertake new explorations, for which a suitable contract would be granted, and

Ponce now set about preparing the expedition that would lead to the discovery of Florida in the spring of 1513.[53] Though in 1514 Ponce was named Captain of Sea and Land he was subsequently more concerned with explorations and the pursuit of Caribs than with governmental matters on Puerto Rico.

Cerón encouraged the search for Indians who had withdrawn into the mountains and away from the northern valleys, sending out a number of expeditions that accomplished little more than the capture of a few caciques and the driving of others more firmly into the Carib alliance; the caciques Daguao and Humacao had especially close relations with the Caribs on Vieques Island. Meanwhile Diego Colón sent a small expedtion from Española to San Germán in December, 1512; it consisted of twenty-five persons, including a number of naborias, under the leadership of comendador Rodrigo Moscoso, whom he named teniente, thus showing he intended for San Germán to succeed Caparra as the main town. He had contracted with Juan Bono de Quejo to carry them; Bono, now back from his voyage to Spain in 1510, was under contract with Ponce to take part in the expedition to Bimini, and would join him at the mouth of the Yuma after depositing his passengers at San Germán.[54]

The cross purposes of the king and Colón were once again to work to the great disadvantage of the settlers. In December, 1512, at almost the same time that Moscoso landed at San Germán, Alonso Manso, the first bishop, reached the port near Caparra with a party of some thirty attendants and artisans from Spain; in June or July, 1513, about six months after they arrived, Caribs, incited by the raids into the Daguao and probably the offshore islands, struck at Caparra up the Loíza river. They killed a number of the inhabitants, set fire to most of the thatch huts including the church, and withdrew with a minimum of losses after dispatching the man-hunting dog, Becerrillo, with a poisoned arrow.[55]

Diego Colón himself had reached San Germán at about the same time as the attack with a larger expedition

—some sixty-five persons, including twenty-three Indians and teniente Cristóbal de Mendoza a replacement for Moscoso. Colón's purpose was apparently to assure San Germán's loyalty by seeing that the city council had the proper membership and to direct the taking of testimony from several participants in Columbus's four voyages who were then resident in one of the two towns. In this way Colón intended to support his claim to all lands touched on by his father. On learning of the attack at Caparra, Colón at once dispatched a ship to Española for reinforcements and supplies, the latter from Tomás de Castellón—a member of the Genoese merchant group who had long supported his father. Cristóbal de Mendoza was sent forward with a caravel to begin an attack on Vieques Island. Colón also sent out Captain Juan Enríquez, his brother-in-law, to march overland from Caparra into the Daguao to establish a fort, and possibly a town, should gold deposits warrant a new settlement. The attacks were only partly successful; Mendoza succeeded in driving the Caribs off Vieques and in capturing some of them, but the town founded by Enríquez, called Santiago del Daguao, lasted only a short time. It has a precarious existence from the outset owing to the local tribes' hostility most of whom withdrew to join the Caribs, to the scarcity of food, and to the failure to find gold placers rich enough to offset these disadvantages.[56] In 1514, Ferdinand ordered that the two be abandoned as an unnecessary expense.[57] Thus, expansion eastward proved a failure. For the indefinite future, the Loíza river formed the eastern boundary of Spanish settlement on Puerto Rico. San Germán enjoyed a brief gold boom, but never attained the political ascendancy desired by Viceroy Colón.

Spanish civilization in Puerto Rico was rooted, though precariously, during a brief gold boom that lasted only a few years. In contrast with Columbus's experience on Española, Ponce, aided by experienced miners, found gold immediately. He enjoyed good relations with his followers because his contract with the king was not a monopoly: he preempted certain placers and conucos in the king's name and operated them with salaried miners and Indians who at first worked voluntarily for barter goods. The remainder of the Spaniards, the great majority, worked other placers on their own, paying only the quinto to the king. This controlled situation broke down as hundreds flocked to the island, a movement that coincided with Diego Colón's successful assertion of his right to name the governing officials, and led to establishment of the repartimiento. This institution, in turn, prompted Indian revolts and withdrawals from the island as the partly Caribized Taínos resisted the incursion.

Puerto Rico well represents the Spanish experience in the Caribbean: hundreds rushed to find gold and a few score remained. Neither the amount of gold nor the number of Indians met the expectations of the immigrants who, toward the end of Colón's first government in the islands, were already drifting back to Española or Spain, or were following up new rumors in Panama or Cuba. Those who stayed generally settled for a prosaic existence, whiling away their time gambling for a hank of velvet and attaching themselves to the more advantaged residents such as Andrés de Haro, the "Pasamonte of Puerto Rico," the treasurer to whom Ferdinand entrusted his farms and mines after 1514.[58] Though gold mining continued on a reduced scale, it was insufficient to attract more than an occasional ship from Spain, for the shipmasters preferred to put in directly at Santo Domingo. The residents complained and eventually decided that they must relocate Caparra on the coast in order to attract more trade and to make a living offshore. The tiny gold-rush towns passed from existence, only Caparra and San Germán remaining for some years.

In these two towns, a few families among the first settlers would become permanent, such as the Ponces and the Diazes and the Troches. There is no firm evidence that the Franciscans tried to convert the Taínos in these early years, and only one priest is known to have been on the island up to 1515, dividing his time between thatched parish churches in the two main towns.[59] By 1515 Bishop Manso left his impoverished rustic bishopric for Spain, vowing never to return.

The expansion to Panama, Jamaica, and Cuba was at times hampered by the same persistent rivalry between the king and Colón as the move onto Puerto Rico had been. Colón was greatly irked on arriving to learn that Diego de Nicuesa and Alonso de Ojeda had signed contracts with the king to settle the region around Urabá, for Colón felt that his father had already touched on that entire bay, so that like the Greater Antilles and the Pearl Coast, it fell rightfully within his domains. However, the expeditions were already forming, and they sailed in November, 1509, in spite of Colón's efforts to delay them. His alguacil mayor, Francisco de Garay, arrested Nicuesa for debts, who quickly found a bondsman and was able to sail that same month.

Colón could, nonetheless, derive some consolation from sending an expedition led by Juan de Esquivel, a former criado of his uncle Bartolomé, to Jamaica in late 1509 or early 1510. Jamaica had been assigned to Nicuesa and Ojeda as a provisioning area for their mainland venture, but they apparently had been unable to persuade any followers to assume the mundane function of supplying cassava and other foodstuffs from an island without gold. They instead relied on their own conucos and those of some followers on Española, and the pugnacious Ojeda confined himself to a stern if futile warning to Esquivel not to settle on Jamaica on penalty of his life.[60] Such threats were commonplace and had no effect on the outcome.

Esquivel departed, presumably from Santo Domingo, with some sixty men and livestock, and put in at St. Ann's bay on the north coast, probably choosing this site because the Indians, source of food and labor, were cooperative with Columbus while he was marooned there six years earlier. Here with the aid of Indian labor he laid out a town, Sevilla la Nueva, and a stone fort. There was apparently no conquest in the usual sense: the Spanish were few, and the Indians apparently offered little resistance; the conucos were numerous, but the gold was vitually nonexistent. Jamaica would only serve as a provisioning station for Panama and Cuba, and the few

Spaniards who would ultimately remain settled for a modest living as domestic merchants exporting cassava, salt pork, and livestock.[61]

The king did not oppose Colón's settlement of Jamaica, perhaps because Nicuesa and Ojeda defaulted on their agreement to settle it; Ferdinand thought it best to dissimulate on this matter, especially since Colón had a clear claim to the island as long as the right of discovery was sustained as a cardinal principle supporting his viceroyalty. He urged Colón to see that the island produced all the food needed for the precarious Panama venture, but he soon lost confidence in Esquivel who failed to find gold, for he judged this to be due to his lack of knowledge or initiative. He felt, moreover, that Esquivel was a poor manager of the royal conucos and farms, which he had been charged with laying out, and he had established but one town whereas the contract of Nicuesa and Ojeda, which Esquivel in effect was carrying out, called for a minimum of two.[62] One was especially needed on the south coast of the island, partly because the main salt deposits for the salt pork trade were there, but even more because by 1513 Ferdinand was planning the great Pedrarias expedition to Panama, largest to America since Ovando's in 1502. The two thousand or so expeditionaries would surely face starvation if not well supplied from Jamaica. His fears proved well founded.

By 1512 Ferdinand ordered Colón to replace Esquivel and the king himself named Pedro de Mazuelo to be the island's factor (and later treasurer). Mazuelo, like his contemporaries Pasamonte and Haro, proved to be reliable, and would serve the Crown in these capacities until at least 1536. He embarked from some port on Española in October, 1514, carrying in his two caravels an unknown number of immigrants and considerable livestock. Meanwhile, Colón had agreed that Francisco de Garay, his ambitious alguacil mayor and his uncle by marriage, should succeed Esquivel. Garay did not take office at once, however, but went to Spain to negotiate a contract with the king. During the some two years between Esquivel's dismissal and Garay's arrival on the island in

May, 1515, Cristóbal Pérez and Diego Camargo, probably followers of Garay, served as tenientes at Sevilla la Nueva.[63]

Soon after his arrival, Garay learned that Ferdinand wanted to revise the contract, for he thought the one-half he had originally granted Garay was too high, since the island produced a great amount of cassava, yams, hammocks, and other cotton goods. Garay, however, forestalled any reduction in his share on the grounds that his initial expenses had been unduly great, and that the number of Indians and anticipated future production would be less.[64] By this time the Indian population was somewhat reduced as a result of exporting them to Española and Cuba, sometimes as slaves, other times, as with Pánfilo de Narváez, as followers. Garay's main contribution to the development of the island was to establish a second town on the southwest coast, Oristán, at approximately the site of the later Bluefields.[65] Although this offered some aid to Panama, many inhabitants of Santa María del Antigua were already dead or dying, and many others had migrated to Jamaica and hence to Cuba, where they would form a good part of the rank and file of the expeditions to Mexico in 1519–1520.

Jamaica was purely provisioning ground, an agricultural colony supplying food and later horses to the other islands and to Panama. Its early history was relatively uneventful compared with that of Española or Puerto Rico. Though it attracted few settlers, its Spanish population was for a time greatly increased as the starving settlers from Panama sought refuge there after 1515. The island was remarkably fertile, though its large and varied agricultural production probably owed as much to the necessity of producing what was possible, as to the quality of the soil. The Indian population—estimated at about sixty thousand—declined even without gold mining,[66] as the result of shipping Indians off the island and from the epidemics that ravaged all the islands settled by Spaniards. Only the Garay family was prominent on the island, and the Franciscans led by the veteran French Recollect Friar Juan de la Duele, established a monastery at Nueva Sevilla about 1511 in order to instruct caciques'sons and to hold religious services for the small Spanish population.[67]

Ferdinand was as zealous in urging exploration for signs of gold on Cuba as he had been in fostering settlements of the other islands of the Antilles and mainland: he had strongly supported the exploration and settlement of Urabá by Nicuesa and Ojeda in 1509. The promise of gold on Cuba had thus far been slight: Columbus had seen a few signs of it in 1492 and during his explorations along the south coast two years later. Still other explorers had passed along its southern shores: Juan de la Cosa, probably Vicente Yáñez Pinzón, and Juan Díaz de Solís in 1508, and in that year or 1509, Governor Ovando had presumably sent Sebastián Ocampo to circumnavigate the island. None of these voyages had stimulated great interest.

In these years interest in Cuba sprang more from a need for labor than from any hope that the island contained important deposits of gold. Then, too, the obligation to evangelize was increasing, since Ferdinand had just acquired complete patronage of the Church in 1508, and Española was receiving an ever greater number of Franciscans and, by 1510, Dominicans. Governor Ovando had apparently transported a few Indians from Española to Cuba as agents of goodwill, hoping to win over the Cuban Taínos. But the possible benefits of this overture seem to have been offset by an unauthorized slave raid conducted by a ship captain from Española, as well as by the earlier flight to Cuba of Taínos from Jaraguá, led by the cacique Hatuey, who was convinced that making peace with the Spaniards was tantamount to inviting destruction.[68]

Diego Colón needed little urging from Ferdinand to settle the island, since the maximum claims which were his main pursuit until his death would be much enhanced by an expedition under his direction. He was, however, unable to devote his attention to the project for nearly two years after his arrival, being too preoccupied with other matters of higher priority, such as counter-checking the independent power of Juan Ponce de León on Puerto Rico, and with pre-empting Jamaica before Ojeda and Nicuesa might act on their contract and occupy it. It is likely, too, that Ojeda and Nicuesa had first claim on voluntary migrants, for Panama had a reputation as a source of gold, deserved or not, which Cuba did not enjoy, and an expedition to the latter place, if mounted in 1509 or 1510, would have had but slight chance of drawing recruits. By 1511, however, the initial attraction of Panama had been snuffed out by the return of starving, ship-wrecked men, and Colón, after first considering his uncle Bartolomé for leader of the Cuban expedition, selected Diego Velázquez, very likely on Bartolomé's recommendation.

By this time Velázquez was likely to have found his income to be in decline, owing to the tendency of mine labor to depopulate the periphery. For this reason, he was surely receptive to Colón's offer to head up an expedition to Cuba. Still the genial attractive conqueror, and still possessed of various conucos and hog farms (although not so wealthy that he did not request some provisions on credit from the Franciscan monastery in Santo Domingo),[69] he was able to attract some three hundred recruits at Salvatierra de la Sabana by the time he departed in January, 1511.[70] In addition to his numerous relatives, many of the expeditionaries were debt-ridden encomenderos from the southwestern pueblos, Azua, Jacmel, Verapaz, and Salvatierra, who were eager to escape Colón's rigidly enforced laws against debtors. The mining industry was moving toward concentration into ever fewer hands. Later prominent among the rank and file were Hernando Cortés, who had served as town scribe at Azua, and Pedro de Alvarado, both to achieve fame in the conquest of Mexico. Perhaps to bolster protection of his interests, Colón sent Francisco de Morales, his father's trusted follower since 1493, as captain and second in command. The ships were laden with the usual provisions, and Velázquez planned to return for additional supplies from time to time, until the Cuban natives could cultivate and harvest additional conucos at his request.

The occupation was intended to be slow, gradual, and humane; four friars went along.[71]

What little is known of Velázquez's early activity on Cuba is derived from Diego Colón, who wrote the Archbishop of Toledo in January,1512,[72] conveying the contents of a letter he had received from his teniente; Velázquez had apparently put in at or near Guantánamo bay, and soon established on the north coast a fort surrounded by thatch huts. Since this first Spanish town on Cuba was christened Nuestra Señora de Asunción de Baracoa, it may have been formally founded on August 15 (1511), the date marking this holiday. He was apparently harassed by Hatuey who wished to dislodge the Spaniards from the island, and many of the Indians, probably at the cacique's urging, withdrew to the mountains to avoid contact. Several months were spent in forcing and cajoling the Indians to make peace, although Hatuey himself was not captured by the date Colón received Velázquez's letters and we have only Las Casas's word that Hatuey was later burnt alive.[73] If the event occurred, it would have been in 1512 prior to Las Casas's arrival on Cuba. At some point during the campaign, Velázquez sent for his friend Pánfilo de Narváez on Jamaica, who was summoned, it may be supposed, not because Velázquez lacked sufficient men, but because Narváez must have had, even then, a reputation for carrying out difficult tasks such as subduing rebellious Indians. Narváez arrived with thirty Spaniards and some Jamaican Indians in late 1511 or 1512. With the aid of Narváez and Francisco de Morales, Velázquez was able to assure, at least temporarily, peaceful relations with Taíno tribes in three regions: he himself probably established control in the vicinity of Baracoa. He sent Francisco de Morales a short distance along the north coast to the Bay of Nipe and the mouth of the Sagua, which became for a time a supplementary port for Baracoa, probably to transport foodstuffs to the latter town. Narváez with his thirty men were dispatched southward to the Cauto basin, around Bayamo, where he established at best precarious relations with the Indians and sustained a surprise but miscarried night attack in the region called the cacicazgo of Guaranamo.[74]

The behavior of the Indians, here as elsewhere on the islands, hardly typifies the tactics and strategy of resistance fighters. Caciques sometimes gave shipwrecked Spaniards considerate treatment for months or years and turned them over safely to their countrymen. Other times they drowned or hanged them, to see if they were really mortal, or because their *cemi* had commanded it; in so doing, they seemed to have no conception that such acts would certainly provoke a full scale counterattack, and were usually unprepared for it. They also practiced deception, concealing an intent to kill behind a mask of obsequiousness and ceremonialism, and while such ruses are perhaps necessary for a weaker opponent in warfare, unfortunately for them, the Spaniards were past masters at such tactics, and the deceiver was all too often himself deceived.

For approximately one year, the Spanish occupation of Cuba was confined to present-day Oriente province, with Baracoa the only town worthy of the name. From this port Spaniards fanned out with small squads of Indians, combing the rivulets for placer gold, but sifting out only small quantities. Velázquez, ever mindful of the king's interests, had royal conucos laid out to support himself and a few others nominally on royal salary.[75] How some three hundred men managed to content themselves with such a modest enterprise for a year can only be surmised. It may be that fear of a debtor's jail kept them languishing at Baracoa; it may be, too, that foodstuffs and even enslaved Indians were sent to Española, which returned a modicum of profit pending a chance discovery of greater gold deposits.

Certainly Velázquez tried to prevent harassing the Indians, and laid on them a very modest work requirement—one month's labor a year for any one Indian male—without breaking up villages or even assigning encomiendas.[76] When Morales provoked an Indian revolt near the Sagua, resulting in deaths on both sides, Velázquez expelled him to Santo Domingo.[77] Of course the paucity of gold found made unnecessary a more intensive exploitation of Indian labor, which Velázquez would have probably found impossible to control. After this

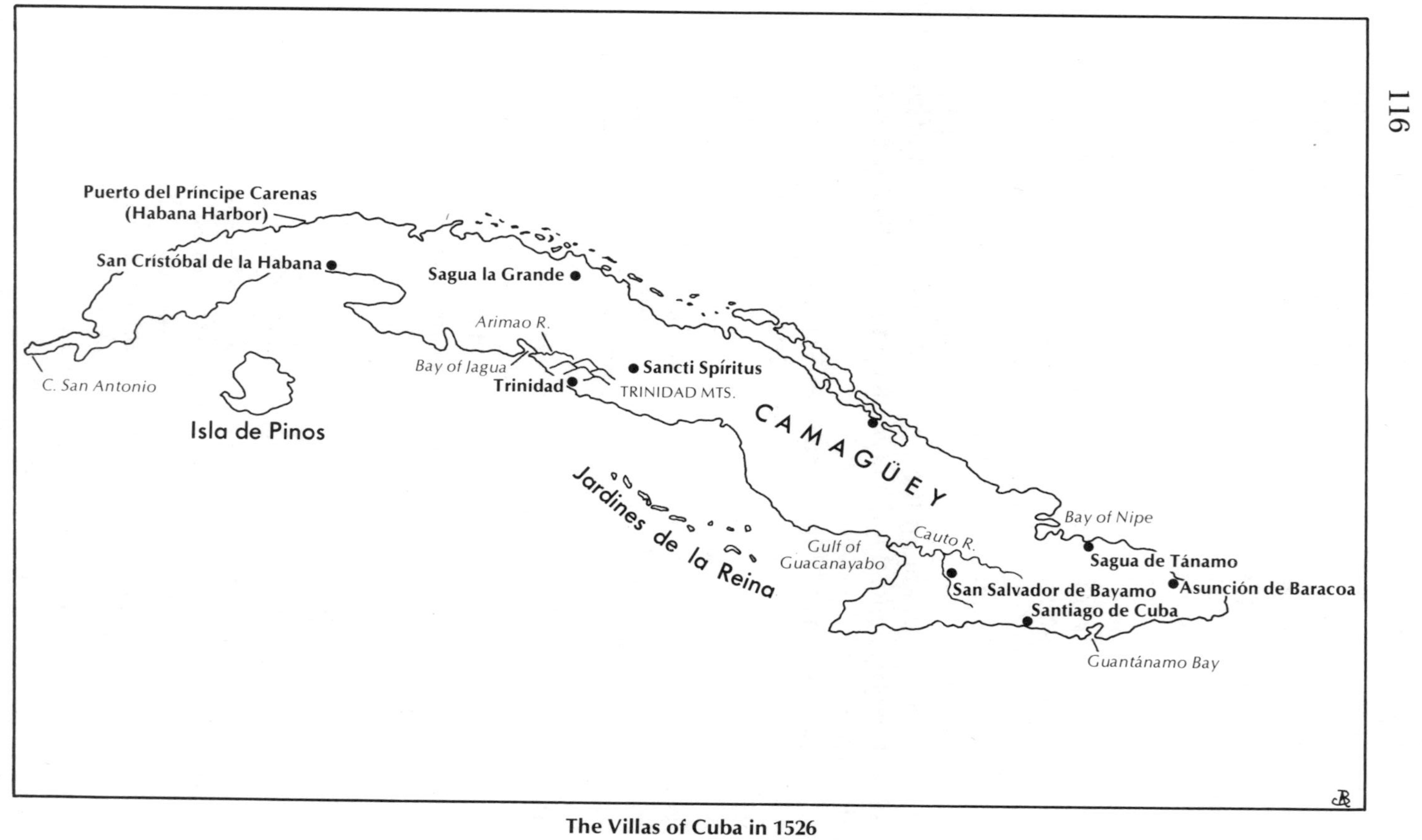

The Villas of Cuba in 1526

slow beginning, the expansion south and west during 1513–1515 occurred with dramatic suddenness. In those brief two years or less, Spaniards settled along the south coast and expanded into the interior, fixing the demographic stamp for some years, altered only by the founding of Havana, which responded to the conquest and settlement of Mexico. Velázquez's slowness in exploring the whole island is not completely explicable; it may be that the placers near Baracoa were sufficiently rewarding for a time. It may also be that he had orders from both Colón and the king to avoid as much as possible provoking the Indians, for criticism of the conquest was voiced well in advance of the promulgation of the Laws of Burgos, which did not reach the islands until 1514. But by 1513 the best placers were probably playing out, and further explorations became obligatory if Cuba was not to become another Jamaica.

Velázquez planned the exploration logically and thoroughly. There would be three expeditions, more or less contemporary: one, led by Narváez, would pass through the interior of the island; the other two would be coastal explorations, one each along the north and south coasts. Velázquez would himself lead the south coast explorations (which were partly by land); an unidentified lieutenant would command fifteen men in canoes to reconnoiter the north coast.[78] The explorations, however, were not carried out exactly as planned. Narváez learned in Baracoa that Indians had killed nine Spaniards, shipwrecked on the island while attempting to return from Panama, and he would also follow up rumors, heard later, that another three Spaniards—two of them women—were somewhere in the far western part of the island. The urgency imparted by this prompted Narváez to combine his explorations by land with sailings along both coasts; when he had accomplished his mission. he would finally join Velázquez in early 1514 at Jagua, near modern Cienfuegos on the south coast.

Narváez's first objective was the Cauto basin in Oriente. He led more men than the other lieutenants, about a hundred, probably because the Indians around Bayamo were known to be unpredictably hostile. After camping there some time, he marched northwestward, finally reaching a large Indian village, Caonao, which may have been situated approximately at the site of Sancti Spiritus, later established by Velázquez. Here Spaniards were greeted by two thousand Indians and their cacique, Caguax, in the main plaza; another five hundred remained inside a large *caney* (ceremonial hut). Nervous because of the fate of the nine Spaniards, apprehensive because of the cords the Indians had, the guests thought it expedient to disarm their polite ceremonialism and launch a surprise attack, which Las Casas, an eyewitness, described as one of the worst atrocities ever committed on the islands, leaving such an ineffaceable imprint on his soul as to contribute strongly to his life-long crusade against conquests and encomiendas.[79] It is difficult, however, to accept Las Casas's evaluation of the event as one in which innocent Indians were butchered, and who were themselves incapable of stealthy attacks. No one, not the least Las Casas, has tried to explain why five hundred of the Indians, described as naively curious to ogle the Spaniards, remained discreetly inside a caney, instead of satisfying their presumedly avid curiosity. That the affair was as bloody as Las Casas remembers it, there seems no reason to question; some one hundred Indians were killed in what was the last resistance of consequence until caciques wiser in Spanish ways would revolt six or seven years later.

While camping at this village, Narváez received word from Indians that three Spaniards were held captive by a cacique to the northwest, who was, as Narváez's party later learned, Caguionex, cacique of Havana. Narváez then turned northward, probably to reach the coast and travel as much as possible by canoe or, if he could find it, by the brigantine sent from Baracoa. In December, 1513, his party reached the village of Carahate where Indian messengers they had sent out returned with two Spanish women. They had been released by the Havana cacique, who had doubtlessly gotten word of Caguax's fate at Caonao.[80] As Velázquez had previously instructed Narváez to meet him in Jagua at Christmastime, Narváez now sent word to the south coast that he would rejoin Velázquez as soon as he had recovered the one remaining Spanish captive. He and Las Casas, with a small party, then sailed to the site of Havana, where they effected the recovery of a Spaniard who had lived among the Indians for two or three years, ever since he was shipwrecked at the western end of the island, en route from Panama. Narváez then journeyed to Jagua, possibly on the brigantine which by this time reached him.

Meanwhile Velázquez had set out from Baracoa in October, 1513,[81] coasting along the north shore the short distance to Sagua el Tánamo, and from there marched overland to the Cauto basin. While at an Indian village here, he received letters from the king, dated April 8, 1513,[82] which greatly clarified his powers and his responsibilities. He was authorized to assign the Indians to encomiendas, to establish such additional towns as his discoveries warranted, and especially to found towns along the southern coast that could offer provisions and relief to expeditions from Panama, which were borne along that passageway by prevailing currents and winds.

Velázquez now sent word to Baracoa for some of his followers to transfer themselves to the Cauto basin, and soon after this, in November, 1513, he established a town, San Salvador de Bayamo, on the Yara river, about five or six miles from the south coast.[83] Undoubtedly his empowerment as *repartidor* greatly encouraged settlement, for Spaniards could at least be assured of encomiendas, whether or not gold would be discovered. From Bayamo, Velázquez traveled by canoe along the south coast, where at Manzanillo he learned of Narváez's progress westward, and in or about January, 1514, he and his lieutenant met at Jagua. In this large bay, Velázquez had decided to establish a town, initially as a supply base for ships from Panama; he christened it Trinidad.[84] At about the same time, gold was discovered along the Arimao, which flowed into the bay, and as Spaniards fanned out up river, finding ever more deposits, he established another town, Sancti Spiritus, in the interior. Access to encomiendas seemed to have whetted the prospecting ardor of still others, for now gold was found not only in the interior stream beds of Oriente province, and among the *sierras* of Camagüey, but a little later, toward the north of the former province in valleys of the area of Holgüín. Cuba now entered into a brief gold boom that lasted until about 1520.

Narváez was sent westward from Jagua to determine whether gold deposits were situated in that area; although he did not find gold, he established a town among populous Indian tribes on the south coast, at San Cristóbal de Habana, sometime in the first seven months of 1514.[85] By 1514, Velázquez judged it advisable to abandon Baracoa because it was too far from the main goldfields and the trade that would follow the gold discoveries; he relocated the town on the large harbor of the southeast coast, thus establishing Santiago de Cuba.[86] With this town, and a port called Puerto de Príncipe founded after the gold discoveries in the Holgüín area, seven settlements had been established.

The initial Spanish occupation of Cuba differed from that of the other three islands in that sharp Taíno resistance was offered at the outset and was sustained for a year or more in Oriente. Eastern Cuba had been occupied by Taínos probably during the fifteenth century;[87] they were culturally similar to the perceptive tribes at Jaraguá, some of whom fled to give warning and reinforce the Cuban Taínos in advance of the expedition of 1511. One may perceive, therefore, that southwestern Española and southeastern Cuba comprised a common region supporting the highest Arawak or Taíno culture on the islands. The defense put up by Hatuey is but a sequel to that offered at Jaraguá earlier and the Cuban cacique is a forerunner of the astute and partly Hispanized Enriquillo at Jaraguá who successfully withdrew from Spanish control in 1519.

After Taíno resistance was overcome in Oriente, occupation of most of the north and south coasts followed rapidly. The personal motive of the explorers was to find gold, but the laying out of ports, especially Santiago de Cuba, Trinidad, and San Cristóbal de Habana responded to the need to support the large colony at Panamá, thereby showing that the occupation of Cuba owed as much to external influences as to internal needs. The Indian tribes west of Oriente, who were chiefly Siboneys, offered little resistance to this advance.

Otherwise early Cuban history repeated essentially the same pattern of development as that on Española and Puerto Rico: the working of placers by encomienda labor, trade with the other islands and with Panama, and the rise of a main port—Santiago de Cuba—as the chief entrepôt on the island. A few missionaries came by 1515. The Dominicans may even have preceded Velázquez as they claimed a few years later, but there is no record of their activities. Several Franciscans accompanied him and the secular priest Bartolomé de las Casas soon followed.

But it was as a rendezvous for luckless settlers that the large, fertile island was chiefly distinguished. Immigrants from Spain and the other three islands were at first attracted by the gold discovered in 1514, others fled there from Panama to escape starvation, and most of these newcomers tarried but a few years before joining the great rush to New Spain. In their wake, they left few of the original settlers, notably Diego Velázquez, who with a handful of supporters, mostly late arrivals, controlled the wealth of the island, its rapidly declining towns, and its thatch parish churches that awaited in vain for a resident bishop.

The occupation of Cuba brought Ferdinand's expansionist aims in America to their apex: only the great expedition of Pedrarias in 1514 raised his hopes for a vast gold discovery to a still higher peak. America was the easiest area for expansion in terms of royal expenditures and military power: the Mediterranean and Jerusalem remained as his major aims, for the king planned personally to lead the series of naval attacks in the Mediterranean in 1511.[88] This had followed the victories of Pedro Navarro, beginning at the Peñón de Vélez in 1508 and climaxed by the great victory at Tripoli in 1510.

This was the crest of Ferdinand's expansionist dreams.

He had in 1510 called the Cortes of Monzón, a great political event since for the first time representatives of his eastern peninsular kingdoms and Italian possessions met in one great convention, to vote generous subsidies for the monarch who was bound for Jerusalem in the name of the Christian faith.[89] The victories won by Navarro and the promise of still greater success helped the king unite factious Castilian nobles for the time being. He was careful, however, not to press Castile for subsidies, but to draw on his regalia, on his more loyal and interested eastern possessions, and on the gold from the Caribbean and the revenue from all his royal farms and mines. Half of this had to be paid to Juana and her household, but the other half could be spent as he wished.

But the crest passed quickly. Navarro suffered a great reverse at Djerba in August, 1510;[90] this might not of itself have checked Ferdinand's drive against the Turks, but before new forces could be raised the conflict in Italy between Louis XII, Maximilian, and Pope Julius II had reached the point where he had no recourse but to divert his Mediterranean expedition to the Pope's defense. By 1512 he was involved in Italy and in trying to detach Navarre from an alliance with France. After these wars, which left him rather worse off in Italy, Ferdinand's health was broken along with his dreams; weary and irascible, surfeited with Diego Colón's antics, he would recall his troublesome viceroy in 1515. Before he made that decision, however, the king had put up with years of intrigue, evasion, and conflict on Española, now an island of somnolence and disappointment compared with its bright Ovandine days; to follow this conflict on Española is to unravel an important political thread of Caribbean history closely entwined with the expansion of which Ferdinand was himself the chief architect.

4

Diego Colón and Española (1509-1515)

The Spanish civilization that was to spread out so dramatically from Española throughout the Greater Antilles and the vast mainland beyond was initiated through the precarious occupation of the main islands adjacent to Española and the tenuous foothold on Panama. However, the expectations of wealth that accompanied this expansion greatly exceeded the actual realizations. The king added his encouragement, even his insistence, to hidalgo ambitions as he helped finance, arm, and provision the many explorations and expeditions. But the results were uneven. The gold placers on Puerto Rico were rich but shallow;[1] new beds were found every year or two, resurrecting hopes that untold wealth was at hand, but the gold was never enough to do more than help keep the royal treasury solvent and contribute to the modest fortunes of a few settlers. Panama proved more of a graveyard than a gold mine, although it was the Lorelei of Spanish hopes during these years, for Nicuesa and Ojeda in the beginning, and for the feckless hundreds who accompanied Pedrarias there in 1514. Even the pearl bartering, so promising during the days of Niño and Guerra, proved overly hazardous; the roving Caribs with their poisoned arrows made the Spaniards extremely wary of voyages to the Spanish Main or the Lesser Antilles until a build-up of armaments gave them new courage. Jamaica never yielded more than a pittance of gold, none till after Ferdinand's death, and Cuba yielded only small amounts until the discoveries on the Arimao in

1514. This last gold strike, together with new signs of gold on Panama, made Ferdinand's last year on earth happier than it might otherwise have been. Death, however, spared him the realization that even these last discoveries were much like the others, of some substance but hardly, as in the case of Panama, sufficient to warrant a bishopric and creation of the grandiose title of Patriarch of the Indies.

The years were no less disappointing to the bishops, to the Dominicans and Franciscans who became critical of the forced labor regime, to disappointed vecinos, and to Diego Colón who waged a competitive struggle with the royal officials and their followers over the meager and diminishing wealth in the Indies, offset somewhat by the brief Puerto Rican gold boom and the delayed strike on Cuba. Ferdinand alternately counterchecked Colón and appealed to his loyalty; the king could manipulate the proportionate amount of income going to the Crown and the vecinos in order to allay discontent, and he could support an inexpensive evangelistic movement to the other islands and ultimately, in his last year of life, to Venezuela. He had the great majority on his side as against the pleas of the few reformers to abolish the forced labor system. But one conflict he could not resolve—though it was muted by episcopal absenteeism. This was the conflict between his stated purpose to establish bishoprics in the Indies and the pursuance of his expensive foreign policy in the Mediterranean. The second purpose defeated the first; the price of peace at home and war abroad was the collection of gold from the Indies that might have paid for the cathedrals—so long unconstructed.

These years of expansion and hope had dispersed much of the population from Española and had attracted immigrants from Spain to the newly occupied lands. The island of original settlement was thus considerably depopulated by 1515, a tendency that would be continued and accelerated. The regions of greatest population loss were the eastern and western ends of the island, which reflected a double movement: the departure of expeditions to new areas, and the concentration of Indians in the mining zones of the Cibao and San Cristóbal. The movement of Spaniards out of these two zones was not represented only by the initial expeditions of Ponce de León, Nicuesa and Ojeda, Esquivel, and Diego Velázquez. It continued less noticeably during all these years as debtors fled the island, encomenderos lost out in the shuffling and reshuffling of encomiendas, and word of gold booms or at least numerous Indians filtered in from Cuba or Panama or elsewhere. The exodus was not only of Spaniards but of Indians. The western town of Lares de Guahava was nearly depopulated when the cacique Hatuey fled to Cuba with his people prior to 1511, and hundreds of other Indians accompanied the Spanish expeditions as migrants, voluntarily or involuntarily.[2] The absolute decline of Indians on Española seems to have been due as much to migration as to death during these years.

An internal migration on Española involved both Spaniards and Indians, who relocated in the mining zone. Sometimes caciques were persuaded to relocate; others undoubtedly were forced to do so, and still other Indians simply remained in the central zone towns, after being sent there for mine labor. Fewer Indians on the whole island made this centripetal movement necessary if mining was to continue. By 1514, Santa Cruz de Aycagua was non-existent in the eastern area,[3] and certain other peripheral towns were greatly reduced in size. The tendency to concentrate in the center zone was illustrated in the redistribution of Indians in 1514. The king held 1,367 Indians in various towns, but of these, 967 were in the San Cristóbal mining area. The tendency to resituate Indians in the center could be seen in transfers made as part of the repartimiento of 1514. For example 533 Indians were transferred from Salvaleón de Higüey and Azua to Santo Domingo, 156 from Jacmel to Santiago de los Caballeros, and 301 from Vera Paz to San Juan de la Maguana.[4] These relocations were presumably only the most recent of many preceding ones, which together constituted the first stage in a contraction of the demographic pattern on the island. Somewhat later the population would be concentrated in a still smaller configuration especially around Santo Domingo and the south coast, and agriculturally based on sugar, cassia fistula, (a tree of medicinal value) and livestock.

When Ferdinand reassumed power in 1507 after the brief hiatus under Philip and Juana, he had great faith in the potential wealth of America. He turned with characteristic Aragonese business acumen and energy to organize the overseas enterprise into a mining industry profitable alike to himself and the hidalgo-bureaucratic class on which his power chiefly rested. These were the years of his unlimited ambitions—the dreams of a Spanish-dominated Mediterranean, of a Jerusalem liberated from the infidel in realization of that boyhood vision of himself as the great paladin of Christendom. But he had great ambitions and a small income; Castile could not be insistently pressed for subsidies lest he erode his precarious popularity. Like other Iberian monarchs later, he must make the most of America where his power was unlikely to be challenged, as it might be in Castile, by a major revolt. The ambitious Ferdinand was consequently to be the prime mover of Caribbean expansion, with the potential hidalgos as his agents.

Had his economic base at home been larger, or his ambitions less, the king might have contented himself with the traditional royal taxes and monopolies, the almojarifazgo, the judicial fines, the monopolies on salt, minerals, dyewood, and later, Negro slaves. But the king had entered directly into mining with Governor Ovando as his manager, and his interest in expansion was in part directly related to his incessant need for funds derived from establishing royal mines and farms in whatever newfound profitable areas. "I have ordered gold from the richest mines reserved for the Crown," he advised Colón.[5] Ovando had already done this on Española, for there the pit mines were mainly royal mines; the *panes de laves* (placers) were opened to private prospectors. The same policy was followed on Puerto Rico, except that there were no pit mines, so Ferdinand claimed the richest placers. This royal pre-emptive policy was necessarily carried over to Indian labor, indispensable to the mining operation. The king advised his managers (Pasamonte on Española) to put the best Indians in the royal mines, to trade Indians with private parties if necessary. When mining seemed to be in a slump in 1510 he advised Pasamonte to take Indians from those least deserving and put them in the royal mines.[6]

The royal mines on Española were operated in what became the typical mode by squads with Indian helpers, all salaried. The administration and supply of the operation was placed in the hands of the treasury with general supervision entrusted to Pasamonte, with tools furnished by the royal factor, and with provisions arranged for by the veedor, the only official more or less constantly at the main site.

Whether the adjacent islands contained gold in quantity was problematical in 1508; thus the impecunious king preferred letting private entrepreneurs take the initial risk, while he participated as a major partner. The first such partner was Ponce de León who had contracted with Ovando to exploit whatever mines might be found on Puerto Rico on terms of his furnishing all provisions and tools in return for one-third the gross profits. When this proved disadvantageous the contract was renegotiated in 1509 on an equal basis.[7] Diego Colón made a similar contract with Juan de Esquivel in 1509 and with Diego Velázquez two years later.[8] In this way the king's royal mines and farms expanded with the conquest. He insisted on having one thousand Indians at work in the royal mines on Española and, by 1514, five hundred in the Puerto Rican mines.[9] His conucos on Jamaica employed about two thousand Indians, and an unknown number in Cuba.[10] As a result he was the chief miner and encomendero on the islands, in essence, the principal rival of the encomenderos who did not deign to criticize the right of their monarch to engage directly in economic enterprise.

Though the king was the encomenderos' chief competitor, holding perhaps 10 to 15 percent of the Indians on all four islands[11] and the best mines and farms, statism was not resented as much as absenteeism—the holding of encomiendas by court favorites. The trend toward increasing numbers of absentee encomenderos was begun after Ferdinand's restoration to power in 1507 and represented the king's way of assuring loyalty, which was still much needed owing to threats to his power from dissident factions in Spain. The effect of this tendency in the Indies was the dispossession of encomenderos on various grounds—mistreatment of Indians, failure to bring their wives from Castile, too long a sojourn in Spain; the effect was also to swell the ranks of recruits for the expeditions leaving Española in 1508–1511. Furthermore, the absentee policy heightened the competition for Indians, contributing to deepening factionalism, and gave Diego Colón, for a time, the opportunity to act as a forerunner of *criollismo*, championing local interests against the absentee Spaniards viewed as covetous courtiers who had never ventured to leave the peninsula. Ferdinand was usually willing to make concessions to the *procuradores* (delegates) from the islands, but as for dispossessing his supporters in Spain of Indians, he limited himself to replying in 1512 that he would make no further grants to absentees.[12]

With an intensity hitherto unsuspected, Ferdinand urged onward expansion in the Caribbean. If Prince Henry of Portugal merits his title of Navigator for inspiring the Portuguese advance southward along the African coast, Ferdinand might well be called the "Explorer" of the Caribbean. No monarch's hand would ever guide events in the Indies so closely again, not even Philip II's who in any case had virtually a world enterprise to look after. The Aragonese king congratulated every small discovery of gold, urged explorers to "spy out the secrets" of unknown islands, and suffered with them when their enterprises ended in disaster.[13] Mismanagement of his enterprises he found intolerable; he was tireless in his search for an honest, efficient manager. Pasamonte was virtually peerless in this respect, and had it not been for Diego Colón's unpredictable maneuverings, Ferdinand would have had no cause for worry about his Española mines. Although his first appointees to the treasury, other than Pasamonte, proved unsatisfactory, for one reason or another, he had by 1514 rounded out the treasury staff with two able men: Gil González Dávila, later more prominent in Central America, as contador, and another Aragonese like Pasamonte, Juan de Ampies, as factor.[14] He was early dissatisfied with the management of the Puerto Rican enterprises. Ponce had virtually an uncontrollable situation when Juan Cerón and Miguel Díaz arrived in 1509–10, along with a horde of gold-seekers, for in the ensuing manipulation of encomiendas the royal mines were virtually disregarded. In the rapid changes of command that followed, Ferdinand lost much of the income that he should have received under the Ponce contract.[15] In 1512 he appointed Sancho Velázquez, the fiscal at Santo Domingo, to take Ponce's *residencia* and audit the accounts of the partnership he held with the Crown. Velázquez obliged Ponce to pay some 1,300 pesos, which he judged had been earned by the king's Indians.[16] Ponce paid, but appealed on the grounds that Cerón's repartimiento removed some of the Indians and that he had resigned from the company in May, 1510. He was finally cleared of culpability in 1519, though his money could not be refunded because the treasurer who had received it in 1512 had sent it to Spain and disclaimed personal responsibility for repayment.[17]

Only in 1514 did the king manage to find a capable treasurer in Andrés de Haro, who efficiently managed the royal mines and farms. At about the same time the king appointed Baltasar de Castro as contador, Antonio Sedeño as factor, and Diego de Arce as veedor. All three officials would serve until 1520, the latter two somewhat longer.[18]

The king was similarly dissatisfied with the management of his farms on Jamaica. Since gold had been found on two of the other islands, he naturally presumed it should also be discovered there. "What kind of man is this Esquivel?" he queried Pasamonte.[19] To Colón he expressed the opinion that Esquivel must know little about how to prospect for gold.[20] Colón was, like the king, interested in finding new wealth; he removed his retainer on Jamaica in 1512, and substituted, over the next two years, two others without effecting any noticeable improvement. Finally in 1514, with the needs of Panama in mind, the king contracted with Francisco de Garay, on the basis of equal shares, to stimulate the development of agriculture on the island. To make certain that royal income would be adequately collected, he named Pedro de Mazuelo factor (later treasurer) and both men would serve the Crown many years in these capacities.[21] Cuba was the only island where the king left management of his properties in the hands of the original contractor, for he remained satisfied with Diego Velázquez and the initial treasury perhaps because Velázquez found just enough gold to prove he was prospecting and furnishing provisions for the Panama venture at a time when they were sorely needed.

Although Ferdinand implanted many royal enterprises in the Caribbean—a tendency referred to in our day as statism—he was by the same token sensitive to the complaints and needs of the encomenderos who participated with him and his officials in the common enterprise of mining gold. The encomenderos varied their approach to the monarch, now channeling their requests through local treasuries or the governor, now authorizing procuradores, who typically had additional private interests in mind, to represent them at the court. In 1508 two procuradores for Española were elected from Concepción de la Vega and Santo Domingo, the two main towns on Española. These officials, Diego de Nicuesa and Antonio Serrano, were to request the following measures: extension of the *merced* of paying one-fifth severance tax on privately mined gold; the building of churches from durable material; subsidies for roads; the right to build ships; to engage in island trade; and to bring Indians from other islands to Española.[22] The monarch modulated these requests with an eye to protecting his own interests without overly discouraging his necessary allies in the American enterprise. These requests for concessions were also voiced, in one form or another, by procuradores from towns of the other islands, such as Juan Bono de Quejo and Pedro Moreno for Puerto Rico in 1510 and 1511, respectively; Bartolomé Colón, Francisco de Garay, and Gil González Dávila for Española in 1510, 1512, and 1515; and Pánfilo de Narváez and Antonio Velázquez, the first procuradores for Cuba in 1515.[23] In general, the king refused to relinquish his monopoly on dyewood and salt, but granted small subsidies for roads, and adjusted taxes on the use of Indians in accordance with the risk of obtaining them and the volume of complaints from debt-ridden miners.

The king's policies towards economic opportunities for the islanders were thus characterized by a tendency toward limited liberalization to offset mounting disadvantages. Although he entrusted Diego Colón to assign encomiendas, as Ovando had done, the king himself exercised close supervision over the process to assure that the size of encomiendas accorded with social position and merit. With the transportation of Indians from the island, the slower attrition by death owing to various causes, and the assignment of encomiendas to absentees and local officials, there was grave need to find an encomienda policy that would keep a sufficient number of islanders content to remain on Española.

The king's encomienda policy at the outset of Colón's first governorship, which he entrusted to the Viceroy to carry out, was to assign Indians on the basis of a maximum of one hundred and a minimum of thirty. Officials would receive one hundred, *caballeros* with their wives, eighty, *escuderos* with their wives, sixty, and *labradores* with their wives, thirty.[24] But the distinction between caballeros (or hidalgos) and labradores was not always possible to draw because claims to hidalgo status by humble persons could not be verified or refuted. Owing to a long tradition of leadership by the nobility, however, the Spaniards apparently took it for granted that vice and mistreatment of Indians was exceptional among men of higher social status and typical among the plebeians. Since many of the latter were among the first settlers, their mistreatment of the Indians seems to have been taken for granted and they were, in many instances, among the first to be dispossessed. The king granted the encomienda for the lifetime of its holder, with the proviso that he pay one *peso de oro* per year for each Indian.[25] Ferdinand's purpose was not primarily to raise revenue but to assure that the Indians would be profitably employed, for he suspected that many encomenderos worked their Indians very little. For the same purpose he constantly enjoined that encomenderos employ one third of their Indians in the mines at all times.[26] Inflation proved that one hundred Indians were too few to provide a living for the encomenderos, for even the reformer Las Casas believed in 1516 that the maximum should be one hundred fifty and the minimum forty Indians for encomenderos.[27] Such suggested revisions were rather specious, since there were, at least by 1514, a year for which records are available, too few Indians to satisfy this distribution. Except for a favored few, the average encomendero of some prominence was fortunate to hold sixty to eighty Indians.[28]

The holding of Indians by absentee and resident officials continued during and for some years after Ferdinand's reign and was increasingly resented by the vecinos. The king decreed in 1510 that officials would hold two hundred Indians, but his penchant for multiply rewarding his favorites at court soon greatly raised this figure, especially for Lope de Conchillos and Rodríguez de Fonseca.[29] On repeated protests from the islanders, he promised in 1512 that no more encomiendas would be given to absentees. He agreed, in order to mollify the vecinos, to subsidize roads on Española by setting aside a certain amount of the gold they turned in at the foundries, and on Puerto Rico he granted his court fines for the same purpose.[30] By 1514 he allowed miners a liability for debts limited to the value of tools they had bought on credit.[31]

More important than trying to distribute Indians equitably was the king's encouraging the importation of Indians from other islands to offset the dwindling labor supply. Ferdinand's policy in this matter was that the royal conscience would not be burdened by the removal of Indians from islands that were devoid of gold—useless islands—since they would be converted and their souls saved. The question arose in Columbus's time whether Indians could be enslaved and Queen Isabel had ruled against it.[32] At about the same time, however, Ojeda, Bastidas, and other explorers voyaging along the Spanish Main had been attacked by Indians with poisoned arrows—all such Indians were considered Caribs—which took a considerable toll of Spanish lives. These attacks and the evidence some of the perpetrators, at least, were cannibals, provided the rationale for the decree authorizing enslavement of Caribs.[33]

The Spaniards distinguished between slaves and peaceful non-cannibalistic Indians brought from other areas to Española for conversion and forced labor. In practice, there was often little difference and, in some cases, none at all. The Lucayos of the Bahamas, the Taínos shipped to Española from the other three main islands (not very many, apparently), and the peaceful non-cannibals of the Venezuelan coast were called naborias. Spaniards claimed permanent custody of these Indians, and typically used them as household servants or for other forms of personal service on their estancias. Virtually every resident had at least a few naborias, though vecinos did not always succeed in keeping all of those they claimed. The naborias were for all practical purposes indistinguishable from slaves for they were subject to forced labor, were branded to facilitate recovery should they run away, and were even illegally sold, in most instances, when an islander wished to liquidate his property.[34]

The procurement of offshore Indians became, after 1508, a valuable adjunctive enterprise to the mining industry, sustaining it at a higher level than would otherwise have been possible. The business, like mining, was operated as both a state and a private enterprise, for the king supplied caravels from the Casa de Contratación to his treasury officials on all the islands, although Española was the main island participating up to 1515. The typical method of operation was for Diego Colón and the treasury to let contracts to private merchants or shipowners. The king suggested that such contracts be granted with the Crown reserving three-fourths of the Indians acquired. He also felt that holders of these naborias should pay the annual peso tax, and that they should be assigned them only for two to three years, at whatever price was feasible.[35] His purpose again was to assure that the Indians would be put to good use.

Although a vast area both south and north of Española was thus thrown open to catching of Indians, it is virtually certain that the Bahamas were the best hunting grounds during the years prior to 1515. One cannot know whether forty thousand Lucayos were removed as Las Casas estimated, but the islands were ultimately depopulated. Among the main *armadores* were Rodrigo de Bastidas, the merchant-shipowner of Santo Domingo, and Miguel Diaz and Francisco de Garay, both active merchants and shipowners during these years.[36] Through mercantile connections in Seville, it is relatively certain that the Manzorro-Becerra clan of Santiago participated, and may even have been the leading Bahama slavers, owing to their location.[37] Local ships were probably built, but shipmasters plying the Atlantic trade sometimes laid over a year or two, perhaps even permanently, to engage in Indian slaving. Antón Cansinos of Palos, for example, remained at Santo Domingo in 1513.[38]

Capturing the docile Lucayos proved easy, but few wished to take advantage of the invitation to capture Caribs. The islanders had already resisted the king's offer to sign contracts in which they would receive only one-fourth the Indians taken: the king reduced his share to one-half later in 1509 and to one-fifth in 1510.[39] Still greater inducements had to be offered before the armadores would fit out for the Lesser Antilles or eastern Venezuela. Garay sent a ship to Guadaloupe in 1510, but there is no evidence that his crew captured any Caribs.[40] The fates of Nicuesa and Ojeda's men further paralyzed the desire to make such voyages: forty-six of Nicuesa's expeditionaries were killed on Los Gigantes (Curaçao) in a single engagement and the veteran navigator Juan de la Cosa was killed at Urabá in 1510 from wounds inflicted by a poison arrow.[41] Not many wanted to utilize Ojeda's cure of red hot iron to cauterize the wound.[42] In 1511, Caribs joined the Taínos on Puerto Rico to wipe out the small town of Sotomayor and to kill a number of the Spanish settlers.

In reprisal for these attacks, the king declared official war on the Caribs on June 3, 1511,[43] and orders poured into the Casa de Contratación for quilted vests, shields, and harquebusses; the king sent an order for the round shields of Naples—the best in the world.[44] In 1512, the monarch waived all taxes for anyone waging war against the Caribs. Non-Caribs captured on the coast of Venezuela could be held permanently as naborias and passed on to heirs. "I grant all these concessions," the king wrote his treasury, "that the vecinos may produce more gold. The more gold they produce, the more mercedes I will grant."[45] Still there were few forays to the south during most of these years. Not even the additional lure of pearls, whose barter the king opened to all vecinos subject to licensing by his treasury, sufficed to impel many voyagers to the Pearl Coast before 1515.[46] Gradually, as more small arms and shields were shipped to the alcaide at Santo Domingo, and as Lucayo Indians became fewer, expeditions began to hazard penetrating the poison-arrow curtain. One armador brought back two hundred Indians from Curaçao in 1514, and it was reported that a total of twelve hundred had been captured by the end of the following year.[47] These are not likely to have been Caribs, for that tribe was seaborne and apparently had no fixed habitat on the Spanish Main, unless it was around the mouth of the Orinoco.

The procurement of offshore labor was thus a hazardous affair in the Carib zone, although relatively easy to the north. Like most other enterprises of the time, the results were less than expected and were often disappointing. This was especially true to the south, for Ferdinand had counted on a renewal of the valuable pearl trade but only a small number of pearls were obtained, mainly during 1508–1510, before the Carib menace reached its greatest proportions.

The king was sympathetic with these disappointments and remained responsive to the economic needs of the hidalgo-letrado class on whom continued occupation of the islands depended. Even so, these were restless times: many encomiendas changed hands on Española two and three times. Migration among the islands and to and from Panama was virtually constant and many islanders must have returned to Spain aboard the scores of caravels that sailed yearly in the Atlantic trade.[48] Las Casas's estimate of twelve thousand Spaniards on Española in 1508 may be too high, but the 718 vecinos estimated for the island in 1514 is doubtless an index of population decline, whatever had been the earlier apex of population.[49]

One may appreciate that Diego Colón's first governorship coincided, unfortunately for him, with a depression and an ebb tide—more Spaniards returned to Spain than came to the New World. Not even Ferdinand's indefatigable encouragement, his guarantee of the quinto, his progressive reduction and eventual cancellation of the tax on Indian slaves, and his elimination of the interisland almojarifazgo,[50] were sufficient to check the decline. Vecinos who chose not to return to Spain could join an expedition to Panama or one of the other islands. But for these expeditions—excepting Panama—and for casting one's lot on Española, official favor was much needed. The king's favor helped explorers such as Ponce de León; the favor of the king's officials—Bishop Rodríguez de Fonseca or Lope de Conchillos—helped the Tapia brothers at Santo Domingo. But in the short run, Diego Colón's favor was necessary to fare well on Española and some combination of royal approval and Colón's was the best guarantee of success on the other islands. As the *repartidor de indios,* Colón held the key to the labor supply for the mines and farms of Española; he alone could decide, sometimes in spite of conveniently ignored royal cédulas, who deserved to hold encomiendas. As governor he could send out expeditions to occupy new territory, so that it is not surprising to find that the Díazes, Velázquezes, and Garays whom he favored were to be counted among the most prominent and successful families in the islands.

The return of the Columbuses in 1509, led by the proud hidalgo Diego, was a small triumph vindicating the disgrace of the deposition by Bobadilla. He was accompanied by a splendid entourage: his wife, Doña María, the first *gran dama* of the New World, the Duke of Alba's niece, with her own suite of *doncellas;* and his immediate relatives—Fernando his half-brother, his two uncles, Diego and Bartolomé, and his cousins, Andrea and Giovanni. Also on the expedition were his criados and his father's old retainers: Marcos de Aguilar, his forthright alcalde mayor, Diego Méndez, his business manager, and Gerónimo de Agüero, his former tutor.[51] Other loyal *Colombistas* met him at Santo Domingo—his uncle by marriage, Francisco de Garay, whom he named alguacil mayor, and Bartolomé's criados, Miguel Díaz, Diego Velázquez, and Juan Cerón.[52] With his palace guard, his one-tenth of the net income to the royal treasury, and his largess, he and his retainers were not the most envied group on the island. Colón doubtless favored his followers but he tempered this spoils system by an encomienda policy that was widely if not universally supported, for he had not done so it is unlikely that he could have remained governor even until 1515. Although Diego's fortunes would rise and fall over the years, his coming represented the permanent establishment of the most titled and notable family in the islands, at least for many years.

The mantle of Diego Colón's favor helped greatly in surviving the economic vicissitudes on Española, but it is unlikely that favoritism alone was sufficient for success. As in most business enterprises, willingness to risk, business acumen, and luck were even more important in the long run. Francisco de Garay, perhaps following a Basque tradition, had turned to the Atlantic trade after the arrival of Ovando, was the owner of one or more caravels, and had made several voyages to Cádiz.[53] What he exported to the Spanish port is nowhere directly stated, nor do the detailed shipping records compiled by Chaunu include cargo manifests. On this mysterious matter, both for Garay and for shipping generally, certain other of his actions are instructive. About this time he was also named alcaide of a fort at Jacmel, where he stocked arms and emplaced several small cannon.[54] That a fort was necessary at this place on the south coast would be inexplicable if it were not that the island's best dyewood stock was found there. Garay apparently needed the fort to protect the king's dyewood from unscrupulous shipmasters. The arms were undoubtedly also used on Indian slaving expeditions in which he engaged. As a shipper of dyewood, Garay was trusted both by Colón and the king. For these reasons, he was chosen in 1514 as teniente of Jamaica and as holder of a royal contract to develop the island. His assumption of the governorship in 1515, and his taking up residence with his family at Sevilla la Nueva, signified the establishment of the most prominent family on the island. Rodrigo de Bastidas also profited during these years as a merchant-navigator in both the Atlantic and inter-island trade and as an armador, although he was not considered closely linked with the Colón family.[55] The Tapias at Santo Domingo owed their position largely to Juan Rodríguez de Fonseca, who had personally recruited them for the New World. Francisco de Tapia held the position of alcaide in Santo Domingo until his death in 1533, and his brother, Cristóbal, was for a time veedor in the San Cristóbal mines.[56]

In the Cibao region, the Manzorro-Becerra clan at Santiago de Caballeros retained firm roots during these years, although a few of its members migrated to Puerto Rico or Cuba. They may not have been favored in the first voyages to the Bahamas for naborias, however, for Santiago and Santo Domingo were the cities most clearly anti-Colón. But they were prominent armadores about 1512 or soon thereafter, and one may suppose that the coming of Vázquez de Ayllón as judge of appeal in 1512 facilitated their slaving expeditions to the Bahamas.[57]

On Puerto Rico, two important families were established with the migrations to that island: the Ponces at Caparra, and the Miguel Díaz clan at San Germán. Though Ponce was pitted against Colón in the conflict between the viceroy and the king, he was nonetheless able to survive these turns of fortune. Ferdinand had granted him triple *solares*, or town lots, (the usual reward for hidalgo settlers was double solares) and Ponce built the only stone house in the village, which for years functioned additionally as the Casa de Contratación, the archive, and the arsenal.[58] He profited from his early contract with the king and was the owner of two ships by 1513;[59] he was granted the coveted title of adelantado in 1512 for his projected settlement of Bimini.[60] Caparra proved to be Ponce's permanent home; he brought his family there in 1509, and was joined by some relatives and their families: his first cousin, Juan González Ponce de León, his nephew, Hernán Ponce, and his criado, Ovando's former secretary, Pedro Moreno, who returned to Puerto Rico from Spain in 1512 with his family and several criados.[61]

Like Garay, Miguel Díaz had the support of both Colón and the king. Colón had named him alguacil mayor of Puerto Rico in 1509, and on the former's reinstatement in 1511 following a favorable decision of the royal council, Colón named Díaz to found the second town of importance on the island, San Germán. Ferdinand, perhaps aiming to detach Díaz from his close relationship with Colón, named him factor, and from then on he held various city council positions in the new town.[62] Here he established his household and to this town soon came various relatives from Spain, including his brother Vasco de Tiedra.[63]

The career of Diego Velázquez paralleled those of these other early figures in the settlement of the Caribbean. He had been accompanied by numerous relatives and followers to Cuba in 1511, who became the main holders of encomiendas and town offices in the years immediately following. Owing to chance, Velázquez did not establish a family on Cuba, for his young bride, the daughter of Cristóbal de Cuéllar, died soon after their marriage and Velázquez, in spite of future plans to do so, failed to remarry.[64]

No settlement was more tenuous and restless than the one in Cuba for gold had hardly been discovered in 1514 before the lure of Mexico, initiated by the Hernández de Córdoba voyage in 1517, turned the islanders' attentions to the west. Then, too, Ferdinand's death, the Cisnerian interregnum, and Charles's early callow years followed hard on the discovery of gold—the only attraction for most of these Spaniards—and contributed to the uncertainty of holding encomiendas or land grants. For these reasons, few of the early settlers proved permanent. Velázquez did not establish a family; of those who came with him to the island in 1511, only Andrés de Duero, about whose family nothing is known, and Vasco Porcallo de Figueroa, about whom many unfortunate things are known, settled down in spite of the lure of Mexico. Narváez's Castilian wife, María de Valenzuela, joined him sometime after 1515, but most prominent families came later and were friends or relatives of Valázquez. These were people who had lost encomiendas on Española or Puerto Rico, or emigrated from Spain shortly before 1520 and found that the opportunities on a depopulated Cuba offset the temptation to risk their fortunes elsewhere.[65] Thus several prominent families were, by 1515, settled in the towns of the four islands where they would remain, at least for many years. They had taken up this residence during the period of Fernandine expansion (1509–1515) and most of them had been offered and had profited from a second chance to find wealth and social prestige in the New World. They had gained valuable experience on Española and they put this to good use on their second island home. Colón, who had also insisted on a second chance for the Columbuses, dominated Española and had facilitated the success on other islands of his father's and uncle's former criados. A few others attained success by direct royal favor or, as in the case of Bastidas, by mercantile acumen.

Though Ferdinand was fairly successful in harmonizing his royal interests with those of the hidalgo-letrado class, or at least a sufficient number of them to retain occupation of the islands, he could try to smooth over, though not repair, a growing rift with Diego Colón. His mounting irritation with Colón would culminate with the recall of that proud courtier in 1515. Still less could the king understand or sympathize with the mystifying criticism of the Dominicans concerning the fundamental position of the Indian in Spanish society, although he was concerned enough to promulgate the Laws of Burgos in 1512–1513. Finally, he was unable to satisfy the needs of his first bishops, whose entrance into America was so long delayed, for the shrinking source of Indian labor could not support so many institutions and groups—the encomenderos, the treasury officials, the *audiencia*, and finally the Church—all of which Ferdinand believed could be sustained by encomiendas.

The conflict with Colón was presaged in the capitulations of 1492 and was enhanced and animated by vested interests choosing to support the Viceroy. It was complicated by vagueness about the exact routes of Columbus's third and fourth voyages, and was fueled by Ferdinand's incessant need for gold. Finally it was vivified by the contentious personality of Diego, who was not always completely honest with his overlord, in spite of his many protestations of loyalty. The main questions were over just what territory Columbus had discovered which entitled Colón to rule it and to exact one-tenth of the royal income from it; and what powers Colón could exercise as distinguished from royal residual powers; and lastly, which of Colón's powers and privileges were hereditary. The conflict had already begun before Colón sailed from Sanlúcar de Barrameda in 1509, it was especially active when he returned in 1515, and it would persist long thereafter.

Even before he sailed, Colón had received word that Ovando had begun the settlement of Puerto Rico in contravention of Colón's rights and he at once had his attorney file a protect. His legal representative was Juan de la Peña, criado of the powerful Duke of Alba who had so influentially supported Colón as Ovando's successor.[66]

The ducal house apparently had considerable connections with Diego; apart from the marriage that linked him with that family, Colón was a creditor of the Duke's son, the Marquis of Villa-Franca, having lent him five hundred fifty ducats.[67] Then, too, the financially powerful Genoese mercantile community saw Colón as the instrument that would open up the Indies trade for them and they surely helped finance the court battle in addition to supporting Colón in other ways.

The conflict over territorial rights for Colón concerned mainly Puerto Rico and Panama (Urabá), where gold had been discovered; there was virtually no conflict over Jamaica and Cuba where gold was either nonexistent or undiscovered in quantity before 1514; a conflict over Colón's rights on the Pearl Coast was postponed by the hesitation to re-enter that area during the height of the Carib threat. Ferdinand was not on solid legal ground with respect to Puerto Rico: his needs for funds must have prompted him to urge exploitation of the island. For the same reason, he was reluctant to disapprove of Ponce's coup of 1510, which would break the contract he then felt was very promising, unaware that Ponce had already resigned. He was on more solid, if disputed, ground in sending out Nicuesa and Ojeda to Urabá and Veragua, but Colón was equally certain that this expedition violated his inherited rights. He confiscated the two expeditionaries' Indians in their absence and obstructed sending them provisions, which so angered Ojeda that he threatened, according to the rumor that came back to Santo Domingo, to decapitate the Viceroy and kidnap the *virreina*.[68] After Ojeda returned to Española to find provisions for the starving garrison, Balboa overthrew Ojeda's *alcalde mayor;* on learning of this, Colón was only too happy to name Balboa interim governor in 1511, thus hoping to secure his claim to the area.[69] Ferdinand finally put an end to these machinations by sending out Pedrarias in 1514.

Meanwhile the question of Colón's rights and privileges had been referred to the royal council, which heard arguments presented by Peña, by Fernando, Colón's half-brother, and by Pedro Ruiz for the Crown.[70] The council handed down its decision on May 5, 1511, and the king approved it on June 17.[71] The four main islands were conceded to fall within Colón's powers, by right of his father's discovery. But Urabá and Veragua were excluded owing to the voyage in 1500–1501 of Rodrigo de Bastidas who was regarded as the discoverer of that part of the coast. By the same decision, Colón's political powers, besides those of general and administrative nature adhering to his office of governor, included the right to name officials—alcaldes, alcaldes mayores, and *escribanos* for purposes of judicial matters only. His titles of Viceroy and admiral were considered hereditary but honorific, without the right to exercise power by reason of the title. The right of one-tenth of the net royal income was confirmed for Colón and his heirs. The king, on the other hand, reserved the right by the Laws of Toro of 1480 to name judges of residencia, appoint judges of appeal or an audiencia, and name all non-judicial officials—alcaides, *regidores, escribanos de número,* and repartidores de indios.

The decision represented a qualified victory for Colón, who soon saw his officials restored to power on Puerto Rico, and his appointments, in effect, confirmed on Cuba and Jamaica. He might have been wise for the time being to have rested his case there, but his attorney at court at once appealed the decision with respect to residencias, judges of appeal, and repartimentos, claiming that such powers so limited Colón as to make his rule impotent. He further contended that Urabá and Veragua had been first touched on by Columbus on his fourth voyage.[72] On his part, Colón was no sooner in the islands than he asserted the right to nominate (and if the king did not act, to appoint) regidores, and he would later, in 1514, insist that he could name interim judicial officials to serve while his appointees were undergoing residencia. He claimed that he himself could not be removed from office, a legality the king did not challenge but would circumvent by recalling him for consultation as an overlord might recall a loyal but headstrong vassal. Contemporary with his council's decision, the king had decided to check his errant Viceroy further by asserting his right to name judges of appeal. The threatened strife between Ojeda and Colón, the latter's removal of encomiendas from expeditionaries who had sailed with the royal promise their Indians could be retained for four years, his conflicts with the treasury officials, and his continued claims of disputed territory, all led the king to establish this royal body, emblematic of regal power since the late Middle Ages.[73]

The three judges, accompanied by a royal fiscal and various other minor officials and criados, reached Santo Domingo in May, 1512.[74] The king had balanced legal experience with firsthand knowledge of the island in his selection of the judges. Juan Ortiz de Matienzo, a nephew of the veteran treasurer of the Casa de Contratación, Sancho Matienzo, was experienced in the courts at Seville, and Marcelo de Villalobos, a *sevillano* by birth, had served in the city assizes of Jerez de la Frontera. Lucas Vázquez de Ayllón had been the alcalde mayor of Concepción under Ovando with whom he left the island in 1509; he had then gone on to earn a law degree from Valladolid.[75] The fiscal, Sancho Velázquez, was expected to defend the royal interests against any unwarranted claims by Colón. Ferdinand now hoped that he had set up a system of checks and balances that would ensure justice for encomenderos and expeditionaries and keep peace between Colón, the royal officials, and himself. Instead, the lines of conflict were to be more tightly drawn and the next two to three years saw an intensified struggle move toward its denouement.

Neither the territorial or the hereditary claims were the crucial matter, as events revealed, although both continued to be debated at court while the opposing sides solicited sailors' statements in the Caribbean and Spain that could be used as evidence. The conflict arose, rather, from the reassignment of vacant encomiendas, which Ferdinand wished to bestow on various members of his council or administrative staff, or upon veterans of the wars in Italy or Navarre. In his capacity as repartidor,

Colón had meanwhile become the leader, though tenuously, of the great majority of encomenderos. The reasons for this become clear when it is recalled that the one principle upon which all towns agreed was that encomiendas should not be granted to absentees. Colón did not dare to prevent absenteeism completely, but on at least one occasion he held up a royal cédula that called for granting to Hernando de Vega, Comendador Mayor of Castile, an encomienda of three hundred Indians. In a letter of explanation, which he sent to his uncle Bartolomé in 1510, Colón explained that this could not be done without doing injustice to a number of the original settlers. Losing his usual control, the king hotly penned this retort: "Carry out the cédula, then consult. Remember—one good work is worth ten finely worded excuses in the eyes of God."[76]

However, this was only the surface manifestation of the struggle for the control of encomiendas; Colón learned to exercise this control covertly. There was, in fact, a curious scarcity of announced vacant encomiendas in spite of the almost constant movement of encomenderos to other islands and back to Spain. Colón appears to have reached an understanding with all or most of the town officials on the island that vacant encomiendas would be kept secret and assigned to resident vecinos without formal notification to Spain of the vacancies. This apparent understanding furnishes the only probable explanation for the disputed town elections of 1513.

Under Governor Ovando the towns had exercised considerable autonomy, electing their own alcaldes and regidores. After Colón arrived, he contrived to have the towns nominate a double list of alcaldes and regidores from which he would appoint four regidores and two alcaldes.[77] He presumably acted on the premise that the capitulations of 1492 gave him the right to nominate regidores to the king, and if the king was too preoccupied to make the appointments (which had called for nominating three times the number to be elected, but which the present small population made impractical), he could himself make them. He managed to institute this procedure because he gave encomiendas to local residents and set aside or otherwise procrastinated on royal cédulas calling for the assignment of Indians to absentees; only the coming of the judges of appeal arrested the functioning of this entente of local interests.

The judges of appeal challenged Colón's right to appoint city officials, claiming it to be illegal, for officials were either to be elected as during Ovando's governorship, or the regidores were to be appointed for life by the king himself.[78] Marcos de Aguilar so strongly argued the case for Colón, however, that the judges decided to yield (to avoid worse conflict, as they wrote the king) and to permit Colón once more to name the officials to take office on January 1, 1513. Had there been a widespread anti-Colón feeling, one would suppose that the towns would now have been encouraged to nominate officials hostile to him. Only two towns did so, Santo Domingo and Santiago de los Caballeros, and in the latter town, the officials were so badly divided that the pro-Colón faction jailed their enemies, causing Judge Matienzo to intervene. He arrested Colón's supporters and held them for trial in Santo Domingo where, as he wrote the king, Colón saw to their every comfort while they remained in jail.

The episode served to demonstrate the extent of Colón's power and to reveal to the judges, informed by those left outside the system, that Colón left the majority of royal cédulas unfulfilled that called for assigning encomiendas to immigrants from Spain who had served the king. These revelations prompted Ferdinand to take the final steps in reducing Colón's power, and ultimately in removing Colón himself. He no doubt now perceived that, in spite of repeated requests, Colón's failure to submit an accurate, detailed, and complete statement of encomiendas on Española was another tactic in fending off the assignment of encomiendas to absentees or recent arrivals.[79] By 1514, Ferdinand decided that he must exercise his prerogative by naming officials with the combined powers of *juez de residencia* and *repartidor de indios* for Española and Puerto Rico. On Cuba, where

Velázquez had served without complaint from the vecinos, the king had earlier named him repartidor, and now waived his residencia. On Jamaica, Garay, the newly appointed *teniente de gobernador* was also named repartidor, to share his powers jointly with the factor Pedro de Mazuelo, neither of which had been in office long enough to require a residencia. More stringent accounting, however, was considered advisable for Puerto Rico and paramount for Española. The king named the licentiate Pedro Ibáñez de Ibarra to take the residencia of Colón's officials and to carry out a new and just distribution of Indians. He deferred appointment of an official with similar duties for Puerto Rico to the judges of appeal, who named the fiscal, Sancho Velázquez, to take the residencia of Colón's teniente there, Cristóbal Mendoza, and to reapportion the Indians in response to the complaints reaching the court from a number of the early settlers.[80] Ibáñez reached Santo Domingo sometime before July, 1514, bringing with him the first copies of the famous Laws of Burgos, which were to be put into effect on Española and the other islands, contemporaneous with the new distribution of Indians.[81] Velázquez reached Caparra on September 22, 1514.[82]

When Ibañez arrived, Española was bitterly divided into factions as the result of Colón's protracted galvanizing of loyal elements and the sharp but so far ineffectual opposition of the judges of appeal and the treasury officials. The anti-Colón faction doubtless welcomed the arrival of Ibáñez, but his unexpected death before he had scarcely begun his duties created an opportunity, under legal pretense, to seize power. Claiming the right to act in the king's name to replace interimly a royal appointee, the judges named Rodrigo de Alburquerque as repartidor de Indios.[83] Alburquerque, a vecino of Concepción, was friendly to the faction that was more or less lined up behind Pasamonte and the judges. He in turn named *visitadores* in the towns to enforce the Laws of Burgos; the visitadores would also declare the number of Indians available for repartimiento. The *cabildo* of Santo Domingo, which worked closely with the officials, at the same time elected Alburquerque alcalde mayor on the grounds that they could exercise this right pending the king's confirmation or appointment of a replacement.[84] Their action was surely inspired by the judges of appeal, who had stoutly upheld the king's right to name judicial officials while Colón was under residencia (as he technically was, in spite of Ibáñez's death).

What action Colón took following this regalist seizure of power cannot be known, but Ferdinand feared that a civil war was imminent and recalled the impetuous viceroy sometimes in the latter half of 1514.[85] He had heard rumors that the pro-Colón faction urged the admiral to assert his position and claim jurisdiction over the upcoming redistribution of Indians.[86] The king later had Amador de Lares, a veteran of the Italian wars en route to Cuba as contador, inspect Colón's mansion to see whether it was built and equipped as a feudal fortress, a move Las Casas termed ridiculous.[87] The incident points up Ferdinand's characteristic fear of feudalism, even toward the end of his life.

Colón named Doña María and Gerónimo de Agüero to represent his governorship (they would be essentially powerless), and obediently sailed for Spain in late 1514. There he would remain for five long years, futilely pressing his claims till circumstances played into his hands when he found the young king Charles in a receptive mood in 1520. The king named another juez de residencia, Cristóbal Lebrón, who arrived in June, 1515,[88] but he would find little to do. The judges had removed Colón's appointees, who had already gone into hiding or secretly taken ship for Spain, where some were jailed in Seville pending the king's decision.[89] Whether Lebrón even proceeded with a residencia is not known; in any case before he could have made much progress the king died, which suspended the juez de residencia's powers pending new orders from the successor.

Ferdinand V's aim in the Indies was to discover new wealth and to expand into unknown lands while maintaining to the degree possible peace and harmony between himself, Diego Colón, and the vecinos. Though this aim had proved impossible to fully attain owing to the intensified struggle for control of Indian labor, he had fared somewhat better at the outset in his relations with the Church. The missional Church, almost purely Franciscan until the coming of the Dominicans in 1510, tended gradually to overcome its initial monastic tendencies, and Franciscans had accompanied the expansion to the other islands and the mainland at Panama. The establishment of the bishoprics also seemed promising, at least from Ferdinand's point of view, for by 1511 he had secured the bulls in final form that guaranteed royal control in the Indies against possible inroads by the papacy or the bishops themselves.

The Church was still inchoate on Española toward the end of Ovando's governorship. About twenty Franciscans were divided among the central friary at Santo Domingo and the three residences at Concepción, Buenaventura, and Vera Paz.[90] This was scarcely more, and perhaps less, than had been on the island after the arrival of Ovando. Certain of the Franciscans served as parish priests, supplemented by a few seculars, Benedictines, and Mercedarians.[91] The acephalous Church on Española tended to languish, and Diego Colón on his arrival saw that no few priests led completely secular lives amid the gold-rush mentality of the times.[92]

But on the eve of expansion important changes in Franciscanism were taking place in Spain. The work of reformers was beginning to have effect, for to Jiménez de Cisneros's notable early efforts were added those of the Franciscan general, the Pope's nuncios in Spain, Queen Isabel, and after 1504, Ferdinand. The effect of the reform, most clearly seen when the bull of 1517 merged the Conventual Franciscans with the reformed Observants, was on the one hand to detach Conventual Franciscanism from secular laxity, and on the other, to persuade Observantism to be less inward-looking.[93] The result was an emerging Franciscanism cast rather more in a Cisnerian mold: disciplined, austere but not purely mendicant, living the common life, and willing to accept the challenge on the mission frontiers of the expanding New World.

These new Franciscans were often called *reformados*, though it is not to be supposed that every Franciscan coming to the Indies after 1508 had necessarily been touched by reform. But most took the great task of evangelism seriously, which meant they would be aware of whatever obstructed their task. They were, in short, of a potential mind to protest against mistreatment of the Indians even without the catalyst of Dominican leadership, which would be provided.

In this prevailing new mood, Franciscans were ready to answer the call of their general, who was requested by Ferdinand to send out friars to accompany the expeditions to the islands and Panama. Only two friars are known to have come to Española in 1509, but in 1511 a record contingent of twenty-three came over, and an unknown number in 1513 sailed under the leadership of Friar Espinar, now the provincial and decidedly reformist in outlook.[94] Friar Espinar, however, died enroute to Española.[95] From that island the Franciscans were sent out to the new settlements; several accompanied Friar Deule to Sevilla la Nueva in Jamaica where they established a residence and apparently baptized in a brief time many of the docile Jamaican Taínos. Friar Tisín, like Deule a veteran Belgian friar on Española, accompanied Valázquez to Cuba, along with three other Franciscans; there they began work among the Taínos at Nuestra Señora de Asunción de Baracoa. Two Franciscans may have gone to San Germán, Puerto Rico, in December, 1512.[96]

Ferdinand's decision to send the Dominicans—another medicant order—to Española was only partly due to the need for additional priests. The Dominicans had been looked upon since their order was founded as the guardians of orthodoxy in matters of faith. By 1508, Ferdinand had received various reports that heresies had come to the island;[97] the source is a matter of conjecture, but one supposes such reports to have originated with Friar Espinar, who frequently corresponded with Jiménez de Cisneros. As a result, Ferdinand called upon the Dominican provincial of the monastery of San Pablo at Burgos to send out good, virtuous, conscientious friars who could defend the purity of the faith by their theological knowledge and preaching ability.[98] Friar Alonso Loaisa succeeded in recruiting fifteen friars by 1510, although only nine are known to have sailed that year, led by the vicar, Friar Pedro de Córdoba.[99] This first company of Dominicans, including the later famous Antonio de Montesinos, arrived at Santo Domingo in September, 1510.

The Dominicans began their work on Española as they were expected to do, setting a good example of morality and poverty in their personal lives, preaching in the church at Santo Domingo and probably at Concepción, and establishing a Dominican monastery. They soon perceived unorthodoxy in the sermons of the newly arrived Carlos de Aragón, provisor for the bishop of Concepción, who seems to have learned a new theology at Paris that greatly reduced the number of venial sins, as these had been conceived under Thomist doctrines. The Dominicans nailed a refutation to the church door at Concepción, an action which probably led to Bishop Pedro Suárez de Deza expelling Aragón back to Spain, soon after the former's arrival in 1513.[100]

Meanwhile the Dominicans had been preaching at Santo Domingo and Concepción, and from what they witnessed during their journeys between these two main cities on the island, they became convinced that cruelty to the Indians was widely practiced. The reasons for their attitude have been variously explained. Venancio Carro has expatiated on the Dominican tradition of viewing all men as free and equal in the sight of God, a deeply ingrained belief, presumably not shared equally by others such as the Franciscans.[101] Giménez Fernández believed that only certain Dominicans, whom he calls reformandos,[102] were possessed with this keen sense for the equality and dignity of men, an explanation which at least has the merit of accounting for the failure of the Dominican general in Spain to share the views of the reformers on Española. It may be, furthermore, that the Bahama slave trade was presenting during these years an unusual spectacle of brutality, a reality embroidered by tales of horror supplied by Juan Garcés, who took refuge in the Dominican monastery after several years of hiding in the mountains to escape punishment for murdering his Indian wife.[103] Whatever the reasons, they inspired Friar Antonio de Montesinos, as is well known, to denounce from the pulpit the system of forced labor as morally wrong, and to condemn its unregenerate perpetrators to hell. His sermons, delivered on the fourth and third Sundays of Advent in December, 1511, created a great stir among the vecinos of Santo Domingo. Friar Montesinos, supported by the vicar Friar Pedro de Córdoba, returned to Spain in the spring of 1512 to defend his views, and Friar Espinar returned at about the same time to defend the system on the grounds that the Dominican accusations were greatly exaggerated.[104]

The sermons had no immediate effect on Española's economic life; in Spain, the denunciations led to the drafting of the Laws of Burgos, designed to ameliorate the working and living conditions of the Indians. These laws, however, were not put into effect until late 1514. Even then, they were unlikely to have significantly altered conditions of life for the Indians, partly because such conditions may not have been as bad as the reformers thought, and partly because the causes for death were not discerned and hence could not, given the lack of knowledge of disease, be eliminated. The sermons, however, united with reforms in Spain to inspire others to join the Dominican cause. The supporters included various Franciscans,[105] already inclined toward such protest, and notably the great reformer Bartolomé de las Casas.

The great controversy over freeing the Indian is the subject of a vast literature by writers among whom Professors Lewis Hanke and Manuel Giménez Fernández come most readily to mind. The controversy need not be followed here for its outcome is later expressed in the rather fruitless and tenuated reforms undertaken by the Jeronymites and several judges on Española. But the issue of Spanish cruelty to the Indian seems to have acquired even more distortion in recent years than it commonly carried, having become entangled with racism, modern ideas of liberty, and other notions inappropriate to the historical context. One need not deny or defend that the Taínos were whipped for what the Spaniards considered dereliction of duty. But Spaniards of the lower class, who were the vast majority, had been whipped for centuries and would be for several centuries longer. Columbus, one may recall, slit the noses of Spaniards who pilfered gold from the factoría. Cruelty, moreover, has been considered by the slightly informed as the most sweeping cause for death, thus looking upon the decline of the Taínos as the result of haphazard genocide, Spanish style. This writer's experience is that this emotion-laden falsehood will find a hundred ready adherents who lack the curiosity or mental toughness to deal with a more complicated truth. Though at this point further analysis of the causes for Indians deaths will be postponed, it is held probable that had the Spaniards come over only to sell roses, the results for the Indians would have been about the same—a fairly rapid population decline. Finally, the issue of liberty, the pathetic twentieth-century existential liberty, has been read into the controversy where it is markedly anachronistic. No reformer seriously advocated that the Indian be left to do whatever he wanted, with or without an encomienda system.

The immediate practicable effect of Montesinos's sermons, however, was for Ferdinand to give even more support than ever to the Franciscans. It was now that he urged the vicar general to send out forty friars as soon as possible,[106] and granted the friary in Santo Domingo three hundred *pesos de oro* a year for ten years from the *penas de cámara*, a fund from which he had never before permitted any local expenditures.[107] The Franciscans had, by 1514, given up their encomiendas, though one cannot be certain to what degree this was due to necessity rather than stricken consciences.

Nonetheless Ferdinand held no long grudge against the Dominicans for whom, he said, he had an especial affection. The Dominicans held their peace for a time, and Ferdinand later granted them annual alms of one hundred *pesos de oro;*[108] he told Colón to encourage them to move into new mission fields. At least two Dominicans were sent to Cuba sometime in 1511; four others began work there in March, 1515, joining the Franciscans and the recently ordained priest, Bartolomé de las Casas.[109] Las Casas, the erstwhile encomendero, had decided to enter the priesthood and was ordained several years earlier.[110] Apparently Ferdinand then decided to make Cuba a Dominican province, for he named a bishop of that order in 1512, although the nominee failed to take office. Since the four Dominicans arrived in Cuba just as the gold rush was in full swing, they were as much incensed at treatment of the Indians here as they had been on Española. Friar Bernardo de Santo Domingo's fiery denunciations from the pulpit at Sancti Spiritus greatly inspired Las Casas, who was himself delivering his first sermons denouncing the holding of encomiendas. By July or August, 1515, the Dominicans and Las Casas had decided that only a journey to the court would halt what they saw as the threatened extermination of the Indians. At that time Las Casas and two of the Dominican friars departed for Santo Domingo from where they planned to sail for Spain to advise the king that the Indians would never be preserved by the Laws of Burgos, for they felt that far-reaching reforms—free Indian villages in Las Casas's opinion—were mandatory.[111] Friar Ampudia fell ill and died at Vera Paz; Las Casas and Friar Alberca continued on to Santo Domingo to find that both orders—Dominicans and Franciscans—were vivified by a like reform spirit.

The religious were in agreement that they must adopt a twofold approach in behalf of the Indians: one, to urge the king to have the Indians brought into Spanish-type towns, and, further, to reduce the labor demands made upon them under the Laws of Burgos (some, of course, advocated freedom); and two, to establish missions in areas aloof from the Spaniards in order to carry on the work of teaching and conversion unmolested by any deleterious contact. Sending Dominicans to Cuba had been part of that venture, on the premise that Velázquez maintained a humane labor regime, but they had unfortunately arrived contemporary with the first real gold rush. Dominicans had already sent a small mission to Venezuela, which had departed Santo Domingo in November, 1514, and consisted of the friars Francisco de Córdoba, Antonio de Montesinos, and the lay worker Juan Garcés. Montesinos fell ill enroute and, after a layover in Puerto Rico, had returned to Santo Domingo. The other two friars established a mission at Piritú, not far from the later Caracas, where they would be murdered by Indians in December, 1515.[112]

About the time that Las Casas and Friar Alberca arrived, two additional missionary expeditions were ready to depart for the Venezuelan coast, of which pearl barterers had brought word that the tribes were peaceful and would be receptive to evangelization. The Franciscans, now as zealous as the Dominicans, had on July 14, 1515, held a chapter meeting in which they elected Friar Diego Torres provincial and voted to ask for an additional nine friars to bring up their present staff to a total of twenty-eight.[113] They had especially in mind the needs of a planned mission at Cumaná. Their first *procurador*, Friar Torres, died enroute[114] but they subsequently dispatched Friar Juan Altemang to represent their needs to the Franciscan general. The two missionary expeditions to Venezuela left Santo Domingo in August or September, 1515, bound for the coast at the Cumaná river. Each order sent six friars, with Friars Juan Garceto and Tomás Ortiz heading respectively the Franciscan and Dominican contingents.[115] The Franciscans would locate at the mouth of the Cumaná; the Dominicans established a mission some miles in the interior, on the same river. Las Casas, meanwhile, joined by Friar Montesinos, left for Spain in September, 1515.[116]

The missionary movement was in this way perceptibly broadened and resuscitated between 1509 and 1515, and was fully in accord with Ferdinand's aims. He encouraged it and underwrote the board, passage fare, clothing, and the church equipment of the friars.[117] Equally in accord with his announced aims was establishment of episcopal churches on the islands, but on Ferdinand's death there would not be a single resident bishop in the Greater Antilles, a situation that would prevail until 1519. It may now be appreciated why no bishops arrived before 1512, eight years after the first bull establishing these institutions was issued. The 1504 bull had omitted royal patronage, which raised the specter for Ferdinand of papal intrusion into the distant domains that had somehow miraculously been bestowed on the Crown of Castile. He could not be expected to forget his earlier experience with feudal, rebellious prelates, and nepotistic Popes. There followed the period of uncertainty over succession to the Crown—until 1507. But even the bull of 1508 was unsatisfactory to the king, for though it granted the necessary patronage, it failed through a misunderstanding to grant collection of the tithe, and in any case the occupation of Puerto Rico and the decline of population on Española made necessary a redivision of Bishoprics.[118] Not until 1511 was the new bull in royal hands and in the proper form.[119] He had meanwhile, by a special bull of 1510, which reflected his great need for funds to wage the Mediterranean wars, excluded gold production from the tithe.[120]

The first bishops to America, like Ferdinand, had great expectations for their sees. They modeled these islands episcopacies after the bishopric of Toledo, though they were realistic enough to restrict the projected *cabildos* to about half the number of positions for that ancient Spanish see.[121] Bishop Alonso Manso, former canon at Salamanca,[122] reached his episcopacy at Caparra on December 25, 1512,[123] apparently having travelled by way of Española where he must have conferred, indeed established good relations, with the Viceroy Diego Colón.[124] Bishop Pedro Suárez de Deza, nephew of the archbishop of Seville, arrived in Concepción, second of the established episcopacies, in the following year.[125] But Bishop García de Padilla, designated for the see at Santo Domingo, was in ill health and died in Spain in 1515 without taking possession.[126] The first resident bishop for Santo Domingo arrived only in 1519.

But the reality of serving as a bishop in the Caribbean during this time was as disappointing to the two prelates as being viceroy was to Colón, for the islands enjoyed a reputation for wealth that exceeded their present economic capacity to sustain expensive institutions, always taking into account the decisions already made about distribution of the existing wealth. Manso arrived with only three prebends, who were the lowest salaried officials of his staff, though he planned to send for dignities and canons at a later date.[127] His three years at Caparra were marked by frustration and disappointment. Sancho Velázquez assigned him only one hundred fifty Indians—a small fraction of the number he considered proper for a bishop's cabildo; but his repeated protests brought only the response that there were few Indians to go around.[128] Caribs attacked and burned Caparra in 1513, leaving even his humble thatched church in ruins. Prohibited from exacting a tithe on gold, and finding that the predial tithe was too meager from a small society with only a nascent agriculture and livestock economy, he arranged with treasurer Haro to exact a four percent personal tithe. But the vecinos stoutly resisted this, claiming that such a tithe had no precedent in these new lands.[129] Bishop Manso then abandoned his rustic, impoverished island see in November, 1515, vowing never to return.[130]

His contemporary at Concepción, Bishop Súarez, fared no better. He, too, established a skeletal ecclesiastical cabildo, slightly larger than Manso's,[131] but found that his income would not even support a staff of this size. Indians for encomiendas were relatively fewer than on Puerto Rico, and the several naborias assigned him in the Alburquerque repartimiento of 1514 were not even enough to aid in collecting the tithes, which the parishioners insisted should be paid in kind.[132] Bishop Suárez fulminated interdictions and excommunications, loudly announced from the front of his thatch church, but these had no significant results. "It was a case of grab a shovel and begin mining or take ship for Spain," Las Casas commented. Bishop Suárez took ship for Spain, departing on January 20, 1516, where he remained as absentee bishop until his death in 1522.[133] All three episcopal cabildos then remained inchoate over the next five years, without bishops, and as the clerics had to find other income to supplement a haphazardly paid tithe, half of which went to Spain to the absentee prelates, they improvised a melange of small fees, about which the vecinos soon complained.[134]

The failure to establish bishoprics in the islands was thus owing to a collaboration of causes. The height of Ferdinand's ambitions and his greatest need for funds coincided with the belated attempt to establish episcopacies. The exemption of gold from the tithe removed in advance a vital part of the financial base given the present state of the economy. But the hidalgo-letrado settlers had also made a choice that prevented their more adequately supporting the Church, for many looked first to their own stone manses and velvet caps, while the cathedrals remained unbuilt—this in spite of the king's sending a band of artisans for their construction in 1510.[135] Though they later complained about paying tithes to absentee bishops, such complaints ignored the earlier situation that caused the bishops to return to Spain. Cathedrals need not, of course, be built of stone, nor need bishops have an impressively numerous staff, but to argue for austere simplicity for a bishop is to ignore a thousand years of Church history and to divorce unrealistically the expression of a faith from its specific culture.

The two bishops, then, joined the caravan of disappointment in 1515 that filed to the court of the moribund king. The prelates fell in line with a chagrined, suspended viceroy; anguished reformers; frustrated, dispossessed encomenderos; and the procuradores from Cuba, who still looked to a sanguine future. Spanish civilization in the Caribbean had truly advanced under Ferdinand's leadership, but as so often in human affairs, to many it seemed an era of regression and despair.

5

Reform and Readjustment (1515-1520)

Between 1514 and 1515, there was a redistribution of Indians on three of the islands—recently occupied Cuba was the exception. This redistribution left a number of settlers greatly dissatisfied for many received about half the number they expected, and still others, less influential, were given only a few naborias as household servants. These unhappy vecinos directed their bitter complaints to the dying king and the future regent, Cardinal Jiménez de Cisneros. The settlers who remained on the islands, especially Española, flooded the audiencia with suits that had backed up to some four hundred by 1517. "We prepared a table to which others have been invited," was their typical complaint as stated by Judge Alonso Zuazo in 1518.[1] As is typical where total wealth declines in relation to the population, suspicions arose—partly justified—that some encomenderos were favored because of bribery or favoritism by the repartidores de indios, and factions arose on the three islands. The have-nots included a fair number of Diego Colón's followers but the lines were not sharply drawn. Most *Colombistas* who were deprived of encomiendas had either offered active opposition to Cristóbal Lebrón, the juez de residencia who arrived in June, 1515, and to the judges of appeal, or had resorted to intrigue or acts of disrespect or disloyalty. Those staying aloof from such tactics fared reasonably well.

Discontent and bitterness owing to the despoilment of what early settlers felt was their rightful due was nonetheless uneven on the islands. The conflict was most intense on Española where Lebrón overpowered Colón's judges. These, the viceroy maintained, had the right to rule during the residencia of his pre–1514 appointees. Lebrón had broken their *varas* (official staffs), while all those opposing the Alburquerque repartimiento were threatened, jailed, and deported until the king's confirmation, which reached the island in October, 1515, put an end to intrigues. The opposition was then partly drained off by migrations to Cuba, Panama, or Spain. In Puerto Rico, Sancho Velázquez also broke the varas of Colón's officials, though there was generally less to contend for on this island and discontent was confined to the representation of claims before the Spanish court.[2] Jamaica and Cuba were reasonably peaceful since the former island had no gold and the latter was still producing enough from newly found placers to satisfy the majority of settlers. The relative peace in Cuba was not due, however, to a small population and rich gold mines. The large, fertile island absorbed the dispossessed encomenderos from the other three islands, the starved émigres from Panama, and a small but steady stream of immigrants from Spain. But few or none of these had any basis for claiming that they were cheated of Indians; the refugees from Panama were probably thankful just to have something to eat. Most of the Spaniards who did not hold encomiendas—the majority—attached themselves as criados of wealthier men on one of the four islands, biding their time. Then, too, before greater discontent might have arisen, the spectacular discoveries to the west, beginning with the voyage of Francisco Hernández de Córdoba in 1517, soon drained Cuba of its surplus, leaving it sparsely populated. The other three islands were similarly affected a year or so later.

In spite of the many complaints about Rodrigo de Alburquerque's unfair distribution of Indians on Española and Sancho Velázquez's on Puerto Rico, the repartidores seem to have been as just as the situation allowed, making exception for a few personal enemies. Alburquerque's repartimiento was virtually a model for the petty encomendero, because the great majority of Spaniards received less than thirty Indians, surely an effort to satisfy as many persons as possible. Even a Spanish blind man was given a Taíno to beg for him.[3] Sancho Velázquez was faced with more claims for encomiendas than he had Indians with which to fill them, and resorted to the necessary expedient of proportionately reducing the number for each encomienda while portioning out a few Indians—defensively classified as naborias—to the rank and file of settlers.[4] In Cuba, Diego Velázquez likewise scaled down encomiendas to accommodate certain newcomers,[5] and presumably Francisco Garay and Pedro de Mazuelo, joint repartidores on Jamaica, did the same.

Underlying the discontent was the attrition in the Indian population, typically slow but continuous, though occasionally, as in 1518–1519, accelerated by an epidemic. Forced and voluntary migrations of Indians from Española, the absorption of Indian women into Spanish households, occasional suicides and flights into the canyons (*arcabucos* as the Spaniards then called them) of the interior, all took their toll year by year upon the Indian population under Spanish control. But disease was doubtless the most persistent and pervasive cause for this population decline.

The decrease in population would have been more rapid had the Laws of Burgos been promptly and fully executed. The Laws called for resituating the Indians in villages near the Spaniards for the primary purpose of facilitating their education in the faith and their adoption of a Spanish life style. The Laws, which were to be implemented in these and certain other respects by the repartidores, did not, however, immediately result in the establishment of villages, though some tribes were persuaded to relocate. As seen earlier, Indians were resettled near Santiago de los Caballeros and Santo Domingo around 1515; at about the same time Indians from Higüey were transferred to Salvatierra de la Sabana and still others were resituated near Santa María del Puerto de Yaguana.[6] The reasons for the transfers into the mining zones are obvious; the transfers to Salvatierra and Yaguana, with the simultaneous abandonment of Jacmel, probably meant that the dyewood trees had all been cut down around Jacmel, obliging this industry to shift westward. Yaguana, situated approximately on the site of modern Port-au-Prince, was surely oriented commercially to the rise of Santiago de Cuba and perhaps trade with Panama. On the whole, however, Indians stoutly resisted leaving their widely dispersed thatch settlements or *yucayeques;* efforts to remove them often resulted in suicides, flight, or rebellion.[7] Though the population was generally concentrated in the mining zones and at a few peripheral ports, it was still unconsolidated in 1515, and Spaniards and Indians tended to live apart, brought into direct contact only slightly and temporarily by the Indian's forced labor.

The decline of the Indian population and, necessarily, the encomiendas in Española and Puerto Rico, like a house crumbling on its foundations, signified that virtually all of the policies pragmatically worked out by Ferdinand must be modified if not abolished, for the Caribbean economy and the needs of the islanders were undergoing transition after 1515. A new source of labor, whether from the Indies, Spain, or Africa must somehow be found at an affordable price; the king's share of the profits must be reduced if the islands were to remain inhabited by Spaniards; agriculture, the only alternative to mining, must be subsidized, and its products made more profitable by tax relief and by liberalizing the restrictions imposed on a gold economy and administered by the Casa de Contratación; the Church, with its absentee bishops and diversion of the tithe to Spain, must somehow find a financially viable basis and acquire a leadership under resident bishops.

Especially was there a need to curtail absentee holdings or even to eliminate the Crown and its courtiers, councillors, secretaries, and its island officials from the encomienda system. Ferdinand had been sensitive enough to encomendero desires to check his penchant for granting absentee encomiendas in 1512. Still, absentee holding increased greatly in his latter years owing to the tendency of Lope de Conchillos, his secretary, to exact and receive favors through his influence and friendship with Pasamonte. Indeed, if Giménez Fernández's suspicions are correct, Conchillos may have issued cédulas for emoluments in the Indies without the king's knowledge.[8] Certainly there were opportunities during Ferdinand's last two years that invited such chicaneries; the king was often ill, shunned the court, and customarily spent more time crow hunting than conducting affairs of state.[9] By 1515, and especially during the preceding two years, the number of Indians held in encomiendas by officials, both absentee and resident, had burgeoned to somewhere between six and eight thousand. Treasury officials and judges on the islands had been granted two hundred Indians each in lieu of salary. Conchillos and Juan Rodríquez de Fonseca apparently held about one thousand each, distributed more or less equally on all four islands. Ferdinand had earlier granted two hundred or more to his chamberlain, Martín Cabrero, to his councillor, Hernando de Vega, the comendador of the order of Santiago, and to a second councillor, Luis Zapata, the influential "rey chiquito," considered second only to the king himself in power and influence.[10] The treasury officials normally held only two hundred Indians, but Pasamonte held about seven hundred, distributed among all the islands except Jamaica. The Crown was the largest absentee-holder of all, with several thousand, including Indian slaves and naborias on Española (one thousand were employed in the mines during Ovando's time), and five hundred on Puerto Rico. The king was a partner with Garay in Jamaica and in a less formal way with Diego Velázquez in Cuba, thus drawing profits from an unknown number of Indian laborers. Statism, which involved not only encomiendas, but mines, plantations and onerous fees, weighed heavily on the island; it would be the aim of the procuradores after 1515 to eliminate the state as a competitor, a goal made easier of attainment since it coincided with that of the moral reformers led by Bartolomé de las Casas.

The repartimientos of 1514–1515 on the islands were closely followed by an exodus of town procuradores and individual encomenderos, bishops, and reformers to Spain, each hoping to get a royal order reinforcing his patent to hold a certain number of Indians, or, in the case of reformers, to secure a decree abolishing or altering the encomienda system. The Caribbean towns, in practice the more important ones, had elected procuradores to represent their needs before the court since 1502, a time-honored procedure dating from the early Middle Ages. Far from discouraging such a practice, the kings regarded it as cementing ties between them and the towns, who counterbalanced the turbulent nobility. Only the meetings of procuradores from many towns, representing a sizable and dangerous constituency—should the kings find their requests difficult to meet—were forbidden; the kings preferred to call all the estates together, the traditional Cortes, at the time and place of their choosing, and only when the financial needs of the Crown made such convocation necessary.

The procuradores of 1515 spoke for typical island aspirations. Gil Gonzáles Dávila, the contador of Española and later an explorer along the Central American coasts, represented Española; Puerto Rico sent Martín de Eguiluz and Alonso de Mendoza to represent Caparra and San Germán respectively; Pánfilo de Narváez and Antonio Velázquez represented Cuba. Francisco de Garay was the procurador for Jamaica, though he had gone to Spain earlier and returned before May, 1515.[11] The procuradores did not as a rule present the repartimiento as being unjust, for they themselves had usually fared well. Rather, they sought to have the encomiendas made hereditary as a preventive to such redistributions as had just been carried out, and to limit the holding of encomiendas to married men who were permanent residents of the island; non-residents were to have their encomiendas removed—thus they struck at the king's secretaries and other officials, though they did not then mention the king himself, and still less the island officials with whom, especially after 1515, they maintained cordial relations.

They also asked that licenses be granted freely to any *armadores* desiring to make a slaving expedition to the so-called Carib areas of the Venezuelan coast. Trade among the islands in all local produce should be permitted without the payment of taxes, and relief to debtors—an indication of the decline of mining—should be afforded by smelting gold more often, introducing coinage or both. Fines should be reduced for minor violations of the law and legal fees should be charged in strict accordance with a publicly posted rate schedule. Bishops should be obligated to live in their sees, and tithes must be spent only for legitimate purposes such as the building of stone and masonry churches.[12] The encomenderos aimed at a readjustment of the economy and of the state and Church to accord with their more straitened financial circumstances. Less fortunate encomenderos, and the bishops of Puerto Rico and Concepción who either went to court or found someone to represent them there, additionally filed complaints to recover Indians lost in the redistributions and to forbid anyone's holding more than eighty Indians[13]—this to effect a still broader sitribution.

Bartolomé de las Casas and the Dominican friar Antonio Montesinos had radically different aims from these complainants. They viewed the entire labor system as destructive of the Indian population and were prepared to ask that it be abolished in favor of a system in which Indians would work voluntarily for themselves as miners and farmers after being situated in villages near the Spaniards.[14] Like Ferdinand and Isabel, Las Casas had faith that Indians living in daily contact with Spaniards would be slowly instilled with the Christian faith and Spanish civilization—the capillary method implicit in the law of March, 1503, and the Laws of Burgos. Here, too, they could be additionally instructed by clerics, untrammeled by the demands for labor presently put upon them by their encomenderos. Las Casas, through his persistence and great moral courage, would prove to be the conscience of the court during the next five years.

Ferdinand was not well enough to grapple with the many requests that inundated his royal council and required his decision in the autumn of 1515. He had held Cortes at Monzón and Burgos and led his ambulatory court toward Seville in November, where the archbishop had told him that the climate was kind to old and ailing men.[15] Few of the importunate islanders managed to get an audience with him; Las Casas succeeded in holding a private conversation on Christmas Eve, and came away with the expectation that the king would grant him an audience again in Seville.[16] Had he lived, or had he been in the vigor and mood of his days as the great expansionist and director of colonial government, the king might well have expedited the transition in the islands from gold mining to the production of sugar by authorizing the importation of Negro slaves. Just now he could only express his pity that his advisers had shielded him from the worst effects of his mining policy; he journeyed on southward, hunting crows on the way, till he was so stricken by dropsy in January that he was put to bed in the tiny village of Madrigalejo. On January 16, he died, unrecognizably swollen, unwilling to believe that the Lord would claim his soul before he had achieved the reconquest of Jerusalem—that exhalted aim of his Mediterranean policy and one he clung to till the very end.[17]

Spain and the Indies were now left in uncertainty and apprehension, which would be relieved only temporarily in September, 1517, with the coming of the young grandson Charles from Flanders. Meanwhile the government of Spain devolved upon Cardinal Jiménez de Cisneros, who would hold the kingdoms and the estates together, as he had done in 1506–1507, until the Habsburg king assumed the throne. At eighty, the cardinal himself was less than two years from death; "vigorous and spare, as if made of roots,"[18] he lived long enough to fulfill this last important obligation. Though Las Casas and Montesinos were sanguine that their requests for reform would be favorably viewed by the stern, uncompromising, and principled cardinal, the main attributes of his character and his earlier governing style would seem to explain, in retrospect, why he acted too cautiously and moderately to effect more than slight change in the Indies.

Jiménez de Cisneros believed deeply in the mission of the Spanish people, as leaders of Christendom, to spread the faith to the infidel and to defeat and convert the heretic. He apparently believed this mission reflected the common aim of all true Spaniards; he considered, though, that the lower classes, uncorrupted by wealth and power, were especially selfless in their willingness to sacrifice themselves for the faith. He had himself taken part in organizing the militant spread of the gospel along the African coast, shunting off warnings of personal danger with the famous comment that "gunpowder smells as good to me as incense."[19] Possessed of this conviction, it is understandable that he would strive to preserve the unity of the Spanish people at all costs, organize the popular militia against the turbulent and (as he saw it) selfish nobility, underwrite the missionaries in the New World as they moved onto the Venezuelan mainland, inaugurate the Inquisition on the islands, and by the same token, be disinclined to support abolition of encomiendas if it meant disinheriting the hidalgo class and producing deep divisions within Caribbean society. He shared with traditional Christianity the conviction that men—not institutions—must be reformed, and his fame as the quintessential Spaniard rests in part on his insistence on honesty, morality, and, of course, religious purity in government officials and the governed. Such insistence is a perennial wellspring of Spanish history, though the motives are sometimes less pure than the aim.

Jiménez de Cisneros was formally vested in office in February, 1516, and Charles confirmed his powers in April and titled him Chancellor Mayor of Castile in June.[20] Meanwhile the cardinal had heard from Las Casas and Montesinos that the encomienda should be abolished, and the rewards for conquerors commuted to a pension; the Crown and its officials should likewise withdraw from using encomiendas for income, and the Indians should be relocated in free communities, near the Spanish towns but with autonomy. At the same time, certain Franciscans, and above all, the encomenderos, reported to him that the encomienda was not as harmful to the Indians as Las Casas claimed, Narváez adding that the priest knew little of what he talked so much about.[21] Jiménez de Cisneros convened a junta composed of the most informed persons together with members of the royal council; this body sat for some two months between April and June, 1516.[22] The junta generally agreed that the plight of the Indians should be at once alleviated, whether or not their complete freedom could be squared with the aim of converting them. Jiménez de Cisneros was likewise convinced that investigatory and corrective action should be taken, but not by lay persons like Alburquerque who were susceptible to bribery, and not by (unreformed) Franciscans or (reformed) Dominicans who had differed sharply on the question since the days of Espinar and Montesinos six years earlier. Rather, persons without concern for worldly gain, disinterested and impartial, would be most suitable. Thus he decided that the Jeronymites would best serve, and he at once asked the Jeronymite general to select three friars for this highly important commission.

With great reluctance, the Jeronymite general prevailed upon Luis de Figueroa, Bernaldino de Manzanedo, and Alonso de Santo Domingo to offer themselves as commissioners to Jiménez de Cisneros. The Jeronymites had been affected by that spiritual movement dating back a century in which Spanish friars had been so repelled by the secularization of society—perhaps typified by the court of Henry IV—that they turned to the austerity and simplicity of the monastery. They were of the same mind as Friar Bernardo Boyl who had spurned America in 1494 to return to his monastery and order. "Can we save the souls of others without losing our own?" was the question put to Jiménez de Cisneros by the Jeronymite general, almost at the outset.[23] But after the cardinal's insistence, the duties were accepted. Rather by coincidence, the Jeronymites would agree with Jiménez de Cisneros that the issue of the encomienda should not be made a cause for alienating the settlers should they oppose its abolition. The friars lacked Las Casas's appetite for controversy about moral matters; Jiménez de Cisneros could withstand any amount of opposition to reforms that would convert men but he doubted whether the encomienda was directly related to these aims. The survival of the encomienda could well be predicted.

The three Jeronymites were granted specific, enumerated powers; they were commissioners, not governors.[24] Their main assignment was to conduct a hearing on the encomienda system, and if such a hearing made the establishment of free Indian villages advisable, they were to establish them. Their instructions on this point were written by Las Casas, and they called for villages of three hundred vecinos, who would own their own land communally, work voluntarily in the mines with the Crown taking one-third of the gold produced (the mine labor was not Las Casas's suggestion but was added by Jiménez de Cisneros), and pay tribute and tithes.[25] Should the friars decide that free villages were inadvisable, they were to form such towns but continue the encomienda system under the Laws of Burgos, amended to eliminate the carrying burden and to add a longer midday rest period.

Furthermore, they were to remove the Indians from all non-residents and from resident officials, a measure bound to meet with the approval of most encomenderos as it did with Las Casas and part of the royal council, though for different reasons. Jiménez de Cisneros was adamant on this point—though the Jeronymites were to prove tractable when face-to-face with the situation on the island. The removal squared with the cardinal's convictions about moral idealism in government and Church leaders, and he had by June removed both Lope de Conchillos and Juan Rodríguez de Fonseca from office as much for their involvement in economic interests in the Indies as for Las Casas's charges against them of callousness with respect to the Indians.[26]

Since judges and officials (including the jurist Sancho Velázquez, justicia mayor of Puerto Rico) had been accused of bribery, favoritism, and undue investment in the thriving Venezuelan slave trade, Jiménez de Cisneros named the licentiate Alonso Zuazo to take these officials' residencia.[27] Zuazo was also instructed to act in concert, however indirectly, with the Jeronymites, especially in matters relating to the Indians. Zuazo held a bachelor's degree in canon and civil law from the University of Salamanca, where he claimed to have studied for twenty years, and was at the time of his appointment in the summer of 1516 connected with the *colegio* of Valladolid, presumably as a teacher of law.[28] The functions of government were thus divided in a way that would have been unworkable had not Zuazo and the Jeronymites been generally of the same mind. Jiménez de Cisneros compensated, however, for this division of powers by investing his delegates with absolute power in their own spheres; this was more significant for Zuazo than for the Jeronymites, because the judge would act forthrightly, suspend the judges, and himself exercise their appellate powers. Finally, in what proved to be an ineffective assignment for Española and the Indies, Jiménez de Cisneros named Las Casas "Universal Protector" of the Indians.

The reformers—the Jeronymites, Zuazo, and Las Casas—all sailed for the Indies at approximately the same time, though Zuazo was delayed by certain council members' objections to his absolute powers. He finally departed in February or March, 1517, whereas the Jeronymites and Las Casas had left, in separate ships, the previous November.[29] Together they planned to carry out what Giménez Fernández calls the "Casas-Cisneros Reform Plan"; they would implement, in however limited a form, the first phase of reforms largely inspired and instigated by Las Casas with his extraordinary perseverance; the second phase, carried out in 1519–1520 and also inspired by Las Casas, would fall under the aegis of the young Charles and his Flemish courtiers. Jiménez de Cisneros, ever cautious about causing divisiveness in the small discontented New World society, sent an announcement prior to the reformers' departure that he would guarantee justice for all, and he instructed the Casa de Contratación at Seville to intercept the mail and determine whether rumors of their coming might cause a revolt;[30] he ordered ships embargoed for a month before their departure to ensure that false rumors were not spread to the Indies.[31] The complaints of individual encomenderos asking for the restoration of their Indians who had been taken from them in the 1514–1515 distributions, were sent to the Jeronymites in Santo Domingo. Jiménez de Cisneros advised only that "justice be done," thereby showing his conviction that such rewards were only proper for the hidalgo class, the standard bearers of the Spanish mission in the Indies.

The cardinal also supported the missions of the Dominicans and Franciscans on the Venezuelan coast, for at the request of Las Casas he recruited sixteen Picard Franciscans who sailed for Española at the same time, and possibly with, the ships carrying the Jeronymites.[32] The latter had been instructed to furnish all support possible to these fledgling missions, and as Las Casas had carried complaints of slaving operations threatening the missions, the Jeronymites were to name supervisors who would accompany all expeditions to the Spanish Main, and were to see that only "true Caribs" were enslaved. The supervisors seem to have had little effect on the slave trade, though this was largely because it was impossible to distinguish Caribs from others, even had there been a genuine interest on the armadores' part in doing so.

The missions and the Indian slave trade to the south of Española had begun at approximately the same time, and remained in peaceful co-existence, except for the killing of two Dominicans in 1515, until the fall of 1520. The slaving operations had been encouraged by the late king, and by 1514 were probing the southern islands of the Lesser Antilles, Trinidad, and what would later be called Curaçao, Aruba and Bonaire—the latter islands brought to the attention of armadores through certain voyages to Panama. This southward orientation of the Española (and a little later Puerto Rico) armadores signified that the Bahamas had been largely depopulated by earlier raids, and that the decline of Indians on Española was partly offset by the procurement of offshore labor. How many

Indian slaves were taken from the Venezuelan region cannot be estimated; Zuazo understood that fifteen thousand had been brought to Española by 1518.[33] But this vague estimate has little significance; however many Indians were enslaved, they did not substantially check the decline of population, whether because many soon died or because they were too few to offset substantially the general decline. The operations continued throughout the tenure of the Jeronymites and later, for the attraction of potential Indian slaves was strongly supplemented by the great salines on the Peninsula de Araya (presumably the salt was mainly used in the hide trade), by barter for gold and pearls, and by pearl fishing which began at about the same time on Cubagua.[34] The majority of the Indians captured were not Caribs, for those doughty warriors were seldom taken; an expedition in 1515 landed on St. Vincent island just long enough to suffer three Spaniards killed, before sailing on toward Trinidad where there were less ferocious Indians.[35]

The parallel movement of missionaries began in 1514 with two Dominicans, Friars Francisco de Córdoba and Juan Garcés, boldly beginning their labors among the tribes at Piritú, rather too close to the raids at Curaçao for their own safety. These two friars were killed in 1515 after an armador had seized Indians near their mission. But they were merely the vanguard in a movement of friars propelled by revulsion with the continuing deaths of Indians, which they saw as inseparably connected with the encomienda system. Their sentiment was shared by certain Franciscans as well as Dominicans, and especially by the Franciscans caught up in the reform movements of Europe, of which Jiménez de Cisneros was the great Spanish leader. These friars were not only inspired by ideals of austerity and the inward life, such as the Jeronymites and the Minims, but by the inestimable possibilities of converting the heathen in the Indies. When the encomienda system on the islands proved unbreakable, as it seemed in 1515 and intermittently thereafter, they turned away from civilization in search of virgin fields.

Small contingents of six Franciscans and a like number of Dominicans left Santo Domingo in September, 1515, to establish missions on the Venezuelan coast. Their choice for these fields was probably directed by reports of peaceful Indians on this coast, and the Franciscans erected their mission near the mouth of the Cumaná river; the Dominicans situated themselves about fifty miles upstream, establishing a mission they called Santa Fe de Chichiribichí.[36] The Franciscans were slightly reinforced in 1517 by the sixteen sent out by Jiménez de Cisneros; not all the friars went to Venezuela, mainly owing to the discouraging reports that unless Indian slaving was stopped, the mission had a dismal future.[37] They preferred to use their influence against this practice. The missions continued to thrive, although slowly, and according to one report the Franciscans were teaching forty Indian boys at Cumaná in 1519.[38] Though the missions were doomed, as it turned out, by 1520, they seemed so promising up until that time that Charles I named a bishop for the Paria coast, and the friars of both orders planned an extensive expansion in Venezuela.[39]

The Jeronymites docked in Santo Domingo on December 25, 1516, after a pleasant voyage; en route they had stopped at Caparra, where they removed two hundred Indians assigned to Lope de Conchillos, and reassigned them to the city to build a road and causeway linking the mainland with the islet, on which San Juan de Puerto Rico would be situated five or six years later.[40] In spite of Jiménez de Cisneros's precautions, the rumor had reached Santo Domingo that the friars came to remove encomiendas; they arrested Cristóbal de Tapia who was accused (falsely as it turned out) of spreading such rumors and they deterred Pasamonte and other officials from sending a procurador, Juan Carrillo Mexía, to Castile in protest.[41] After Zuazo arrived in April,[42] they conducted a hearing of the main vecinos on the question of the encomienda and ways of resolving the economic depression on the island.[43] As was to be expected, two positions emerged: the vast majority of the encomenderos predicted economic ruin, desertion of the island by

Spaniards, and relapse of the Taínos to idolatry, if the encomienda were abolished. They favored making the encomienda hereditary—a standard encomendero position. A few—especially the temporarily deposed judge, Ayllón—differed with the consensus that the Indians should be regrouped into villages near Spanish towns.[44] Ayllón argued that most Indians would resist such relocation, as he had seen them do when visitadores tried to implement the Laws of Burgos. They might be gradually persuaded to relocate over the years, he counseled, but abrupt removals would provoke flight, suicide, or revolt. Ayllón was prescient; though he apparently was a typical encomendero and Indian slaver during most of his life (like several others, he changed his views in his last years), he was probably the most knowledgeable, intelligent, and articulate Spaniard of long residence on Española.

The Dominicans and Franciscans, bolstered and led by Las Casas who had arrived in January,[45] argued strongly for abolition of the encomienda and the establishment of free Indian communities—the long desired integration advocated since 1510. Convinced that the Jeronymites were too timid to oppose the encomenderos, Las Casas, strongly encouraged by the priors of the two religious orders, once more set sail in early June for Castile, with the Jeronymite Figueroa's warning lingering in his ears: "Don't go. This candle will burn everyone."[46] Soon afterward, and partly to counteract Las Casas's version of affairs with a good dose of Jeronymite realism, the governing friars dispatched one of their members, Friar Bernaldino de Manzanedo.[47] Meanwhile, the Jeronymites recommended to Jiménez de Cisneros that the encomienda be retained, with the Laws of Burgos fully enforced under salaried visitadores, thus detaching those officials from the encomienda system. They further recommended that the Indians be grouped into villages as soon as feasible. They recognized, however, as the encomenderos did, that if retention of the encomiendas was important, the economy of the island could not be revitalized on that basis, and that wider participation in the

Carib slave trade, increased Negro slave importation, and the encouraged immigration of Spanish peasants were necessary to hasten the transition from gold mining to agriculture. Free trade with all ports of Spain was also recommended to afford wider outlets for such produce as sugar, *cassia fistula,* cotton, and dyewood.[48]

Jiménez de Cisneros agreed with these recommendations and authorized Casas to begin recruitment of Spanish peasants for Española. The great cardinal, however, was nearing the end of his government and his life, and lacked the time for further action. He was already informed that Charles would soon set sail from Flanders for Castile, by way of England.

Meanwhile Zuazo was engaged chiefly in holding a secret *pesquisa,* or special investigation, of the conduct in office of the three judges, Ayllón, Matienzo, and Villalobos who were, in accordance with custom, suspended. They would return to office either in 1519 or 1520; the time of resumption remains unclear. Zuazo's investigation was inconclusive, for he had by July, 1517, only taken declarations on Matienzo, who asked for a separate pesquisa; after this he suspended proceedings apparently because Charles's arrival in Spain, which occurred in September, left his instructions in abeyance. The investigation uncovered nothing that was not well known about Matienzo—and for that matter the other two judges.[49] They were, to some extent at least, personally involved in Indian slave trading and pearl bartering. Less likely and less provable were charges of acceptance of bribes, favoritism in hearing court cases, and persecution of Spaniards outside their cabal. As was customary in such pesquisas, the personal morality of the officials was brought into question, with Matienzo's nightly escapades related with all the detail garnered by the bored inhabitants of a tiny town. He was in one instance cut on the cheek by an angry husband who found him in his wife's bedroom, a wound that Matienzo first sought to hide by some balsam sent him by Diego and Maria Colón and when that failed, by a velvet patch; he explained to visitors in his court that he was nicked by a cane stalk. Such episodes might have prompted his recall by Jiménez de Cisneros, but the profligate court of young Charles doubtless took a more tolerant view. Though the pesquisa was unfinished, Zuazo's conduct of it and his known enmity toward the oidores, emboldened the anti-Pasamonte bands on the island to participate in the general junta of April 1518, and the Council of Castile used their complaints in drawing up instructions to Zuazo's successor, Figueroa, in 1519.

The Jeronymites devoted the rest of their time—they would remain on the island until August, 1519—to removing the Indians held by absentee Spaniards—whether officials or private vecinos—and reassigning them to resident encomenderos with the provision that the natives be employed in raising sugar cane or building mills.[50] They also reduced smelting fees by one-third, thus cutting into emoluments granted to courtiers and pensioners of the late Ferdinand, such as Miguel Pérez de Almazán.[51] These actions were applied both to Española, and in consequence of orders to Sancho Velázquez, to Puerto Rico. They seem also to have been applied to Cuba and Jamaica, though the evidence is not clear, and there is reason to suspect that Diego Velázquez kept in the good graces of Juan Rodríguez de Fonseca by a merely nominal removal. Garay may have removed Conchillos's Indians, for the secretary's influence was by then nearing an end.

The friars also initiated the resettling of the Indians into villages near Spanish towns. By the fall of 1518, sites had been selected for thirteen villages and by spring, 1519, five had been occupied. A smallpox epidemic beginning in October, 1518, and lasting at least into January may have so reduced the Indians intended for certain of the villages as to make occupation of them merely nominal.[52] The villages were grouped around Santiago de los Caballeros, Bonao, Jaraguá, San Juan de la Maguana, and especially in the environs of Santo Domingo. In addition, and apparently not regarding the settlements as new, the Spaniards resituated some Indians in the previously depopulated Jacmel and at Sabana de la Salvatierra and

Yaguana.[53] Such Indians as had already been relocated, and there is no evidence as to numbers, apparently did not revolt, though some of them may have fled. Revolts came later in 1519, after the arrival of Figueroa.

The reforms as carried out by the Jeronymites and Zuazo were thus partial and inconclusive; neither finished the tasks they set out to do, partly because the coming of the new king stifled their initiative, as in Zuazo's case, and partly because they were unwilling to risk inciting the encomenderos to rebellion by abolishing the encomiendas, as was true of the Jeronymites.[54] Their net contribution was to remove Indians from all or most absentees on two islands, to reassign them to sugar planters, and partly to consolidate the Indian population, thereby making the Indians, as critics wryly observed, more accessible to their encomenderos. They left the encomiendas of resident officials intact. In keeping with their reluctance to assume the duties of reformers, and with the spirit of Jiménez de Cisneros which they doubtless shared, their reforms redounded to the benefit, small as it was, of the encomenderos. Whether there actually was another feasible choice, as Las Casas argued, is uncertain. Certainly the reformers had been unable or unwilling to act with the forthrightness and dispatch envisioned in their instructions, even in areas not directly affecting the Indians. Zuazo was to have conducted a residencia of the justicia mayor, Sancho Velázquez, in Puerto Rico; when he proved too busy, the Jeronymites and Zuazo were authorized to name a judge,[55] but they did not do so. Thus the justicia mayor was extended for five years in an office that was originally intended to be temporary pending a solution of the case of Diego Colón versus the Crown.

The seeming listlessness with which the reforms were carried out was partly due to the change of government in Spain. Jiménez de Cisneros ceased to offer direction after July, 1517,[56] for he had word of the coming of Charles, who landed at Tazona, Asturias, in September and made his way toward Tordesillas to pay respects to his demented mother. He came as a young Flemish stranger without knowledge of the Castilian language, and some grandees attempted to put forward his younger, Spanish-born brother Ferdinand, as a rival for the throne. But this weak movement collapsed when Charles finally incurred greater wrath from the Castilian towns and healed the rift with the nobility as they united forces against the rebellious municipalities in 1520. Charles and his council acted slowly and erratically on Indies affairs, for the young monarch was preoccupied with winning the loyalty and financial support of his new subjects, and, for months, in holding Cortes in each of his three kingdoms. Hardly had he gained some measure of support in 1519 than the unexpected opportunity arose to be Holy Roman Emperor, which would erode a great part of the Castilian loyalty he had so patiently sought to garner.

The news of his arrival had prompted much the same response in the Indies as had the unpopular repartimientos of 1514–1515. Procuradores were once more elected among the island towns, partly to seek redress of grievances and new privileges, including a new redistribution of Indians, partly to seek confirmation of privileges already granted. Garay sent a procurador to get confirmation of his partnership with the Crown in the royal farms on Jamaica, which he secured in 1519 for an additional three years.[57] In October, 1517, Bernaldino Velázquez, who had been exploring the Mexican coasts, brought back reports of stone cities and numerous Indians in Yucatán. This news so excited Diego Velázquez that he sent Bernaldino Velázquez and Gonzalo de Guzmán to enter into capitulations on his behalf with the young king.[58] Puerto Rico elected Francisco de Barrionuevo and Cristóbal de Mendoza as procuradores in an effort to obtain various economic privileges.[59] On Española the election of a procurador proved a long and difficult matter, owing to a number of factors: the factionalism that had rent the island since at least 1515; the prospect that Diego Colón might be restored to the viceroyalty; and especially the leadership and encouragement Alonso Zuazo gave to the anti-Pasamonte cabal on the island.

Rumors of the pending arrival of Charles in Spain had encouraged Pasamonte and the Santo Domingo cabildo to initiate a petition listing various requests and grievances. These they initially presented to the Jeronymites who they supposed would soon be reaffirmed in office and could therefore act upon their requests.[60] The needs sought by the petition were repeated at the April hearings. They asked for the inportation of Negro slaves, the right to trade with all ports of Spain, and lower Church fees; they added several new requests—that the severance tax on gold be reduced to one-tenth to relieve the depressed mining industry, and that a mint be established as a means of stimulating agricultural production and commerce.

The clergy had been charging fees at a rate five times that of Castile, but the high assessment was a key to the poor economic base on which the churches rested during these years of transition between mining and a plantation agriculture. Ferdinand, it will be recalled, had exempted precious metals from the tithe in 1510, a measure which, coupled with the decline of Indians that denied the churches an encomienda base for their support, caused the bishops of Concepción and Puerto Rico to return to Spain where they hoped to renegotiate a contract for financially viable bishoprics. Lacking any share in the encomiendas which the encomenderos had successfully defended, the leaderless parish priests were obligated either to abandon, or at least perfunctorily perform, their duties while making a living at whatever means lay at hand. Raising the fees was one of the few means available. The episcopacies of Concepción, Santo Domingo, Puerto Rico, and Cuba, and the abbacy of Jamaica were all held by absentees during these years;[61] even afterward only Santo Domingo and Puerto Rico would have resident bishops in 1519 and 1520, the other sees remaining vacant until 1527. A large part of the tithe paid on agricultural products was sent to the bishops in Spain; seeing this, the vecinos began to withhold or circumvent paying the tithe, while demanding that bishops fulfill their duties by taking up residence in the islands. The cathedrals thus had a very late beginning in the Caribbean.

The petition put forward in the fall of 1517 by the Santo Domingo cabildo, however, did not broadly represent interests on the island; when the Jeronymites failed to act promptly, or perhaps to give sufficient reassurance that they would, the Pasamonte cabal quietly selected Francisco Lizaur to bear their requests, and especially their charges against Zuazo, directly to the king.[62] These included (it may be presumed, for they were aired again when Zuazo's residencia was taken in 1519) the accusation that Zuazo had obliged Pasamonte to demonstrate that he was not circumcised, and that he had accused Pasamonte and Lebrón of committing sodomy.[63] Though such charges reflect unfavorably on Zuazo's character, they can be explained by the great hatred engendered between him and the judges as the result of his conducting their residencias. Zuazo otherwise possessed many fine attributes; he was well educated and more appreciative than any other islander of the immense possibilities inherent in the search for a westward passage that began in 1517, and even more by the discoveries that by1519 had unveiled a good part of the Mexican coast.[64] Against this move of Lizaur, Zuazo acted swiftly; having got word of his leaving, he apprehended Lizaur aboard a caravel and jailed him for perhaps a month.[65]

The Jeronymites, less bold than Zuazo, were now taken aback as the officials of Santo Domingo, especially the cabildo members, threatened to send a procurador to the king no matter what resistance was offered; since by this time the friars had word that the other towns on the island also had requests that should be heard, they suggested convening a single junta, representing all the towns, for the purpose of selecting one or two general procuradores as representatives to the king. As a result, the Jeronymites and Zuazo called for town elections of procuradores in February, 1518; the procuradores, with the exception of one or two of the dozen towns, had been elected by March, and the general junta, presided over by one or other of the two Jeronymites, opened on April

21.[66] Though the meeting bears a superficial resemblance to the *comunero* movement, still inchoate at this time in Castile, its more primary cause was a desire by the interior towns to break the restrictive hold of the city of Santo Domingo on the procurement of offshore wealth, now so important to the declining hinterlands. Otherwise, the interior towns would have had little reason to journey the many and often roadless miles to the capital.

The delegates quickly passed proposals of general benefit for the economic development of the island: requests for the importation of more Negro slaves and commerce with all Spanish ports, which had been put forward earlier in the previous fall's petitions; the request that the nascent sugar industry be subsidized by the Crown and that only a 2 percent tithe be paid on sugar production while the industry was getting started. They were likewise in agreement that 20 percent of the Indians removed from absentees should be distributed as naborias among the vecinos, which would have the effect of attaching them permanently to Spanish families.

Other issues showed a clear division between those towns where the cabildos were dominated by former followers of Diego Colón or were simply anti-Santo Domingo by reason of the main city's dominance of trade and control of most economic life. The anti-Pasamonte towns asked for the right to engage in offshore barter and trade without going to the expense of getting a license from the treasury officials in Santo Domingo, and they asked that visitadores be locally elected—a move calculated to prevent control of encomiendas by the Pasamonte cabal. All these issues reflected the factionalism that by 1515 had been engendered under Diego Colón's leadership and which lingered on in expectation of his momentary restoration to the governorship. Naturally those who supported Colón proposed that the island be placed under a hereditary governor with virtually autonomous towns (Colón might not have agreed to the latter provision); the opposition, led by the cabildo of Santo Domingo, favored Crown-appointed governors. The pro-Colón group favored abolition of the court of appeals because it was burdensomly expensive. The opposition, led by the cabildo of Santo Domingo, favored a Crown-appointed governor, ruling with an audiencia, and both subject to residencia after three years. They hotly debated this matter which, as it turned out, they could little influence after the monarchy have solved its internal problems in Spain. In the spring of 1518, however, with the new monarch holding Cortes in Valladolid, the delegates believed that what was decided at this local junta might determine the future of the island for decades to come. Hence they considered critically important the matter of who should be elected procurador general to represent the island at the court. When in the May balloting it appeared that Lope Bardeci, a vecino of Santo Domingo but considered a friend of Diego Colón, would be elected, the cabildo of that city recalled their delegate and replaced him with Cristóbal de Tapia, a staunch *Pasamontista;* this alteration, considered illegal by the *Colombistas,* was followed by the winning over of one of the Colombista delegates and by the election of the oidor Ayllón as procurador general. Judge Zuazo now intervened, branded the election illegal (though his enemies felt he acted out of enmity for Ayllón and sympathy for the Colombistas), and impounded the written petitions, declaring the proceedings null and void.[67]

The Colombistas lacked the funds to send a procurador representing their towns, or it may have been that rumors of Diego Colón's return made such representation unnecessary. The city of Santo Domingo, which had more wealth and connections, elected Antonio Serrano in 1519[68] who took to the court many of the requests that had been advocated in 1517–1518. Thus the island-wide meeting had no direct results. The vecinos lacked an important unifying idea such as the *comuneros* of Castile shared in 1520, and the divisiveness born of years of squabble over diminishing wealth easily overrode the vague idea of communes standing together against encroaching state power.

Continuity in the Caribbean social reform movement has long been recognized as due mainly to the great reformer Bartolomé de las Casas.[69] From his arrival in Spain in July, 1517, until his departure to the Indies in December, 1520, Las Casas sought tirelessly to awaken the court to the need to save the Indians before they should be totally eliminated from the islands; he found friends at court to support his cause: such Erasmian humanists as the Grand Chancellor Jean Sauvage; the royal chamberlain, Carlos de Poupet, Monsieur de la Chaulx; and finally the third Grand Chancellor, Mercurino Gattinara, who took office in October, 1518, after Sauvage's death.[70] He also had Dominican friends, a group of Salamanca theologians, and finally, about 1520, the young Charles himself. Partly by Las Casas's efforts, the Jeronymites were removed by 1519, and his influence lay behind the order issued with the approval of Gattinara that Indians be taken away from officials in Española and Puerto Rico, a provision that Figueroa was expected to carry out. The reforming priest also secured the long-sought decree on May 18, 1520, freeing the Indians as soon as present encomienda holders had died. This gradualist emancipation was of course ineffective, since the larger part of the Indians had died (for reasons presumably unconnected with the encomienda) long before it was put into effect. Finally, Las Casas was one of the supporters for the restoration of Diego Colón.

Given the sense of urgency shared by Las Casas and his supporters, the reforms unfolded with agonizing slowness. Charles was largely preoccupied with other matters, at first with the pretty *doncellas* thrust into his eager arms by his young widowed grandmother, whom Castilians viewed as disgracefully carnal,[71] later with the alluring opportunity posited by the death of his grandfather Maximilian who left the throne of the Holy Roman Empire open to the successful maneuverings of Charles's supporters, and finally with the complications ensuing from that election—mainly the vain effort to placate the jealous Francis I at the convention at Montpellier in May–June, 1519.[72] In between these matters, he found it unexpectedly a delicate and difficult matter to placate, as he believed he did, the resentful comuneros at Valladolid in

1517, and the equally suspicious and unmanageable Castilian procuradores at Zaragoza and Barcelona in 1518–1519. A vast part of his official energy went into winning acceptance of himself as king and emperor in his three kingdoms, with the Castilian comuneros finally rejecting him when he departed for the Germanies. Meanwhile the Indies received only erratic attention.

Owing to these circumstances, as well as to the influence of Juan Rodríguez de Fonseca—who was restored as Secretary of the Indies in March, 1518,[73] and who was at times able to postpone action on reform cédulas while expediting the granting of petty patronage—cedulas affecting the Indies were only occasionally signed and were executed, if at all, still more slowly. The influence of Las Casas with his friend Sauvage was responsible for the confirmation by Charles V on March 15, 1518, of the removal of Indians from certain absentees by the Jeronymites.[74] These deprived courtiers at once claimed compensation for what their encomiendas had earned since approximately April, 1517, when the Indians had been removed, but there is no clear evidence that Pasamonte had the funds to meet such claims. To relieve the labor shortage on the islands and at the same time to save the Indians from hard labor, Charles granted in August, 1518, that four thousand Negro slaves be sent to the Indies,[75] pro-rated among the four islands in accordance with population and need. Las Casas urged this solution to the labor problem, though he later regretted it; since Negro labor had been asked for since 1515, the court doubtless would have granted it in any case, and Negro slaves, of course, had been sent in illegally, although not in enough numbers to satisfy the demand. Charles granted the contract as a favor to one of his chamberlains, Lorenzo de Gorrevod, who twice subcontracted the privilege.[76] The result was that an excessive number of middlemen raised the price higher than most could pay, and few Negroes reached the islands through this agency.

While this rather piecemeal approach toward socioeconomic reforms unfolded, the court machinery moved slowly to replace the main officials on Española and

Puerto Rico. Las Casas's argument that they should be removed because of insensibility to the Indian problem was not the main reason for their removal. For months, the Jeronymites had been pleading to be allowed to return claiming they could do no more even "if they had a thousand years." Zuazo, whom Las Casas would feign have left as judge on Española, was the bête noire of the Pasamontistas. By the summer of 1518, they had reported to Rodríguez de Fonseca and the king Zuazo's arbitrary conduct in arresting Francisco Lizaur and impounding the petitions of the general junta of April–May. Then there were the suspicions, perennial in Spanish administration, that the royal fifth was not always collected on the pearl trade from Cubagua, as suggested in the testimony taken by Zuazo in the Matienzo residencia.[77] An auditing, the first since Gil González Dávila performed that function in 1509, was clearly in order. Both Las Casas and Rodríguez de Fonseca were in agreement, too, that Sancho Velázquez should be removed as justicia mayor of Puerto Rico. Las Casas judged that he cared nothing for the fate of the Indians there, and Rodríguez de Fonseca had no reason to support him over another appointee. The auditor for Española was also to scrutinize the treasury accounts of Puerto Rico as well as those of the other islands.

All three of the new officials—the replacements for Zuazo and Sancho Velázquez and the auditor had been selected by August, 1518—were apparently the result of Rodríguez de Fonseca's having asked for recommendations from Dr. Sancho de Matienzo, the veteran treasurer of the Casa de Contratación. The licentiate Rodrigo de Figueroa, who had served as judge of customs revenue at Seville, was named as juez de residencia and justicia mayor of Española; Dr. Juan Fernández de la Gama, legal counselor to the *corregidor* of Seville, was named to the same offices for Puerto Rico, and Pedro de Isásaga, brother of the Casa's factor, Ochoa de Isásaga, was appointed to audit the accounts on the four islands, beginning with the Española treasury.[78] Pasamonte contemplated returning at last to Castile, after his long tour of duty on

Española, when Isásaga had finished his audit,[79] but the investigation dragged on for months, while the Comunero revolt had the Spanish court officials running for their lives and Pasamonte lingered on to die in office.

Las Casas's influence was nowhere clearer than in the instructions given to Figueroa.[80] He was to remove the Indians of resident officials as well as those of any remaining absentees, and was to see that these and all other Indians be placed in villages, as soon as such towns could be laid out. Though the Jeronymites had already removed the Indians of most absentees, a few remained, notably those of Diego Colón and María, his wife, who returned to Castile in 1518.[81] Still the council was unwilling to risk freeing the Indians from Spanish control without more evidence, and Figueroa was to hold hearings again to determine whether he should create free villages, or retain the encomienda system with a village organization. If the consensus was against relocating the Indians, he was to leave them in their yucayeques, rather than risk their destruction; but he was to see in any case that the modified Laws of Burgos were fully enforced. The justification for rehearings was that the Jeronymites had listened mainly to the encomenderos. Figueroa was further instructed to complete the residencias of the three judges and to take Zuazo's residencia. He was authorized to name an alcalde mayor on Cubagua to see that only Caribs were enslaved and that the king's fifth was collected on the pearl trade. Figueroa also carried provisions that responded to the requests of the procurador Antonio Serrano, though some of these orders followed him to Española; these included granting the cabildo of Santo Domingo appellate jurisdiction over civil cases involving less than twenty-five *pesos de oro*, various measures of tax relief, the right to take on and discharge cargo at Cádiz providing no gold were carried, and the right to grant subsidies to sugar mill owners—all indices of an island moving out of a mining economy and into agriculture.

The instructions to Gama (actually issued to his son) generally duplicated Figueroa's with respect to the removal of Indians and the establishment of villages, and he was to take the residencia of the Licentiate Sancho Velázquez and his main judicial officials.[82] Gama also carried privileges, asked for by the Puerto Rican procuradores, granting the cabildo of Caparra appellate powers like those of Santo Domingo, a five-year extension of the right to use money from judicial fines to build roads and bridges, and tax relief including the privilege of mining salt on the island and the Venezuelan coast, free of royal tax. Isásaga's instructions were routine for auditors of treasury accounts.

Though instructions were drawn up by December, 1518, at least for Figueroa, the three officials did not sail from Spain until June, 1519, some six months later.[83] The reasons for so long a delay had to do with the preoccupations of the court already mentioned, and with the resignation of Dr. Gama owing to illness and advanced age; he recommended that his son, Antonio de la Gama, like himself a professional lawyer, be appointed in his place, and the younger Gama was named in March, 1519.[84] Figueroa at one point considered resigning because of the apparent procrastination in sending him out on his new duties. The three men sailed in June, reaching Caparra on or before July 13, when Figueroa and Gama both inspected the site where the city was to be relocated.[85] Figueroa and Isásaga were in Santo Domingo by July 27.[86] Meanwhile the epidemic of 1518–1519 had further depleted the Indian population on Española, thereby making certain of the projected social reforms appear rather pointless.

After holding a brief hearing in August, Figueroa decided to carry out the formation of villages along with an experimental autonomous government in at least one—Cayacoa in the Vega. He removed Indians from the treasury officials and the Colón family, which they greatly resented, and partly to provide for these Indians, laid out four villages.[87] He did not remove the Indians of the three judges.[88] The Jeronymites had already selected the sites for thirteen villages of which they had populated five (though, in fact, flight and epidemic scattered the

Indians from all but one village). Figueroa initiated the populating of an additional seven villages. All this required planning and time, the selecting of sites (two villages in Higüey, one on the Vega, three in San Juan de la Maguana area, and one in Santo Domingo), and the naming of administrators.[89] The Indians he removed from absentees were reassigned to encomenderos—including some of his own *allegados* (companions who came with him)—for the purpose of building sugar mills. Finally, soon after May, 1520, came the decree freeing all Indians on Española and Puerto Rico as soon as the encomienda fell vacant, a gradualism that mocked—assuming one accepts the interpretation that encomiendas caused the depletion of the Indian population—the intent of the reforms.[90] Figueroa carried out the rest of his instructions routinely, taking Zuazo's residencia, and naming Antonio de Flores, a young man who accompanied him from Spain, to the newly created position of alcalde mayor on Cubagua.[91]

The Licenciate Gama had much less to do on Puerto Rico, for that small island contained only two towns and few Indians. Much of the furor that followed in the wake of the 1514-1515 repartimiento had passed away along with many of the Indians, and the islanders listlessly gambled at *a la flux* for a piece of cloth, a canter of wine, or perchance a chicken or an old nag, if nothing better was at hand. Sancho Velázquez was a hail-fellow-well-met, who spent much of his time gambling, sometimes with Spaniards he jailed in his own *posada*, for want of a public jail. Gama found from the extensive pesquisa he held from July to December, 1519,[92] that Velázquez was well liked by some and hated by others, a fairly typical state of affairs for a governor in the Indies. He was accused of the same offenses as the judges on Española, as was, for that matter, Diego Velázquez in Cuba—accepting gifts, lax and capricious law enforcement, winking at concubinage and other carnal sins. Gama fined him a few hundred pesos for various of these offenses, and obliged him to restore 1,352 *pesos de oro* which Gama judged he had wrongfully collected from

Ponce de León in 1512. Velázquez protested and appealed to the Crown, but by 1520, when Bishop Manso had returned with the title of *Inquisidor General* of the Indies, he was removed from Gama's custody and remanded to house arrest, where he died on May 17, 1520.[93] Otherwise, Gama removed the Indians of local officials, of Pasamonte who seems to have temporarily recovered his after the Jeronymites ordered them removed, and those of Diego Colón. They were relieved of work pending further decision of the Crown (the May, 1520, cédula), and at least one village was established in conformance with Gama's instructions.[94]

The more active phase of the reform era ended in 1520 with the gradualist law of May 18, the departure of Charles to northern Europe, and the comunero revolt that virtually cut off the Indies from Spain and from any direction by a regency in wild and desperate flight. In spite of Casas's admirable tenacity, his reforms seemed devoid of efficacy, for even if they might have retarded the decline of Indian population, especially on Española and Puerto Rico, the measures of apparent preservation seem too little, too late, and too slowly implemented. The reforms were only partly implemented in Cuba and Jamaica where Crown enterprises, linked with Diego Velázquez and Francisco de Garay, continued to flourish; though other courtiers had been dispossessed, the Crown on these two islands had not even detached itself from the presumably destructive encomienda system.

The causes of Indian deaths have been considerably elaborated since Las Casas first wrote of their dying from starvation, overwork, suicide, inability to procreate, and general extermination by Spanish swords thrust through their unprotected bellies. The break-up of families, the tendency of Spaniards to congregate Indian women as household servants on their haciendas (which probably did give rise to an extensive if uncounted mestizo population), the breakdown of a balanced cassava-fish diet[95]—all these and others have been adduced as causes. Still it seems unlikely that all these taken together account for more than a small part of the population decline. As suggested earlier, the relatively large number of old persons included in the Alburquerque repartimiento of 1514 would belie to a large extent the thesis of cruelty, overwork, and even starvation. Moreover, after the Laws of Burgos were put into effect with respect to the provision of food, there is evidence that some encomenderos assigned Indians to fisheries, from which the natives were regularly supplied.[96]

But even after 1515 when officials and encomenderos were cognizant of and worried about the decline in the Indian population, the deaths continued. The treasurer Haro on Puerto Rico wrote the king in 1518 that the Indians were well treated but that they died regularly "as weak in the body as they are in the faith."[97] Ayllón, as experienced and observant as any resident of Española, told the Jeronymites that he had observed that the Indians died as rapidly in Spanish households, without ever doing any hard labor, as they did in the mines.[98] Clearly hard labor, or the encomienda system, is too simply an explanation though the immense historiography on the encomienda shows that moral righteousness usually prefers a simple falsehood to a complex truth.

In essence, the simpler explanation has been that the Spaniards killed the Indians with hard work and replaced them with Negroes. Actually, *bozales,* or Negroes from Africa, had been imported since at least 1505 and been put into the mines where they were in direct contact with Indian laborers. Negroes were imported thereafter in increasing numbers—though illegally and doubtless with the connivance of the treasury officials—to all the islands, and especially to Española and Puerto Rico. This cumulative importation in small numbers was more important than the Gorrevod contract of 1518. Various islanders brought in a dozen or more slaves by special contracts. Complaints arose that there was too much contact between Negroes and Indians, or simply too many Negroes were being imported. Juan de Ampies, the royal factor on Española, warned in 1517 that Negroes must be kept away from the Indians because they seized the Indian girls for sexual relations and caused the tribe to flee to the *arcabucos*.[99] On complaints of the Española vecinos, the court in 1519 prohibited temporary residents from working Negroes in the mines. The most telling evidence that bozales were imported in quantity between 1515 and 1520 is the *probanza* drawn up by the merchant Rodrigo de Bastidas in 1521; residents of Española testified that more Negroes were imported in a single year before the Gorrevod contract than since it had been awarded.[100]

The increase of Negroes and the decrease of Indians, who as a result did less and less of the hard mine labor (pick and bar work), brings one squarely to face the long published but insufficiently appreciated Ashburn thesis.[101] P. M. Ashburn, a medical colonel who practiced for years in the tropics, concluded after examining the sources containing accounts of disease in colonial Latin America, that both Spaniard and Negro carried diseases that were lethal to the Indian. Of the two, the Negro from Africa, who brought not only smallpox from the Spaniard but malaria and yellow fever from Africa, was the single greatest cause for the demise of the Indian. Thus, the Negro did not simply replace the Indian, but by causes little appreciated and impossible to avoid in the sixteenth century, he helped eliminate him. The epidemic of 1518–1519, which erupted significantly in the mines, was only an intensified aspect of what had been occurring continually, if at times slowly, since at least 1505. Since Spaniards typically kept Negroes as household servants, the deaths of Indians there are thus readily explained.

The causes for the decline of the Indian population, then, need to be separated from ill treatment with which these causes are often conjoined. The documentary evidence on which this work rests, confirms Ashburn's assumption that disease was the main killer of the Indians. Spaniards carried diseases to the Indians to which the latter had no immunity, and Negroes carried diseases contracted from the Spaniards and the African coast to which they were immune, but the Indians were not. Indians died as readily from light work as from mine labor or idleness. Haro's descriptions of Indians weakening daily, though labor was light and food supply adequate, would suggest that malaria was the probable cause. When to disease are added migrations from the island and the tendency to concentrate Indian women in haciendas and Indian males in the mines with the resultant reduction in the Indian birthrate, the decline of the Indian population is largely accounted for. Cruel treatment, harsh labor, and battle deaths taken together could only account for a minority of the total depopulation. We may rightly deplore oppression of the weak by the strong, but we can be more discriminating about the results of such oppression.

The regrouping of Indians into villages, whether as free communities or owing service to encomenderos, potentially hastened the demise of the Indians by reason of greater contact with Spaniards and Negroes. This was illustrated by the 1518–1519 epidemic that coincided with the Jeronymites' effort, minimally successful, to congregate Indians into villages near the Spaniards. Still other Indians resisted the attempt to relocate them and fled to the mountains giving observers the specious appearance that the decline in Indian population was worse than it actually was. On Puerto Rico in 1517, where an attempt was made to form villages in response to Jeronymite orders, an estimated one-third of the Indians fled to the mountains.[102] Few, if any, were recovered. In Española, the storied revolt of Enriquillo near Jaraguá in 1519, while attributed by Las Casas to the rape of the cacique's wife by a local encomendero[103] (it has since become almost mandatory that revolts be instigated by the rape of someone's wife, sister, or mother), is much more likely to signify resistance to the attempted consolidation of villages in that region by Judge Figueroa. This would tend also to account for the revolts of other caciques in the Vega soon afterword, and it is surely no coincidence that the major early revolts on Española, in 1504 and 1519, erupted in the region of the most perceptive Taíno culture on the island. Small wonder that with Indian labor at its scarcest in 1519, the importation of Negro slaves temporarily cut off by the adverse effects on shipping of the Magellan expedition, Charles's great fleet enroute to Flanders, and the comunero revolt,[104] the vecinos turned in 1520 to the Venezuelan coast where in a more aggressive search for Indians they inadvertently destroyed the fledgling missions, thus bringing two contradictory strains of Spanish civilization into destructive contact.

6

The Restoration of Diego Colón (1520-1523)

The hapless son of the Discoverer had the misfortune to rule only at the wrong times. He took command in 1509 just as the first of several depressions set in on Española and he was recalled because of the bitter factionalism engendered by the struggle for control over a declining number of Indians. He would return in 1520 during a hardly more propitious time—the young monarch who restored him was absent in northern Europe, the reformers who deemed him their champion were incapable of defending him from his many enemies, and the comunero revolt was acting as a catalyst, spurring on a nascent centralism by the Crown which mistrusted Colón's anachronistic feudalism and his vague claims to virtual autonomy in the Indies.

Thus he ruled, unfortunately, during years of unusual instability both in Spain and the Indies, where to the rebellion of Cortés and the massacres of missionaries on the Venezuelan coast, Colón added his own futile efforts to regrasp the reins of power that had, during his five-year absence, been in his rivals' hands. These few years obscured, as will be shown, the slower, less conspicuous movement toward stability in the islands and the mother country. The Spanish Caribbean was moving toward a tropical agriculture based on Negro slavery and Spanish peasants, and on this base—so much firmer than gold mining—the episcopacies would finally be erected, and the invigorated and enlarged audiencia would extend its authority over the islands and the mainland. They obscured, too, the incalculable power that accrued to Charles as Holy Roman Emperor, his connection with the great Austrian bankers—the Fuggers and Welsers—and the royal income brought to him by taxes on commerce with Flanders, Naples, and southern Europe. These movements promised a stability, a base on which royal authority could finally be laid down as a dike against the great comunero upsurge and the smaller whirlpool of Colón's tenacious struggle to uphold the rights his famous father had bequeathed him.

Why Colón should have been restored at all is not easily explained. His deposition in 1515 was not, so far as the Crown announced, meant to be permanent. But with the death of Ferdinand, whatever influence that ailing monarch actually exercised in Colón's removal, the viceroy perforce had to turn to Jiménez de Cisneros, and very soon thereafter to Charles, to seek restoration of his governorship and the powers and emoluments that he considered clearly implied in the original capitulation with Columbus. While pressing the cardinal, unsuccessfully as it turned out, to restore his judicial officials to office of the Indies,[1] Colón sent a trusted retainer, García de Lerma, ("better with the tongue than the lance" in Oviedo's scornful appraisal) to Flanders to urge upon Charles that his case be heard before the Council of Castile.[2] The rule of such remote islands must have appeared unimportant to the young Fleming, who in early 1517 directed that Colón's case be heard at once;[3] four months later, however, doubtless advised by his secretary Francisco de los Cobos, the king ordered that the suit be suspended until he reached Spain, for he now understood that it involved his *señorio*.[4]

After Charles arrived in Spain in September, 1517, Colón won over the young king; one can reach no other conclusion, for Colón's gains were made in spite of Rodríguez de Fonseca's opposition among others, and Colón was almost constantly at the lavish court where he must have become well known to the king. Colón apparently possessed all the charm of an educated courtier who had been raised as a royal page,[5] and he was devoted and attractive to his friends, many of whom, such as

Diego Méndez,[6] were his lifelong intimates. Besides force of personality, Colón enjoyed the prestige of the Duke of Alba and his large following as well as the friendship and support of the Genoese mercantile community on whom the spendthrift Charles would often depend for loans. His acceptance to Charles and his court was enhanced by his loyalty and willingness to be of service, for in November, 1518, he accompanied Charles's sister, Leonor, to Portugal where he attended the important event of her marriage to Manuel I.[7] Finally, as Charles prepared to leave for the Germanies and his coronation as Emperor, having spent all available funds including the exaction of double subsidies from the Castilian towns, Colón lent him ten thousand ducats.[8]

Meanwhile Colón had other supporters who urged upon the council and the king his restoration to office in the Indies. He had like his father retained a special devotion for the Franciscan order, bestowing on the monastery at Santo Domingo his private patronage;[9] then, too, he had the reputation of being more humane in his treatment of the Indians than the average encomendero. For these reasons, the Franciscans at court, prompted by Friar Juan Vithern who had returned by 1518 from the Franciscan mission at Cumaná urged that the king return Colón to the governorship so that he might supervise the Venezuelan coast, protecting the missions and keeping the slavers at bay.[10] Some towns on Española had added their voices in support of Colón during the general junta of 1518, for his popularity in the islands, quite apart from ties of personal loyalty and affection, lay in the excess of Spanish inhabitants in relation to the available wealth. Colón's influence was thus partly due to those vecinos on Española who had lost out after he left in 1515; they awaited his return with great hope for rewards. Then, too, there was the irresistible argument for unity of rule in the islands as against the fragmented government—up to 1519—of justicia mayores, juezes de residencia, and the Jeronymites. Zuazo, with characteristic eloquence and persuasiveness, had written Chievres in January, 1518, that Colón would be the best choice for governor of the Indies, whether or not his privileges were fully restored. Unlike opportunists, Zuazo argued, "Colón loves the land his father discovered," and had a personal interest in its development, since he received one-tenth of the Crown's income. He alone should rule for "it is as natural as a bee leading a hive that power flows harmoniously from top to bottom, thus preventing factionalism." Then, shifting from Aristotelianism to the Bible, he concluded: "A kingdom divided against itself cannot stand."[11]

Since Colón was actually restored to power in 1520, it seems obvious that he had succeeded in persuading Charles, through whatever combination of personal charm and support, that he was the rightful governor of the Indies. Yet this hardly accounts for his five-year sojourn in Spain. That he might be restored was already apparent by 1518 for documents pertaining to the Indies were often addressed to him (though he exercised no actual power) as viceroy, admiral, and governor; at about the same time he was authorized to name subordinate judicial officials[12]—a recognition that such officials ought not to have been forcibly removed in 1514–1515.

Still, he did not return for two more years. Las Casas's pleas that the Jeronymites be replaced with someone less timid in the face of the encomenderos had resulted, though not solely because of Las Casas, in the sending of the licentiate Figueroa, rather than Colón, who otherwise would have been acceptable to the reformers given his humane reputation. His tardiness in returning can only be due to his insistence that certain powers and rights, pressed on the court by his newly engaged attorney, Alonso Romano,[13] at Valladolid in 1518, be granted him, and to the royal attorney's resistance to these overtures. Colón's eagerness to return to Española was thus offset by his determination to secure from the Crown acknowledgment of what he considered his full political and judicial powers and his right to one-tenth of the royal income from the lands his father had discovered.

An appreciation of the powers granted Colón and the situation that would confront him in the Indies in 1520 is impossible without taking into account the instability of Spanish government during the early reign of Charles V. Colón was supported by a conglomerate of forces, in and out of the government, including Las Casas, the representatives of the Franciscans and Dominicans, the Flemish courtiers (especially the Grand Chancellors Sauvage and Gattinara) the Salamancan theologians, and by some members of the Council of Castile. These were the forces that together supported and helped win the king's approval of the restoration document of May 17, 1520. Actually this coalition lacked coherence and was dispersed even before Colón sailed for the New World. Charles and Gattinara sailed for the Germanies, and Las Casas, supposing the main issue settled, especially since the law of that same month freed the Indians, likewise prepared to leave Spain for the Indies. The government was left by Charles in the hands of Adrian of Utrecht, supplemented a few months later by the prestigious Constable and the Admiral of Castile; none of these three governors had more than passing interest in the Indies. The actual direction of the overseas governments reverted to the experienced Bishop Rodríguez de Fonseca who rapidly put forward for the unknowledgeable governors' signatures, legislation which largely eroded or curbed Colón's powers, and that, furthermore, had support in the islands for it coincided with certain local economic interests and political aspirations antagonistic to Colón. No wonder Colón felt the need, even the right, to interpret his powers as he saw fit, once he had been reinstated in Santo Domingo.

From the time of the first Cortes held in Valladolid by Charles in February, 1518, when Colón's suit with the Crown was first advanced, until his powers were approved at La Coruña in May, 1520, Colón made great headway with his arguments; though introduced by the attorney Romano, his final proposal was laid before the Council in 1519 by his half-brother Fernando,[14] who was as embued as Diego with the rightness of the cause and possessed of a fine literary style.

The proposal drafted by Fernando Colón,[15] which was

approved by the king, with certain exceptions, would have given Diego such extensive powers as to place the Indies virtually under his control, thus tying the four islands back together under a centralized command from which they had virtually escaped since 1515. It would have, at the same time, relegated the audiencia to a position of sharing, but never overruling, Colón's power in an arrangement sometimes referred to as the *Acuerdo*, meaning that decisions were jointly reached by the viceroy and the oidores. On his authority as viceroy, Colón would himself appoint *tenientes de gobernador* or alcaldes mayores in such towns as he saw fit. He would act in concert with the audiencia, to be composed of three oidores as it had been, in proposing to the king three candidates (theoretically) for the eight *regimientos* (office of regidor) for each town. The king would then name one—a traditional compromise between local and royal power called the ternary system. Colón was also to act in concert with the oidores in distributing land and water, an indication that the measure of potential wealth was no longer the encomienda. Even in these concessions to royal power, Colón proposed the safeguard that he carry the decisive vote in the event of split decisions, which applied both to political or administrative matters and to judicial ones. Still more remarkable, considering how little power it left the audiencia, was the proposal that the line of appeal in civil cases would extend from local alcaldes who were the judges in the first instance, to the tenientes and from the latter to the admiral; finally—should it ever go so far—the case would pass to the audiencia where the admiral had a decisive vote. It was precisely this concentration of judicial power at both the intermediary and appellate levels in the hands of one man—Colón—that prevented the functioning of a real audiencia (though the term is used for convenience) until after the viceroy's final suspension in 1523.

That these proposals were approved by the king, quite apart from his relationship with Diego Colón, can only be explained by the drastic circumstances facing Charles in 1520. Certain of the Castilian towns were already up in arms against him; he was deluged with petitions of all sorts at Santiago de Compostela and La Coruña, and a large, exorbitantly expensive armada awaited him at the port, ready to sail northward. One suspects that in these circumstances, preoccupied with the immensely important matter of securing the Emperorship, thankful like his grandfather for what loyal support he had, he hastily empowered Colón and let matters work their way out as they would. The state was thus weak at this juncture. What he approved on May 17 did reserve to the towns the right to elect *alcaldes ordinarios,*[16] a slight concession to localism that Colón nonetheless protested.[17] The Crown retained the traditional regalia of the royal patronage, including the appointing of oidores, judges of residencia (though the admiral was to be irremovable with the right to appoint substitute judges during the hearings), treasury officials, and *escribanos de número* (town scribes). The document was silent about Colón's control of repartimientos, which were left in charge of the licentiates Figueroa and Gama for Española and Puerto Rico, respectively. The power to distribute Indians had never been removed from the tenientes Diego Velázquez and Garay in Cuba and Jamaica.

Obviously the decision on Colón's powers left matters about as untidy, as likely to cause friction among authorities, as prevailed before 1515. Nor had any advance been made on the geographical definition of the Columbian viceroyality. Though the document stated that the admiral was to receive one-tenth of the royal income, excepting certain parts of the regalia, from the area discovered by Columbus, there was still no agreement on exactly what Columbus had discovered. Colón still insisted that he was entitled to a tenth from Panama, which the treasury at Santo Domingo had always resisted, and certainly to a tenth of the income from Venezuela, now increasingly lucrative owing to an expanded pearl fishing operation. But whether Columbus had actually discovered that part of Panama (Urabá) from which gold came, and whether he had actually discovered the islands of Cubagua and Margarita was, given the geographical knowledge of the time, certainly questionable. Colón had of course gathered detailed evidence from mariners, immediately prior to and just after his deposition in 1515, that purported to prove his father's discovery of these lands. But the matter was unresolved by 1520, for even the definition of discovery—whether merely by sailing in the general area or formally taking possession of it—remained a moot point. Though the case remained in abeyance, Colón, hard pressed for income since Española was in economic ebb tide, would enforce collection of his tenth on Venezuela while continuing to press his rights to Urabá. But the latter was isolated from Española by distance and ocean currents, whereas the Venezuelan coast was an easy five-days' voyage away and under Santo Domingo's political control. Doubtless Bishop Rodriguez de Fonseca viewed the influence of Colón, which was inseparably part of the influence of the still more radical group composed of Las Casas and other advocates of the encomienda's abolition, as baneful for the royal regalia, with the young king taken in by arguments appealing to a vague, unworkable idealism. Colón had withdrawn from the court after Charles's departure, and at least by August was in Seville, [18] While waiting for the fleet that would return him to Española, he filed a protest against the restrictions still encumbering his powers. Had he known of legislation passed on Rodríguez de Fonseca's initiative, he would have had much more to protest about.

In September, 1519, Rodríguez de Fonseca had put through a provision that assigned to the audiencia the sole right to distribute lands and water, and he later dispatched an order to Diego Velázquez to refer any such allotments he made to the Crown for approval.[19] Rodríguez de Fonseca apparently felt that the capitulations with Columbus did not warrant assigning these powers to Colón. At about the same time, he created what is actually the first regular audiencia in the New World,[20] though it never functioned as envisioned until 1527. Earlier, in 1516, the judges of appeal had advocated that their court should be modeled on the Spanish audiencias and invested with all the powers and officials which made that body a key agency of royal power.[21] Their proposal called for four oidores and a president, a membership that would have had the effect of nullifying Colón's decisive vote, though that may not have been the sole reason for expanding the court. A larger court was in any case needed by 1520, for the area subject to it was becoming larger, with the Spanish expanding into Mexico, Panama, and Venezuela. In actuality, Rodríguez de Fonseca had Cristóbal Lebrón (though Figueroa briefly preceded him) named as the fourth oidor,[22] but did not find a suitable candidate for president, probably owing to difficulties connected with the comunero revolt. In any case, Colón must work with four oidores, rather than three, who were apt to oppose him on various issues. In the naming of life-time regidores for the towns, Rodríguez de Fonseca (who of course only rubricated the cédulas that were officially signed by the governors and the Council), continued what the Crown had done up to 1520, though he violated the Colón contract in so doing. The initiative for the appointing of life-time regidores came from the early settlers on all four islands and was connected in part with a desire to assure retention of an encomienda by reinforcing such tenure with an official position, as against the changes that were apt to follow the naming of a new repartidor. In additon, since no few regidores were appointed to Cuban towns in 1519–1520,[23] it can only be supposed that Rodriguez de Fonseca had warned Diego Velázquez, if not the island's procurador in Spain, that these positions should be filled before Colón had time to act with the audiencia in proposing a list of nominees. Finally, the issuance of a cédula in 1520,[24] reducing the severance tax on gold to one-tenth on Española, and other cédulas the same year applicable to all the islands, had the effect, if enforced, of reducing Colón's income in that sector by one-half, for his tenth was tied to the Crown's income. All these measures were passed after Colón had left the court, and they likely had been earlier rejected by him in discussions leading up to the restatement of his powers and privileges of May 17. Such tactics place Rodríguez de Fonseca in the light of carrying out illegal maneuvers, but that guardian of royal financial interests probably felt he was protecting the Crown from those who had taken advantage of the young and inexperienced king.

Colón apparently knew nothing before his departure from Spain of these sub rosa restrictions on his power and income; had he done so, he would have branded them as illegal, issued without the king's knowledge and against the spirit and letter of the royally approved document. The Cuban procuradores, who were in Seville simultaneously with Colón, somehow managed to learn that Colón planned to send Judge Zuazo to take the residencia of Diego Velázquez, and sent this information to Rodríguez de Fonseca.[25] The latter then issued an order prohibiting Zuazo's leaving Española on the grounds that his own residencia was incomplete.[26] But Colón would ignore the order, even though it was repeated. That he contemplated naming Zuazo *juez de residencia* makes clear that Colón interpreted the king's powers as devolving on him, as viceroy, during the monarch's absence. Such an interpretation was not mentioned in the document setting forth his powers.

The viceroy left Sanlúcar de Barrameda in October, 1520,[27] probably with a sizable retinue that included his wife, Maria, his children, and a number of his loyal retainers, some of whom had faithfully served his father. It was, and was intended to be, a triumphal return. After all, he sailed with a patent from the king of Spain and Holy Roman Emperor, and with the moral support of the reformers, so recently influential with Charles and the grand chancellor. At a comfortable distance from the realities he soon would face, Colón might well have felt he could look forward to years, perhaps to the rest of his life, as the viceroy of a rich, justly governed, expanding New World. The encomienda was in its final stage; the Indian was to be freed as present holders died or proved themselves abusive lords. The new enterprise on the Venezuelan coast was to be managed for the good of all: pearls for the Spaniards, Christianity for the peaceloving Indians, and slavery for their enemies—the cannibalistic Caribs.

The coast of Paria, as the Spaniards then called the

hundreds of miles stretching from the Orinoco to Santa Marta, was now thought of as the new land of hope by missionaries and slave hunters, enterprises that would have been mutually contradictory even at the outset had it not been for the great sweep of the coast and the small mission enterprise. Here on this coast, Colón would lose his reputation for humaneness in treatment of the Indians. Paria was one of the ambushes of reality lying in wait for him as he sailed into the Caribbean in November, 1520. By this time, unfortunately, the contact between Spaniards and Indians had long passed the friendly stage and a brief war was already begun.

The Franciscan and Dominican missions established on the Cumaná river in 1515 had been successful small outposts, winning the riparian tribes to friendship and to Christianity. The Franciscans by 1520 were training forty young neophytes in the mission, surrounded with fruit trees, near the mouth of the Cumaná;[28] up river, about fifty miles, the Dominicans worked among the Tagares in the mission called Santa Fe de Chichiribichi.[29] Though the friars were at times apprehensive of Spanish slaving operations, the menace remained more potential than real; it failed to dim the Franciscans' hope that with the coming of the humane, amply empowered Colón, they could look forward to great expansion of missions in the future. Both orders had in 1518 sought to get exclusive mission grants from Charles extending up to a hundred leagues;[30] apparently the grants were not made, probably because the grant made to Bartolomé de las Casas in May, 1520,[31] harmonized with their purposes. Las Casas had contemplated in 1518 returning with Licentiate Figueroa to help supervise freeing the Taínos. He now decided, after learning of the 1518–1519 epidemic and after hearing the glowing reports of mission work on Paria, to secure a contact authorizing him to establish three towns and demonstrate that Spanish peasants could co-exist peacefully with the Indians—the same idea underlying the Cisneros-Casas reforms, but now to be worked out in an unspoiled Indian world.[32] How far the sanguine Franciscans had affected Charles with their accounts of Paria's great future is shown by the monarch's request that his ambassador in Rome obtain papal bulls naming Pierre Barbier, his chaplain, the Bishop of Paria.[33] Before this could be acted upon, however, peace on the coast was rudely broken.

The two very different aims—peaceful conversion of the Indians and enslavement—could hardly have co-existed in the same general area for long. When the missions were first established, and for some time thereafter, the armadores concentrated on Los Gigantes (Curaçao) and smaller islands surrounding it. They were drawn to these, one would expect, by reports brought back from shipmasters trading between Santo Domingo and Panama. A little later, a ship captain touched on the large island of Trinidad where he captured Indians considered Caribs, thus beginning more or less regular slaving expeditions to that island.[34] None of these expeditions threatened the missions, which lay between these two distant points. But by 1519 Spaniards began to draw ever closer to Cumaná. Barter for pearls on Cubagua and Margarita had by that year proved that pearls were available in great number if organized pearl fishing, rather than barter, was established. By authorization of the Crown, Licentiate Figueroa named a young companion of his, Antonio Flores, alcalde mayor of Cubagua; Flores established a formal town, Nueva Cádiz,[35] and was to supervise pearl fishing, to see that the Crown received its one-fifth, and to see that friendly Indians were well treated and only Caribs enslaved. That same year, Figueroa declared certain areas of the coast to be Carib lands, and others to be inhabited by *guatiao* or friendly Indians.[36] Meanwhile armadores attracted by pearl fishing and slaving converged on Cubagua in great numbers; to older investors such as Rodrigo de Bastidas and the Becerros were now added Juan Fernández de las Varas, who farmed the almojarifazgo tax, and Diego Caballero el Mozo, among others. The judges and treasury officials were regular investors in these enterprises, or at least claimed a share in them as compensation for granting a sailing license.[37] The Puerto Rican vecinos were equally interested in pearl fishing—indeed they vainly asked for a monopoly on the enterprise owing to their poverty and geographical position.[38] The treasurer Andrés de Haro had entered into a partnership with the Palos ship captain Antón Casinos;[39] Francisco de Barrionuevo, who had married into the Becerro family on Española and later relocated in Puerto Rico, was among the most enterprising. He transferred some of his Bahama Indian slaves to Cubagua (they live in the water, he explained when asking permission of the Santo Domingo authorities), and secured use of the island of Mona and its Indians as a provisioning ground for supplying cassava for his own and other expeditions bound for the pearl fishing grounds.[40]

Another enterprise brought Spaniards even closer to the missions on the Cumaná river. Southward from Cubagua lay the Peninsula of Araya with its great salt beds, increasingly a necessary commodity for preserving meat and especially, one supposes, for curing hides to be exported to Spain. Finally, since Cubagua or Margarita lacked a water supply, all enterprises were dependent on the mouth of the Cumaná for fresh water, thus bringing many Spaniards into contact with the Franciscan mission situated nearby.

Though contacts between ship captains and missionaries were usually friendly, it was predictable that sooner or later Indians would be seized as slaves; even if not neophytes, the potential captives at least lived near the missions and were on friendly terms with the friars. The older slave hunting grounds were probably desolate by this time, for the Indians who had not been captured had fled to the interior—a continuous process along the Spanish Main during the sixteenth century. Indians were becoming scarcer, but tribes living near the missions had thus far known only friendly Spaniards and were caught off-guard. Captain Alonso de Ojeda (presumably unrelated to the deceased explorer) precipitated events leading to the destruction of the missions by capturing thirty Tagares Indians at a village, Marapacana, on September 1, 1520.[41] The village was near the Dominican mission on the Cumaná. When a local cacique, Gil González de Avila, who had adopted the Espanola contador's name, learned of this, he at once (September 3) attacked the Dominican mission, killing the two Dominicans, a friar and a lay worker, as well as nine neophytes. A few days later he fell upon the unsuspecting Captain Ojeda, and after first feigning friendship, attacked the Spaniards, killing the captain and seven of his men; the remainder escaped by *barco* to Cubagua where an Indian interpreter from the Dominican missions had already preceded them with news of the rising.

The exact order of events over the next several weeks—or months—is not clear, owing to inadequate and contradictory information. Flores sent out reconnaissance ships but even as he did so, armadores, who did not realize that the Indians were in revolt, called at or near Marapacana. They were greeted by the Indians with the usual outward friendliness, and then were attacked. In September alone, if dates are correct, two expeditions lost a total of thirty-three men killed. Flores meanwhile evacuated the Franciscans to Cubagua and apparently because aid from Santo Domingo was tardy in coming, withdrew with all settlers, arriving in Santo Domingo on November 30. The Indians followed up their attacks by burning the Franciscan missions. The coast and the pearl fishing islands were for the time being swept free of Spaniards.

Diego Colón, whose presence was counted on to prevent just such a disaster as this, arrived in Santo Domingo on November 12[42] to find the officials fitting out an expedition of one hundred men under the armador Gonzalo de Ocampo. When Flores reached the port with news of still more serious attacks, Colón and the officials thought it expedient to enlarge the expedition to two hundred men and six ships.[43] These preparations—the purchase of ships and provisions, the recruiting of men (presumably Colón insisted that the men sail on salary rather than with license to capture and sell Indians, which led to indiscriminate attacks)—all took time. Ocampo's mission was to punish the guilty Indians, to capture and enslave all those he could, and to restore the Franciscan mission.[44] Friar Vithern, believing he could re-establish friendly relations with his surviving neophytes and Indian friends, went along. Friar Córdoba, the Dominican provincial, evidently thought better of continuing the Cumaná mission and concentrated on establishing additional monasteries in the islands, finally choosing Puerto Rico in 1521.[45] Ocampo departed Santo Domingo in January, 1521, with five ships, stopped in San Germán, Puerto Rico where he bought a sixth, and by March was seeking out and capturing the Indians along the coast.[46]

The vecinos were even more anxious to re-establish the pearl and salt trade on which Española now greatly depended. Flores, whose conduct was felt to be less than heroic, had in any case to be replaced since he was a Figueroa appointee. The appointment of a new alcalde mayor fell to Diego Colón who by the same token gained control of the pearl trade and was in a position to see that his one-tenth, still disputed in Spain, would be collected in spite of the opposition of the veteran treasurer Pasamonte. Colón selected, on whose recommendation is unknown, Francisco de Vallejo, a resident of Santo Domingo since Ovando's time who had formerly served under Pedrarias in Panama and had reconnoitered the Paria coast after the Indians killed two Dominicans at Piritú in 1515.[47] Vallejo sailed in April, 1521,[48] for Cubagua where he re-established Nueva Cádiz, resuming pearl fishing there and on the adjacent island of Margarita.

Thus far Colón had apparently lived up to expectations for by his efforts the Venezuelan coast was made safe for the Franciscans, with the pearl and salt trade re-established under supervision of his alcalde mayor. But the situation and his reputation were alike vulnerable. Even Las Casas, however, must have conceded that Colón had perforce to deal with a situation not of his own making and that, with closer supervision in the future, the Franciscan missions and his own projected peaceful colonization could look forward to progress. Las Casas had reached Puerto Rico in January, 1521, just in time to meet Ocampo and protest his armed expedition to Venezuela. But the desertion of most of the men Las Casas brought from Spain, the condemnation of the vessel he brought in Puerto Rico as unseaworthy, and the scant funds at his disposal, all combined to oblige him to make a contact with the officials in Santo Domingo. This contract formed a joint stock company for the purposes of settling the long stretch of coast granted Las Casas and engaging in peaceful barter with the Indians. The document was drawn up in July, 1521;[49] the investors included Colón who put in one-eighth, and Ocampo, whose expedition had by this time returned with slaves. Ocampo, with Las Casas and his few companions, then sailed from Santo Domingo in late July and after stopping in Puerto Rico, reached Cumaná in August.[50]

Las Casas soon perceived that both his own enterprise and the Franciscan mission, near which he put up his warehouses, were doomed to an early extinction if the Indian slave raids continued. Vessels from Cubagua, which Vallejo either could not or would not control, called on pretensions of renewing friendships, wheedled the Indians out of the bush with offers of wine, and dragged them aboard while drunk. Ocampo's men who were, had the contact been taken seriously, under Las Casas's orders, gradually drifted away to Cubagua, and in November, Las Casas made the short trip to the island to warn Vallejo of the probably disastrous consequences of slaving in the proximity of the missions. He received no assurances, and after returning to Cumaná, decided, after many misgivings, to sail for Santo Domingo to appeal either to Diego Colón or directly to the king. He departed on a salt ship from the Peninsula de Araya in December, reaching Santo Domingo after some delay, in March, 1522.[51]

During his absence, Indians attacked the small settlement on the Cumaná, killing five persons, including Las Casas's second in command. The mission and warehouse were burned to the ground, and the few survivors fled to the coast where they managed to hail a brigantine coming for fresh water.[52] Las Casas was mortified on learning of the tragedy; he subsequently wrote to the king, who returned to Spain in July, 1522, that this second destruction of the mission would not have occurred except for the negligence of Colón's alcalde mayor.[53] This report, with another supplied by Las Casas's contador, Miguel de Castellanos,[54] went far toward turning the king against Colón, though his part in the Venezuelan fiasco was but one of the bad marks set down against him. Clearly the viceroy had made himself partner to the unsavory matter of Indian slavery, for he had invested in expeditions that soon went far beyond mere punitive action. Colón was trapped by his accustomed lifestyle and his large body of retainers, impossible to support on the declining Española economy without participating in whatever enterprises were profitable. The Paria coast venture cost him the support of the reformers, which was not regained even though he replaced Vallejo in September, 1522, with Jácome de Castellón, who erected, by March, 1523, the first fort at Cumaná beside a town that he christened Nuevo Toledo.[55] The water supply was thus assured, but the missionaries now turned away, for some years, to other parts of the New World.

When Colón returned to the islands, he needed to reassert control over the area that fell within his viceroyalty, and the instrument at hand was his power to appoint tenientes and alcaldes mayores. He had stopped at San Juan de Puerto Rico en route to Santo Domingo, where he named Pedro Moreno, then an alcalde ordinario, his teniente.[56] Antonio de la Gama, who already was on notice that he was to be relieved as justicia mayor, reverted to *juez de comisión* (commissioner) in charge of Indian affairs.[57] How Moreno, who was at one time secretary for Governor Ovando, came into Colón's confidence is not clear, but since he was alcalde ordinario at least by 1519,[58] following Colón's reauthorization to name justices in the Indies, he must have been recommeded, perhaps by the Cerón-Díaz families who had long supported his father. The change of command here was devoid of friction, though members of the city council protested Colón's insistence that no meeting could be held without

Moreno being present. At Santo Domingo, Colón named Gonzalo de Ovalle, former criado of the Duke of Alba, his teniente,[59] a position not considered necessary before. Colón felt the need to shore up his authority at all points, and Ovalle had served him loyally since 1509. Colón left Jamaica untouched, where his uncle by marriage, Francisco de Garay, still governed as teniente; but in contrast with Colón's earlier governorship, when Cuba was left alone under Diego de Velázquez while Puerto Rico was the scene of forcible changes of command, it was Cuba that now claimed his attention.

Though a full explanation by Colón of his motives in sending Alonso Zuazo to Cuba has not been found, it is clear that Velázquez had long since thrown off the substance, if not the form, of Colón's authority over him, represented by the title teniente de gobernador. After Colón's deposition in 1515, the Cuban treasury had withheld paying Colón one-tenth of the royal revenue, on various excuses.[60] Moreover, Valázquez's close relationship with Bishop Rodríguez de Fonseca was well known, and his acquiring title of *adelantado* of Yucatán was a move of at least dubious loyalty, from Colón's point of view. It is likely, too, that Colón, who put in a claim to one-tenth the income from the Mexican mainland, had in mind legitimizing Cortés's break with Velázquez by naming Zuazo the effective teniente of Cuba, thereby inducing Cortés, presumably grateful for such protection, to agree that the newly conquered land was an addition to the viceroyalty from which his expedition had originated. This aim of Colón was illustrated, after Zuazo reached Cuba, by his suspension of Velázquez's pesquisa of Cortés on the request of Francisco Altamirano, the conqueror's cousin;[61] Zuazo would later serve Cortés as alcalde mayor. Of course neither Diego Velázquez nor still less Diego Colón found their claims to New Spain supported by Charles who in 1522 named Cortés governor.

Zuazo reached Santiago de Cuba in early January, 1521, vested with Colón's full powers, indeed with more than his legitimate powers in the judgment of the Council of Castile. Zuazo was empowered to hold Velazquez's residencia, to name tenientes and city officials, and to redistribute encomiendas.[62] Though available documents furnish a sparse picture of his actions, he set about with characteristic vigor to hold a pesquisa on Velázquez's long governorship. He appointed various officials including Vasco Porcallo de Figueroa as teniente at Trinidad.[63] In sending Zuazo to Cuba, Colón defied the orders of the government in December, 1520,[64] repeated several times in 1521,[65] to restore Velázquez to command and recall Zuazo, since the latter was himself still under residencia. Colón apparently saw in the orders not the power of the Crown but the machinations of Rodríguez de Fonseca, and must have felt that the king would concur with his actions when he returned to Spain. Since certain of the cédulas were sent direct to Velázquez, and Zuazo continued as teniente until early 1523, it may be surmised that Zuazo set aside these cédulas with Colon's approval.

Two serious matters occurred in Cuba that required the personal investigation of Colón and the oidores Villalobos and Matienzo in early 1522. Both matters related to Vasco Porcallo. He was accused of the especially brutal act, justified by the circumstances in his opinion, of cutting off the genitalia of several Indians, and stuffing them into their mouths. This was done, he claimed, in a desperate effort to prevent the Indians from committing suicide by eating dirt, a method which had become fairly widespread.[66] The reason for suicide, as the Spaniards understood it, was their horror at being torn from their native villages and sent to New Spain, as had been done with hundreds who had been put aboard the expeditions of Cortés, and more recently, in 1520, of Narváez. The matter did not relate to Zuazo's government but was serious enough to require the personal investigation of the two oidores. Vasco was presumably acquitted for he is known to have lived on Cuba as a prominent vecino many years thereafter.

In a second incident, Vasco Porcallo and some twenty followers learned that, in defiance of his authority as teniente, the city council at Sancti Spiritus had, in 1521, elected alcaldes ordinarios. The election represented the clash of authority resulting from instructions issued by the Governors in Castile, prompted by Rodríguez de Fonseca, and those given Zuazo by Colón, whose authority Vasco Porcallo represented. Vasco and his men invaded the town, seized what they considered the rebel officials, and dragged one of them to jail, tearing his clothing and pulling out his hair as he sought to resist.[67] Between January and March, 1522,[68] while in Santiago de Cuba, Colón and the two oidores resolved these issues and also investigated the reasons that the renter of the almojarifazgo had gone bankrupt; the three officials then returned to Española, leaving Zuazo as judge; finally, in March, 1523, Colón replaced Zuazo with Gonzalo de Ovalle.[69] Ovalle was himself deposed by Velázquez at least by July,[70] for by this time Colón himself had been finally relieved as viceroy and was soon to make his last voyage back to Spain. The Council of Castile, with Charles agreeing, decided that Colón had exceeded his powers in Cuba.

The destruction of the missions on Paria and the defiance of royal power on Cuba were only two instances of Colón's unfortunate and futile struggle to assert a viceregal power that went against the grain of bureaucratic and, to a degree, localist sentiment. His final term, lasting less than three years, saw the Acuerdo, the warnings of Rodríguez de Fonseca notwithstanding, dissolve after the first few months to such an extent that Colón wielded virtually all power in spite of the audiencia. Colón, like an angry lion, thus sought to disentangle himself from the net woven by Rodríguez de Fonseca after the restatement of his powers won from the king after five long years.

Though he had the support of various Colombistas in Santo Domingo, such as Gonzalo de Ovalle and Diego Méndez who served as alguacil mayor, he was perhaps unexpectedly bolstered by the gravitation of Licentiate Figueroa to his side. Finding himself by 1520 much hated for removing Indians from encomenderos who mistreated them and also resented by Pasamonte and other officials, Figueroa became Colón's legal adviser even as he continued to serve as commission judge in charge of the Indians.[71] With Figueroa's advice, Colón would carry out certain of the maneuvers that largely offset or nullified the effects of legislation curbing his power. Earlier he had himself resorted to using unauthorized powers adhering to the title of admiral. Since his contract prohibited naming alcaldes ordinarios, Colón, with dubious legality in this case, decided that as admiral he could appoint *alcaldes del mar*, or judges with cognizance in the first instance of maritime matters in seaports.[72] Since most important economic questions in the islands, such as Indian slaves, pearls, and salt, fell within this category, the maneuver largely compensated him for the deprivation in the contract. After Lebrón's appointment as the fourth oidor, rendering it less likely that Colón's vote would be decisive, Colón arrogated to himself, as viceroy, cognizance of cases affecting royal interests,[73] which had the effect of leaving the audiencia with only cases between private parties.

These tactics eventually drove Colón and the oidores so far apart that they were scarcely on speaking terms. Colón also lost the support of many vecinos, some of whom had believed in 1518 that he should be recalled to govern the island. Colón had found himself with much less income in 1520 than he had during his earlier governorship. His encomiendas had been removed, gold mining was but a third of what it had been before,[74] and various concessions made by the Crown—no tax on Indian slaves or on inter-island trade—had additionally reduced royal income. As a result, Colón's one-tenth amounted to much less than it had before. He believed it within his rights to repudiate some of these measures, for they had been carried out without consulting him. Thus he reinstated a tax on Indian slaves, quietly put aside the cédulas reducing the fifth on gold to one-tenth, and sought to make up for his declining income in other ways, by investing in slaving expeditions and by imposing annoying fees, such as one for anchorage in Santo Domingo port.[75]

By 1522 complaints of his illegal and arbitrary acts began to pile up at court; the oidor Ayllón departed in the fall of 1521 with a lengthy memoir indicting Colón for wrongfully appropriating cognizance in cases of royal interest.[76] Las Casas's damaging reports about Colón's failure to protect the missions followed the next year, and by early 1523 Charles had neard other details from Las Casas's contador Castellanos, along with complaints from the Santiago de Cuba city council of Zuazo's unauthorized actions. Colón no doubt grew uneasy, for Charles had returned in July, 1522, and had for a time issued neither assurances of support nor criticism in response to the reports he was surely familiar with. Perhaps more sensitive to the case building up against him, Colón sought harmony on his island appendages. Hence his replacement of Zuazo with Ovalle in Cuba in 1523, his appointment of Castellón to replace Vallego on Cubagua, and his temporary replacement of Pedro Moreno, as teniente on Puerto Rico, with Bishop Manso in 1522.[77] This last alteration was due to a conflict that had risen between Moreno and Francisco Valázquez, borther of the deceased Sancho, who had been sent out to audit the treasury accounts (since Isásaga had taken too much time on Española) and had become involved in a dispute with Moreno over his brother's properties and debts.[78] Colón probably realized that he had lost the confidence of the king, for the latter named Ayllón in April, 1523, to investigate the matter as well as to act as juez de residencia for Colón's appointees on Puerto Rico.[79]

In March, 1523, Charles issued an order reprimanding Colón for exceeding his powers, arrogating to himself virtually all appellate cognizance, intervening in Indian affairs, collecting his one-tenth from illegal sources and exercising Church patronage—he had named one or two canons and rationers at Santo Domingo.[80] The same order revoked all such acts. It was not publicized until August by which time the king had decided to recall him for discussions. In the Crown's view, he had clearly infringed royal residual power by exercising patronage, though this charge was probably selected as the most palpable. Colón was probably induced to make the appointments by Bishop Geraldini, owing to the king's absence.

Colón drew up his last will before embarking for Spain on September 8, 1523.[81] He expected to return, for he asked that he be buried in the Franciscan monastery in Santo Domingo if he died in that city. But as it turned out, his departure marked the end of the effective Columbian viceroyalty and almost the end—he would die in Spain in 1526—of Colón's long struggle to maintain and enhance it. As he set sail, he did not view himself as capriciously disobedient, but as the faithful son of the Admiral, "my Lord and father," devoted to protecting the mayorazgo he courageously won, and obediently returning to consult with his overlord. Tenacious as he was in upholding a cause in which self-interest was prominent, Colón believed unshakably in something outside himself. Committing his soul to the Creator and espousing loyalty to his king, he prepared himself to run the gauntlet of French corsairs on the Atlantic, leaving María, who was about to give birth to their eighth child, as *virreina.*

7

Church, State, and Society by 1526

Diego Colón's departure for Castile came at a time when Spain was beginning to strengthen its position in Europe and the Indies, while the Church was finally becoming reasonably solvent. Early Spanish Caribbean society was entering its second generation, thus demonstrating its viability in spite of all the restlessness, the almost constant migrations, the Indian population's attrition, the decline of the mines, and the slow evolution toward a sugar cane economy. The audiencia was intended to be, from its inception in 1512, the chief representative of royal power in the Indies. Yet it had remained weak for several reasons. The vestigial feudalism so casually passed to Christopher Columbus in 1492, and so adamantly advanced by his son, Diego, had greatly hampered the effectiveness of the judicial body. Colón had interposed his own appellate powers between the towns and the audiencia, and virtually nullified the latter's effectiveness during the years of his government. Then, too, the audiencia came under the weakening influence of Las Casas's attacks as he accused it of being callous to the condition of the Indians and financially interested in encomiendas, forced labor, and Indian slavery. Finally, the unusual personality of Pasamonte, his long (seventeen years) service as treasurer and the power accruing to him from his control of the largest capital resources available, further prevented the audiencia from exercising the general governmental powers that would distinguish it in later years.

It could not be expected that the judges would derive much advantage from Colón's absence between 1515 and 1520, for Zuazo was empowered to suspend the judicial body during what became a long, interrupted, and incomplete residencia. The audiencia's recovery even after its restoration in 1519 was very slow. The first effort to exert its powers outside Española met with failure: the sending of Ayllón in 1520 to Cuba, and hence to Veracruz, in a vain effort to prevent the sailing of Narváez's large expedition to New Spain. Ayllón's mission ended ignominiously with Narváez shipping him back to Cuba. All Ayllón could do on reaching Santo Domingo was to file charges of *lese majeste* against Diego Velázquez and Narváez—even though such charges were of no consequence to a harried Spanish government fleeing from the comuneros. The judges had then so little prestige that Narváez's representatives could plausibly argue at Guaniguanico in March, 1520, that the audiencia had been suspended and they had not seen the order officially restoring it to power.[1] From that nadir, the judges began slowly to acquire a stronger position. In 1521 the addition of a fourth judge, Cristóbal Lebrón, often made it possible for one or two judges to be off conducting investigations on other islands. Even before Colón left, two of the judges, Villalobos and Matienzo, had asserted their power at Santiago de Cuba. The government in Spain henceforth began to use the judges as juezes de residencia, naming Lebrón in 1523 to take the residencias of Rodrigo de Figueroa and Antonio Flores, Figueroa's alcalde mayor on Cubagua;[2] in 1523, Ayllón was appointed juez de residencia for the officials in Puerto Rico.[3] The audiencia's scope of authority was further broadened with the sending of Pedro de Moreno, the fiscal, to Honduras in 1525 to mediate a dispute between Gil González Dávila and Cortés's lieutenant in Trujillo.[4] That same year, the king authorized the audiencia to name a governor for that newly occupied region.[5]

The audiencia's earlier weakness was in part related to the concomitant weakness of the government in Spain. Not until the return in 1522 of the matured Charles did any regent or monarch firmly grasp the reins of power that had fallen from Ferdinand's slackened hands in his late, ailing years. Cardinal Jiménez de Cisneros's rule was too short and too tentative to permit formulation of a policy for the Indies; then, too, his Christianity was more militant and impatient than the reformers desired in Indian relations, an attitude that resolved few if any of Española's problems in 1516 and 1517. From the outset Charles had more sources of revenue than his grandfather ever enjoyed, for he was king of all Spain and had the right—necessarily to be tempered with good judgment—to draw upon all the kingdoms for subsidies. He thus had access to considerable funds which he misspent on court festivals and capricious patronage, resulting in a weakly supported social reform in the Indies and an alienated constituency in Castile among the *meseta* towns. He soon became wholly preocuppied with acquiring the Holy Roman Empire and he left Spain in 1520, entrusting to three inexperienced governors the immensely critical task of maintaining royal authority. In this power, vacuum, Colón enjoyed, or at least resurrected, a final Indian summer of political feudalism, and Cortés with his luck and genius, confronted the returning Emperor with an irreversible fait accompli in New Spain, thus demonstrating that if one would rebel, he must do so grandly, and above all, successfully.

The monarch who returned to Spain in 1522 was very different from the naive youth of 1517. The threat of the comunero revolt, though broken at Villalar in 1521, combined with the demonstrated audacity of the French king who had twice invaded northern Spain, to impel Charles to deal forthrightly with disloyalty, and to consolidate and strengthen royal power in all ways feasible. Soon after he reached Spain in July, 1522, he had some two hundred comunero ringleaders tried and executed, and in the next year he incorporated the four remaining military orders into the Crown and acquired patronage over the Spanish Church;[6] in 1524 he reorganized the Council of the Indies as an independent body, putting at its head the Dominican bishop of Osma, Friar García de Loaísa.[7]

These actions paralleled measures taken about the same time in the Indies. Though Charles and his council saw fit to name Cortés governor in New Spain, Colón had nothing to extenuate his misgovernment of the Indies—neither great wealth nor new conquests. With his removal, and the strengthening of the audiencia's power, the only official still needed was a president for that judicial body—someone trained in the law, honest, moral and above the petty squabbles over Indians and pearls. As he had done with the Council of the Indies and the Santo Domingo audiencia, the king sought a friar or priest. But a long delay ensued as the first three appointees died before taking office. The bishop of Concepción, Pedro Suárez de Deza, died in September, 1522, and the next two appointees, Luis de Figueroa and Alonso de Santo Domingo, died in 1524 and 1525, respectively.[8] Bishop Sebastián Ramírez de Fuenleal was finally selected in 1526, and he sailed for Santo Domingo the following year. He was to be bishop of both Concepción and Santo Domingo, as well as president of the audiencia—an arrangement that economized on the treasury's inadequate funds.

The island episcopacies, like the state institutions, also moved during these last years toward greater solvency, though the progress was slow and uneven. Since Suárez de Deza's departure in 1516, there had been no bishops in the Indies for three years, until Bishop Alexandre Geraldini finally arrived in Santo Domingo to occupy his see.[9] Bishop Manso of Puerto Rico returned in 1520[10] after an absence of five years. But not until after 1526 did Cuba have a resident bishop or Jamaica, a resident abbot. The Church's financial problems had been virtually unsolvable as long as mining was the main economic activity, since Ferdinand had exempted precious metals from the tithe. Though all four of the bishops had skeletal staffs after 1515, even those few canons or rationers had, as we have seen, to resort to devious means to support themselves, such as exacting inflated fees and entering into mining covertly with one or more partners.

Though a tithe was collected on agriculture and livestock during these years, the total amount was too meager even to support such priests as were resident on the islands. A great many of the islanders were temporary residents, soon to migrate to Cuba and from there to Mexico, or to return to Spain. They defaulted on their obligation to pay tithes, leaving the Church with little income from that source. On the other hand, the tendency for the bishops to remain in Spain and collect the tithe, or at least half of it, caused many vecinos to evade payment while at the same time demanding, as was done in 1518–1520, that bishops reside in their sees. All the episcopacies thus floundered until after 1520.

Charles placed the bishoprics on a better financial base than Ferdinand could afford to do, for after 1520 he could count on wide resources, such as those connected with the Fugger and Welser financial empires. Beginning in 1518 he gave over the *tercia,* the traditional one-third of the tithes, to the episcopacies for construction of stone cathedrals;[11] in 1519 the tithe on dyewood, previously exempted whether by the king's orders or the local treasury's decision, was granted for Cuba and was probably in effect for the other islands.[12] In 1523, the king extended to Cuba an earlier general order for the Indies that the tithe be paid on royal haciendas, which the island treasury had heretofore considered exempt.[13] The base for tithing thus became broader by official action; at the same time increased agricultural production raised the tithe on sugar, livestock, and cassia fistula.

In 1523 Bishop Geraldini was able to begin, after so many years' delay, the construction of a stone cathedral in Santo Domingo. The labor was largely performed, one may suppose, by Negro slaves who were more numerous by this time. Bishop Manso might not have been much better off in 1520 than he was five years earlier, had it not been that he came out as Apostolic Inquisitor, for which he drew an additional salary; furthermore he served as teniente of the island from 1522 to 1524. How his financial problems were otherwise solved is not clear, but he had not begun building a stone cathedral by 1526. Though Cuba did not have a resident bishopric, the episcopal see was put on an improved basis by its transfer to Santiago de Cuba in 1522, and by the several orders of the king assuring it a good basis for tithing.

The two main religious orders, the Dominicans and Franciscans, had also gained markedly in influence since the early days when the reformados sought vainly to abolish the encomienda outright, and the conventual Franciscans contented themselves with converting a few caciques' sons. The Dominicans had abandoned for the time being their aim to convert Indians in isolated lands and established a second monastery in San Juan de Puerto Rico (1521) where they planned to train young neophytes for mission work; in Santa Marta, and especially in New Spain, they and the Franciscans would find their work crowned with much greater success than had been possible in the islands. The Franciscans remained the leading order in Santo Domingo, but both orders continued in the king's favor; in 1525 Charles turned over supervision of the Indians to the friars, thus abolishing the position of civil commissioner which had existed since the Cisneros-Casas reforms.[14] There were still Indians to convert or catechize on all four of the islands, with an unknown number in the mountainous interiors where, wiser to Spanish ways, they long survived ultimately to be absorbed by the complex process of *mestizaje*. Enriquillo's forces still held out in the mountains of Jaraguá and were to be won over only in the 1530's when they were offered advantageous terms; some Indians were also rebelling in Cuba's Oriente.[15] This was one more manifestation of the Taínos' astuteness and intelligence in what was presumably a single cultural zone: southwestern Española and eastern Cuba.

Of the several thousand Spaniards who emigrated to the islands during the first twenty-five or thirty years, a few score settled permanently to establish Spanish society in the Caribbean. Economic survival, however, depended on adjusting to economic change, and on moving with the peripheralization of settlements that was everywhere the tendency as mines declined and greater dependence on offshore trade followed. The interior of

Española hollowed out as Santo Domingo and Puerto Plata, suitable sugar ports, absorbed vecinos who did not leave the island; Caparra passed from existence about 1520 when the port of San Juan de Puerto Rico was founded; Sevilla la Nueva on Jamaica was only resituated a short distance to make it a better port.[16] Santiago de Cuba soon became the early leading port in Cuba, although contemporary with the conquest of Mexico, the northern port of Havana came into existence[17] as settlers at San Cristóbal de Habana on the southern coast sought to take advantage of the new shipping lane from Veracruz through the Florida channel to the Atlantic and Spain.[18]

Flexibility as the key to economic survival is well illustrated by Francisco de Barrionuevo's relocations from Española to Puerto Rico and, finally, once more to Española at Puerto Plata. Barrionuevo migrated to Puerto Rico from Santiago de los Caballeros shortly after Ponce's initial settlement of the island. He remained there about ten years during which time he married Elvira, the wealthy *mestiza* heir of Rodrigo Manzorro of Santiago. Barrionuevo engaged in the Venezuelan Indian slave and pearl trades profiting additionally from the grant of Mona Island which armadores used for provisons. In 1519, perhaps because the pearl trade was temporarily in decline, he relocated in Puerto Plata where he went into business with Pedro de Barrionuevo, presumably a relative, who owned a sugar plantation back of the port.[19] Puerto Plata was evidently growing in population, for several Spaniards reported that Santiago was almost depopulated in 1520 and should be combined with Puerto Plata to make one sizable town.[20] Near the port, Ayllón owned cassava plantations which he drew upon in outfitting his expedition to the coast of North Carolina in the mid-1520's.[21]

A much greater convergence of Española's remaining population occurred in and around Santo Domingo. Many vecinos from the hinterland moved to the capital by 1520, among them Juan de Villoria, formerly of Concepción, and García de Lerma and Gonzalo de Ocampo, formerly of Buenaventura.[22] The capital functioned as a magnet with the decline in mining. One, however, had to be on good terms with the Santo Domingo officials in order to get permission to sail to Venezuela for salt, slaves, or pearls. Yet trade alone was not the capital's only attraction; the rivers flowing southward from the central range, several near the capital, furnished the water power and the means of transportation for an incipient sugar industry.

Columbus had brought the first sugar cane to Española on his second voyage and its adaptability to the climate and soil was soon appreciated, though cane was raised only for molasses during the early years.[23] The commercial growing of sugar cane was advocated as early as 1515;[24] within five years a few *ingenios* (water powered mills) had been established along the south coast. By 1520 the few surviving Indians were unavailable for mine labor; this spurred on many Spaniards to form partnerships, secure land and water rights, import Negroes legally or illegally, and establish water-powered mills. Investing in sugar mills was the way local officials absorbed the loss of encomiendas; by 1520 or after, such officials as the treasurer Esteban Pasamonte (after his uncle Miguel Pasamonte's death in 1525), the fiscal Pedro Vázquez de Mella, the contador Alonso de Avila (relative of Gil González Dávila and his successor about 1520), the oidores Lebrón and (after 1525) Zuazo—all owned mills singly or in partnerships.[25] Diego Colón's plantation near Santo Domingo was supported by at least forty Negro slaves as early as 1522.[26] One of the most successful sugar planters was Hernando Gorjón of Azua, who after 1526 became famous for endowing a *colegio* in Santo Domingo, forerunner of the first university in America.[27]

Though Negroes were never imported in accordance with demand until 1526,[28] there were already nineteen mills, the single greatest concentration on Española, dotting the coastal river valleys from Azua to Santo Domingo.[29] The commercial production of sugar was barely begun in Puerto Rico, where Tomás de Castellón had established a mill at San Germán,[30] and in Jamaica where

Garay and Mazuelo owned a few mills. In Cuba, where mining still held up fairly well for the dwindling number of vecinos, the cultivation of sugar cane was not begun until much later.[31]

Few, if any, vecinos on Española had weathered the economic vicissitudes of the preceding decades better than Rodrigo de Bastidas, the merchant-navigator from Seville. One of the first shipowners on the island, he had relied upon the maritime trade, farmed the almojarifazgo, and hunted Indians along the Spanish Main, rather than seek encomiendas and mines. By the time of his death, about 1527, he owned thousands of head of livestock and several ships, and was publicly known to put up scores of criados and *estantes* (temporary residents) in his *posada.* He had realized the seignorial dream and had privately supported the Church in Santo Domingo when its financial resources were meager. Perhaps for this reason his son, Rodrigo, was appointed dean of the cathedral there (by 1527) and subsequently became the second bishop of Puerto Rico.[32]

As the placer mines were played out on Puerto Rico, the inhabitants converged on San Juan, the northern port whose settlement was initiated about 1520 and completed by 1522. Juan Ponce de León, who had built his stone house at Caparra in 1509, disapproved of the relocation but the majority felt that commerce must be given every advantage if the island was to have a future. San Germán soon declined, for its placers were overrated; Miguel Díaz, founder of the *villa,* thrived for a time there as a merchant, importing goods on credit from the Grimaldo family of Seville. Early settlers in San Germán included Vasco and García Troche, who were joined in 1514 by a third brother, Gaspar, from Panama.[33] Though the Troches fared well through the changes of government, partly because they, like Sancho Velázquez, were former residents of Olmedo, Spain,[34] by 1519 they had moved to the capital in keeping with the gravitation to the best commercial ports.

In Cuba by this time, several recently-arrived families were already well established: Gonzalo de Guzmán, who arrived in 1517, was by 1524 royal treasurer and heir to Velázquez's vast land holdings and encomiendas;[35] his brother-in-law Pedro Núñez de Guzmán came the following year,[36] possibly accompanied by his own brother-in-law, Pedro de Paz. These new arrivals, all royal officials as well as city officers at Santiago de Cuba, the main town and capital, formed with Duero and Narváez a closely knit clique which successfully opposed official intervention represented by Zuazo and later Juan de Altamirano.

The most prominent settler in Jamaica was Francisco de Garay who remained until 1523 as co-partner with the king in a company supplying cassava, cotton, and livestock to Panama and Cuba. After Garay died in 1523, his properties, including livestock, land, and two sugar mills,[37] passed to his son.

In spite of the thirty years of restlessness and discontent that characterized the early Spanish Caribbean, a small social hierarchy had appeared by 1526. The highest title then attained, discounting Diego Colón's often vague viceroy and admiral, was that of adelantado, granted in the islands to only three persons: Bartolomé Colón, Juan Ponce de León, and Diego Velázquez. But at the pinnacle of Caribbean society during this time was undoubtedly the Colón family. Diego Colón not only inherited his father's titles of viceroy and admiral, but in 1514 his uncle Bartolomé's title of adelantado as well; moreover he more than anyone else could give substance to the social rank he held by use of the one-tenth of income guaranteed him and the many emoluments that accrued to him as a result of the power he periodically exercised. From his father, too, he held a mayorazgo thus assuring his ownership of lands on Española and his right to the coat of arms received by his father.

Given the underpopulation of the Spanish Caribbean at this time, Colón's children could hardly hope to marry upward in the New World. The best marriage on Española would link the family with the letrado class, and of the eight children Diego Colón left, only one, Cristóbal, the next to the oldest son, would make this kind of marriage. He was united with Leonor Zuazo, daughter of the brilliant but controversial Licentiate Alonso Zuazo who, by 1526, had returned to Española to live out his life as oidor in the now fully constituted audiencia. Otherwise, the oldest son and heir to the mayorazgo, Luis Colón, by his second marriage, wed Maria de Mosquera, daughter of Juan de Mosquera of Santo Domingo.[38] Later, the often married wastrel Luis, acquired the empty titles of Duke of Veragua and Marquis of Jamaica as the long suit between the Crown and the Columbus family was finally settled in essentially monetary terms. Diego Colón's widow Maria managed rather better for two of her daughters, after she returned to Spain. Isabel, the youngest, married Don Jorge de Portugal, Count of Gelves, and Juana married Luis de la Cueva, brother of the third Duke of Alburquerque.[39]

The first family of early Puerto Rico was undoubtedly that of Ponce de León, the first settler and loyal vassal of Ferdinand during the early conflict with Columbian feudalism. Ponce largely turned away from Puerto Rican affairs after his second deposition in 1511, and had discovered Florida in 1513 for which he was named adelantado. But he was unable to follow up on this discovery until 1521. Ferdinand commissioned him in 1515 to make war on the Caribs and open up a wood-and-water station for the Panama route in the Lesser Antilles. This mission proved impossible to execute owing to Carib ferocity and the desertion of most of his salaried crew, attracted by freelance slaving opportunities with the Santo Domingo armadores.[40] Ponce then found it necessary to get confirmation of his contract to settle Florida with the new king, a matter that kept him in Spain until 1518; in order to clear his name of charges of defalcation in the royal company of 1508–1510, he preferred charges against Sancho Velázquez in the pesquisa of 1519. By 1520 Ponce was a widower with the need to marry off his three daughters. His youngest daughter Isabel, married Licentiate Antonio de la Gama in 1520, a marriage signifying a hidalgo-letrado alliance, and for Gama, a sharing in the honor of a great explorer's family. Juana and Maria, the older daughters, married the Troche brothers, Garcia and Gaspar, merchant entrepreneurs.[41] Gaspar was subsequently engaged in shipping livestock to the newly established Trujillo, Honduras, in the mid-1520's.[42] Since Ponce's only son, Luis, entered the newly established Dominican order at San Juan, the Ponce name was not directly perpetuated, but bore the name of Troche. Antonio de la Gama's marriage to Isabel was childless, for she died shortly after.[43]

Although Diego Velázquez's marriage plans failed, and though he has been most well known in history for losing control of his bold lieutenant Cortés, he died a wealthy man in early Caribbean terms. No one, perhaps not even Diego Colón, owned more lands and livestock and controlled more Indian labor than he did. His will showed that his life was bound up in small casual dealings with many friends: he owed three hundred *pesos de oro* to Narváez's wife, Maria de Valenzuela, and he was in debt for horses and cows bought from various acquaintances over the years. He was not inhumane, even Casas conceded that, and he left "five hundred *pesos de oro* for clothing and other things for my Indians, and to discharge my conscience."[44] Dying with faith and dignity, he bequeathed his holdings to his close associate Gonzalo de Guzmán.

Other settlers of the Caribbean could not hope to equal the social pretensions of a Diego Colón: a few aspired to coats of arms for individual deeds but apparently did not attain them. It is significant that these requests, except for that of Diego Méndez who understandably wished to commemorate his hazardous canoe voyage from Jamaica to Española, were for coats of arms to honor action against the formidable Caribs, not the more docile Taínos. Years later, Diego Ramos and Baltasar de Castro requested they be thus honored for fighting Caribs on Puerto Rico in 1513–1515,[45] and the Hispanized Genoese, Jácome de Castellón, felt he merited a coat of arms for establishing the first permanent fort and town on the Venezuelan coast.[46]

The more typical marriages of the first (partly) creole generation united offspring of the merchant-planter class to those of letrados, or were marriages within their own professional group. The encomendero-miner at Concepción, Juan de Villoria, relocated in Santo Domingo by the 1520's as a merchant and sugar planter, married his daughter, Maria de Villoria to the Licentiate Pedro Vázquez de Mella, a new arrival and fiscal of the audiencia; a second daughter, Aldonza, married the son of the merchant-planter Francisco de Tapia, bearing the same name as his father.[47] The daughter of Licentiate Juan Becerra at Santiago de Caballeros had married, as observed earlier, the judge Lucas Vázquez de Ayllón. Other marriages merely crossed lines of fairly successful merchant-planter families such as Francisco Barrionuevo's marriage to the *mestiza* daughter of Rodrigo Manzorro; Elvira Manzorro, Rodrigo's only heir in spite of his marriage to a Castilian woman, was known as the rich *mestiza* of Española and for a time resided in Castile. In Puerto Rico, Miguel Diaz's widow married Antonio de la Gama, after the latter's first wife died.[48]

On the whole, then, the Ponces and Colóns were the two most prominent families as the founding generation of Spanish civilization in the Caribbean neared an end. The principal men of this generation were remarkable for their persistence, their consuming ambition, and sense of adventure. All the prominent men had had two main opportunities, in somewhat different senses, by the early 1520's. Diego Velázquez had been wealthy on Española and again on Cuba, and yet sought the final goal of New Spain. Diego Colón had experienced wealth and power, however frustrating, in 1509–1515, and again in 1520–1523. He died in 1526, still trying to achieve a second restoration vested with all the feudal grandeur and pretensions he had claimed during his lifetime. As for Francisco de Garay and Miguel Diaz, those partners in the discovery of gold on Española and in maritime trade during the Ovandine period, they joined in one last adventure in 1523. Aimed at the partial occupation of New Spain, the venture ended in death for both men that same year.[49] Their lives in the Indies always had a marked symmetry and parallelism.

Yet not all men merely sought adventure or wealth.

The experience of the conquest, the wealth acquired from Indian slavery, the assault upon their consciences by Las Casas and the reformed Dominicans and Franciscans (whose reforms were partly written into the laws of 1526), were all external influences at work upon the inner man who considered himself Christian. There would seem to be no other explanation for the circumstances leading to the deaths of some of the earlier settlers. The rich merchant Rodrigo de Bastidas, now about sixty, sailed for Santa Marta in 1525 as a transformed man, to establish a colony based on peace and harmonious relations with the Indians; his defense of the natives resulted in his being fatally stabbed by rebel Spaniards. He was evacuated to Santiago de Cuba where he died from his wounds about 1527.[50] Vázquez de Ayllón was similarly motivated in his attempt to establish a peaceful colony on the coast of South Carolina, but the same forces that had largely determined the history of the islands, which he at that time incarnated, worked against him and he lost his life in the venture from hardship or disease. Earlier, in 1521, Ponce de León died in Cuba from an arrow wound received on the Florida coast where he had refused to take revenge on the Indians for killing a Spaniard.[51] Few historians allow for the changes that take place within men, but prefer to manipulate such handy blocks as classes, races, nations, ethnic groups, and social systems in an unconscious form of propaganda, which their readers, trained to play the same game, often seem to accept with enthusiasm. Yet history ought to go beyond the manipulatable norms; to write only what is generally true is to romanticize reality. Spaniards were lazy nd energetic, cruel and kind, covetous and self-denying; some Taínos resisted the invasion and others accepted it with wonder and enthusiasm; some resisted the forced labor and a surprisingly large minority worked voluntarily in the mines for pay; some committed suicide at the thought of leaving their islands and others saw the expeditions as an exciting challenge. Herdlike behavior by any people is not more common than individualism, though the latter is harder to discern and more difficult to convey.

On the whole, however, the first settlers had been only average in their regard for the Church, which they professed to support but did so less than sacrificially. Diego Colón left an endowment for a Franciscan nunnery and Diego Velázquez bequeathed some alms for the future *Iglesia Mayor* in Santiago de Cuba. But Colón and Velázquez, the two wealthiest men in early Caribbean history, set aside much more for requiem masses for their own souls. This was customary, but of course custom is rarely ideal and only occasionally admirable. Like most average Christians, they looked to their own affluence first, just as Ferdinand looked to the leadership and presumed glory of Spain first, rather than to the needs of the Church. For all protestations and laws to the contrary, individual wealth and glory took precedence over mere spiritual matters; the renaissance spirit, germ of humanism, glowed more brightly than that of the professed, institutionalized, and inevitably compromised. faith.

* * *

Early Caribbean history cannot be well understood without realizing that a weak monarchy directed its slow and haphazard course. To account for the slow advance of Spain in America by assuming cautiousness in the face of the unknown, or to account for the slow implantation of the main institutions of Church and state by attributing it to an exotic environment, is to miss the mark. The Atlantic was crossed in three weeks; almost twenty years passed before there was a settlement on the mainland, a short distance from the Caribbean islands. The Church was established in 1504 but the first stone for a cathedral was laid barely twenty years later. These two decades, extending from the death of Isabel until the genuine assertion of Charles's power are a significant hiatus in the general tendency toward centralism under the Spanish monarchy.

How else to appreciate that only one island—Española—had been occupied sixteen years after Columbus's discovery of America. It is true that the discovery of gold about 1500 on that island diverted attention from the mainland, but still more did the interregnum of 1504–1507 oblige Governor Ovando to accommodate a surplus of men to a single island. Conversely one may appreciate that the second wave of expansion, which saw the occupation of the other three islands of the Greater Antilles and Panama, occurred during 1508–1511—the high noon of Fernandine expansionism in the Mediterranean and the Caribbean. Afterward, expansion occurred only as the incidental result of seeking Indians as laborers to keep a mining industry viable that had already plateaued by 1515. In these enterprises, the Greater Antilles was neatly divided in two halves: Española and Puerto Rico, flanked by the Carib wall to the east, were oriented to the Pearl Coast by ocean currents and economic opportunities; Jamaica and Cuba were likewise tied closely to Panama, until the unexpected great discoveries to the west beginning in 1517.

The parallel slow establishment of the main institutions of Church and state likewise reflect the interregnums, preoccupations, and weaknesses affecting the Spanish monarchy. The establishment of the Church was delayed because of Ferdinand's experiences and ambitions as well as by hidalgo desires for the trappings of seignorial life. The state institutions, the audiencia with its president or governor, could not function properly until the monarchy became strong enough or rich enough to remove the Columbus family from its quasi-political position. But this could not be accomplished by the precarious regency of Ferdinand or the unrooted kingship of Charles. They could not afford financially or politically to dismiss these claims, no matter how pretentious and inconvenient they were.

Nor could the monarchs afford, for the same reasons, to fully support the moral idealism that Las Casas espoused. The Caribbean islands balanced political and economic power in Spain for a monarchy that could not risk demanding too much from its constituents in the peninsula or the islands; then, too, the state was engaged, during most of these years, in the same enterprises in America that Las Casas sought to abolish. Only a wealthy state based on broad financial resources can afford to implement rather than merely to declare and legislate ideals that would adversely affect important elements of society. This, of course, is to view the matter as they did and to ignore whether the implemented ideals would have accomplished their purposes.

Too much was asked of the four islands. They could not support the thousands of immigrants who camped restlessly in their towns, and they supported only precariously the permanent bureaucracy and the encomenderos. When the restless winds of change had stilled, only a few score of the early settlers had committed their families to the islands, among whom the Columbus family enjoyed the eminence to which the great Genoan had originally aspired.

Notes

NOTES TO THE INTRODUCTION

1. He ruled as Ferdinand II of Aragón and Ferdinand V of Castile.

2. Tarsicio de Azcona, *La elección y reforma del episcopado español en tiempo de los reyes católicos.* (Madrid, 1960), pp. 44–48, 54.

3. José Maria Doussinague, *La política internacional de Fernando el Católico* (Madrid, 1944), p. 32.

4. Ibid., p. 416 AND *passim.*

5. He was Charles I of Spain and Charles V as Holy Roman Emperor.

6. Melquiades Andrés Martín, "Reforma y estudio de teología en los franciscanos españoles," *AA,* 8 (1960): 43, 73; Andrés Martín, "Evangelismo, humanismo, reforma y observancias en España (1450–1525)," *MH,* 23, No. 67 (1966): 6; Angel Ortega, O.F.M., *La Rábida, historia documental crítica indiana* (Mexico, 1870), 1, 257–59.

NOTES TO CHAPTER 1

1. Ruth Pike, *Enterprise and Adventure: the Genoese in Seville and the Opening of the New World* (Ithaca, 1966), pp. 3, 6.

2. The final form of the capitulations, issued at Granada on April 30, 1492, clearly stated that the title of viceroy, among others, was hereditary. The document furnished the basis for the long court case between the Columbuses and the Crown. The latter's attorney argued that regardless of the literal wording, the king had no intention of permanently alienating royal power, and indeed could not by law. In their time, Fernando Colón, Columbus's natural son, stoutly supported his father's claims as did Bartolomé de las Casas, *Historia de las Indias,* 3 vols. (Mexico, 1951), 1, p. 175. Writers have made various observations about the significance of the title. Altolaguirre concluded that titles such as viceroy were never hereditary in Castile. Angel de Altolaguirre y Duvale, "Estudio jurídico de las capitulaciones y privilegios de Cristóbal Colón," *BRAH* 38 (1901): 297–94. In an article, "Precedentes mediterráneos del virreinato colombino," *AEA* 5 (1948): 592, Jaime Vicens Vives found that the title was of Aragonese origin and without precedent in Castile, implying that the authors of the

capitulation must necessarily have been vague regarding the powers they were granting Columbus. Still more recently, Sigfrido A. Radaelli stated that making the viceregalship hereditary was clearly against Spanish law but that the monarchs did not want to hold up the enterprise on that point alone. "La institución virreinal en las Indias," *RI* 14, Nos. 55–56 (January–June, 1954): 44, 49.

3. There are innumerable accounts of the first voyage, none superior to Samuel Eliot Morison's, *Admiral of the Ocean Sea. A Life of Christopher Columbus* (Boston, 1946).

4. Charles H. McCarthy, "Columbus and the Santa Hermandad in 1492," *CHR* 1 (1915): 38–50.

5. Columbus was aided financially by the Florentine Juanoto Berardi and by the Di Negro, Sapatal, and Doria families, who were Genoese residents in Spain. Antonio Ballesteros y Beretta, *Cristóbal Colón y el descubrimiento de America,* 2 vols. (Barcelona-Buenos Aires, 1945) (Vols. 4 and 5 of *Historia de América y de los pueblos americanos*), 4, pp. 530–31.

6. Angel Ortega, O.F.M., *La Rábida, historia documental crítica indiana,* 4 Vols. (Seville, 1925–26) 1, p. 320.

7. A sailor from Palos, Roldán made several additional voyages before settling in Santo Domingo where he owned a number of houses. He was known to Las Casas and contemporaries as "the pilot Roldán" and customarily signed his documents with the figure of an anchor, since he was illiterate. Las Casas, *Historia* 1, p. 312; "testimony on Columbus's discoveries of Tierra Firme, Santo Domingo, Nov. 10, 1513," *CDIU* 7:299–300.

8. Manuel A. Amiana, "La población de Santo Domingo," *Clio,* 27, No. 115 (July–December, 1959), 118. Angel Rosenblat, *La población indígena y el mestizaje en América* (Buenos Aires, 1954), p. 102.

9. For Columbus's uncle.

10. Sven Loven wrote one of the best descriptions of the cacicazgos in *Origins of the Tainan Culture, West Indies* (Gotemburg, 1935), pp. 71–78. See map showing the cacicazgos.

11. Las Casas, *Historia,* 1, p. 291; Alicia B. Gould, "Nueva lista documentada de los tripulantes de Colón en 1492," *BRAH* 85 (October–December, 1944): p. 151.

12. Morison, *Admiral,* p. 309.

13. Jesse Walter Fewkes, *The Aborigenes of Porto Rico and Neighboring Islands* (Washington, D.C., 1907), pp. 26–27. The warlike Caonabó was believed to be a Carib immigrant. Ballesteros, *Cristóbal Colon* 5, p. 224.

14. The Indians must have been adept in the use of cords. Las Casas wrote that when Columbus and his men were returning from the Cuban explorations, and were off the coast of southeastern Española, there were threatened by Indians with poisonous arrows (showing Carib acculturation) who made gestures with cords suggesting they would bind the Spaniards if they could. *Historia,* 1, p. 402. In Cuba, Spaniards once attacked Indians in an apparently peaceful village

because they carried so many cords that the Spaniards suspected a surprise assault.

15. The letter has been published by Martín Fernández Navarrete, *Colección de los viages y descubrimientos que hicieron por mar los españoles desde fines del siglo XV*, 5 vols. (Buenos Aires, 1945–46), 1, pp. 297–303, and twice in English translation in *Works of the Hakluyt Society*, 1st ser., 43, pp. 1–18 and 2nd ser., 65, pp. 3–18. Though Columbus wrote to Luis de Santangel, treasurer of the Santa Hermandad, as if he were at the Canary Islands, he was actually near the Azores. Editorial note by F. Navarrete, *Colección*, 1, p. 303, and Morison, *Admiral*, p. 323.

16. Instructions of the Catholic kings to Columbus, Barcelona, May 29, 1493, *CDIA*, 21: 352–53; E. Ward Loughran, "Did a Priest Accompany Columbus in 1492?" *CHR* 16, April, 1930–January, 1931): 165; Rev. C. Jesse, "The Papal Bull of 1493 Appointing the First Vicar Apostolic of the New World," *CQJ* 11, Nos. 3–4 (September–December, 1965): 62–71; Melquiades Andrés Martín, "Evangelismo, humanismo, reforma y observancias en España (1450–1525)," *MH*, 23, No. 67 (1966): 17.

17. Jesse, "The Papal Bull," p. 69; Ballesteros, *Cristóbal Colón* 5, 179.

18. Francis Borgia Steck, "Christopher Columbus and the Franciscans," *The Americas* 3, No. 3 (January, 1947), 331–32; Las Casas, *Historia* 1, p. 349.

19. That thirteen Franciscans sailed is virtually certain as a coordination of names mentioned in the following studies shows: Ortega, *La Rábida* 1, pp. 264–66; Dr. Apolinar Tejera, "Párrafos históricos," *BAGNSD* 11, No. 56 (January–March, 1948): 50–51; Pedro Borges, O.F.M., "Primeras expediciones misioneras a América," *AIA*, n.s., 27, No. 106 (April–June, 1967): 122–25; Fidel Fita, "Frey Jorge y el segundo viaje de Cristóbal Colón," *BRAH* 19 (1891): 235–37.

20. Juan Pérez de Tudela Bueso, "La negociación colombina de las Indias," *RI*, No. 57–58 (July–December, 1954): 289–357. In this and other articles, Pérez has greatly clarified Columbus's purposes and illuminated the conflict he was to face on Española.

21. The Spaniards who took the oath in Seville had had no experience with a disciplined factoría system, and their outlook had been influenced by the *Reconquista*, that is, to acquire booty by individual initiative. Pérez de Tudela, "La negociación," p. 343.

22. Ballesteros, *Cristóbal Colón* 5, p. 666.

23. Manuel Giménez Fernández, *Bartolomé de las Casas*, 2 vols. (Seville, 1953–60), 2, p. 1011.

24. Ortega, *La Rábida* 2, pp. 312–13; Vicente Murga Sanz, *Juan Ponce de León, fundador y primer gobernador del pueblo puertorriqueño, descubridor de la Florida y del Estrecho de Bahamas* (Rio Piedras, 1959), p. 15. Since nothing is known of Ponce de León's

activities until after the arrival of Ovando, Manuel Ballesteros Gaibrois thought it likely he came to the Indies only in 1502. *La idea colonial de Ponce de León* (San Juan de Puerto Rico, 1960), pp. 32–33. This argument is not strong, however, for neither is anything known of Diego Velázquez during the early years.

25. Las Casas, *Historia* 1, p. 353; Ballesteros, *Cristóbal Colón* 5, p. 175.

26. Fr. Cipriano de Utrera, "Roldán, el ingrato," *Clio* 20 (1952), p. 115.

27. Pérez de Tudela, "La negociación," p. 325; Néstor Meza Villalobos, "Significado del período 1493–1508 en el proceso de la conquista," *RCHG*, No. 110 (July–December, 1947): 43.

28. The cemi was similar to the Peruvian *huaca;* it was typically a tiny image vaguely resembling a human form; the Taínos believed it had the power to bring about good or ward off evil.

29. Morison, *Admiral*, p. 423; Dr. Chanca to cabildo of Seville, Isabela, n.d., F. Navarrete, *Colección* 1, p. 339. The Genoese eyewitness Michele de Cuneo wrote that "our men were dead and without eyes, which we thought to have been eaten, for Indians as soon as they behead anyone scoop out the eyes and eat them." Cuneo to Hieronymo Annari, Savona, Oct. 28, 1495, Morison, *The Second Voyage of Christopher Columbus from Cádiz to Hispaniola and the Discovery of the Lesser Antilles* (Oxford, 1939), p. 213. The Indians removed eyes in the belief that only then was the person fully dead.

30. Gonzalo Fernández Oviedo y Valdez, *Historia general y natural de las Indias*, 6 vols. (Vols. 117–21 of *Biblioteca de autores españoles*) (Madrid, 1959), Vol. 118, pp. 99–101.

31. Dr. Diego Alvarez Chanca, a physician from Seville, whose letter to Spain is one of the main sources for the second voyage. Detailed knowledge of Española up to 1500 depends heavily on the histories of Las Casas, Oviedo, Peter Martyr, and Fernando Colón, with occasional information from Andrés Bernáldez. I have compared all these accounts, but considered it superfluous to cite them in support of generally accepted facts.

32. Las Casas, *Historia* 1, pp. 369–70; Ballesteros, *Cristóbal Colón* 5, p. 205.

33. Pérez de Tudela, "La quiebra de la factoría y el nuevo poblamiento de la Española," *RI*, No. 60, 15 (April–June, 1955): pp. 208–10.

34. A distribution of Indians on Española in 1514 included the proviso that children of Christians are not subject to the repartimiento. Repartimiento de la Isla Española, La Concepción, 1514–15, *CDIA* 1: 80–81 and *passim*.

35. Morison, *Admiral*, p. 434.

36. *Pietro Martire d'Anghiera, Décadas del Nuevo Mundo*, 2 vols. (Mexico, 1964–65), 1, p. 113. The author's name is often Anglicized as Peter Martyr.

37. Cuneo to Annari, Savona, Oct. 28, 1495, Morison, *The Second Voyage of Christopher Columbus from Cádiz to Hispaniola and the Discovery of the Lesser Antilles* (Oxford, 1946). p. 215.

38. Andrés Bernáldez, *Historia de los reyes católicos D. Fernando y Doña Isabel*, 2 vols. (Seville, 1870), 2, pp. 37–38.

39. By September, 1494, Guacanagarí was supporting one hundred Spaniards in his cacicazgo. Las Casas, *Historia* 1, p. 414.

40. Las Casas, *Historia* 1, p. 468. Diego Márquez, who came out on the second voyage, was veedor for Española and later treasurer in Panama. Morison, *Admiral*, p. 406; Las Casas, *Historia* 1, p. 352.

41. Columbus called the later Jacmel, Puerto Brazil, presumably because of the dyewood trees there. Dyewood is rarely referred to in the chronicles and documents of the time, and then in such a way as to give little emphasis to its importance. Nonetheless a great amount was probably cut and shipped to Spain, for otherwise one cannot account for the large number of ships in the Indies trade (about forty a year on the average, from Ovando's time, and sixty or more after 1520). Huguette and Pierre Chaunu, *Seville et l'Atlantique* (1504–1650), 8 vols. in 12 (Paris, 1955–59). Though gold and later pearls were probably the main attractions, shipmasters needed a bulk cargo which must have been dyewood, supplemented after about 1515 by hides and agricultural products.

42. Tejera, "La Cruz del Santo Cerro y la batalla de la Vega Real," *BAGNSD* 8, Nos. 40–41 (May–August, 1945): 108, 119. According to a later legend Columbus was supposed to have erected, on the day before the battle, a large cross which mysteriously turned the tide of battle for the Christians. Tejera shows that the battle, which occurred on March 24, 1494, was earlier and farther westward from where the cross was subsequently implanted.

43. Columbus's will, n.p., Feb. 22, 1498, *CDIA* 30: 481–500. The document also appears in Navarrete, *Colección* 2: 264–74, and in John Boyd Thacher, *Christopher Columbus*, 3 vols, in 6 (New York, c. 1903–04), 3, Part 2, pp. 646–54.

44. Las Casas, *Historia* 1, p. 441. Oviedo, *Historia* 117, pp. 50–51. Oviedo wrote that Díaz and Garay reached the site of Santo Domingo on Aug. 5, 1494, which is undoubtedly too early.

45. Fr. Cipriano de Utrera, "Isabel la Católica, fundadora de la Ciudad de Santo Domingo," *Clio* 19 (1951), p. 132.

46. The Taíno word for cultivated field; it was adopted by the Spaniards.

47. Both Tejera and Cipriano de Utrera reject Oviedo's date of Aug. 5, 1494, for the founding of Santo Domingo. Tejera considers the date too early for Bartolomé Colón to have participated, but concentrates mainly on refuting the myth initiated by Oviedo that the town was begun after Miguel Díaz, fleeing from Bartolomé because of a crime he had committed, fell in love with an Indian cacica whose village was at the site of the later city. Tejera, "La fundación de Santo Domingo,"

BAGNSD 11, No. 57 (April–June, 1948): 103–18; Fr. Cipriano de Utrera, in a later detailed analysis, shows that Santo Domingo could not have been founded even in August, 1496, as Las Casas rather unclearly suggested, because the king had not authorized the founding of a second town, nor was Columbus planning to found one. It was only later in 1497, when Columbus learned that gold had been discovered on the Haina, that he obtained authorization to found a town. The document was carried by Pedro Hernández Coronel, whose expedition, the first to sail directly to the south coast, arrived in March, 1498. Utrera estimates the city was founded in June, 1498. Utrera, "Isabel la Católica," 124, 131. Of course, an informal settlement had been started in 1496, though not in August, thus giving a choice between 1496 and 1498, of a *de facto* or *de jure* founding. But the date of Aug. 5, 1496, would seem to be a case of erroneous precision.

48. The Indian custom of changing names. The Spaniards later used the word on the Venezuelan coast to mean friendly Indians, as distinguished from actual or presumed Caribs.

49. Utrera, "Roldán," pp. 111, 113.

50. Dr. Chanca to the cabildo of Seville, Isabela, n.d., F. Navarrete, *Colección* 1, p. 348.

51. A detailed account of Pane's work appears in Juan Bautista Múñoz, *Historia del Nuevo Mundo* (Madrid, 1793), pp. 263–66.

52. Fr. Pane's account of Indian legends and customs appears in Fernando Colón, *Historia del Almirante de las Indias, Don Cristóbal Colón* (Buenos Aires, 1944), pp. 163–85.

53. Múñoz, *Historia*, p. 306.

54. Pérez de Tudela, "La quiebra," p. 204.

55. Details of Carvajal's contact with Roldán are supplied by Casas, *Historia* 1, pp. 577–79, and Colón, *Historia*, pp. 219–20.

56. Las Casas, *Historia* 2, pp. 9–10.

57. Columbus's negotiations with Roldán are described in Las Casas, *Historia* 1, pp. 584–96; 2, pp. 6–22; Colón, *Historia*, pp. 221–34, with corrections of the latter's dates by Ballesteros, *Cristóbal Colón* 5, p. 400.

58. Ojeda's maneuvers on Española are described in Las Casas, *Historia* 2, pp. 26, 40–42, 57–66; Colón, *Historia*, p. 234, and Morison, *Admiral*, p. 568.

59. Fr. Juan de Trasierra to Archbishop of Toledo, Hayti, Oct. 12, 1500, in Ortega, *La Rábida* 2, p. 305.

60. John S. Fox, "The Beginnings of Spanish Mining in America: the West Indies and Castilla del Oro," Ph.D. dissertation, University of California, Berkeley, 1940, p. 40.

61. Colón, *Historia*, p. 238.

62. Research by Incháustegui Cabral shows that Bobadilla, a comendador of the Order of Calatrava, has been confused by Oviedo, whom many writers have followed, with another Francisco de Bobadilla, a corregidor, who was of a humble and peaceful nature. The

Bobadilla who deposed Columbus had a long record of contentious actions in Spain. Joaquín Mariano Incháuestegui Cabral, ed., *Francisco de Bobadilla* (Madrid, 1964), pp. 469–74.

63. Fr. Juan de Trasierra to Archbishop of Toledo, Hayti, Oct. 12, 1500, in Ortega, *La Rábida* 2, p. 304–5.

64. Columbus to Doña María María de Guzmàn, [Granada?], [December?], 1500, F. Navarrete, *Colección* 1, 390.

NOTES TO CHAPTER 2

1. Pérez de Tudela, "Castilla ante los comienzos de la colonización de las Indias," *RI* 15, No. 59 (January–March, 1955): 49–50.

2. Because of illness, the Friar had returned on the same fleet bearing Columbus. Bobadilla to Archbishop of Toledo, Santo Domingo, Oct. 12, 1500, *BAGNSD* 8, Nos. 38–39 (January–April, 1945): 72–73.

3. Cédula, Sevilla, May 20, 1500, *CDIA*, 38:, 425–29.

4. The first merchants to contract with the king for the dyewood trade were Juan Sánchez and Francisco Riberol. King to Treasurer of the Indies, Granada, Aug. 26, 1500, *MRAE* 12: 33–34. Sánchez was a native of Zaragoza and at the time was a merchant in Seville. Pérez de Tudela, "Política de poblamiento y política de contratación de las Indias (1502–1505)," *RI* 15, Nos. 61–62 (January–March, 1955), 405–6; José Antonio Saco, *Historia de la esclavitud de la raza africana en el nuevo mundo y en especial en los paises americo-hispanos* (Barcelona, 1879–1893), pp. 132–133.

5. Fr. Trasierra to Archbishop of Toledo, Hayti, Oct. 12, 1500, Ortega, *La Rábida*, 2, pp. 304–5.

6. Azcona, *La elección*, pp. 87–97 and *passim*. The Catholic kings at first sought the right to nominate bishops only. The papal review still collected from benefices in Spain is well brought out by Justo Fernández, "Don Francisco des Prats, primer nuncio permanente en España (1492–1503)," *AA* 1 (1953): 67–154.

7. Ursula Lamb, *Frey Nicolás de Ovando. Gobernador de Indias (1501–1509)* (Madrid, 1956), pp. 24–25, 48–52.

8. Two caravels put in at Portugal, presumably Lisbon, in late 1504. King to Ovando, Toro, Feb. 8, 1505, *CDIA* 31, 277.

9. Lamb, *Frey Nicolás*, p. 12.

10. Antonine S. Tibesar, "The Franciscan Province of the Holy Cross of Española," *The Americas* 13 (April, 1957), 380.

11. The great shipwreck of 1502 has been variously described and will perhaps never be known about fully. Fernando Colón reported that only three or four of twenty-eight ships were saved, with only one of these reaching Castile. *(Historia* 2, pp. 248–49). Secondary accounts have followed this or Las Casas's description, which is approximately the same. Yet Bernáldez understood that most of the ships reached

various ports in Spain and Portugal after the fleet was dispersed by the storm. (*Historia* 2, p. 253). At least two ships, neither being the one Bastidas sailed on, reached Spain, for they brought dyewood to Seville. Pérez de Tudela, "La quiebra," p. 248. Though the number of ships reaching Spain remains vague, two other equally vague matters have been clarified. On the basis of a 1505 cédula calling for Roldán's residencia, Prof. Lamb assumed that the rebel did not die in the shipwreck, but Incháustegui Cabral reported that a document drawn up in Seville, Aug. 5, 1504 (cited in another secondary work), showed that Roldán's widow, Juana Martínez, had drawn up a power of attorney to handle her deceased husband's properties. This is almost conclusive evidence but in 1511 the king advised Colón, in a statement to Bartolomé, to treat Roldán (among others) well. King to Bartolomé Colón [Seville?], June 11, 1511, *CDIHA* 6, 347. But was the mention of Roldán based on specific knowledge that he was alive? If so, it is remarkable that nothing had been heard from so forceful a character for nine years, except that his widow had drawn up a power of attorney. Incháusteguí Cabral, *Francisco de Bobadilla* (Madrid, 1964) pp. 515–16. Finally, though chroniclers and secondary accounts based on them assume that Antonio de Torres, veteran fleet captain, died in the shipwreck, Incháustegui Cabral found that Torres was named governor of Gran Canaria on Feb. 21, 1502, and died in a shipwreck in the bay of Cádiz in the autumn of 1503. (p. 517). The queen spoke of him as if he were still alive on June 5, 1503, in a royal provision addressed to the Casa de Contratación. *CDIU* 5, 53–55.

12. Las Casas reported that Esquivel led 300–400 men against the Indians of Higüey in two separate campaigns (*Historia* 2, pp. 160–62, 187–98. This has been repeated by secondary accounts. Two such campaigns would not have been necessary. Moreover, even had there been a second campaign in 1504, it is unlikely to have been led by Esquivel who was in Spain in late 1503 and probably later, Pérez de Tudela, "Politica," p. 383. Spanish writers closer in time to the event do not mention two campaigns. Dominicans and Franciscans to Monsieur Chievres, Santo Domingo, June 4, 1516, *CDIA* 7, 405–7; Zuazo to Monsieur Chievres, Santo Domingo, Jan. 22, 1518, *CDIA* 1, 306–7. Nor for that matter does Herrera follow Las Casas in all details. Herrera's interpretation is that the fort was put up after Ovando arrived. However, confronted with two bloody campaigns (as related by Las Casas), he truncates a second one, about 1504, to the capture of Caonabó, presumably sensing that two events could not have been so similar. Antonio Herrera y Tordesillas, *Historia de las Indias Occidentales*, 9 vols. (Madrid, 1726–30) 1, pp. 129; 159–61. The Yuna River flows eastward off the Vega; the Yuma River flows southward through the Higüey.

13. See map of Española in the Appendix.

14. There were 47 encomenderos who held a total of 1,228 Indians. Alburquerque Repartimiento, Concepción, 1514, *CDIA* 1, 144–51.

15. Pérez de Tudela, "Política," p. 379.

16. Las Casas, *Historia* 1, p. 463; Loven, *Origins*, pp. 69, 78.
17. Las Casas, *Historia* 1, p. 455; Martire, *Décadas* 1, p. 154.
18. Lamb, *Frey Nicolás*, p. 126.
19. Las Casas, *Historia* 2, pp. 164–66.
20. The conquest of Jaraguá has been viewed uniformly as the Spanish crushing of a threatened Indian revolt till the reassessments by Prof. Lamb, *Frey Nicolás*, p. 126, and especially Pérez de Tudela, "Política," pp. 378–79. Both authors linked the Indians with Roldanista feudalism, though Prof. Lamb felt that the Indians revolted on their own account (p. 130). Herrera wrote that Ovando marched to Jaraguá partly to deal with "the insolence of Roldanistas." He then forgot all about the Roldanistas and treated the conflict as a purely Spanish–Indian one. Herrera y Tordesillas, *Historia* 1, p. 152. Charlevoix thought the Spaniards trying to save children from the sword were also members of the attacking force, more humane than their fellow soldiers. Pierre F. X. de Charlevoix, *Historie de L'Ile espagnole ou de St. Domingue*, 2 vols. (Paris, 1730) 1, p. 234. Las Casas's statement that 80 caciques were burned alive should not be taken too literally, for Oviedo reported that 40 caciques were burned (*Historia*, Vol. 117, 83) and another source reported that 60 Indians were burned. Dominicans and Franciscans to Monsieur Chievres, Santo Domingo, June 4, 1516, *CDIA* 7, p. 410. One cannot help wondering if the sale of lances, swords, daggers, and shields to the Indians and caciques, a charge made against Bastidas, is not linked with the Jaraguá rising. Bastidas passed through that area in 1502, but denied having made such sales, and said that he could not be responsible for what deserters did. Cédula, Medina del Campo, Jan. 29, 1504, *CDIA* 39: 61–67.
21. Using a definition of petty encomendero to mean a Spaniard holding from 1 to 10 Indians, one finds that there were 314 such encomenderos on Española in 1514 out of a total of 718. Alburquerque repartimiento, Concepción, 1514, *CDIA* 1: 50–236.
22. King to Diego Colón, Sevilla, June 6, 1511, *CDIU*, 5: 314–15. Though issued two years after Ovando's governorship ended, the order is typical of Ferdinand's concern for mine production in contrast with the socially feudal values of many vecinos who were more concerned with holding serfs than working Indians productively. As he told Ovando, some Spaniards hold them as pages and *mozos*. King to Ovando, Valladolid, Aug. 14, 1509, *CDIA*, 31: 446–48.
23. Las Casas, *Historia* 2, p. 322.
24. The shipping records compiled by Pierre Chaunu begin in 1506. See also Pérez de Tudela, "Política," p. 398.
25. Secondary authors have usually accepted this figure, supplied by Las Casas. The figure is probably too high; in 1510 the Dominicans thought there were about 1,500 Spaniards on the island.
26. Since Jaraguá was notable for its carved bowls, it seems probable that *bateas* would come from the same source.

27. Manuel Giménez Fernández, "Las Cortes de la Española en 1518," *AUH* 15, No. 2 (1954), 124.

28. Pedro Mateos, a sailer aboard the *Gallegos* on Columbus's fourth voyage, settled at Salvaleón de Higüey, and Juan Moreno, another sailor on the *Vizcaino* settled at Salvatierra la Sabana, and had migrated to Cuba by 1515. King to Casa de Contratación, Salamanca, Nov. 2, 1505, *CDIA*, 31: 365, 367. Probanza of Diego Colón, Santo Domingo, June 16, 1512, *CDIU*, 7: 151–52; Alburquerque Repartimiento, Concepción, 1514, *CDIA*, 1: 222–23; Testimony taken for Diego Colón, San Salvador [de Bayamo], Cuba, Feb. 16, 1515, *CDIU*, 17: 74. King to Casas de Contratación, Segovia, Aug. 25, 1505, *CDIA*, 31: 344–54; King to Casa de Contratación, Salamanca, Nov. 2, 1505, *CDIA*, 31: 362–78.

29. Chaunu's records show that 119 ships came out from Spain during the years 1506–1509 and only 77 (approximately 65 percent) returned. Chaunu, *Seville* 2, pp. 8–33.

30. Las Casas thought that the Indian population had declined from about 3 million to 40,000 by 1508, though the vecinos were silent about the deaths of Indians till that year. Since Spain was ravaged by a pestilence that took many lives in 1507, I hold it likely that the first noticeable death rate among the Indians occurred as a result of the transmission of this unidentified disease by immigrants. The pestilence is described in Alonso de Santa Cruz, *Crónica de los reyes católicos*, 2 vols. (Sevilla, 1951), 2, p. 103 and Pedro Mexia, *Historia del Emperador Carlos V*, vol. 7, p. 38 of *Colección de crónicas españoles* (Madrid, 1945).

31. Ballesteros, *Cristóbal* Colón, 5, p. 487. King to Rodrigo de Alcázar, Toro, April 16, 1505, *CDIA*, 31: 298–301. (A reappointment made necessary by death of the queen.)

32. Cédula, Medina del Campo, Feb. 15, 1504, *CDIA*, 31: 233–37.

33. King to Ovando, Villa de Arcos, July 13, 1508, *CDIU*, 5: 152.

34. The Crown-Columbus monopoly was first broken by the king in 1495 when he declared the severance tax on gold to be four-fifths. In about 1500 Columbus reduced this to one-third, with an additional one-tenth to be paid to him. Following Bobadilla's brief popular imposition of one-eleventh, the royal tax remained at one-third (though Ferdinand attempted to have one-half collected from newcomers from 1502–1504) till the quinto was declared in 1504. This tax remained standard in the islands until 1520. Cédula, Madrid, April 9, 1495, *CDIA*, 21: 566; Columbus to Doña María de Guzmán, Granada, December?, 1500, Navarrete, *Colección*, 1: 392; Las Casas, *Historia*, 2, p. 153; Lamb, *Frey Nicolás*, p. 11.

35. Cédula, Medina del Campo, Feb. 5, 1504, *CDIA*, 31:216–19.

36. Las Casas, *Historia*, 2, p. 277. See the Appendix for the royal income (essentially the quinto) sent to Spain.

37. Chaunu, *Seville*, 2, pp. 20–23.

38. For example, Ovando left Miguel Ballester unmolested as majordomo of an estancia near Concepción, which Columbus deeded to his son, Diego. Pérez de Tudela, "Castilla," p. 76.

39. In 1508 the king was silent regarding the request from the two procuradores of Española that absentees and transients be prohibited from holding encomiendas, and he upheld, against their wishes, the right of clerics to hold Indians. King to Ovando, Burgos, April 30, 1508, *CDIA*, 32: 14, 16.

40. Lamb, *Frey Nicolás*, p. 148.

41. Fox, *The Beginnings*, pp. 40, 44, 59, 68. According to Fox, only Española and Cuba had gold-bearing viens; Puerto Rico and Jamaica had only placers; the amount of gold found on Jamaica was negligible.

42. Probanza of Bastidas, Santo Domingo, June 22, 1521, *CDIA*, 2: 369. Though the statement was made long after Ovando's time, the measurement of social status by the number of criados kept in one's posada is typical of the seignorial mentality. Many witnesses in documents of the period state that they enjoy room and board in the posada of another vecino.

43. Las Casas, *Historia*, 2, p. 163; Lamb, *Frey Nicolás*, p. 110; Oviedo, *Historia*, 117, p. 78.

44. Ballesteros, *La idea*, p. 173.

45. Cédula, Valladolid, Nov. 12, 1509, *CDIU*, 5: 166–71.

46. Las Casas, *Historia*, 2, p. 278. Ferdinand unceasingly urged collection of the debt but it was still outstanding when the king died, since Santa Clara's properties were sold on credit.

47. Vera Paz was granted an escutcheon on which was inscribed a dove bearing a green branch in its beak, and in the lower half of the shield, a traditional peace symbol. Cédula, Sevilla, Dec. 7, 1508, *CDIA*, 31: 63.

48. The number of elderly persons was not always counted in the repartimiento, but a tally shows that there were 593 at Santo Domingo, 329 at Concepción, and 167 at Santiago de los Caballeros. Encomenderos holding 200 or more Indians often had as many as 40 oldsters. Petty encomenderos held none. Other towns had fewer as they were less populous. In the light of such figures, it would be hard to argue that the Indians were wiped out by hard labor. By this time the gold boom was over, though the decline continued—obviously not directly related to work in the mines. Alburquerque repartimiento, Concepción, 1514, *CDIA*, 1: 50–236.

49. The Indian woman, Luisa, former wife of Alonso de Cáceres, was entrusted to Gaspar de Astudillo so that the latter's wife could teach her in the faith. Alburquerque repartimiento, Concepción, 1514, *CDIA*, 1: 121.

50. Alburquerque repartimiento, Concepcion, 1514, *CDIA*, 1: 138.

51. Statement of Martín Garcés, Residencia of Sancho Velázquez, Caparra, 1519, *MHDPR*, 2: 264–65

52. Cédula, Seville, June 21, 1511, *CDIA*, 32: 169–80. Ovando owned conucos of yuca totalling about 340,000 hills which would have been worth about 8,500 *pesos de oro* when the gold mining was flourishing. About 40 hills were worth 1 peso. Lamb, *Frey Nicolás*, p. 169.

53. Pérez de Tudela, "Política," pp. 402–3.

54. King to Diego Colón, Burgos, June 5, 1512, *BAGNSD* 4, Nos. 14–16 (January–June, 1941), 122; Pérez de Tudela, "Política," p. 402.

55. Pérez de Tudela, "Castilla," p. 76.

56. Testimony taken by Diego Colón, Santo Domingo, Sept. 5, 1514, *CDIU*, 7: 378–80; Pike, *Enterprise*, p. 71.

57. Columbus owed 30,000 Portuguese *reales* to the heirs of Luis Centurión Escoto, Genoese merchant. Ballesteros, *Cristóbal Colón*, 5, p. 734. His son Diego was in debt to Nicolás de Grimaldo, and Gaspar and Melchor Centurión, among others. Promulgation of the will of Diego Colón, Santo Domingo, May 2, 1526, *CDIA*, 40: 214–15.

58. Las Casas, *Historia*, 2, p. 143.

59. By 1509 they owned one-half of the *Santiago*, the other half being held by the shipmaster, Juan de Jerez of Palos, Chaunu, *Seville*, 2, pp. 28–29.

60. Alburquerque repartimiento, Concepción. 1514, *CDIA*, 1: 58, 63–64; "Nombres de la Vega," *Clio*, 22, No. 100 (July–September, 1954), 124.

61. Probanza on the discovery of Darién, Santo Domingo, Dec. 7, 1512, *CDIU*, 7: 222–24.

62. Alburquerque repartimiento, Concepción, *CDIA*, 1: 87, 100, 186, 188, 194, 219, 230; Giménez Fernández, *Bartolomé*, II, 100.

63. Giménez Gernández, *Bartolomé* 1, p. 323.

64. King to Jeronymite friars, Zaragoza, Dec. 12, 1518, *MHDPR*, 3–2: 27–28; King to *juez de residencia* of Puerto Rico, Barcelona, March 10, 1519, Manuel Serrano y Sanz, *Orígenes de la dominación española en América*, vol. 25 of *Nueva biblioteca de autores españoles* (Madrid, 1918), p. dcii; Giménez Fernández, *Bartolomé* 2, p. 223.

65 Las Casas, *Historia* 2, p. 312; Oviedo, *Historia* 119, p. 174.

66. Velázquez must have been close friends with Cuéllar, since he married his daughter, and he would probably have spent considerable time at Santo Domingo courting her prior to 1511.

67. Alburquerque repartimiento, Concepción, 1514, *CDIA*, 1: 209–10, 214, 222.

68. King to Diego Colón, Valladolid, Nov. 14, 1509, *CDIA*, 31: 520; Audiencia of Santo Domingo to Governors of Spain, Santo Domingo, Aug. 30, 1520, *CDIA*, 13: 342; Alburquerque repartimiento, Concepción, 1514, *CDIA*, 1: 80, 204–5; 209–10; Testimony taken by Altamirano, Santiago de Cuba, June 21, 1525, *CDIU*, 1: 213; Governors of Spain to Jeronymite friars, Madrid, Nov. 10, 1516, Serrano y Sanz, *Orígenes*, p. dxlv.

69. Murga Sanz, *Juan*, pp. 21–23.

70. He was co-owner with Alonso Sarmiento of the *Santa María de Regla*, Chaunu, *Seville* 2, pp. 32–33.

71. Empowerment as executors of García Troche and Juan de Soria, San Juan de Puerto Rico, Nov. 4, 1521, Murga Sanz, *Juan*, p. 304.

72. He was subsequently joined by two nephews, both named Hernán Ponce. Murga Sanz, *Juan*, p. 25; a cousin, Juan González Ponce de León, may have been with Ponce from the earliest explorations. Aurelio Tío, *Nuevas fuentes para la historia de Puerto Rico* (San Germán, 1961), p. 164.

73. Tibesar, "The Franciscan," p. 380.

74. Andrés Martín, "Renovación en teología dogmática y ascética en España (1500–1530)," *AA*, 11 (1963): 58, 64.

75. Fr. Juan de la Deule to archbishop of Toledo, Las Indias, Oct. 12, 1500, Ortega, *La Rábida* 2, p. 303. Rev. Livarius Oliger, O.F.M., "The Earliest Record on the Franciscan Missions in America," *CHR*, 6: 60.

76. Royal instructions to officials of Española, Alcalá de Henares, March 20, 1503, *CDIA*, 31: 157.

77. Pedro Borges, O.F.M., *Métodos misionales en la cristianización de América* (Madrid, 1960), p. 420.

78. Tibesar, "The Franciscan," pp. 381–82.

79. The bull, *eximie devotionis*, Rome, Oct. 11, 1503, Balthasar de Tobar, *Compendio bulario índico*, 2 vols. (Sevilla, 1954), 1: 41–42.

80. King to Diego Colón, Monzón, June 15, 1510, *CDIA*, vol. 84.

81. Las Casas, *Historia* 2, p. 390.

82. Pérez de Tudela, "Política," pp. 392–94.

83. The bull *illius fulciti*, Rome, Oct. 17, 1504, Tobar, *Compendio* 1, pp. 42–44.

84. The Sacred Host was made secure in the island towns only about 1511, though this was in stone sacristies or small chapels. King to Diego Colón, Tordesillas, July 25, 1511, *CDIA*, 32: 263.

85. Lamb, *Frey Nicolás*, pp. 204–11. Manuel Giménez Fernández, "Las Cortes," p. 74.

NOTES TO CHAPTER 3

1. Contract between the Crown and Juan de la Cosa, Medina del Campo, Feb. 14, 1504, *CDIA*, 31: 220–29; Contract between the Crown and Vicente Yáñez Pinzon, Toro, April 24, 1505, *CDIA*, 31: 309–17. The 1504 contract with Pinzón has never been found.

2. Pérez de Tudela, "Política," p. 414; King to Ovando, Córdoba, Oct. 6, 1508, *CDIA*, 36: 257. The depression on Española impelled the islanders to find new wealth, which took the form of Indian slaves, pearls, and salt, all of which were found at approximately the same

place in or adjacent to the eastern coast of Venezuela, then called the Paria or Pearl Coast.

3. Karl Joseph von Hefele, *Der Cardinal Ximenes und die kirchlichen Zustände Spaniens am Ende des 15 und Anfange des 16 Jahrhunderts* (Tubingen, 1851), p. 195.

4. Santa Cruz, *Crónica*, 2, pp. 4–9.

5. Barón de Terrateig, *Política en Italia del Rey Catolico, 1507–1516*, 2 vols. (Madrid, 1963), 1, p. 42.

6. Hefele, *Der Cardinal*, p. 197; Santa Cruz, *Crónica*, 2, pp. 40–43, 71.

7. Giménez Fernández, *Bartolomé*, 1, p. 78.

8. Hefele, *Der Cardinal*, pp. 224–25; Santa Cruz, *Crónica* 2, p. 67.

9. Santa Cruz, *Crónica* 2, pp. 65–66.

10. Hefele, *Der Cardinal*, p. 239.

11. Giménez Fernández, *Bartolomé* 2, p. 190.

12. Santa Cruz, *Crónica* 2, pp. 55–56; Doussinague, *La política*, p. 139.

13. Safe conduct issued to Diego Colón, Palencia, July 30, 1507, *CDIA*, 39: 151–52.

14. Santa Cruz, *Crónica* 2, pp. 98–99; 104–14.

15. Doussinague, *La política*, pp. 259–60; 278.

16. Fernando Colón and Hernando de Vega, Comendador Mayor of Castile, each was assigned 300 Indians on Española. King to Colón, Campanario, July 2, 1511, *DCIA*, 32: 200–220; King to Colón, Cantillana, June 24, 1511, *CDIHA*, 6: 365–66. Juan Cabrero, the king's butler, and Bishop Rodríguez de Fonseca were each assigned 200 Indians on Española, as shown in the Alburquerque repartimiento. Lope Conchillas acquired Indians on Puerto Rico. Coll y Toste, "El Alzamiento de los Indios del Boriquén—Rectificaciones históricas," *BHPR*, 9, No. 6 (November–December, 1922), 342.

17. Cédula, Arévalo, Aug. 9, 1508, *CDIA*, 39: 175.

18. Las Casas, *Historia* 2, p. 302; Murga Sanz, *Juan*, p. 44.

19. Las Casas, *Historia* 2, p. 279; Oviedo, *Historia* 117, p. 85; Giménez Fernández, *Bartolomé* 1, p. 29; Ismael Sánchez-Bella, *La organización financiera de las Indias. Siglo XVI.* (Seville, 1968), pp. 166, 323.

20. King to Ovando, Burgos, April 30, 1508, *CDIA*, 32: 6.

21. Oviedo, *Historia* 117, p. 85.

22. The captains of two caravels that put in somewhere in Portugal in 1505 misspent part of the gold intended for the royal treasury. King to Ovando, Toro, Feb. 8, 1505, *CDIA*, 31: 277.

23. Royal Order, Seville, Nov. 29, 1507, *CDIA*, 39: 162.

24. Crown to Ochoa de Isásaga, Valladolid, June 6, 1509, *CDIA*, 36: 277; Memorial of Isásaga, n.p., n.d., *CDIU*, 5: 94–97; Doussinague, *La política*, pp. 163–67.

25. King to Ovando, Villa de Arcos, July 13, 1508, *CDIU*, 5: 515; King to Colón, Cádiz, May 3, 1509, *CDIA*, 23: 290–309.

26. King to Ovando, Villa de Arcos, July 13, 1508, *CDIU*, 5: 153.

27. The tendency to concentrate the remaining population of Española in Santo Domingo and in the mining zone is illustrated by the Alburquerque repartimiento, though such centralization had doubtless been the trend since gold was discovered. Santo Domingo gained 325 Indians from Salvaleón de Higüey and Azua, Santiago de los Caballeros gained 156 from Jacmel, and San Juan de la Maguana gained 301 from Verapaz. Whole pueblos (the casual arrangement of huts that the Taínos called a *yucayeque*) were seldom or never uprooted, even though the cédula of 1503 and the Laws of Burgos of 1512–13 called for the formation of regular towns. The belated effort to form towns in 1519 met with slight success, and provoked, in my judgment, the Enriquillo revolt at Verapaz. Nonetheless, clans apparently moved on occasion even if yucayeques would not be moved. Thus no single generalization can be made about the Taínos' instinctive love for their natal sites.

28. Tío, *Nuevas Fuentes*, pp. 110–13; 168.

29. It would be strange if Ponce de León, a shipowner, had not visited Puerto Rico before 1508, since he had lived adjacent to the island since the conquest of Higüey. Though Ponce's first official expedition was in July, so far as firm evidence shows, Ovando had written the king May 17, 1508, that Ponce had found something on Puerto Rico. One may suppose that the cacique on the south coast gave him a few gold nuggets. King to Ovando, Villa de Arcos, July 13, 1508, *CDIU*, 5: 151.

30. Murga Sanz, *Juan*, pp. 38–39.

31. Residencia of Ponce de León, Caparra, October, 1512, *CDIA*, 34: 493.

32. Residencia of Ponce de León, Caparra, October, 1512, *CDIA*, 34: 456, 480; Ortega, *La Rábida* 2, p. 272; Murga Sanz, *Juan*, pp. 35, 240; Salvador Brau, *La colonización de Puerto Rico* (San Juan de Puerto Rico, 1969), p. 96.

33. Las Casas, *Historia* 2, 290–91.

34. Rafael Delorme Salto, ed., *Los aborígenes de América* (Madrid, 1894), pp. 219–20; Jesse W. Fewkes, *The Aborigenes of Porto Rico and Neighboring Islands*, pp. 23–28; 36–40; Cayetano Coll y Toste, "El repartimiento de los indígenas entre los Españoles—Rectificaciones históricas," *BHPR*, 9, No. 5 (September–October, 1922), 276.

35. Oviedo, *Historia* 118, pp. 99–101. Oviedo remarked their doubt whether Spaniards could really die.

36. Cayetano Coll y Toste, "Exploración de la isla por Juan Ponce de León," *BHPR*, 4, No. 5 (September–October, 1917), 300–330; Murga Sanz, *Juan*, p. 36. Caparra was called Ciudad de Puerto Rico in official documents from 1514, and after about 1521, when the town was relocated on the coast, Columbus's name for the island, San Juan de Bautista and the name of the city became confused and gradually interchanged. Antonio S. Pedreira, "De los nombres de Puerto Rico," *REHNY*, 1 1928): pp. 21–27. I shall refer to the first town as Caparra and the relocated town of 1520–22 as San Juan de Puerto Rico.

37. Murga Sanz, *Juan*, pp. 36–37, 44; Contract between Crown and Ponce de León (paraphrased), Concepción, May 1, 1509, *CDIA*, 34, pp. 357–63. Murga Sanz believed the contract was approved by Diego Colón in July, 1509, after Ponce was blown back from St. Croix island by contrary winds. The event is unclear and seems difficult to explain in the light of Colón's sending soon after a wave of immigrants whose presence in a small goldfield made operation of the company impossible.

38. Murga Sanz, *Juan*, pp. 41–42; Brau, *La colonización*, p. 115.

39. Murga Sanz, *Juan*, pp. 44, 56.

40. Coll y Toste, "El Alzamiento," 342–43.

41. Contract between the Crown and Ponce de León (paraphrased), Concepción, May 1, 1509, *CDIA*, 34: 360.

42. Oviedo, *Historia* 118, pp. 92–93; Cayetano Coll y Toste, ed., "Documentos históricos referentes al pueblo de Guánica," *BHPR*, 7 (1921): 209–10.

43. The cédula naming Ponce governor was issued at Valladolid, Aug. 14, 1509 (*CDIA*, 21: 459–60). Murga Sanz, *Juan*, pp. 50–51; "Autógrafos de Cristóbal Colón y Papeles de América, los publica la Duquesa de Berwick y de Alba, Condesa de Siruela" (excerpted) (Madrid, 1892), *BHPR*, 1 (1914): 132–33.

44. King to judges of appeal, Burgos, Nov. 9, 1511, *MHDPR*, 3-1: 103–4; Cayetano Coll y Toste, "Principios de la colonización de la isla, rectificaciones históricas," *BHPR*, 9, No. 2 (March–April, 1922), 95; Murga Sanz, *Juan*, p. 50.

45. Murga Sanz, *Juan*, p. 51; Juan Martínez Peña said he brought the stone for Ponce's house from the islet (on which San Juan de Puerto Rico would be situated). Testimony taken by Lic. Figueroa on relocation of Caparra, Caparra, July 13, 1519, *CDIA*, 36: 511–15. The document is misprinted as July 13, 1517.

46. Murga Sanz, *Juan*, pp. 52–61.

47. Cayetano Coll y Toste, "Principios de la colonización de la isla, rectificaciones históricas," *BHPR*, 9, No. 2 (March–April, 1922), 101; Coll y Toste, "Documentos," pp 209–10; Las Casas, *Historia* 2, p. 325; Oviedo, *Historia* 118, pp. 92–93.

48. Oviedo, *Historia* 118, pp. 90–95; 100.

49. Ponce's contingent captured 46 males and 21 females; prices for these slaves and others ranged from about 5 to 30 *pesos de oro* each. Murga Sanz, *Juan*, pp. 280–84. King to Cerón and Díaz, Burgos, Sept. 9, 1511, *CDIA*, 32: 275–80; King to Ponce de León, Burgos, Sept. 9, 1511, *CDIA*, 32: 280–83; King to Ponce de León, Burgos, Feb. 23, 1512, Tío, *Nuevas fuentes*, pp. 469–70.

50. Murga Sanz, *Juan*, p. 74; King to Cerón and Díaz, Burgos, Sept. 9, 1511, *CDIA*, 32: 276.

51. Murga Sanz, *Juan*, p. 73.

52. Ibid., pp. 81–83.

53. Characteristically fearing a civil war, the king had written Ponce on July 21, 1511, to come to court on handing over authority to Juan

Cerón, to avoid a possible conflict. Ponce must have explained that this was not necessary, for he made his first voyage to Florida before returning to Spain. Murga Sanz, *Juan*, p. 74.

54. Murga Sanz, *Juan*, pp. 91, 98, 104. Cayetano Coll y Toste, "Nuevo Alzamiento de los Indios del Boriquén y depredaciones de los Caribes—Rectificaciones históricas," *BHPR*, 10, No. 3 (May–June, 1923), 173.

55. Murga Sanz, *Juan*, pp. 91, 98, 133; Coll y Toste, "Nuevo Alzamiento," p. 170.

56. Murga Sanz, *Juan*, pp. 133–39; Cayetano Coll y Toste, "Gobierno de Juan Cerón and demás tenientes de D. Diego, hasta 1515," *BHPR*, 10, No. 2 (March–April, 1923), 79–80; Oviedo, *Historia* 118, p. 106; Probanza of Juan González Ponce de León, México, June 18, 1532, Tío, *Nuevas fuentes* (ed. note by Tío), p. 174.

57. Cédula of Sept. 27, 1514, editorial note by Tío, to Probanza of Juan González Ponce de León, México, June 18, 1532, *Nuevas fuentes*, p. 175.

58. Haro was named treasurer general of Puerto Rico by a cédula issued at Valladolid, May 13, 1513. *MHDPR*, 3-1: 216–18. Gambling seems to have been the main pastime on the island, the currently popular card games being *al flux* and *al parar*. Though traditional history of Latin America often recaptures the inspiration behind the deeds of a Columbus, a Las Casas, or a Cortés, a reader of documents soon realizes that ordinary people continued ordinary lives beneath this more glittering surface. Gamblers quarreled and knifed each other, irate livestock raisers sent their criados to hang planters' dogs that had chewed up their cattle, Spanish boys idly threw rocks at Indians, washerwomen slapped each other on the river banks (one Negro woman knocked a Spanish woman into the river during a quarrel and was held blameless by Sancho Velázquez). Isabel Ortíz ran a boarding house in Caparra where she regularly offered herself, along with her meals, to her customers—for a price. The young Juan Rodríguez Sillero, whose character was impugned as a witness on charges of consorting with the *mesonera*, replied laconically that he paid for what he received, just as others do. Residencia of Sancho Velázquez, Caparra, 1519, *CDIA*, 34: 49, 69, 133–35, and *passim*.

59. Two Franciscans are said to have accompanied Moscoso to San Germán in 1512, but nothing more is known of them. Ortega, *La Rábida* 3, p. 295; the cleric Juan Fernández served the churches at Caparra and San Germán in 1512, at 100 *pesos de oro* a year; he was apparently the only priest in service on the island. Murga Sanz, *Juan*, p. 71.

60. Las Casas, *Historia* 2, p. 312.

61. Irene A. Wright, *The Early History of Cuba, 1492–1586* (New York, 1916), pp. 71–72; Las Casas, *Historia 2*, pp. 314, 327–28.

62. King to Diego Colón, Burgos, Feb. 23, 1512, *EHR*, 36: 79–80. (Irene A. Wright edited the documents published in this review.) King to Diego Colón, Burgos, Feb. 23, 1512, *CDIA*, 32: 338.

63. Francisco Morales Padrón, *Jamaica española* (Seville, 1952), pp. 98, 217; *Auto*, Seville, Jamaica, Feb. 21, 1522, *EHR*, 36: 92–94; Oviedo, *Historia* 118, pp. 184–85. Pedro de Mazuelo to king (Sevilla la Nueva), April 21, 1515, *EHR*, 36: 85–88.

64. King to Francisco de Garay, León, Nov. 28, 1514, *EHR*, 36: 85; Garay to king (Sevilla la Nueva), June 11, 1515, *EHR*, 36: 88–91.

65. Morales Padrón, *Jamaica*, p. 43.

66. Ibid., p. 27.

67. Fr. Deule, apparently with several other Franciscan friars, went to Jamaica with or soon after Esquivel; he was dead by 1511. Tibesar, "The Franciscan," p. 384.

68. King to Ovando, Córdoba, Oct. 6, 1508, *CDIA*, 36: 258.

69. Last will of Diego Velázquez, Santiago de Cuba, June 11, 1524, *CDIA*, 35: 516.

70. Several writers have believed that Velázquez left Cuba in 1510, a possibility enhanced by the dearth of information about his first activities there. Indeed the king wrote Colón on June 6, 1511, purporting to answer Colón's letter of Aug. 22, 1510, which said Velázquez was on Cuba and in another connection that Colón was planning to send Bartolomé, his uncle, to explore the island. That Velázquez might open placer mining in one part of the island, while Colón explored it, is possible, but another explanation seems more likely. The king answered several other letters of Colón on the same day, one of them dated Jan. 15, 1511, and it is likely he or his scribe got the contents of the letters confused. Colón reported nothing of Velázquez's activities till early 1512; that Velázquez could have been silent since 1510 seems improbable. The figure of 300 expeditionaries is doubtless a loose appraisal by Las Casas. It seems little more than a way of speaking, for there were 300 men who invaded the Higüey in the presumed expeditions and 300 who accompanied Ovando to Jaraguá.

71. Las Casas, *Historia* 2, p. 475; King to Colón, Seville, June 25, 1511, *CDIA*, 32: 192. Fr. Juan de Tisín was one of the four friars. Tibesar, "The Franciscan," p. 384.

72. Colón to Archbishop of Toledo, Santo Domingo, Jan. 12, 1512, *CDIE*, 104, 347–49.

73. Las Casas, *Historia* 2, p. 470.

74. Carlos A. Martínez-Fortún y Foyo, "El Casicato de Sabana de Sabaneque," *RBNC*, 2nd Ser., 7, No. 1 (January–March, 1956), 71–72.

75. Velázquez to king [Jagua], April 1, 1514, *CDIA*, 11: 417.

76. Ballesteros, *Cristóbal Colón* 4, p. 42.

77. Ibid., p. 40.

78. *Historia de la nación cubana*, Ramiro Guerra y Sánchez, dir., 10 vols. (Habana, 1952), 1, pp. 66–67.

79. Las Casas, *Historia* 2, pp. 481–85; Martínez-Fortún, "El Casicato," p. 72.

80. Carlos A. Martínez-Fortun y Foyo, "¿Donde estuvo situado 'Carahate?'," *AAHC*, 20, 138.

81. Wright, *The Early History*, p. 44.

82. King to Velázquez, Valladolid, April 8, 1513, *CDIU,* 1: 34–35.
83. Wright, *The Early History,* p. 44.
84. Ibid., p. 58.
85. Irene A. Wright, *Historia documentada de San Cristóbal de la Habana en el siglo XVI,* 2 vols. (Habana, 1927), 1, p. 70.
86. Guerra, dir., *Historia* 1, p. 70.
87. J. A. Cosculluela, "Sincronismo de las culturas indoantillanas," *RAEC* 1, No. 3 (November, 1946), 46.
88. Doussinague, *La política,* p. 332.
89. Ibid., pp. 32, 327–29.
90. Ibid., p. 352.

NOTES TO CHAPTER 4

1. Sancho Velázquez told the king that rich mines had been found near Caparra, but after a few months nothing more was heard about them. Velázquez to king, Caparra, April 27, 1515, *CDIA,* 36: 355. Fox observes that gold on Puerto Rico came only from alluvial river deposits, not from veins. *The Beginnings,* p. 68.

2. Carl O. Sauer, *The Early Spanish Main* (Berkeley, 1966), p. 182; Las Casas, *Historia* 2, p. 452.

3. The town was unlisted in the Alburquerque repartimiento of 1514.

4. Figures based on the Alburquerque repartimiento, Concepción, 1514, *CDIA,* 1: 50–236.

5. King to Colón, Cádiz, May 3, 1509, *CDIA,* 23: 296.

6. King to Colón, Valladolid, Aug. 14, 1509, *CDIA,* 31: 439; King to Pasamonte, Monzón, June 15, 1510, *CDIA,* 31: 99.

7. Contract between Crown and Ponce de León /paraphrased), Concepción, May 1, 1509, *CDIA,* 34: 357–60, 489.

8. King to Colón, Madrid, Feb. 28, 1510, *CDIU,* 5: 204; Wright, *The Early History,* pp. 70–71; king to Colón [Seville], June 6, 1511, *CDIU,* 1: 11.

9. King to Colón, Madrid, Feb. 28, 1510, *CDIU,* 5: 202; king to *repartidores de indios* of Puerto Rico, Valladolid, Sept. 27, 1514, *MHDPR,* 3-1: 276.

10. Pedro de Mazuelo to king [Sevilla la Nueva], April 21, 1515, *EHR,* 36: 86.

11. Since the Indian population was undergoing more or less constant decrease, the Crown's holdings, which were replenished as needed, were probably proportionately higher each year. In 1514, the Crown held about 500 of 5,500 Indian laborers on Puerto Rico. In the same year the Crown held 1,367 Indians on Española out of 22,181 encomienda Indians. Though this is only a little over 6 percent of the whole, the total number declined rapidly after 1514 but the Crown's

holdings, supervised by Pasamonte, are likely to have remained more or less constant. Calculations based on the Alburquerque repartimiento.

12. King to Colón, Burgos, Feb. 23, 1512, *CDIA*, 32: 336.

13. The king urged Colón to find out if there was gold on Cuba (Cádiz, May 3, 1509, *CDIA*, 23: 303); he asked Pasamonte to find out all possible information about Cuba (Valladolid, May 13, 1509, *CDIHA*, 6: 159). He told the officials of the Casa de Contratación to keep funds on hand to enter into contracts to make discoveries (n.p. [1511?], *CDIA*, 32: 399). See also king to Colón, Sevilla, June 25, 1511, *CDIA*, 32: 193.

14. González Dávila served as auditor of the treasury accounts in 1509, then returned in 1511 as contador, serving until about 1519. King to Colón, Cádiz, May 3, 1509, *CDIA*, 22: 290–309; king to González Dávila, Valladolid, July 30, 1511, *CDIA*, 32: 267–70. Juan de Ampiés served as factor from 1511 to 1533. Royal instructions to Ampiés [Burgos?], October, 1511, *CDIU*, 5: 336–41; Giménez Fernández, *Bartolomé* 2, p. 1125; Enrique Otte, "La expedición de Gonzola de Ocampo a Cumaná en 1521 en las cuentas de tesorería de Santo Domingo," *RI*, No. 63 (January–March, 1956), 57.

15. "I marvel at the bad management our enterprises had on San Juan," the king told the treasury officials there. (Burgos, Feb. 23, 1512, *MHDPR*, 3-1: 114).

16. King to Sancho Velázquez, Burgos, Feb. 23, 1512, *CDIA*, 34: 356–57; Residencia of Ponce de León, Caparra, *CDIA*, 34: 469–70.

17. *Demanda* presented by Ponce de León to Sancho Velázquez, Caparra, 1519, *CDIA*, 34: 336–515.

18. King to Arce, Seville, Feb. 26, 1511, *CDIA*, 32: 116–18; king to Castro, Guaza, Dec. 12, 1514, *MHDPR*, 3-1: 358–59. Haro was named treasurer by a cédula, Valladolid, May 13, 1513, *MHDPR*, 3-1: 216–18, and Sedeño was named contador at Burgos, Aug. 10, 1512, *MHDPR*, 3-1: 134–37.

19. King to Pasamonte, Seville, June 6, 1511, *CDIA*, 32: 157.

20. King to Colón, Burgos, Feb. 23, 1512, *EHR*, 36: 80.

21. Garay would serve till 1523 when he left for New Spain, Mazuelo till 1536. Morales Padrón, *Jamaica*, p. 217.

22. King to Ovando, Burgos, April 30, 1508, *CDIA*, 32: 5–24.

23. Ibid., 6–18; Murga Sanz, *Juan*, p. 51; cédula, Burgos, Nov. 8, 1511, *BHPR*, 4: 216–17.

24. King to Colón, Valladolid, Aug. 14, 1509, *CDIA*, 31: 450. The *escudero* was a squire or shield-bearer, the *labrador* a farmer.

25. King to Colón, Valladolid, Aug. 14, 1509, *CDIA*, 31: 451.

26. King to Colón, Seville, June 6, 1511, *CDIU*, 5: 312–13.

27. Las Casas to Cisneros, n.p., n.d., *CDIA*, 1: 255.

28. The Alburquerque repartimiento showed that the most favored resident vecinos held approximately this number of Indians.

29. King to Colón, Monzón, June 15, 1510, *CDIA*, 32: 87; Con-

chillos was assigned 400 Indians on Puerto Rico alone. King to Ponce de León, Burgos, Sept. 9, 1511, *CDIA*, 32: 280–83. Officials soon acquired more than the 200 assigned them, and the king decreed on Feb. 22, 1512, that 300 on any one island would be the maximum allowed. Cédula, Burgos, *CDIA*, 10: 545–49. Casas said that Conchillos held 1,100 Indians and Fonseca, 800. Las Casas, *Historia* 2, p. 443. There are no complete records of encomiendas for Cuba and Jamaica; such holdings on the two islands were usually in partnerships with various vecinos. Conchillos was granted 200 Indians on Cuba. King to Diego Velázquez, Valladolid, May 12, 1513, *CDAHC*, 1: 9–10.

30. In 1508 the king permitted prospectors who discovered mines to work them for one year; he would buy the gold at 400 *maravedís* per peso (the regular rate was 450–475 maravedís), and pay 10 mrs. per peso into a road repair fund. King to Ovando, Burgos, April 30, 1508, *CDIU*, 5: 143–44. King to Consejo of Caparra, Sevilla, Feb. 26, 1511, *CDIA*, 32: 124–26.

31. King to treasury officials of Puerto Rico, Valbuena, Oct. 19, 1514, *MHDPR*, 3-1: 313.

32. Cédula, Granada, Sept. 3, 1501, *CDIA*, 38: 511–13.

33. Cédula [Segovia?], [August, 1503?], *CDIA*, 31: 196–200.

34. King to Colón, Tordesillas, July 25, 1511, *CDIA*, 32: 263; Las Casas, *Historia* 2, p. 499.

35. King to González Dávila, Valladolid, Aug. 14, 1509, *CDIHA*, 6: 168–69; king to Colón, Valladolid, Aug. 14, 1509, *CDIA*, 31: 438–39.

36. Colón made contracts with Bastidas and Garay to bring Indian slaves. King to Colón, Monzón, July 3, 1510, *CDIHA*, 6: 284. The armador fitted out the slaving armadas.

37. Rodrigo Manzorro's son-in-law, Francisco Barrionuevo, transferred certain Lucayo Indians, his mestiza wife's property, from Española to Puerto Rico. King to Lic. Rodrigo de Figueroa, Barcelona, June 19, 1519, *MHDPR*, 3-2: 108.

38. Cansinos was a shipmaster aboard the *San Cristóbal* in the commerce with Spain. He cleared Puerto Plata in 1512, returned to Española in 1513, and remained. Chaunu, *Séville* 2, pp. 52–57.

39. King to Colón, Valladolid, Nov. 12, 1509, *CDIA*, 31: 473; King to Colón, Monzón, June 15, 1510, *CDIA*, 31: 92.

40. Garay's ship, whose master was Juan Bono de Quejo, stopped at Caparra port en route to Guadeloupe where Garay was to establish a fort if signs of gold warranted it. Against orders, Bono took the ship to Spain along with Cerón and Díaz as prisoners. Murga Sanz, *Juan*, p. 50; Coll y Toste, "Principios," p. 99; Autógrafos de Cristóbal Colón y papeles de América, los publica la Duquesa de Berwick y de Alba, Condesa de Siruela (excerpt) (Madrid, 1892), *BHPR*, 1: 132–33.

41. Nicuesa and Ojeda were authorized to enslave the Indians of these islands. Amando Melón y Ruiz de Gordejuela, *Los primeros tiempos de la colonización. Cuba y las Antillas. Magallanes y la primera vuelta al mundo.* Vol. 6 of Antonio Ballesteros y Beretta, dir.,

Historia de América y de los pueblos americanos (Barcelona, 1952), pp. 283–87; Las Casas, *Historia* 2, p. 333; Martire, *Decadas* 1, p. 226.

42. Las Casas, *Historia* 2, p. 338.

43. Cédula, Burgos, June 3, 1511, *CDIU*, 5: 258–62.

44. King to Casa de Contratación, Tordesillas, July 25, 1511, *CDIA*, 32: 248; Oviedo to Royal Council, n.p., n.d., *CDIA*, 34: 121–22 (Oviedo cites arms received about 1512 by Judge Matienzo); King to Casa de Contratación, Burgos, Feb. 23, 1512, *CDIA*, 32: 360.

45. King to Colón, Seville, June 25, 1511, *CDIA*, 32: 187; king to Colón, Burgos, Feb. 23, 1512, *CDIA*, 32: 333.

46. Public Announcement, Seville, Oct. 17, 1511, *CDIU*, 5: 335.

47. King to Colón, León, Nov. 28, 1514, *MHDPR*, 3-1: 356; Treasury officials and judges of appeal to king [Santo Domingo], Sept. 6, 1515, *CDIA*, 36: 412.

48. During 1509–15, Chaunu's records show that 185 vessels sailed from Spain to the Indies and 175 returned.

49. This is the number of persons receiving Indians in the Alburquerque repartimiento. The count of Juan Bautista Muñoz was 715, *CDIA*, 7: 446.

50. King to consejo of Caparra, Sevilla, Feb. 26, 1511, *MHDPR*, 3-1: 49–50. The privilege was gradually extended to other areas.

51. Las Casas, *Historia* 2, p. 302; Ballesteros, *Cristóbal Colón* 5, p. 683; Jose Almoina, "La biblioteca erasmista de Diego Méndez," *PUSD*, 35 (1945) (whole vol.), p. 15; Oviedo, *Historia* 117, p. 89; Gustavo A. Mejía Ricart, *Historia de Santo Domingo*, 8 vols. (Ciudad Trujillo, 1948–54), 4, p. 73.

52. Colón resided in Garay's residence, finest in the city, while his own mansion was under construction. Las Casas, *Historia* 2, p. 309.

53. Garay apparently began his mercantile ventures by buying one quarter of the *Santiago*, whose master was Juan de Jerez of Palos. Jerez owned one half the caravel and Miguel Díaz the other one quarter. Chaunu, *Séville* 2, pp. 28–29. His later stature as a maritime merchant is appreciated by observing that the Crown's gold (in this case from Puerto Rico) was entrusted to his *nao* for shipment to Spain. Cisneros to treasury officials on Puerto Rico, Madrid, July 22, 1517, *MHDPR*, 3-1: 455–56.

54. Dyewood cutting was increasing as Colón told the king he had 500 quintals (the largest amount thus far recorded by documents) ready for shipment. King to Colón, Seville, June 25, 1511, *CDIA*, 32: 194. Garay became alcaide at Jacmel after Diego Colón arrived. Giménez Fernández, *Bartolomé* 2, pp. 1169–70.

55. Bastidas farmed the almojarifazgo tax during 1509–11, though his retention of it may have been lost in a dispute with the Seville merchant Juan Fernández de la Vara; he again farmed the tax in 1519–21; it was a position normally entrusted only to someone the buyers of goods felt had sufficient experience to evaluate imports justly. He had made a voyage to the Pearl Coast by 1512 and sent ships

to the Main more or less regularly after 1515. King to Colón, Seville, June 25, 1511, *CDIA*, 32: 192; Interrogation made by Colón, Santo Domingo, June 16, 1512, *CDIU*, 7: 185–86; Probanza of Bastidas, Santo Domingo, June 21, 1521, *CDIA*, 2: 368.

56. The Tapias, according to Giménez Fernández, were taken off La Feria street, Seville, by Bishop Rodríguez de Fonseca, to whom they owed their start on Española. Cristóbal was best known for his failure to replace Cortés in New Spain, where he had been sent owing to Rodríguez de Fonseca's influence; the Tapias were among those most successful in making the transition from mining to sugar plantations. Giménez Fernández, *Bartolomé* 2, p. 108; Oviedo, *Historia* 117, p. 86; king to Francisco de Tapia, Burgos, June 8, 1508, *CDIA*, 36: 243.

57. Ayllón was the son-in-law of Lic. Juan Becerra of Santiago de Caballeros. Giménez Fernández, *Bartolomó* 1, 323. Diego Colón wrote to the king on July 22, 1512, that vecinos of Santiago asked for a contract to bring Indians "from certain parts." King to Colón, Logroño, Dec. 10, 1512, *MHDPR*, 3-1: 162.

58. King to Ponce de León, Burgos, Nov. 22, 1511, Tío, *Nuevas fuentes*, p. 463.

59. By 1509 he was half-owner with Alonso Sarmiento of the *S.M. de Regla*. Chaunu, *Séville* 2, pp. 32–33. He owned the naos *Santa Maria de Consolación* and *Santiago* by 1513. Murga Sanz, *Juan*, p. 104.

60. King to Ponce de León, Valladolid, Sept. 27, 1514, *MHDPR*, 3-1: 277–78.

61. Murga Sanz, *Juan*, pp. 24, 81, 95; Tío, *Nuevas fuentes*, p. 164.

62. King to Díaz, Seville, June 21, 1511, *MHDPR*, 3-1: 78–80.

63. King to Pasamonte, Valladolid, May 4, 1513, *MHDPR*, 3-1: 212–13. Tiedra was probably a half-brother, though such distinction was not made in this document nor was it customary.

64. Las Casas, *Historia* 2, p. 479. Velázquez had prospects of marrying Bishop Rodríguez de Fonseca's niece. Giménez Fernández, *Bartolomé* 2, p. 225.

65. Oswaldo Morales Patiño, "Los indígenas en los primeros municipios cubanos," *RAEC*, 7, Nos. 13–14 (January–DECEMBER, 1951), 381. Porcallo went native in the manner of the Roldanistas of Jaraguá, and was the father of a numerous progeny, mainly mestizos. Wright, *The Early*, p. 88.

66. Preliminary study by Murga Sanz, *MHDPR*, 3-1: xxv.

67. Promulgation of the will of Diego Colón, Santo Domingo, May 2, 1526, *CDIA*, 40: 219.

68. King to Pasamonte, Tordesillas, July 25, 1511, *CDIA*, 32: 232; King to Nicuesa, Tordesillas, July 25, 1511, *CDIA*, 32: 236–39; King to Ojeda, Tordesillas, July 25, 1511, *CDIA*, 32: 240–44; King to Colón, Tordesillas, July 25, 1511, *CDIA*, 32: 260; king to judges of appeal, Burgos, Oct. 5, 1511, *CDIHA*, 6: 395–96.

69. Melón, *Los primeros*, pp. 312–13.

70. Memorial of Hernando Colón, Seville, March 3, 1511, *CDIU*, 7: 31–32.

71. Decision of the Royal Council, Seville, May 5, 1511, *CDIU*, 7: 42–47; Confirmation, Seville, June 17, 1511, *CDIA*, 36: 345–50.

72. Juan de la Peña to king, Burgos, Jan. 3, 1512, *CDIU*, 7: 59–61. The king never claimed that Veragua fell within Bastidas's discoveries, but the area produced little gold, and was not an object of controversy.

73. Royal Ordinance, Burgos, Oct. 5, 1511, *CDIA*, 11: 546–555. Owing to Colón's exercise of most judicial powers, this court did not function, except rarely, as a regular audiencia till after Colón's death in 1526.

74. The judges left Spain in March, 1512. King to the Casa de Contratación, Burgos, March 20, 1512, *CDIHA*, 6: 433.

75. Giménez Fernández, *Bartolomé*, 1: 36, 324.

76. King to Colón, Burgos, Feb. 23, 1512, *CDIU*, 7: 326.

77. Judges of appeal to king, Santo Domingo, Feb. 22, 1513, *CDIA*, 34: 155–56.

78. Ibid., 34: 158.

79. "Your report on encomiendas is not informative," the king wrote to Colón, "and I marvel at it considering the many times I have told you how to report it." King to Colón, Burgos, Dec. 23, 1511, *CDIA*, 32: 316–17.

80. Their official orders to Sancho Velázquez have not been found; the king had accepted his appointment by Oct. 9, 1514. King to Sancho Velázquez, Valbuena, Oct. 9, 1514, *MHDPR*, 2: lxxxcii.

81. Alburquerque repartimiento, Concepción, 1514, *CDIA*, 1: 50; Giménez Fernández thought Ibañez died July 15, 1514 (*Bartolomé* I, 31), but he was still living on Sept. 5, 1514 and died sometime before November. Interrogation by Colón, Santo Domingo, Sept. 5, 1514, *CDIU*, 7: 362. Antonio Muro Orejón, "Ordenanzas reales sobre los Indios (Las leyes de 1512–13)," *AEA*, 13 (1956): 470.

82. Murga Sanz, *Juan*, p. 169.

83. Residencia of Matienzo, Santo Domingo, 1517, AGI, Justicia, Leg. 42.

84. Ibid.

85. Colón probably reached Spain in late January or early February, 1515. He stated in his will that he arrived in Seville in April. Giménez Fernández states that his uncle, Diego, who accompanied him, died in Seville before Feb. 20, 1515. I would account for this seeming disparity in dates by the probability that the viceroy stayed down river around Palos and Moguer until April to arrange for the taking of testimony to support his claims, while his ailing uncle at once went to Seville. Promulgation of the will of Colón, Santo Domingo, May 2, 1526, *CDIA*, 40: 212; Giménez Fernández, *Bartolomé*, 2: 83.

86. Pasamonte to king, Santo Domingo, Oct. 6, 1515, *CDIA*, 36: 424.

87. Las Casas, *Historia* 2, p. 316.

88. Lebrón to king [Santo Domingo], Aug. 5, 1515, *CDIA*, 36: 374.

89. Giménez Fernández, *Bartolomé* 1, p. 84–85.

90. Tibesar, "The Franciscan," p. 381.

91. Bobadilla brought a Benedictine chaplain in 1500. Ortega, *La Rábida* 2, p. 298. Other than general mention in scattered documents, an idea of the number and names of friars in the Indies to 1509 is best obtained from Ortega and from Borges, "Primeras."

92. Memorial of Don Diego Colón, n.p., n.d., *BHPR*, 1 (1914): 134.

93. Juan Meseguer Fernández, "La Bula 'Ite vos' (29 de mayo de 1517) y la reforma cisneriana," *AIA*, n.s., 18, Nos. 71–72 (July–December, 1958): 260, 266–67, 272–73, 278.

94. Ortega, *La Rábida* 3, pp. 21–217; 224–25.

95. Giménez Fernández, *Bartolomé* 1, p. 44.

96. Tibesar, "The Franciscan," p. 384. Apparently Dominicans were on Jamaica and Cuba by 1512 but neither their names or the number are known. King to Colón, Logroño, Dec. 10, 1512, *MHDPR*, 3-1: 161. In a letter of 1516 the friars said they had begun work on Cuba before Diego Velázquez went there; since the letter is signed by both Dominicans and Franciscans it is not clear which order is meant. Dominicans and Franciscans to Chievres, June 4, 1516, *CDIA*, 7: 427.

97. Persons suspected of heresy who had emigrated to the Indies promoted the issuance of a cédula, Burgos, Oct. 5, 1511, *CDIU*, 5: 307–10, which banned any son or grandson of a *quemado* from holding office in the Indies.

98. Provincial of Dominicans to Vicar General of Indies, Burgos, March 16, 1512, *CDIHA*, 6: 425–26; king to Colón, Burgos, March 20, 1512, *CDIA*, 32: 375–77.

99. Las Casas, *Historia* 2, pp. 318, 321.

100. Ibid., pp. 503–4.

101. Venancio Diego Carro, O.P., *La teologia y los teólogos—juristas espanoles ante la conquista de América*, 2 vols. (Madrid, 1944); Carro, "Bartolomé de las Casas y las controversias teológico-jurídicas de Indias," *BRAH*, 132 (January–March, 1953): 260.

102. Giménez Fernández, *Bartolomé* 1, pp. 47, 155.

103. Las Casas, *Historia* 2, p. 497.

104. Ibid., pp. 390–92.

105. Notably the friars Antonio de Gallegos, Pedro Mejía, Juan Altemang, Tomás Guadalajara, Andrés Ordoñez, Lateranus de Beaurepaire, Fr. de Vallonis, and Tomás Infante. Others were soon of a like mind if indeed they were not already. They asked for the Cisnerian reform of their rule as well as support for evangelization. Franciscan friars to Cisneros, Santo Domingo, Feb. 15, 1516, *CDIA*, 36: 442–45; Giménez Fernández, *Bartolome* 1, pp. 47–48; Dominicans and Franciscan friars to Monsieur de Chievres, Santo Domingo, June 4, 1516, *CDIA*, 7: 397–430.

106. King to Franciscan general, Burgos, June 26, 1512, *CDIHA*, 6: 453–54.

107. King to Treasurer Luis Francisco de Vargas, Burgos, June 27, 1512, Ortega, *La Rábida* 3, p. 224.

108. King to Colón, Logroño, Dec. 10, 1512, *MHDPR*, 3-1: 161. Though they were granted alms of 100 *pesos de oro* yearly by this document, the amount was apparently increased to 300 *pesos de oro* later, if indeed the 100 was not a misprint. King to treasurer at Santo Domingo, Zaragoza, Aug. 2, 1518, Serrano y Sanz, *Orígenes*, p. dlxxx.

109. Colón to Cisneros, Santo Domingo, Jan. 12, 1512, *CDIE*, 104: 348; Las Casas, *Historia* 3, pp. 65–66; Giménez Fernández, *Bartolomé* 2, p. 205.

110. Giménez Fernández decided that Las Casas must have been ordained in November, 1512, by Bishop Manso who stopped off (presumably at Concepción) en route to Puerto Rico. Las Casas then went to Cuba with Narváez in January, 1513. (*Bartolomé* 1, p. 50). The most serious objection to this explanation is that Las Casas said he gave his first mass in Concepción "in the same year and same days" that Fr. Córdoba went to the Vega, which he said was in the same year (1510) that Córdoba arrived in Española. Since this year was of great importance in his personal life, it seems unlikely that Las Casas would confuse it with a later one. If this surmise is correct, then he could only have been ordained, probably in Seville, prior to 1510. (Las Casas, *Historia* 2, pp. 318–21).

111. Las Casas, *Historia* 3, pp. 67–68.

112. Giménez Fernández, *Bartolomé* 2, p. 1109.

113. Franciscans to Cisneros, Santo Domingo, Feb. 15, 1516, *CDIA*, 36: 442–45.

114. Oviedo, *Historia* 119, pp. 249–50.

115. Las Casas, *Historia* 3, p. 74; Giménez Fernández, *Bartolomé* 2, p. 1110; Franciscans to Cisneros [Santo Domingo, 1516], Giménez Fernández, *Bartolomé* 2, p. 1231.

116. Las Casas, Historia 3, p. 74.

117. His support of the missionaries was constant after 1509. A typical document: king to Casa de Contratación, Burgos, July 28, 1512, *MHDPR*, 3-1: 132–33. In *La Rábida*, Ortega carefully records the details of such support for the Franciscans.

118. Tobar, *Compendio*, pp. 45–46; 56–58.

119. The bull *Romanus Pontifex*, Rome, Aug. 6, 1511. Tobar, *Compendio*, pp, 56–58. Dictamen [Rome? July, 1510?], *BRAH*, 20 (1892): 292–94. This anonymously written opinion stated that "as he (Ferdinand) wishes that the tithes of that island of Española belong to the kings by apostolic bulls," which suggests that the 1501 bull was not incorporated in the 1508 bull.

120. Bull issued at Rome, April 8, 1510, *CDIU*, 5: 205–9. W. Eugene Shiels, *King and Church. The Rise and Fall of the Patronato Real* Chicago, 1961), pp. 113–15. Comments by Fr. Fidel Fita, who also published the bull, make clear it was contrary to custom. *BRAH*, 20 (1892): 288–90. The exclusion of gold from the tithe was the main

reason that the archbishopric at Santo Domingo, nominally established in 1504, was not recreated. Dictamen [Rome? July, 1510?], *BRAH,* 20: 292–94.

121. E. Ward Loughran, "The First Episcopal Sees in Spanish America," *HAHR,* 10, No. 2 (May, 1930): 178.

122. Ballesteros, *Cristóbal Colón,* 5, p. 657.

123. Murga Sanz, *Juan,* p. 91.

124. Giménez Fernández, *Bartolomé* 1, p. 50. Manso later served as Colón's teniente on Puerto Rico, after the viceroy's restoration in 1520.

125. Archbishop of Seville to king, Sevilla, Feb. 2, 1514, *BRAH,* 20: 603–4.

126. Fr. Cipriano de Utrera, "Episcopologío Domínicopolitano," *BAGNSD,* 18, No. 86 (July–September, 1955): 235.

127. Bishop Manso was accompanied by a chaplain, mayordomo, and a *maestresala,* as well as some criados and artisans. Murga Sanz, *Juan,* p. 98.

128. Coll y Toste, "Nuevo alzamiento," p. 171.

129. E. Ward Loughran, "The First Episcopal Sees," p. 181. The best evidence of Manso's complaint is found in Cisneros to Jeronymites, Madrid, Nov. 28, 1516 (two letters), *MHDPR,* 3-1: 420–22.

130. Bishop Manso returned in time to officiate at King Ferdinand's funeral. Murga Sanz, Introduction to *MHDPR,* 1, lxiv–lxv.; Introduction to *MHDPR* 2: xcvii.

131. His ecclesiastical cabildo consisted of a provisor, archpriest, canon, and rationer. Alburquerque repartimiento, Concepción, 1514, *CDIA* 1: 73.

132. Loughran, "The First Episcopal Sees," p. 183.

133. Pasamonte to king, Santo Domingo, Feb. 20, 1516, Angel Altolaguirre y Duvale, *Vasco Núñez de Balboa* (Madrid, 1914), p. 115; Giménez Fernández, *Bartolomé* 2, p. 1192.

134. Complaints were made through procuradores and especially at the general junta held in Santo Domingo in the spring of 1518.

135. Notes by Fr. Fidel Fita, *BRAH,* 20 (1892): 291–92.

NOTES TO CHAPTER 5

1. Zuazo to Chievres, Santo Domingo, Jan. 22, 1518, *CDIA,* 1: 311.

2. Judges to the king [Santo Domingo], Aug. 5, 1515, *CDIA,* 36: 375–77. They had jailed Marcos de Aguilar, Gerónimo de Agüero, Fernando de Carvajal, and Lope Vardell [Bardeci], but could only brand as rebels certain of Colón's criados who took refuge in the Franciscan monastery. Lebrón to king [Santo Domingo], Aug. 5, 1515, *CDIA,* 36: 374–75; the vara was a rod carried as the symbol of authority by a town official. The strife on Puerto Rico is described later in king to Royal Council, Zaragoza, May 22, 1518, *CDIU,* 8: 328–29.

3. As noted in Chapter II.

4. Velázquez to king, Caparra, April 27, 1515, *CDIA*, 36: 351. One example is Martin de Eguiluz's complaint that he was authorized to receive 80 Indians and Velázquez gave him less than 50. Cisneros to Jeronymites, Madrid, Nov. 10, 1516, Serrano y Sanz, *Orígenes*, pp. dxliii–dxliv.

5. Cisneros to Jeronymites, Madrid, July 22, 1517, *CDAHC*, 1: 44–45.

6. Zuazo to Chievres, Santo Domingo, Jan. 22, 1518, *CDIA*, 1: 309.

7. Ayllón to Jeronymites, Santo Domingo, 1517, Giménez Fernández, *Bartolomé*, 1: 574–75.

8. Conchillos countersigned a falsified cédula dated Dec. 24, 1515, conferring on Juan de Samano a certain *escribanía* in Cuba. Giménez, *Bartolomé*, I, 116.

9. Santa Cruz, *Crónica* 2, pp. 281, 301, 320.

10. King to Ponce de León, Valladolid, Dec. 18, 1514, *MHDPR*, 3–1: 364; king to Colón, Cantillana, June 24, 1511, *CDIHA*, 6: 365–66; Zuazo to Chievres, Santo Domingo, Jan. 22, 1518, *CDIA*, 1: 308; Las Casas, *Historia* 2, pp. 396.

11. Garay to king [Sevilla la Nueva], June 11, 1515, *EHR*, 36: 89.

12. Cisneros to Jeronymites, Madrid, Dec. 21, 1516, *CDIU*, 1: 68–69; cédula, Madrid, Dec. 21, 1516, Serrano y Sanz, *Orígenes*, p. dxlviii; Manuel Giménez Fernández, "Las Cortes de la Española en 1518," *AUH*, 15, No. 2 (1954). 64; 68–69; 76.

13. Giménez Fernández, "Las Cortes," p. 64.

14. Memorial of Las Casas to Cisneros [Madrid? 1516?], *CDIA*, 7: 14–65.

15. Santa Cruz, *Crónica* 2, p. 302; Las Casas, *Historia* 3, p. 74.

16. Las Casas, *Historia* 3, pp. 74–76.

17. Santa Cruz, *Crónica* 2, pp. 334, 338.

18. Luis Fernández de Retana, *Cisneros y su siglo*, 2 vols. (Madrid, 1929–30), 2, p. 16.

19. Fernández de Retana, *Cisneros* 2, p. 152.

20. Giménez Fernández, *Bartolomé*, pp. 5, 80, 242.

21. Memorial of Casas to Cisneros [Madrid] [March 20, 1516], *CDIA*, 7: 12. Date determined by Giménez Fernández, *Bartolomé* 1, p. 117. Narváez wrote a brief *informe* which was appended to the memorial.

22. Giménez Fernández, *Bartolomé* 1, p. 131.

23. Summary notes by Juan Bautista Muñoz, *CDIA*, 7: 440.

24. Giménez Fernández, *Bartolomé* 1, pp. 212–25.

25. Royal Instructions to the Jeronymites, Madrid, Sept. 18, 1516, *CDIA*, 11: 262, 268; Las Casas, *Historia* 3, p. 98.

26. Giménez Fernández, *Bartolomé* 1, pp. 91, 118.

27. Cisneros to Zuazo, Madrid, Oct. 12, 1516; Giménez Fernández, *Bartolomé* 1, pp. 493–96.

28. Zuazo to king, Santo Domingo, Jan. 22, 1518, *CDIA*, 34: 263; Biographical sketch of Zuazo by M.F.N. [Martín Fernández Navarrete], *CDIE*, 2: 375.

29. Las Casas, *Historia* 3, p. 106.

30. Cisneros to Casa de Contratación, Madrid, Oct. 3, 1516, Serrano y Sanz, *Orígenes*, pp. dxli–dxlii.

31. Cisneros to Casa de Contratación, Madrid, Oct. 24, 1516, Serrano y Sanz, *Orígenes*, pp. dxli–dxliii.

32. Ortega, *La Rábida* 3, 229–30; cédula, Madrid, Nov. 8, 1516, Serrano y Sanz, *Orígenes*, p. dxliii.

33. Zuazo to Chievres, Santo Domingo, Jan. 22, 1518, *CDIA* 1, 312.

34. According to Otte, pearl fishing (rather than mere pearl barter) began about 1515 on Cubagua with Pedro Ortiz de Matienzo, brother of Judge Matienzo, as Colón's alcalde mayor. "La expedición," p. 52. It is doubtful whether this actually occurred, apart from Colón's intent to carry it out. Colón was out of effective power in 1515, and his appointee, if he ever resided on Cubagua, would have been removed. No other official is mentioned as residing there till Figueroa named one in 1520.

35. Statement of Juan García Caballero, residencia of Matienzo, AGI, Justicia, Leg. 42.

36. Giménez Fernández, *Bartolomé* 2, p. 1110.

37. Ibid., p. 233.

38. Ibid., p. 1219.

39. King to Casa de Contratación, Barcelona, May 7, 1519, Ortega, *La Rábida* 3, p. 234; king to Don Juan Manuel, La Coruña, May 17, 1518, Giménez Fernández, *Bartolomé* 2, pp. 1235–36.

40. Order, Santo Domingo, July 4, 1517, *CDIA*, 36: 521–25. The written order confirmed what they had earlier recommended verbally.

41. Jeronymites to Cisneros, Santo Domingo, Jan. 20, 1517, *CDIA* 1, pp. 267–68. Giménez Fernández, "Las Cortes," p. 143.

42. Oviedo, *Historia* 117, p. 94.

43. Interrogation conducted by the Jeronymites, Santo Domingo, [1517], *CDIA*, 24: 201–29.

44. Opinion of Ayllón, Santo Domingo, 1517, Giménez Fernández, *Bartolomé* 1, pp. 573–90.

45. Las Casas, *Historia* 3, p. 106; Giménez Fernández, *Bartolomé* 1, p. 307.

46. Las Casas, *Historia* 3, p. 124.

47. Ibid.

48. Jeronymites to Cisneros, Santo Domingo, June 22, 1517, *CDIA* 1, pp. 286–87.

49. Following comments are based on the residencia of Matienzo, Santo Domingo, 1517, AGI, Justicia, Leg. 42. The court of appeal was reinstated by an order issued Aug. 24, 1518, but it was apparently not sent till at least 1519 (Giménez Fernández, *Bartolomé* 2, pp. 209–10). Even the latter year seems questionable, for officials at Santo Domingo

thanked the governors for reinstating that body only on Aug. 20, 1520 (*CDIA*, 1: 378).

50. Probanza of Bastidas, Santo Domingo, June 22, 1521, *CDIA*, 2, 404. Encomiendas were assigned to Bachelor Pedro Moreno and Pedro García de Villa with the obligation of establishing sugar mills.

51. King to Jeronymites, Barcelona, June 19, 1519, Serrano y Sanz, *Orígenes*, p. dciv.

52. Giménez Fernández, *Bartolomé* 2, pp. 241, 263.

53. Ibid., pp. 499–503.

54. Jeronymites to Cisneros, Santo Domingo, June 22, 1517, *CDIA*, 1: 284.

55. Cisneros to Zuazo, Madrid, July 22, 1517, *MHDPR*, 3–1: 454; Murga Sanz, *Juan*, p. 189.

56. Giménez Fernández, *Bartolomé* 1, p. 354.

57. Wright, *The Early History*, p. 73.

58. Bernaldino de Santa Clara to Francisco de los Cobos, Santiago de Cuba, Oct. 30, 1517, *CDIA*, 11: 556–57.

59. King to Mendoza and Barrionuevo, Barcelona, June 19, 1519, *MHDPR*, 3–2: 108–9.

60. Giménez Fernández, *Bartolomé* 2, pp. 132–35.

61. The treasurer of the Casa de Contratación, Sancho de Matienzo, was named abbot of Jamaica in 1515, a position he held in absentia till his death in 1521. Giménez Fernández, *Bartolomé* 2, p. 113. It is uncertain whether he derived any income from the position, for the vecinos on Jamaica resisted paying tithes and probably paid little if any except to the local Franciscan monastery.

62. Judges to king, Santo Domingo, Jan. 6, 1518, *CDIA*, 34: 236. (Lizaur's name is misprinted as Lozano.)

63. Giménez Fernández, *Bartolomé* 2, p. 142.

64. Zuazo to king, Santo Domingo, Jan. 22, 1518, *CDIA*, 34: 239.

65. Judges to king, Santo Domingo, Jan. 6, 1518, *CDIA*, 34: 236.

66. Giménez Fernández, *Bartolomé* 2, p. 160.

67. Ibid., p. 173.

68. Serrano was in Spain prior to July, 1519, for he had obtained a decree reducing judicial fines by that time. Cédula, Barcelona, July 5, 1519, *CDIU*, 9: 96–98.

69. Lewis Hanke was among the earliest writers to recognize Las Casas's great efforts in behalf of the Indians. See, for example, *The Spanish Struggle for Justice in the Conquest of America* (Philadelphia, 1949), pp. 55–56.

70. Giménez Fernández, *Bartolomé*, 2, p. 177.

71. Ballesteros, *Cristobal Colón* 5, p. 702; Giménez Fernández, *Bartolomé*, 1, p. 343.

72. Giménez Fernández, *Bartolome* 2, pp. 252–54.

73. He exercised little power till after the death of the Grand Chancellor Sauvage on June 7, 1518. Giménez Fernández, *Bartolomé* 2, p. 174.

74. King to Diego Velázquez, Barcelona, April 6, 1519, *MHDPR*, 3–2: 90–91. The documents make clear that the king considered the absentee encomiendas formally abolished on March 15, 1518.

75. Cédula, Zaragoza, Aug. 10, 1518, *CDIA*, 7: 423–24.

76. The first subcontract was to two Genoese at Seville: King to Adán de Vivaldo and Tomas de Forne, Zaragoza, Jan. 14, 1519, *MHDPR*, 3–2: 172–73. It was eventually passed to a Spanish merchant in Seville.

77. Various witnesses testified during Zuazo's residencia of Judge Matienzo that the royal fifth was not always taken out from pearls brought from Cubagua. Residencia of Matienzo, Santo Domingo, 1517, AGI, Justicia, Leg. 42.

78. Dates of formal appointment to office are not available, but all three were named by August or September, 1518. Giménez Fernández, *Bartolomé* 2, pp. 209, 230.

79. Pasamonte to Lope Conchillos, Santo Domingo, Aug. 28, 1520, *CDIA* 1: 414.

80. Instructions to Lic. Rodrigo de Figueroa, Zaragoza, Dec. 9, 1518, Serrano y Sanz, *Orígenes*, pp. dlxxxvii–dxcii.

81. Giménez Fernández, *Bartolomé* 2, p. 122.

82. King to Antonio de la Gama, Barcelona, March 3, 1519, *MHDPR*, 3–2: 50–55.

83. Though Figueroa said in Seville April 7 that he planned to sail soon (Figueroa to king, Seville, April 7, 1519, *CDIA*, 1: 368), he probably left in June with Antonio de la Gama, since they were at Caparra at the same time. For month of Gama's departure, Giménez Fernández, *Bartolomé* 2, p. 1065.

84. King to Antonio de la Gama, Barcelona, March 3, 1519, *MHDPR* 3–2: 48–49.

85. Figueroa to king, Santo Domingo, Sept. 12, 1519, *CDIA*, 36: 529–39. The document is misprinted as Sept. 12, 1517.

86. Treasury officials to king, Santo Domingo, Sept. 14, 1519, *CDIA*, 1: 373. Isásaga arrived on July 27. Figueroa may have arrived in August.

87. Giménez Fernández, *Bartolomé* 2, pp. 499–502.

88. Figueroa to king, Santo Domingo, Nov. 13, 1520, *CDIA*, 1: 421–22. Since he did not mention the treasury officials, I have assumed he removed their Indians. Pasamonte said he had no encomienda Indians on Aug. 28, though he had lost his Indians on Española in the epidemic of 1518–19.

89. Giménez Fernández, *Bartolomé* 2, pp. 497, 499–502.

90. King to Figueroa, La Coruña, May 18, 1520, Serrano y Sanz, *Orígenes*, p. dcv.

91. City of Santo Domingo to king, Santo Domingo, Aug. 29, 1520, *CDIA*, 1: 415.

92. The pesquisa and residencia comprise Vol. 2 of *MHDPR*, and pp. 336–515 OF *CDIA*, 34.

93. Gama to king, San Juan de Puerto Rico, May 30, 1520, *MHDPR*, 2: 11–13; introduction to *MHDPR*, 1: LXX.

94. Gama to king, San Juan de Puerto Rico, Feb. 15, 1521, *CDIA*, 40: 52–54.

95. Sauer, *The Spanish Main*, p. 203.

96. Other than several general statements about Indian fisheries, Francisco de Arbolancho stated in 1517 that he had been on the estancia of Judge Matienzo where he had a fishing boat that Indians used for fishing. Residencia of Matienzo, Santo Domingo, 1517, AGI, Justicia, Leg. 42.

97. Haro to king, Caparra, Jan. 21, 1518, Serrano y Sanz, *Orígenes*, p. dlxxvi.

98. Opinion of Ayllón, Santo Domingo, 1517, Giménez Fernández, *Bartolomé* 1, p. 578.

99. Giménez Fernández, *Bartolomé* 1, p. 313.

100. Statement of Gaspar de Astudillo in Probanza of Bastidas, Santa Domingo, June 22, 1521, *CDIA*, 2: 420. Scelle saw contraband of Negro slaves following a cédula of July 22, 1513, which put a tax on slaves. George Scelle, *La traite negriere aux Indes de Castile*, 2 vols. (Paris, 1906), 1, pp. 126–27.

101. F. D. Ashburn, ed., *The Ranks of Death: A Medical History of the Conquest of America* (New York, 1947). P. M. Ashburn judged that the Negro was the primary carrier of malaria, which thrives in lowlands and in stagnant pools of water. The Taíno custom of frequent bathing must have especially propagated the disease in the Caribbean islands. The work was edited and collated by his son, F. D. Ashburn, after Colonel Ashburn died leaving an incomplete manuscript

102. Fr. Bernaldino de Manzanedo to king, Valladolid, February, 1518, *CDIA*, 34: 296–97.

103. Las Casas, *Historia* 3, pp. 234–39. This revolt was also romanticized in Manuel de Jesus Galván's *indianista* novel, *Enriquillo*, published in 1878–82.

104. The conditions are described by various testifiers. Probanza of Bastidas, Santo Domingo, June 22, 1521, *CDIA*, 2: 366–467.

NOTES TO CHAPTER 6

1. Jiménez de Cisneros issued a cédula on July 28, 1517, suspending the right of Colón to name justices during his officials' residencias. Giménez Fernández, *Bartolomé* 2, p. 362.

2. Giménez Fernández, *Bartolomé* 2, p. 199; Oviedo, *Historia* 119, p. 78.

3. Cédula, Brussels, Jan. 14, 1517, *CDIU*, 8: 317–18.

4. Cédula, Mechlin, April 18, 1517, *CDIU*, 8: 318–19.

5. The queen received him as page on May 8, 1492. Ballesteros, *Cristóbal Colón* 4, p. 539.

6. Méndez epitomizes the loyal followers of the Columbus family. He is most famous for his canoe voyage from Jamaica to Española in 1503, to obtain aid for the marooned Columbus; he returned to Spain with the Discoverer, remained with him until his death, served Diego Colón in Spain and accompanied him to Española in 1509, returned with him in 1523 and served him till near the time of the viceroy's death. He was still aiding the third generation of Columbuses in 1535, the year before his own death. Almoina, "La biblioteca," pp. 15, 21–23.

7. Santa Cruz, *Crónica* 1, p. 184.

8. King to Pasamonte, La Coruña, May 16, 1520, *MHDPR*, 3–2: 369–70.

9. Colón established three chaplaincies in the Franciscan monastery at Santo Domingo, provided he was buried there, and he left the monastery 50 *pesos de oro*. He also provided for establishment of a nunnery of Santa Clara (Franciscan order) at Concepción. Promulgation of the will of Colon, Santo Domingo, May 2, 1526, *CDIA*, 40: 192, 200.

10. Las Casas, *Historia* 3, p. 338.

11. Zuazo to Chievres, Santo Domingo, Jan. 22, 1518, *CDIA*, 1: 322–23.

12. Giménez Fernández, *Bartolomé* 2, p. 182. The cédula applied to Puerto Rico where it was at least partly carried out; it was apparently not implemented on the other islands.

13. He was appointed procurador for Colón at least by March, 1518. Alonso Romano to king, Valladolid, March 18, 1518, *CDIU*, 8: 321–23.

14. Las Casas, *Historia* 3, pp. 338–39.

15. Cédula, La Coruña, May 17, 1520, *CDIU*, 8: 331–40.

16. The measure was not to Colón's liking, but the Council doubtless felt that local peace would be better maintained by this practice, which modified the 1492 capitulations.

17. Appeal of Diego Colón, Sevilla, Aug. 23, 1520, *CDIU*, 8: 340–44.

18. He was in Sanlúcar de Barrameda somewhat later but still knew nothing of the Comunero revolt, at least of its serious turn, as he expressed surprise on hearing news of it when at Santo Domingo,. Promulgation of the will of Colón, Santo Domingo, May 2, 1526, *CDIA*, 40: 227.

19. King to judges of appeal, Barcelona, Sept. 23, 1519, *AHR*, 21: 760–62; Cédula, Valladolid, Aug. 31, 1520, *CDIU*, 1: 105–6.

20. The document establishing the larger audiencia, with a president, seems not to be extant. The first evidence that the audiencia had been modified is in the use of the title President of the audiencia. Governor to President of Aud. of Española, Sevilla, Sept. 21, 1520, *CDIU*, 9: 135–37.

21. Minutes of the Royal Council, n. p., 1516, *CDIU*, 8: 314–16.

22. Oviedo, *Historia* Vol. 117, p. 101.

23. An example is the king's appointment of Fernando de Medina as regidor of Sancti Spiritus. King to Medina, Barcelona, Aug. 6, 1519, *CDAHC*, 1: 83–84. The system of the governor's nominating three

candidates for regidor seems never to have worked during Colón's era in the Caribbean. Both the Crown and Colón would ignore the ternary system after 1520. Appointing regidores was one of the Crown's best ways of assuring local loyalty.

24. Cédula, Valladolid, July 9, 1520, *CDIU*, 9: 132–33.

25. Governors of Spain to Diego Velázquez, Vitoria, Dec. 15, 1520, *CDIU*, 1: 110–11.

26. Cédula, Vitoria, Dec. 15, 1520, *CDIU*, 1: 111–14.

27. He was in San Juan de Puerto Rico by Nov. 4, 1520. Murga Sanz, *Juan*, p. 206.

28. Las Casas, *Historia* 3, p. 355; Giménez Fernández, *Bartolomé*, 2, 1219.

29. Giménez Fernández, *Bartolomé* 2, p. 1109.

30. Las Casas, *Historia* 3, p. 158.

31. Las Casas, *Historia* 3, pp. 257–61; Ballesteros, *Cristóbal Colón* 4, p. 41.

32. Las Casas's attempted colonization of Venezuela is treated succinctly by Hanke, *The Spanish Struggle*, pp. 54–71, and by Giménez Fernández in profuse detail, *Bartolomé* 2, Chs. XI–XIX.

33. King to Don Juan Manuel, La Coruña, May 17, 1518 [*sic*, actually 1520], Giménez Fernández, *Bartolomé* 2, pp. 1235–36.

34. This was Juan Bono de Quejo who had apparently taken slaves on Trinidad by 1517. Bono was among the most active ship captains in the Caribbean, serving all the islands and ending his days on Cuba. Las Casas thought his name should have been Juan Malo. Giménez Fernández, *Bartolomé* 1, p. 327.

35. Ibid., 2, p. 1052.

36. Oidores and treasury officials to the king, Santo Domingo, Nov. 14, 1520, *CDIA*, 1: 422–27. His actual declaration was made earlier than this paraphrased report of it.

37. Residencia of Matienzo, 1517, Santo Domingo, AGI, Justicia, Leg. 42. For details about the Caballero family, see Giménez Fernández, *Bartolomé* 2, pp. 1123–24.

38. Cisneros to Jeronymites, Madrid, July 22, 1517, Serrano y Sanz, *Orígenes*, p. dlxi.

39. Residencia of Sancho Velázquez [Caparra], 1519, *MHDPR*, 2: 103.

40. King to treasury officials on Puerto Rico, Barcelona, Jan. 14, 1520, *MHDPR*, 3–2: 153. King to Figueroa, Barcelona, July 5, 1519, *MHDPR*, 3–2: 121–22.

41. Giménez Fernández, *Bartolomé* 2, p. 1046.

42. Ibid., p. 1084.

43. Ibid., p. 1057.

44. Ibid., p. 1060.

45. Coll y Toste, "Nuevo alzamiento," *BHPR*, 10 (1923): 178.

46. Otte, "La Expedición," p. 63; Giménez Fernández, *Bartolomé* 2, pp. 1139–40.

47. Giménez Fernández, *Bartolomé* 2, p. 1153.

48. Ibid., p. 1146.
49. Ibid., p. 1112.
50. Ibid., pp. 1110; 1135–36.
51. Las Casas, *Historia* 3, pp. 359–61; Giménez Fernández, *Bartolomé* 2, pp. 1138, 1155.
52. Las Casas, *Historia* 3, pp. 359–61; Giménez Fernández, *Bartolomé* 2, pp. 1109, 1157, 1163.
53. Giménez Fernández, *Bartolomé* 2, p. 1192.
54. Miguel de Castellanos to king [n.p., 1523?], *CDIA*, 10: 32–39.
55. Las Casas, *Historia* 3, pp. 383–84; Giménez Fernández, *Bartolomé* 2, pp. 1199–1203.
56. Murga Sanz, *Juan*, p. 206.
57. King to Gama, La Coruña, May 17, 1520, *MHDPR*, 3-2: 164–65.
58. Testimony concerning relocation of Caparra [Caparra], July 13, 1519, *CDIA*, 36: 458. Moreno was presumably unrelated to his homonyn, the later fiscal of the audiencia at Santo Domingo, who first attempted to impose the authority of that body in Honduras.
59. Probanza of Bastidas, Santo Domingo, June 22, 1521, *CDIA* 2: 367.
60. Colón complained of it to Jiménez de Cisneros. Colón to Cisneros, Madrid, Oct. 11, 1516, *CDIU*, VIII, 8: 308–9.
61. Probanza by Diego Velázquez, Santiago de Cuba, 1521, *CDIA*, 35: 489.
62. Diego Velázquez to king, Santiago de Cuba, Feb. 20, 1521, *CDIA*, 11: 443.
63. Diego Velázquez to king, Santiago de Cuba, March 18, 1521, *CDIA*, 11: 447; Zuazo discontinued Velázquez's pesquisa on July 8, 1521. Probanza by Diego Velázquez, Santiago de Cuba, 1521, *CDIA*, 35: 497.
64. Cédula, Vitoria, Dec. 15, 1520, *CDIU*, 1: 111–14.
65. Zuazo's commission was declared void by the governors in Spain in September, 1521, and Diego Velázquez was restored to power on Dec. 23. Wright, *The Early History*, pp. 94–95. Colón set these aside, however, for Zuazo and later Ovalle ruled till early 1523.
66. Testimony concerning the deposition of city officials at Sancti Spiritus [Santiago de Cuba], March 13, 1522, *CDIU*, 1: 119–26.
67. Ibid., 119–26.
68. Ibid., 120; Wright, *The Early History*, p. 92.
69. Residencias of Diego Velázquez and Alonso Zuazo, Santiago de Cuba, March 14, 1525, *CDIU*, 1: 146–47. Francisco Benítez said Ovalle served under Zuazo for 5–6 months, after which Diego Velázquez appointed the tenientes.
70. Order, Santiago de Cuba, July 19, 1523, *CDAHC*, 1: 89–90. This order issued by Velázquez is the only firm evidence of his reassumption of the governorship.
71. Giménez Fernández, *Bartolomé* 2, p. 1112.
72. He instituted this practice at San Juan de Puerto Rico while en

route to Santo Domingo, naming Manuel de Lando to this position. It shows that Colón had decided how he would circumvent the restrictions on his powers, even before he reached the Indies. Murga Sanz, *Juan*, p. 206.

73. Memorial of the judges to the king [Santo Domingo? 1521?], *CDIU*, 5: 106.

74. Witnesses estimated that gold production was only one fifth of what it had been. Gonzalo de Ocampo thought it had dropped from 150,000 *pesos de oro* yearly to 30–40,000. Probanza of Bastidas, Santo Domingo, June 22, 1521, *CDIA*, 2: 392.

75. Statement of the fiscal Prado, Valladolid, Sept. 2, 1524, *CDIU*, 8: 367; 370–71; Memorial of the judges to the king, [Santo Domingo? 1521?], *CDIU*, 5: 107. Colón made certain that his one tenth was collected by appointing persons with that sole duty, as Juan García Caballero and Martín de Vergara. AGI, Patronato 10, Ramo 13.

76. Giménez Fernández, *Bartolomé*, 2, p. 1197.

77. Introduction to *MHDPR*, 2: c.

78. King to Ayllón, Valladolid, April 24, 1523, *MHDPR*, 3–2: 272–74.

79. The first document titling him juez de comisión is king to Ayllón, Valladolid, April 24, 1523, *MHDPR*, 3–2: 272–74.

80. King to Colón, Valladolid, March 13, 1523, *MHDPR*, 3–1: 309–14; Ordinance, Santo Domingo, Aug. 7, 1523, *MHDPR*, 3–1: 308–15.

81. Promulgation of the will of Colón, Santo Domingo, May 2, 1526, *CDIA*, 40: 181–231.

NOTES TO CHAPTER 7

1. Documents treating Velázquez's rejection of Ayllón's cognizance, Puerto de Guaniguanico, Feb. 24, 1520, *CDIA*, 35: 135.
2. Giménez Fernández, *Bartolomé* 2, p. 1054.
3. King to Ayllón, Valladolid, April 24, 1523, *MHDPR*, 3–2: 272–74.
4. Instructions of audiencia to Pedro Moreno, Santo Domingo, [1524?], *CDIE*, 1: 511–20.
5. King to audiencia, Toledo, Dec. 1, 1525, *MHDPR*, 3–2: 395.
6. Introduction to *MHDPR*, 2: xcvii.
7. Santa Cruz, *Crónica* 2, p. 93.
8. All three candidates died in Spain, though Las Casas thought Suárez de Deza died in Concepción (*Historia* 2, p. 378). Giménez Fernández, *Bartolomé* 1 p. 307; 2, p. 378; summary notes by Muñoz, *CDIA*, 7: 447.
9. Utrera, "Episcopología," p. 240.
10. Introduction to *MHDPR*, 2: xcvii.

11. Notes by Fita based on a manuscript by León Pinelo, *BRAH*, 20: 612.

12. Giménez Fernández, *Bartolomé* 2, p. 288.

13. The initial cédula was issued at Victoria, July 25, 1522, Lib. 1, Tit. 16, Ley 16, *Recop.* 1, 148; it was specifically applied to Cuba by the king to treasury officials, Valladolid, July 4, 1523, *CDIU*, 9: 183–84.

14. King to Prior of Dominicans and Guardian of San Francisco, Toledo, Dec. 1, 1525, *CDIU*, 9: 235–36; king to Fr. Antonio Montesinos, Toledo, Dec. 1, 1525, 1: 78–80.

15. First evidence of the Oriente revolt is the Order, Santiago de Cuba, July 19, 1523, *CDAHC*, 1: 89–90.

16. King to Garay, Barcelona, Aug. 29, 1519, *EHR*, 36: 94–95.

17. Jenaro Artiles, "Historia local de La Habana," *RBC*, 40, No. 2 (March–April, 1945): 120–23.

18. Murga Sanz, *Juan*, pp. 120–21.

19. Slaves taken in the first defensive war on Puerto Rico, n.p., January [1511], Murga Sanz, *Juan*, pp. 280–82 (Barrionuevo was a participant); king to Barrionuevo, Toledo, July 28, 1525, *MHDPR*, 3–1: 349–351; Giménez Fernández, *Bartolomé* 2, pp. 1066, 1108; Oviedo, *Historia* 117, p. 110.

20. Interrogation by the city of Santo Domingo on depopulation of the island, Santo Domingo, April 16, 1520, *CDIA* 1: 397.

21. Interrogation by Ayllón, Santo Domingo, March 5, 1526, *CDIA*, 35 p. 552.

22. Their former residence in the interior towns is indicated by the Alburquerque repartimiento. Villoria still claimed to be a vecino of Concepción in the 1520's, but seems nonetheless to be an *estante* in Santo Domingo and owned a sugar mill on the Nizao in that region. Oviedo, *Historia* 117, p. 107; Lerma returned with Colón in 1520 to serve in official capacities at Santo Domingo; Ocampo was a vecino in Santo Domingo by 1521. Probanza of Bastidas, Santo Domingo, June 22, 1521, *CDIA*, 2: 390.

23. Mervyn Ratekin, "The Early Sugar Industry in Española," *HAHR*, No. 1, 34 (February, 1954): 4.

24. Rodrigo Manzorro to the king [Santo Domingo?], Aug. 30, 1515, *CDIA*, 36: 411. He advocated employing Indians in building sugar mills, and thought many would do this if it were not for the ordinance requiring that one third of an encomendero's Indians work in the mines as a condition for retaining them.

25. Oviedo, *Historia* 117, pp. 107–10.

26. Ibid., p. 98.

27. Gorjón's wealth, acquired mainly after 1526, derived primarily from sugar production. For valuable details about an early sugar plantation, owned by Gorjón, see Fr. Cipriano de Utrera, "Almoneda del ingenio de Hernando Gorjón," *Clío*, 16 (1948); 3–18.

28. Six hundred Negroes were sold on Española in 1526. Otte, "La expedición," p. 66.

29. Ratekin, "The Early Sugar Industry," p. 13.

30. Cayetano Coll y Toste, "La propiedad territorial en Puerto Rico," *BHPR*, 1, No. 5 (September–October, 1914), 244. Tomás was a brother of Jácome, who put up the first permanent fort at Cumaná. Pike, *Enterprise*, p. 72.

31. Julio J. Le Riverend Brusone, *Los orígenes de la economía cubana* (1510–1600) (México, 1945), p. 31.

32. Apolinar Tejera, "Las primera iglesias de la Isla Expañola," *BAGNSD*, 10, Nos. 54–55 (September–December,1947), 206; Probanza of Bastidas, Santo Domingo, June 22, 1521, *CDIA*, 2, 466. (The document was shown by a scribe to Dean Bastidas in 1527, whose name appears on this printed copy.)

33. Murga Sanz, *Juan*, p. 252; Statement of Gerónimo Alemán, Valladolid, April 12, 1527, Murga Sanz, *Juan*, pp. 306–7.

34. King to the corregidor of Olmedo, Valladolid, July 4, 1523, *MHDPR*, 3–2: 302–3; Murga Sanz, *Juan*, p. 252.

35. Bernaldino de Santa Clara to Francisco de los Cobos, Santiago de Cuba, Oct. 20, 1517, *CDIA*, 11: 557.

36. Giménez Fernández, *Bartolomé* 2, p. 198.

37. Wright, *The Early History*, p. 76.

38. Ballesteros, *Cristóbal Colón* 4, p. 67; Cipriano de Utrera, "Juan de Salamanca," *BAGNSD*, 13, No. 64 (January–March, 1950): 108. Ballesteros said that María de Mosquera was one of Luis Colón's wives; Utrera relates Juan de Mosquera to the Colón family by marriage.

39. Oviedo, *Historia* 117, pp. 104–5.

40. King to Ponce de León, n.p., [1515?], *MHDPR*, III-I, 375–76; Juan Pedro de Sedeño to king [Caparra], Aug. 7, 1515, *CDIA*, 36: 378–79. Sedeño was apparently veedor on Ponce's small fleet.

41. Murga Sanz, *Juan*, pp. 251–53.

42. Statements about actions of Pedro Moreno, Trujillo, Oct. 20, 1525, *CDIA*, 2: 136.

43. Statement of García Troche, Valladolid, 1527, Tío, *Nuevas fuentes*, p. 419; introduction to *MHDPR*, 2: cix.

44. Will of Diego Velázquez, Santiago de Cuba, June 11, 1524, *CDIA*, 35: 514–18.

45. King to Baltasar de Castro, Madrid, June 16, 1535, *BHPR*, 1: 199–200; King to Diego Ramos, Guadalajara, Sept. 21, 1546, *BHPR*, 1: 201.

46. Giménez Fernández, *Bartolomé* 2, p. 1201.

47. Cipriano de Utrera, "Don Luis Franco de Acevedo," *BAGNSD*, 12, No. 63 (October-December, 1949): 374.

48. Introduction to *MHDPR*, 2: cix.

49. Díaz was surely dead by 1523 for Oviedo states that at the time Ayllón was juez de residencia on Puerto Rico (that is, 1524), Isabel de Cáceres, Diaz's widow, married the widower, Antonio de la Gama. A Miguel Díaz de Aux initiated cirtain legal proceedings on New Spain in 1532. See Donald E. Chipman, *Nuño de Guzmán and the Province*

of Pánuco in New Spain 1518–1533 (Glendale, Calif. 1967), p. 92. But he would necessarily be a homonym, possibly the deceased Díaz's son.

50. Oviedo, *Historia* 119, pp. 64–74.

51. Woodbury Lowery, *Spanish Settlements in the United States,* 2 vols, (Washington, 1901?), 1, p. 167; Ballesteros, *La Idea*, p. 211.

Appendix I

Governors of the Caribbean Islands (1492-1526)

*Cuba**

1511–21	Diego Velázquez
1521–23	Lic. Alonso de Zuazo
1523	Gonzalo de Ovalle
1523–24	Diego Velázquez
1524–25	Manuel de Rojas
1525–26	Lic. Juan de Altamirano
1526–32	Gonzalo de Guzmán

Cubagua

1515?	Pedro Ortiz de Matienzo, alcalde mayor
1519–20	Antonio Flores, alcalde mayor
1521–23	Francisco de Vallejo, teniente de gobernador
1523–	Jácome de Castellón, teniente de gobernador

Española

1492–1500	Christopher Columbus, viceroy
1500–02	Francisco Bobadilla, governor
1502–09	Nicolás de Ovando, governor
1509–15	Diego Colón, viceroy
1515–16	Lic. Cristóbal Lebrón, governor
1517–19	Lic. Alonso de Zuazo, governor Jeronymite friars, commissaries (suspension of the audiencia)
1519–20	Lic. Rodrigo de Figueroa, governor (re-establishment of audiencia)
1520–23	Diego Colón, viceroy**
1523–27	Audiencia

*Jamaica**

1509–13	Juan de Esquivel
1513–14?	Cristóbal Pérez
1514–15	Diego Camargo
1515–23	Francisco de Garay
1525	Alfonso Mendoza
1525–	Juan Mendegurren

*tenientes de gobernador

**Lic. Rodrigo de Figueroa served as oidor and commissioner for Indians, 1520–21; Lic. Cristóbal Lebrón replaced Figueroa as oidor in 1521.

Puerto Rico

1508–09	Juan Ponce de León, governor*
1509–10	Juan Cerón, alcalde mayor
1510–11	Juan Ponce de León, governor
1511–12	Juan Cerón, alcalde mayor
1512–13	Rodrigo de Moscoso, teniente de gobernador
1513–14	Cristóbal de Mendoza, teniente de gobernador
1514–19	Lic. Sancho de Velázquez, justicia mayor**
1519–20	Antonio de la Gama, justicia mayor
1520–22	Pedro Moreno, teniente de gobernador***
1522–23	Bishop Alonso Manso, teniente de gobernador
1523–28	Pedro Moreno, teniente de gobernador

*Title from 1509.

**Juan Ponce de León exercised the offices of Captain of Sea and Land, 1514–21.

***Lic. Antonio de la Gama, commissioner for Indians.

Appendix II
Royal Fifth of Gold Sent to Spain

Year	*Espanola*	*Puerto Rico*	*Cuba*	*Reference*
1494	*25,000			Morison, *Admiral*, p. 434.
1502	*200,000			Ballesteros, *Cristobal*, 5: 556.
1504	*14,000			Ortega, *La Rábida*, 2:319.
1508	38,000	*836		*CDIA*, 36: 224, 257; *CDIU*, 5: 150, 153; *CDIA*, 34: 484.
1509	36,000			*CDIA*, 36: 275, 289.
1510	35,503	3,281		*CDIHA*, 6: 283; Murga Sanz, *Juan*, 57–61; *CDIA*, 34: 455.
1511	48,500	13,530		*CDIHA*, 6: 296; *CDIA*, 32: 186, 300, 310; *CDIU*, 5: 295; Murga Sanz, *Juan*, p. 96.
1514		9,000		*MHDPR*, 3–1: 282, 309.
1515	18,000	17,997	12,437	*MHDPR*, 3–1: 378; *CDIA*, 36, 360, 383, 423, 441; *CDAHC*, 1: 19.
1516	40,920	18,600		Altolaguirre, *Vasco*, pp. 115–116; *CDIA*, 1: 290; Serrano y Sanz, *Orígenes*, p. dlxxvi.
1517	26,307	18,600	21,000	*CDIA*, 11: 255; Serrano y Sanz, *Orígenes*, p. dlxxvi; Wright, *The Early*, p. 81.

1518	21,000	35,000	27,709	*MHDPR*, 3–1: 16; Giménez Fernández, *Bartolomé*, 2: 106, 201; *CDIA*, 34: 268, 274, 320; Serrano y Sanz, *Orígenes*, p. dlxxvii.
1519	15,999	18,000	25,581	*CDIA*, 1: 372; 11: 430; Giménez Fernández, *Bartolomé*, 2:273–75; *MHDPR*, 3–2: 136.
1520		16,140		*MHDPR*, 3–2: 157; 194–96.
1521	519	5,000		Giménez Fernández, *Bartolomé*, 2: 1150; F. Navarrete, *Colección*, 4: 190.
1522	119			Giménez Fernández, *Bartolomé*, 2: 1150.
1523	500			Giménez Fernández, *Bartolomé*, 2: 1150.
1524	4,195			*CDIA*, 1: 440.
1525		7,000	4,000	*MHDPR*, 3–2: 373.
1526			4,000	*CDAHC*, 1: 109.

*Figure represents total production, not the royal fifth only.

Notes: The best one may conclude from these incomplete figures is that between 1515–19 each of the 3 islands produced about 100,000 *pesos de oro* annually. The fifth actually includes income from the royal mines, which is sometimes reported separately in documents, but is not so large as to alter significantly the assumed production figures. If Las Casas's estimate (2: 277) of 450,000 *pesos de oro* annually for Española during the Ovandine period is approximately correct (the figures given above are probably incomplete), then gold production there had dropped 75% by 1515–19, with all three islands producing about the same amount. Where conversion to *pesos de oro* was necessary, I have assumed 450 maravedís to the *pesos de oro*, 50 *pesos de oro* to the marc and 375 maravedís to the gold ducat.

Appendix III
Royal Fifth of Pearls Sent to Spain from Cubagua and Environs

Year	*Española*	*Puerto Rico*	*Reference*
1508	16		*CDIA*, 36: 257
1509	26		*CDIA*, 31: 453
1516	19		Altolaguirre, *Vasco*, p. 116; *CDAHC*, 1: 46.
1518	232	110	Serrano y Sanz, *Orígenes*, p. dlxxvii; *CDIA*, 34: 268–69; Giménez Fernández, *Bartolomé*, 2: 106.
1519	180		*CDIA*, 1: 372; Giménez Fernández, *Bartolomé*, 274.
1520		39	*MHDPR*, III–II, 194–96.
1521	304	7	Giménez Fernández, *Bartolomé*, 2: 1156, 1165.
1522	55		Giménez Fernández, *Bartolomé*, 2: 1217.
1524	448		*CDIA*, 1: 440.
1525	200	120	*MHDPR*, III–II, 373.
1526	626		*CDIA*, 11: 504–5.

Notes: Pearls are worth on the average 20 pesos per marc (Giménez Fernández, *Bartolomé*, 2: 1198). Though the above records are incomplete, there is no doubt that the pearl industry produced much less wealth than gold mining. Española and Puerto Rico refer to the places of immediate shipment to Spain. Jamaica and Cuba were not involved in pearling, and there are no reports for Panama.

Bibliography

With the exception of the typescript document on Matienzo's residencia and a microfilmed document of Diego Colón (AGI, Patronato 10, Ramo 13), the sources used have all been published. Other documents from the AGI that I had microfilmed would have added details about a few early settlers but not any new dimensions to the subject matter; for this reason I decided not to use them. The microfilm included probanzas drawn up by certain of the early settlers' sons or grandsons in the 1560's and 1570's, but they proved to offer disappointingly meager information about the years before 1526. The documentary base, however, is considerably wider than that used in other general assessments of the early Caribbean. Most authors have used the CDIA set supplemented by Las Casas, Martyr, and Oviedo; I have additionally drawn upon the scattered documents in the other sets listed below, as well as the important documents for Puerto Rico published by Murga Sanz.

The great corpus of printed documents pertaining to Española (represented especially by the CDIA set) thin out quickly after about 1512, as the selectors anticipated and probably influenced historiography by concentrating on Panama and especially Cuba with relation to the expeditions to New Spain. By far the great majority of the documents consist of the kings' (or regents') letters to the officials on the islands. Letters from the islands are relatively few by comparison, and one must therefore often discern what had occurred there by the king's mention of it, which is at times vague or cryptic, making it difficult to present many events precisely or vividly. A great part of the correspondence from the islands has never been found, and may have been destroyed.

Many monographs also contained documents of which the most numerous and important were found in works by Ortega, Murga Sanz (biography of Ponce de León), Serrano y Sanz, and especially Giménez Fernández, without whose work one could scarcely deal with the years from 1516.

The best recent research treating this period on Española is represented by the articles of Pérez de Tudela Bueso and the two large volumes by Giménez Fernández. Murga Sanz has made a major contribution to Puerto Rican history with the publication of his documents and biography of Ponce de León, but the numerous articles of Coll y Toste published much earlier also provide a wealth of detail about the conquest and settlement of the island. On Española, the numerous articles of Dr. Apolinar de Tejera and Fr. Cipriano de Utrera comprise the greatest body of information other than that in the documents themselves, much of it revising earlier works. No important new documents for the early histories of Cuba and Jamaica have been found, though Morales Padrón has supplied details that make the origins of Jamaica somewhat clearer.

PRINTED DOCUMENTS

Colección de documentos. Academia de la historia de Cuba. 2 vols. in 1 (Havana, 1931).

Colección de documentos inéditos de Ultramar. 25 vols. (Madrid, 1886–1932).

Colección de documentos inéditos para la historia de España. 113 vols. (Madrid, 1842–95).

Colección de documentos inéditos para la historia de Hispano-America. 14 vols. (Madrid, 1927–32).

Colección de documentos inéditos relativos al descubrimiento . . . de las antiguas posesiones españolas de América y Oceanía. 42 vols. (Madrid, 1864–84).

Konetzke, Richard, ed., *Colección de documentos para la historia de la*

formación social de Hispano-América, 1493–1810. 3 vols. in 5 (Madrid, 1953–62).
Murga Sanz, Vicente, ed., *Historia documental de Puerto Rico*. 4 vols. in 3 (Río Piedras, 1956–64).
Navarrete, Martín Fernández, ed., *Collección de los viages y descubrimientos que hicieron por mar los españoles desde fines del siglo XV*. 5 vols. (Buenos Aires, 1945–46).
Recopilación de leyes de los reynos de las Indias. 3 vols. (Madrid, 1943).
Tío, Aurelio, ed., *Nuevas fuentes para la historia de Puerto Rico* (San Germán, 1961).

BOOKS AND DISSERTATIONS

Altolaguirre y Duvale, Angel. *Vasco Núñez de Balboa*. Madrid: Patronato de huérfanos, 1914.
Ashburn, F. D., ed. *The Ranks of Death: A Medical History of the Conquest of America*. New York: Coward McCann, 1947.
Azcona, Tarsicio de. *La elección y reforma del episcopado español en tiempo de los reyes catolicos*. Madrid: Consejo superior de investigaciones científicas, 1960.
Ballesteros Gaibrois, Manuel. *La idea colonial de Ponce de León*. San Juan de Puerto Rico: Instituto de cultura puertorriqueña, 1960.
Ballesteros y Beretta, Antonio. *Cristóbal Colón y el descubrimiento de América*. Vols. 4 and 5 of *Historia de América y de los pueblos americanos*, Ballesteros, ed. Barcelona-Buenos Aires: Salvat editores, S.A., 1945.
Bernáldez, Andrés. *Historia de los reyes católicos D. Fernando y Doña Isabel*. 2 vols. Sevilla: Impr. que fué de J. M. Geofrin, 1870.
Borges, Pedro, O.F.M. *Métodos misionales en la cristianización de América*. Madrid: Departmento de misionología, 1960.
Brau, Salvador. *La colonización de Puerto Rico*. 2d ed. San Juan: Instituto de cultura puertorriqueña, 1930.
Carro, Venancio Diego, O.P. *La teología y los teólogos—juristas españoles ante la conquista de América*. 2 vols. Madrid: Talleres gráficos marsiega, 1944.
Charlevoix, Pierre F.X. de. *Histoire de l'ile espagnole ou de St. Domingue*. 2 vols. Paris: J. Guerin, 1730.
Chaunu, Huguette and Pierre. *Seville et l'Atlantique* (1504–1650). 8 vols. in 12. Paris: A. Coling S.E.V.P.E.N., 1955–59.
Chipman, Donald E. *Nuño de Guzmán and the Province of Pánuco in New Spain* 1518–1533. Glendale, Calif.: A. H. Clark Co., 1967.
Colón, Fernando. *Historia del Almirante de las Indias, Don Cristóbal Colón*. Buenos Aires: Editorial Bajel, 1944.
Delorme Salto, Rafael, ed. *Los aborígenes de América*. Madrid: F. Fé, 1894.

Doussinague, JoséM. *La política internacional de Fernando el Católico.* Madrid: Espasa-Calpe, 1944.

Fernández de Retana, Luis. *Cisneros y su siglo.* 2 vols. Madrid: El perpetuo socorro, 1929–30.

Fewkes, Jesse W. *The Aborigenes of Porto Rico and Neighboring Islands.* Washington, D.C.: U.S. Bureau of American Ethnology, 1907.

Fox, John S. *The Beginnings of Spanish Mining in America: the West Indies and Castilla del Oro.* Ph.D. diss. U. of Calif., Berkeley, 1940.

Giménez Fernández, Manuel. *Bartolomé de Las Casas.* 2 vols. Seville: Publicaciones de la escuela de Estudios Hispano-Americanos de Sevilla, 1953–1960.

Guerra y Sánchez, Ramiro, ed. *Historia de la nación cubana.* 10 vols. Habana: Editorial historia de la nación cubana, 1952.

Hanke, Lewis. *The Spanish Struggle for Justice in the Conquest of America.* Philadelphia: University of Pennsylvania Press, 1949.

Hefele, Karl J. von. *Der Cardinal Ximenes und die kirchlichen zustände spaniens am ende des 15 und anfange des 16 jahrhunderts.* Tübingen: H. Laupp, 1851.

Herrera y Tordesillas, Antonio de. *Historia de las Indias Occidentales.* 9 vols. Madrid: Imprenta real de Nicholas Rodriguez, 1726–30.

Incháustegui Cabral, Joaquín M., ed. *Francisco de Bobadilla.* Madrid: Ediciones cultura hispánica, 1964.

Lamb, Ursula. *Frey Nicolás de Ovando. Gobernador de Indias* (1501–1509. Madrid: Consejo superior de investigaciones científicas, 1956.

Las Casas, Bartolomé de. *Historia de las Indias.* 3 vols. Madrid: Fondo de cultura económica, 1875–79.

Le Riverend Brunsone, Julio J. *Los Orígenes de la economía cubana* (1510–1600). México: El Colegio de México, Centro de Estudios Sociales, 1945.

Loven, Sven. *Origins of the Tainan Culture, West Indies.* Gotemburg: Elanders boktryckeri aktiebolag, 1935.

Lowery, Woodbury. *Spanish Settlements in the United States.* 2 vols. New York: Putnam, 1905.

Martire d'Anghiera. *Décadas del Nuevo Mundo,* 2 vols. México: J. Porrúa, 1964–65.

Mejía Ricart, Gustavo A. *Historia de Santo Domingo.* 8 vols. Ciudad Trujillo: Pol Hnos., 1948–54.

Melón y Ruiz de Gordejuela, Amando. *Los primeros tiempos de la colonización. Cuba y las Antillas. Magallanes y la primera vuelta al mundo.* Vol. 6 of Historia de América y de los pueblos americanos, Ballesteros, ed. Barcelona: Salvat, 1952.

Mexía, Pedro. *Historia del Emperador Carlos V.* Vol. 7 of Colección de crónicas españolas. Madrid: Espasa-Calpe, 1945.

Morales Padrón. Francisco, *Jamaica Española.* Seville: Publicaciones de escuela de estudios Hispano-Americanos de Sevilla, 1952.

Morison, Samuel E. *Admiral of the Ocean Sea. A Life of Christopher Columbus.* Boston: Little, Brown and Co., 1946.

———. *The Second Voyage of Christopher Columbus from Cádiz to Hispaniola and the Discovery of the Lesser Antilles.* Oxford: The Clarendon Press, 1939.

Muñoz, Juan Bautista. *Historia del Nuevo Mundo.* Madrid: Por la viuda de Ibarra, 1793.

Murga Sanz, Vicente. *Juan Ponce de Len, fundador y primer gobernador del pueblo puertorriqueño, descubridor de la Florida y del estrecho de Bahamas. Rio Piedras: Ediciones de la Universidad de Puerto Rico,* 1949.

Ortego, Angel, O.F.M. *La Rábida, historia documental crítica indiana.* 4 vols. Seville: Impr. y editorial de San Antonio, 1925–26.

Oviedo y Valdez, Gonzalo Fernández. *Historia general y natural de las Indias.* 5 vols. Vols. 117–121 of Biblioteca de autores españoles. Madrid: Gráficas Orbe, 1959.

Pike, Ruth. *Enterprise and Adventure: the Genoese in Seville and the Opening of the New World.* Ithaca: Cornell University Press, 1966.

Rosenblatt, Angel. *La población indígena y el mestizaje en America.* 2 vols. in 1. Buenos Aires: Institución cultura española, 1954.

Saco, José A. *Historia de la esclavitud de la raza africana en el nuevo mundo y en especial en los países america-hispanos.* Barcelona: Cultural, S.A., 1879–93.

Sánchez-Bella, Ismael, *La organización financiera de las Indias. Siglo XVI.* Sevilla: Escuela de Estudios Hispano-Americanos de Sevilla, 1968.

Santa Cruz, Alonso de. *Crónica de los reyes católicos.* 2 vols. Seville: Escuela de Estudios Hispano-Americanos de Sevilla, 1951.

Sauer, Carl O. *The Early Spanish Main.* Berkeley: University of California Press, 1966.

Scelle, George. *La traite negriere aux Indes de Castile.* 2 vols. Paris: L. Larose, 1906.

Serrano y Sanz. Manuel. *Orígenes de la dominación española en América.* Madrid: Bailly-Bailliere, 1918.

Shiels, William E. *King and Church. The Rise and Fall of the Patronato Real.* Chicago: Loyola University Press, 1961.

Terrateig, Barón de. *Política en Italia del rey católico,* 1507–1516. Madrid: Consejo superior de investigaciones científicas, 1963.

Tobar, Balthasar de. *Compendio bulario índico.* Manuel Gutiérrez de Arce, ed., 2 vols. Seville: Escuela de Estudios Hispano-Americanos de Sevilla, 1954–66.

Wright, Irene A. *The Early History of Cuba,* 1492–1586. New York: The Macmillan Co., 1916.

———. *Historia documentada de San Cristóbal de la Habana en la primera mitad del siglo XVII.* La Habana: Imprenta "El Sigol XX," A. Muñiz y hno., 1930.

Almoina, José. "La biblioteca erasmista de Diego Méndez." *PUSD,* 35 (1945).

Altolaguirre y Duvale, Angel de. "Estudio jurídico de las capitulaciones y privilegios de Cristóbal Colón." *BRAH,* 38 (1901): 279–94.

Amiama, Manuel A. "La población de Santo Domingo." *Clio,* 27, No. 115 (July–December, 1959): 116–34.

Andrés Martín, Melquiades. "Evangelismo, humanismo, reforma y observancias en España (1450–1525)." *MH,* 23, No. 67 (1966): 5–24.

———. "Reforma y estudio de teología en los Franciscanos españoles." *AA,* 8 (1960): 43–82.

———. "Renovación en teología dogmática y ascética en España (1500–1530)." *AA,* 11 (1963): 127–57.

Artiles, Jenaro. "Historia local de La Habana." *UHPB,* 10, Nos. 58–60 (January–June, 1945): 88–115.

"Autografos de Cristóbal Colón y Papeles de América, los publica la Duquesa de Berwick y de Alba, Condesa de Siruela." (Madrid, 1892) (excerpt), *BHPR,* 1.

Borges, Pedro, O.F.M. "Primeras expediciones misioneras á América." *AIA,* n.s., 27, No. 106 (April–June, 1967): 121–33.

Carro, Venancio Diego. "Bartolomé de la Casas y las controversías teológico-jurídicas de Indias." *BRAH,* 132 (January–March, 1953): 231–68.

Coll y Toste, Cayetano. "El alzamiento de los Indios del Boriquén—rectificaciones históricas." *BHPR,* 9, No. 6 (November–December, 1922): 342–49.

———, ed., "Documentos históricos referentes al pueblo de Guánica." *BHPR,* 7: 199–210.

———. "Exploración de la isla por Juan Ponce de León." *BHPR,* 4, No. 5 (September–October, 1917): 296–301.

———. "Gobierno de Juan Cerón y demás tenientes de D. Diego, hasta 1515, que vuelve a gobernor Juan Ponce de León—rectificaciones históricas." *BHPR,* 10, No. 2 (March–April, 1923): 76–86.

———. "Nuevo alzamiento de los Indios del Boriquén y depredaciones de los Caribes—rectificaciones históricas." *BHPR,* 10, No. 3 (May–June, 1923): 169–80.

———. "Principios de la colonización de la Isla, rectificaciones históricas." 9, No. 2 (March–April, 1922): 93–102.

———. "La propiedad territorial en Puerto Rico." *BHPR,* 1, No. 5 (September–October, 1914): 239–310.

———. "El repartimento de los indígenas entre los Españoles—rectificaciones históricas." *BHPR,* 9, No. 5 (September–October, 1922): 276–85.

Cosculluela, J.A. "Sincronismo de las culturas indo-antillanas." *RAEC.* 1, No. 3 (November, 1946), 27–51.

Fernández, Justo. "Don Francisco des Prats, primer nuncio permanente en España (1492–1503)." *AA,* 1 (1953): 67–154.

Fita, Fidel. "Frey Jorge y el segundo viaje de Cristóbal Colón." *BRAH,* 19: 234–37.

Giménez Fernández, Manuel. "Las Cortes de la Española en 1518." *AUH*, 15, No. 2 (1954): 47–154.

Gould, Alicia B. "Nueva lista documentada de los tripulantes de Colón en 1492." *BRAH*, 85: 34–49; 145–59; 353–79.

Jesse, C. "The Papal Bull of 1493 appointing the first Vicar Apostolic of the New World." *CQJ*. 11, Nos. 3–4 (September–December, 1965): 62–71.

Loughran, E. Ward. "Did a Priest accompany Columbus in 1492?" *CHR*, 16 (April, 1930–January, 1931): 164–74.

———. "The First Episcopal Sees in Spanish America." *HAHR*, 10, No. 2 (May, 1930): 167–87.

McCarthy, Charles H. "Columbus and the Santa Hermandad in 1492." *CHR*, 1: 38–50.

Martínez-Fortún y Foyo, Carlos A. "El Casicato de Sabana de Sabaneque." *RBNC*, 2nd Ser., 8, No. 1 (January–March, 1956), 41–90.

———. "¿Å Donde estuvo situado 'Carahate?' " *AAHC*, 20, 127–49.

Meseguer Fernández, Juan. "La Bula .Ite vos' (29 de mayo de 1517) y la reforma cisneriana." *AIA*, *n.s.*, 18, Nos. 71–72 (July–December, 1958): 257–361.

Meza Villalobos, Néstor. "Significado del período 1493–1508 en el proceso de la conquista." *RCHG*, No. 110 (July–December, 1947): 41–56.

Morales Patiño, Oswaldo. "Los Indígenas en los primeros municípios cubanos." *RAEC*, 7, Nos. 13–14 (January–December, 1951): 368–87.

Muro Orejón, Antonio. "Ordenanzas reales sobre los Indios (Las leyes de 1512–13)." *AEA*, 13 (1956): 417–71.

"Nombres de la Vega." *Clío*, 22, No. 100 (July–September, 1954): 123–25.

Oliger, Livarius, O.F.M. "The Earliest Record on the Franciscan Missions in America." *CHR*, 6: 59–65.

Otte, Enrique. "La expedición de Gonzalo de Ocampo a Cumaná en 1521 en las cuentas de tesorería de Santo Domingo." *RI*, No. 63 (January–March, 1956): 51–84.

Pedreira, Antonio S. "De los nombres de Puerto Rico." *REHNY*, 1 (1928): 18–33.

Pérez de Tudela Bueso, Juan. "Castilla ante los comienzos de la colonización de las Indias." *RI*, 15, No. 59 (January–March, 1955): 11–88.

———. "La negociación colombina de las Indias." *RI*, Nos. 57–58 (July–December, 1954): 289–357.

———. "Política de poblamiento y política de contratación de las Indias (1502–1505)." *RI*, 15, Nos. 61–62 (January–March, 1955): 371–420.

———. "La quiebra de la factoría y el nuevo poblamiento de la Española." *RI*, 15, No. 60 (April–June, 1955), 197–252.

Radaelli, Sigfrido A. "La institución virreinal en las Indias." *RI*, 15, Nos. 55–56 (January–June, 1954): 37–56.

Ratekin, Mervyn. "The Early Sugar Industry in Española." *HAHR*, 34, No. 1 (February, 1954): 1–19.

Steck, Francis B. "Christopher Columbus and the Franciscans." *The Americas*, 3, No. 3 (January, 1947): 319–42.

Tejera, Apolinar. "La Cruz del Santo Cerro y la batalla de la Vega Real." *BAGNSD*, 7, Nos. 40–41 (May-August, 1945): 101–19.

———. "La fundación de Santo Domingo." *BAGNSD*, 11, No. 57 (April–June, 1948): 103–118.

———. "Párrafos históricos." *BAGNSD*, 11, No. 56 (January–March, 1948): 50–54.

———. "Las primeras iglesias de la Isla española," *BAGNSD*, 10, Nos. 54–55 (September–December, 1947): 179–211.

Tibesar, Antonine S. "The Franciscan Province of the Holy Cross of Española, 1505–1559." *The Americas*, 13 (April, 1957), 377–89.

Utrera, Cipriano de. "Almoneda del ingenio de Hernando Gorjón," *Clío*, 16 (1948): 3–18.

———. "Episcopologío domínicopolitano." *BAGNSD*, 18, No. 86 (July–September, 1955): 228–49; No. 87 (October–December, 1955): 324–49.

———. "Isabel la Católica, fundadora de la Ciudad de Santo Domingo." *Clío*. 19 (1951): 116–32.

———. "Juan de Salamanca." *BAGNSD*, 13, No. 64 (January–March, 1950): 104–8.

———. "Don Luis Franco de Acevedo." *BAGNSD*, 12, No. 63 (October–December, 1949): 372–85.

———. "Roldán, el ingrato." *Clío*, 20 (1952): 110–17.

Vicens Vives, Jaime. "Precedentes mediterráneos del virreinato colombino." *AEA*, 5 (1948): 571–614.

Index

Acculturation: rebel Spaniards at Jaraguá, 39, 61; Spaniards and Indian food, 23, 26
Acuerdo: defined, 199; set aside by Colón's arbitrary actions, 213
Adrian of Utrecht: capture by *Comuneros* when governor of Castile, 7–8; mentioned, 198
Afonso V, King of Portugal, 2
Aguado, Juan de: arrival at Isabela, 30; return to Spain, 30
Agüero, Gerónimo de: former tutor of Diego Colón, 137; named co-governor of Española in 1514, 148
Agueybana, cacique, 97
Aguilar, Marcos de, 137
Alba, Duke of: recommends Diego Colón as governor of Indies, 92–93; son of debtor to Diego Colón, 142; supporter of Ferdinand V, 5, 91
Alberca, Diego de, 154
Alburquerque, Rodrigo de, 147, 160–61, 168
Alcázar, Rodrigo de, 67
Alexander VI, Pope, 16
Altamirano, Francisco, 211
Altemang, Juan, 155
Alvarado, Pedro de, 113
Ampies, Juan de: mentioned, 190; named factor on Española, 129
Ampudia, Gutierre de, 154
Anacaona, *cacica:* assumes leadership at Jaraguá, 60; execution of, 63; widow of Caonabó, 35
Añasco, Luis de, 96, 102
Aragón, Carlos de, 151
Arango, Sancho de, 103–4
Arawaks. *See* Taínos
Araya, Peninsula de, 172, 206
Arce, Diego de, 129
Arriaga, Luis de, 26
Ashburn thesis, 191
Assembly of town procuradores: convenes at Santo Domingo in 1518, 180–81; reforms sought by, 181, 182, 196
Audiencia: accrual of power after 1520, 217–18; conflict with Diego Colón over naming town officials, 146; crippling effect on Colón's powers, 199; established on Española, 144; established with full powers, 201–2; suspended in 1517, 175
Avila, Alonso de, 224
Azua: established, 63; salt deposits at, 66

Ballester, Miguel: *alcalde* at Concepción, 36, 41; majordomo of Columbus's *estancia,* 77
Baracoa, Asunción de, 114
Barbier, Pierre, 204–5
Bardeci, Lope, 182
Barrionuevo, Francisco de: investor in Paria trade, 206; migrations of, 223; *procurador* for Puerto Rico, 178; son-in-law of Rodrigo Manzorro, 80, 229
Barrionuevo, Pedro de, 223
Bastidas, Rodrigo de, merchant: *armador* in Indian slave trade, 134, 138; career summarized, 225, 255–56*n;* escapes drowning in 1502, 55; last years and death of, 230; mentioned, 191; voyage to Urabá, 49, 242*n*
Bastidas, Rodrigo de, son, 225
Bayamo, San Salvador de, 119

Becerra, Juan, 229
Beehechio, cacique, 29
Bishoprics: better financial base after 1520, 221; delay in establishing, 2–5, 87–88, 179
Blois, Pact of, 92
Blois, Treaty of, 90
Bobadilla, Francisco de: death of, 55; departure from Spain, 45; identity clarified, 239–40*n;* mentioned, 3, 43; *residencia* taken, 54
Bonao: established as mining town, 57–58; mentioned, 40
Bono de Quejo, Juan: *armador* and ship captain, 267*n;* pilot for Díaz and Garay, 78; pilot on Ponce de León's Florida expedition, 106; *procurador* for Puerto Rico, 101, 131
Boyl, Bernardo: mentioned, viii, 21; Minim friar and diplomat, 16; return to Spain, 27
Brazilwood: discovered on Española, 27; first cargo loaded at Jacmel, 35; first private contract for, 240*n;* importance at Jacmel, 138, 238*n*, 255*n;* made item of royal monopoly, 52
Bribiesca, Jimeno de: death of, 94; first *contador* of the Casa de Contratación, 53
Buenaventura, 66
Burgos, Laws of: amendments to, 169; and relocation of Indians, 161–62, 174; introduced on Española, 147; mentioned, 116, 141, 152, 165

Cabrero, Martín, 163
Caballero el Mozo Diego, 205
Cacicazgos, 14, 56–57
Caguax, cacique of Caonao, 118
Caguionex, cacique of Havana, 118
Camargo, Diego, 110–11
Cansino, García, 103
Cansinos, Antón, 134, 206, 254*n*
Caonabó, cacique: capture of, 29; fear of attack from, 24; mentioned, 14, 21
Caonao, battle of, 118
Caparra, 99
Capitulations of 1492: mercantile aspects, 9–10; titles granted Columbus, 10, 234–35*n*
Carahate, 118
Caribs: attack and burn Caparra, 106, 157; attack on Columbus at St. Croix, 20; migrations of, 12; relations with Taínos on Puerto Rico, 97, 102, 106, 135; use of poisoned arrows, 49; war declared on by king, 135. *See also* Slavery, Indian
Carrillo Mexía, Juan, 173
Casa de Contratación: established, 4, 53; reform of, 94
Castellanos, Miguel de, 210
Castellón, Jácome de: mentioned, 228; named *alcalde mayor* of Cubagua, 210
Castellón, Tomás de: establishes sugar mill on Puerto Rico, 224; Genoese merchant at Santo Domingo, 107
Castro, Baltasar de: mentioned, 228; named *contador* of Puerto Rico, 129
Cattaneo, Juan, 77
Cattaneo, Rafael, 77
Cayacoa, 187
Cemi, 237*n*
Cerón, Juan: arrested by Ponce de León, 101; *criado* of Bartolomé Colón, 137; named *alcalde mayor* of Puerto Rico, 99; restored to office as *alcalde mayor*, 104–5
Chanca, Dr., physician on second voyage, 21
Charles I, king of Spain. *See* Charles V
Charles V: arrives in Spain in 1517, 177, 195; early reign characterized, 7; economic resources after 1520, 221; mentioned, 1; reign after 1522 characterized, 8, 219; returns to Spain in 1522, 210, 215; unpopularity with Castilian towns, 7, 177–78, 199–200
Cibao, 13
Cobos, Francisco de los, 195
Colombo, Giovanni: discovers gold on Haina River, 50; mentioned, 40; voyage to Española in 1509, 137
Colón, Andrea, 137
Colón, Bartolomé: arrives at Isabela, 27; campaign against Ciguayos, 40; establishes Fort San Cristóbal, 34; mentioned, 19; *procurador* for Española, 131; titled *adelantado*, 31, 37, 73–74; voyage to Española in 1509, 137
Colón, Cristóbal, son of Diego, 226–27
Colón, Diego, brother of Christopher: death of, 257*n;* in command at Isabela, 35; mentioned, 19; voyage to Española in 1509, 137
Colón, Diego, Indian interpreter, 13

Colón, Diego, son of Columbus: appointment as governor, 92–93; arrives at San Germán, 106–7; arrives at Santo Domingo in 1520, 207; at court of Charles V, 195–97; connection with Duke of Alba, 5, 91, 92–93; death of, 216; departs Spain for Española in 1509, 93, 137; departs Spain for Española in 1520, 203; embargoes Ponce de León's property, 101; hinders Nicuesa-Ojeda expedition, 109, 142; last will of, 216; mentioned, ix, 95, 99; plans to regain control of Puerto Rico, 105; powers conceded in 1511, 143; recall in 1514–15, 6, 93, 122, 148, 257*n;* recalled to court in 1523, 215; restoration in 1520, 7, 194–95, 197, 199–200; struggle over rights and privileges, 4, 5–6, 99–107 *passim,* 124, 141–43, 200–201; supporter of Ferdinand V, 91; visits Santiago de Cuba, 212

Colón, Fernando: defends family privileges at court, 142–43, 198; legatee of Columbus, 31; voyage to Española in 1509, 137

Colón, Isabel, 227

Colón, Juana, 227

Colón, Luis, 227

Columbus, Christopher: arrest of by Bobadilla, 46; arrival at Santo Domingo on third voyage, 40; as Genoese merchant, 9; Cuban explorations, 27; discovery announced from Azores, 15; first voyage, 10–15; fourth voyage, 55, 243*n;* mentioned, vii–viii; property on Española, 77; reaffirmation of powers in 1497, 31; reports gold discovery to Ferdinand, 49; returns to Spain in 1496, 30; second voyage, 17–21; will of in 1498, 31. *See also* Factionalism

Comendador: as political official, 4. *See also* Nicolás de Ovando

Commerce: *almojarifozgo* tax imposed on, 68, 72; between Spain and Española, 65, 66; crown establishes monopoly on Española, 52; domestic commerce on Española, 66; royal monopoly on relinquished, 67–68, 71; ships engaged in with Española, 68

Comunero revolt, 1, 7, 186, 189, 194, 219

Comuneros, 183–84

Concepción de la Vega, 30, 57–58

Conchillas, Lope de: continues granting income to absentees, 163; dismissed from office, 169; encomienda removed on Puerto Rico, 173; imprisonment in Flanders, 67, 90–91; receives encomiendas, 92, 100, 163

Córdoba, Francisco de: death of, 172; in Venezuela, 155, 172

Córdoba, Pedro de, 151

Cortés, Hernando: mentioned, vii; named governor of New Spain, 220; on Cuban expedition, 113

Cosa, Juan de la: death of, 135; mentioned, 112; voyage to Urabá, 89

Cotubanamá, cacique: capture and execution of, 58; mentioned, 56

Cuba: exploration of under Velazquez, 116; motives for occupation of, 112; towns of as provision stations for ships from Panama, 88, 119–20

Cuéllar, Cristóbal de, 80

Cumaná, 173

Demora, 65

Deule, Juan de la: leads Franciscans to Jamaica, 111–12, 150; mentioned, 16; missionary work on the Vega, 38–39

Díaz, Miguel: arrested by Ponce de León, 101; *criado* of Bartolomé Colón, 137; death of, 229, 271–72*n;* favored by Columbus, 19; founds fort on Ozama River, 34; founds San Germán, 105, 139, 225; discovers gold on Haina River, 32; legendary liaison with a *cacica,* 56; named *alguacil mayor* of Puerto Rico, 99, 139; named factor on Puerto Rico, 139; restored to office as *alguacil mayor,* 104–5; shipowner, 78, 134

Díaz de Solís, Juan, 112

Dominicans: critical of Indian labor, 6–7, 151–52; establish monastery at San Juan de Puerto Rico, 222; mentioned, 6–7; missions in Venezuela, 155, 172–73, 204–7; on Cuba, 121, 154; why recruited by Ferdinand, 150

Duero, Andrés de, 140

Eguiluz, Martín de, 164

Encomienda: abolition of in 1520, 183, 188–89; acceptance of by Franciscans, 86; controversy about in literature, 152; desertion of by Indians, 75; established on Cuba, 119; established on Española, 64; held by absentees and officials, 92, 125–32 *passim*, 162–63, 169, 176, 184–88 *passim*, 247*n*, 252–54*n*, 264*n*; investigation of by Figueroa, 187; investigation of by Jeronymites, 174–75; junta of 1516 on, 168; mentioned, 72; size of, 70, 131–32; supervision of assigned to friars, 222; time granted for, 2, 74. *See also Repartimiento*

Enrique, Duke, 91

Enríquez, Juan, 107

Enriquillo, 75, 192, 222

Escobar, Diego de, 58

Española: decline of Spanish population on, 124–25; island named by Columbus, 15; migrations on, 222–23

Esperanza, 30

Espinar, Alonso de: death of, 150; Franciscan prior on Española, 54, 84; returns to Spain in 1512, 152

Esquivel, Juan de: as manager of royal interests on Jamaica, 129–30; establishes first town on Jamaica, 79; in war with Taínos in Higüey, 57–58; leads expedition to Jamaica, 109; mining contract with king, 127; *procurador* for Española, 57, 71

Factionalism: allayed under Ovando, 68, 78; and Diego Colón, 128, 148, 181; Columbus and Roldán, 3; on Puerto Rico, 100; on second voyage, 19–20; over encomiendas, 4, 144–46, 159–60; relation to abolition of encomienda, 4

Factoría: connection with second voyage, 17–18; mentioned, 9; system at maturity on Española, 30

Ferdinand II, king of Aragón. *See* Ferdinand V

Ferdinand V, king of Castile: conflict with Castilian nobles, 5–6, 91–92; control established over Española, 53; death of, 92, 166; departure to Italy, 90; expansionist policy in the Caribbean, 89, 92, 95, 121–28 *passim*, 232; fear of feudalism and civil war, 1, 46, 60, 74, 89–90, 92–93, 148; Mediterranean policy, 3, 4, 50, 72, 121–26 *passim;* mentioned, viii; patronage and Church, 1–3, 50–51; reassumption of reign in 1507, 126; support of missionaries, 153–55; unpopularity with Castilian nobles, 4, 5, 90–91

Fernández de la Gama, Juan: named *juez de residencia* of Puerto Rico, 185; resigns, 187

Fernández de las Varas, Juan, 205

Figueroa, Luis de: death of, 220; selected as commissioner on Española, 168

Figueroa, Rodrigo de: arrives at Santo Domingo, 187; departs Spain for Española, 187; legal counsel for Diego Colón, 213–14; named *juez de residencia* of Española, 185; official instructions to, 186

Flores, Antonio de: evacuates Spaniards from Cubagua, 207; named *alcalde mayor* of Cubagua, 188, 205

Francis I, king of France, 183

Franciscans: accompany Bobadilla to Española, 45, 83–84; accompany Ovando to Española, 84; accompany Velázquez to Cuba, 121; baptize Indians on Española, 84; contingent to Indies in 1511, 150; contingent to Indies in 1516, 171; converts on Espanola, 85; establish monastery on Jamaica, 111–12; give up encomiendas, 153; in Burgundy and Picardy, 6, 171; mentioned, 6–7; missions in Venezuela, 155, 173, 204; monasticism, 6, 83, 86; number on Española about 1509, 149; on second voyage, 17; Province of the Holy Cross established, 85; reform of in Spain. 149–50; secularism, 83, 86; Venezuelan mission burned by Indians, 207, 209

Gama, Antonio de la: arrives in Puerto Rico, 187; departs Spain for Puerto Rico, 187; marries Isabel Ponce de León, 227; marries Miguel Díaz's widow, 229; named *juez de residencia* of Puerto Rico, 187; official instructions to, 186–87; removes Indians held by absentees, 189; replaced as *justicia mayor*, 210

Garay, Francisco de: agricultural contract with king, 130, 138; *alguacil mayor* for Diego Colón, 109, 137; brother-in-law of Columbus, 19; death of, 226, 229; discovers gold on Haina River, 32; named *alcaide* at Jacmel, 138; named governor of Jamaica, 110, 138; *procurador* for Jamaica, 164; *procurador* for Española, 131; property on Española, 73; shipowner, 134, 137, 255*n*

Garcés, Juan: becomes Dominican lay worker, 155, 172; death of, 172; marriage to a *cacica*, 86–87; murders Indian wife, 152

Garceto, Juan, 155

García, Gil, 36

Garrido, Juan, 96

Gattinara, Mercurino, 183

Geraldini, Alessandro: begins construction of stone cathedral, 221; mentioned, 216, 220

Germana of Foix, 90

Gold: severance tax on, 68, 71, 202, 243*n*

Gold, Cuba: discovered in quantity, 119, 123–24; early placer mining, 115

Gold, Española: decline in production of, 214, 269*n;* first major discovery on, 43–44; first substantial amount acquired, 24; royal mines on, 68, 71, 126–27

Gold, Puerto Rico: mined in 1508–11, 99, 102, 104; mining soon declines on, 108, 123; royal mines on, 126–27

Gómez, Diego, 96

González, Juan: interpreter of Taíno language, 103; mentioned, 96

González Dávila, Gil, cacique, 207

González Dávila, Gil, *contador:* named *contador* on Española, 129; on Honduras, 218; *procurador* for Española, 131, 164

González Ponce de León, Juan, 139

Garbalán, Francisco, 23

Gorjón, Hernando, 224

Gorrevod, Lorenzo de, 184

Gricio, Gaspar, 92

Guacanagarí, cacique: simulates wound, 21; first meeting with Spaniards, 13–14; peaceful character of, 15

Guanahatabeys, 12

Guanines, 13

Guarionex, cacique ón Española: capture of by Spaniards, 40; gives obedience to Columbus, 30; leads revolt on Vega, 35, 39; resentment at increased tribute, 33–34

Guarionex, cacique on Puerto Rico, 102–3

Guatiguaná, cacique, 28

Guerra, Cristóbal, 50

Guevara, Hernán, 43

Gutiérrez de Alcántara, Pedro: factor in Seville for Ovando, 76; mercantile connection with Santa Claras, 76

Guzmán, Gonzalo de: arrives in Cuba, 225–26; *procurador* for Cuba, 178

Haro, Andrés de: investor in Paria trade, 206; mentioned, 190; named treasurer of Puerto Rico, 108, 129

Hatuey, cacique: flees to Cuba, 112; resists Spaniards on Cuba, 114

Havana, 119

Henry IV, king of Castile, 1

Hernández Coronel, Pedro, 37

Hernández de Córdoba, Francisco, 160

Hidalgo aspirations: in Indies, 18–19, 52–53, 64, 69, 71–74, 225–29; retard progress in building stone churches, 87–88, 158

Higüey, *cacicazgo* of: geographical aspects, 56–57; Taíno resistance in, 56–58. *See also* Higüey campaign

Higüey campaign, 241*n*

Hurricanes, 30, 55

Ibáñez de Ibarra, Pedro: death of, 147, 257*n;* named *juez de residencia* on Española, 147

Indians: encomienda, released from, 7; humane treatment of, 74–75; kinds of labor employed in, 74; population estimate for Española, 12–13; survival of in 1526, 13; voluntary labor decree of 1503, 59, 84–85. *See also* Taínos

Inés de Cayacoa, *cacica*, 84

Isabel I, queen of Castile: death of, 89; mentioned, 1; opposition to Indian slavery, 3, 45; popularity of, 4

Isabela: establishment of, 22; depopulation of, 44; starvation at, 25

Isásaga, Ochoa de, 94

Isásaga, Pedro de: arrives at Santo Domingo, 187; departs Spain for Española, 187; named auditor of accounts, 185

Jacmel: decline of brazilwood cutting at, 162; established, 63; main brazilwood port, 61

Jamaica: early history characterized, 111–12; lack of gold on, 123; royal farms on, 127; settled by Juan de Esquivel, 109
Jaraquá, *cacicazgo* of: geography and Taíno culture, 60; location of, 29; resistance of Spaniards to Ovando in, 60–63, 242*n*
Jeronymites: arrival at Santo Domingo, 173; asked to serve as commissioners on Española, 168; convene assembly of town *procuradores* on Española, 180; depart Spain for Española, 170; evaluation of reforms by, 177; instructions from Jiménez de Cisneros, 169; mentioned, 7; recommend reforms for Española, 174–75
Jiménez de Cisneros, Francisco: concern for political unity, 1, 7, 167, 170–71; evangelism encouraged by, 7, 54, 83–84, 167; named a cardinal, 91; regent in 1506, 91; regent in 1516, 166–67; reformer of Franciscan order, 83
Juana I, queen of Castile: mentioned, 4; unfitness to rule, 91
Julius II, Pope, 122

La Magdalena: besieged by Taínos, 28; burned by Taínos, 38; established, 26
La Navidad: destruction of, 21; established, 14
Land grants: first made to Francisco Roldán, 42–43; issued by Ovando, 63; issued by Roldán, 61
Lares, Amador de, 148
Lares de Guahava: depopulation of, 125; established, 63
Las Casas, Bartolomé de: arrives in Puerto Rico and Española in 1520, 208–9; arrives in Spain in 1517, 183; arrives at Santo Domingo in 1517, 174; asks abolition of encomiendas, 165–66, 174; departs Cuba for Santo Domingo and Spain in 1515, 154–55; departs for Española in 1520, 183; departs for Spain in 1517, 174; departs from Spain in 1516, 170; departs Venezuela for Santo Domingo, 209; effect of battle of Caonao on, 118; effect of Dominicans on, 152–53; forms colonization company, 209; influence at court, 1517–20, 182–84, 186; in Higüey campaign, 57–58; mentioned, vii; named Protector of the Indians, 170; on Cuba, 121; ordained a priest, 154, 259*n;* plans to colonize Venezuela, 204; reform efforts evaluated, 189; writes instructions for Jeronymites, 169
Lebrón, Cristóbal: arrives at Santo Domingo, 159; named *juez de residencia* on Española, 148; named *oidor* at Santo Domingo, 202, 218; takes *residencia* of Figueroa and Flores, 218
Lerma, García de, 195, 223
Lizaur, Francisco, 180
Loaisa, Alonso, 151
Loaisa, García de, 219
López de Recalde, Juan, 94
Louis VIII, king of France, 15
Louis XII, king of France: presses claims in Italy, 90, 122; war with Ferdinand, 33
Lucayos, 133

Manso, Alonso: arrives at Caparra, 106, 156; holds encomienda at Caparra, 157; named apostolic inquisitor, 221; named *teniente* of Puerto Rico, 215, 221; returns to Puerto Rico, 189, 220; returns to Spain, 80, 113
Manuel I, king of Portugal, 196
Manzanedo, Bernaldino de: departs for Spain, 174; selected as commissioner on Española, 168
Manzorro-Becerra clan: mentioned, 134, 138. *See also* Manzorro, Rodrigo
Manzorro, Rodrigo, 79
Margarit, Pedro: captain of Fort Santo Tomás, 25; returns to Spain, 26–27
Márques, Diego, 26, 238*n*
Marriage, interracial: in Jaraguá, 60–61; of Spaniards and *cacicas,* 59–60; on Española, 75. *See also* Garcés, Juan
Matienzo, Sancho de: first treasurer of Casa de Contratación, 53; mentioned, 185
Maximilian, Emperor, 92, 122
Mazuelo, Pedro de, 110, 130
Medina Sidonia, Duke of: mentioned, 90; revolt of, 91
Méndez, Diego: acquires coat of arms, 228; *alquacil mayor* at Santo Domingo, 213; at Jacmel, 61; career sketched, 266*n;* voyage to Española in 1509, 137

Mendoza, Alonso de, 164
Mendoza, Cristóbal de: *procurador* for Puerto Rico, 178; replaces Moscoso as *teniente* at San Germán, 107
Mestizos, 23
Mejía Trillo, Rodrigo, 63
Migrations, 125–26, 225, 270*n*
Miners, 73
Missionary work: on Española, 37–39; scarcity of friars, 54
Mona Island: leased to Barrionuevo, 206; provision station for Puerto Rico, 97
Montesinos, Antonio de: arrives at Santo Domingo, 151; asks abolition of encomiendas, 165–67; departs for Spain, 1515, 155; on mission to Venezuela, 155; preaches against encomienda, 152; returns to Spain, 1512, 152
Monzón, Cortes of, 122
Morales, Francisco de: at the Bay of Nipe, 114; expelled from Cuba, 115; on Cuban expedition, 113
Moreno, Pedro, fiscal of *audiencia*, 218
Moreno, Pedro, vecino of Puerto Rico: ejected from Ponce de León's house, 101; named *teniente* of Puerto Rico, 210; *procurador* for Puerto Rico, 131; returns to Puerto Rico in 1512, 139
Moscoso, Rodrigo, 106
Mosquera, Juan, 78–79
Mújica, Andrés de, 43

Naborias: defined, 14; mentioned, 84–85, 133–34
Narbonne, Treaty of, 15
Narváez, Pánfilo de: arrives in Cuba from Jamaica, 114; exploration of Cuba, 117–19; joins Velázquez at Jagua, 118–19; mentioned, 81, 111; *purcurador* for Cuba, 95, 164, 168
Navarro, Pedro, 121–22
Nicuesa, Diego de: at Concepción, 80; mentioned, 53; *procurador* for Concepción de la Vega, 130; sails for Panama, 109, 134–35; signs contract to settle Panama, 95
Niño, Peralonso: departs Cádiz for Española, 33; returns from Española, 31–32; voyage to Pearl Coast, 50
Nitainos: defined, 12, 14; given title as caciques, 64
Nueva Cádiz: established, 205; reestablished in 1521, 208
Nuevo Toledo, 210
Núñez de Balboa, Vasco, 142
Núñez de Guzmán, Pedro: arrives in Cuba, 226; member of Velázquez clan, 81

Ocampo, Gonzalo de: heads expedition to Venezuela, 207–9; mentioned, 223
Ocampo, Sebastián, 112
Ojeda, Alonso de, explorer: *alcaide* at Santo Tomás, 25; explores inland from Isabela, 23; inaugurates Pearl Coast voyages, 49; intrusion at Jacmel, 43; mentioned, 19–20; returns to Española from Panama, 142; sails for Panama, 109; signs contract to settle Panama, 95
Ojeda, Alonso de, slaver in Paria trade: captures Indians on Cumaná River, 206; killed by Indians, 207
Oristán, 111
Ortiz, Tomás, 155
Ortiz de Matienzo, Juan: appellate judge on Española, 144; charged with immoral conduct, 175–76; conducts investigation at Santiago de Cuba, 212–13
Ovalle, Gonzalo de: named *teniente* at Santo Domingo, 211; named *teniente* of Cuba, 213
Ovando, Nicolás de: accomplishments of, 68; appointed governor of Española, 51; departure for Jaraguá, 61; expedition to Española, 53–54; expropriated Diaz's and Garay's gold mines, 78; local government under, 145–46; makes contract with Ponce de León, 96, 99; mentioned, ix, 3; property on Española, 73, 76, 245*n*
Ozama River, 34

Padilla, García de, 156
Pane, Ramón: contribution to anthropology, 39; mentioned, 16; missionary work in the Vega, 38–39
Pasamonte, Esteban, 224
Pasamonte, Miguel de: arrival at Santo Domingo, 94; as manager of royal mines, 128; career sketched and appointment as treasurer general, 93–94, 217; encomiendas held, 100, 163
Patronato Real: and bulls of 1504 and 1508, 156, 259–60*n;* bull issued in

final form, 149, 155–56; bull of 1510, 259–60*n*
Paz, Pedro de: arrives in Cuba, 226; member of Velázquez clan, 81
Pearls: few obtained owing to fear of Caribs, 135–36; first acquired by Columbus, 40–41; fishing for regularized in 1520, 205; obtained off Cubagua, 172
Pedrarias, 121
Peña, Juan de la, 141
Pérez, Cristóbal, 109–10
Pérez de Almazán, Miguel, 176
Philip the Handsome, king of Castile: death of, 4, 91; mentioned, 4; negotiations with Ferdinand V, 89–90
Pinelo, Francisco, 53
Pinzón, Martín Alonso: arrival in Galicia, 15; barters for gold, 14; mentioned, 10; rejoins Columbus off La Navidad, 14
Piritú, 155, 172
Ponce, Hernán, 139
Ponce de León, Isabel, 227
Ponce de León, Juan: arrests Cerón and Díaz, 101; career after 1511, 227; *criado* of Don Pedro Núñez de Guzmán, 19, 82; death of, 230; explorations and settlement of Puerto Rico, 96–98; in Higüey campaign, 58; in Taíno revolt of 1511, 103–4; marriage, 82; mentioned, ix, 95, 256*n;* mining contract with king, 96, 127; named *adelantado*, 139; named Captain of Sea and Land, 106; named governor of Puerto Rico, 100; residence at Salvaleón de Higüey, 58, 73, 82; resigns mining contract, 100
Ponce de León, Juana, 227–28
Ponce de León, Luis, 228
Ponce de León, María, 227–28
Population: decline of Indians, 74, 95, 124–25, 161–62, 176, 189–90, 191–92, 265*n;* of Indians on Jamaica, 111; of Spaniards on Española, 65, 136
Porcallo de Figueroa, Vasco: conduct investigated by *audiencia*, 212–13; mentioned, 140; named *teniente* at Trinidad, Cuba, 212
Poupet, Carlos de, Monsieur de la Chaulx, 183
Puerto de Príncipe, 120
Puerto Plata, 66, 79
Puerto Real, 63
Ramírez de Fuenleal, Sebastián, 220
Ramos, Diego, 228
Repartimiento: and royal mines, 71; assigned in Higüey, 59; of 1514, 159, 164, 171, 244*n;* on Cuba, 115; on Puerto Rico, 100; origins under Columbus, 44–45; under Ovando, 64. *See also* Encomienda
Rodríquez, Cristóbal, 86–87
Rodríquez de Fonseca, Juan: dismissed from office, 169; mentioned, 15; outfitter of ships for Indies, 31, 52; receives encomiendas, 92, 163; replacement considered, 32; restored to office in 1518, 184; supporter of Diego Velázquez, 80–81; tries to offset Diego Colón's powers, 198, 201–3, 212
Roldán, Bartolomé: death of, 11; property in Santo Domingo, 73, 235*n*
Roldán, Francisco: agreement with Columbus, 41–43; death of, 55, 240–41*n;* heads revolt on Vega, 35; mentioned, viii; negotiations with Bartolomé Colón, 37; with Columbus, 41–42; recommended by archbishop of Toledo, 19–20; *residencia* taken, 54; succeeds to position of *alcalde mayor*, 36; withdrawal to Jaraguá, 37, 39
Romano, Alonso, 197
Royal Council, 5
Ruiz, Francisco de: baptizes Indians on Española, 84; recruiter of Franciscans, 54; reports gold discovery to Ferdinand, 49
Ruiz, Pedro, 142–43

Salazar, Diego de: escapes Taíno attack, 103; founds Sotomayor, 102
Salvaleón de Higüey, 58
Salvatierra de la Sabana: base for Cuban expedition, 113; established by Diego Velázquez, 63
Sánchez de Carvajal, Alonso, 40
San Cristóbal, 34
San Cristóbal de Habana, 120
San Germán: expedition to in 1512, 106; founded, 105
San Juan de la Maguana, 63
San Juan de Puerto Rico, 223
Sancti Spíritus, 119
Santa Clara, Bernardino, 76
Santa Clara, Cristóbal: merchant and treasurer at Santo Domingo, 76; misspends treasury funds, 73
Santa Catarina, 30

Santa Cruz de Aycagua: depopulation of, 125; established, 58; producer of cassava, 66
Santa Fe de Chichiribichí, 173, 204
Santiago de Cuba, 120
Santiago de los Caballeros, 30, 57
Santiago del Daguao, 107
Santo Domingo: destroyed by hurricane, 55; early growth of, 41; establishment of, 44, 238–39*n;* rebuilt in 1502, 55
Santo Domingo, Alonso de: death of, 220; selected as commissioner on Española, 168
Santo Domingo, Bernardo de, 154
Santo Tomás, 24
Saona Island, 57
Sarmiento, Alonso, 96
Sauvage, Jean, 183
Sedeño, Antonio, 129
Serrano, Antonio: *procurador* for Española, 182; *procurador* for Santo Domingo, 130
Sevilla la Nueva, 109
Siboneys, 12, 121
Slavery, Indian: first incident of on Cuba, 112; in Higüey campaign, 58; on Bahamas, 133, 171; on Puerto Rico, 103–4, 249*n;* on Spanish Main, 133, 171–72, 205–6, 209; origins on Española, 28–29; on Pearl Coast, 50; practiced by Bartolomé Colón, 42; slaves carried by Niño, 32
Slavery, Negro: connection with Indian death rate, 85, 190–91, 265*n;* contract of 1518, 184; employed in mines, 74, 190–91; mentioned, 64
Smelters, 67
Sotomayor, Cristóbal de: immigrant to Puerto Rico, 99; killed by Taínos, 103; mentioned, 100, 102; settles at Guaymá, 100
Sotomayor, Diego de: killed by Taínos, 103; mentioned, 102
Suárez de Deza, Pedro: arrives at Concepción, 151, 156; death of, 220; departs for Spain, 157
Sugarcane: origins of on Española, 224; redeployment of Indian labor in, 176, 188

Taínos, Cuba: naive strategy of, 115; resistance to Spaniards, 120
Taínos, Española: belief in animism, 21; goldbeating practiced, 13; migrations of, 12; partial resettlement of on Española, 176, 187–88, 192, 248*n;* weapons of, 15
Taínos, Puerto Rico: estimate of population, 97; location of, 97; resistance to Spanish control, 75, 102–4
Tapia, Cristóbal de: arrested by Jeronymites, 173; elected to assembly of Española *procuradores,* 182; mentioned, 256*n; veedor* in San Cristóbal mines, 138
Tapia, Francisco de: *alcaide* at Santo Domingo, 138; marriage of son, 229; mentioned, 256*n*
Tiedra, Vasco de, 139
Tisín, Juan: accompanies Velázquez to Cuba, 150; mentioned, 16
Tithes: Bull of 1501 acquired by king, 51; gold excluded from, 156; increase after 1520, 221
Toledo, Cortes of, 3
Toledo, María de: mentioned, 137; named co-governor of Española in 1514, 148; returns to Española in 1520, 203; returns to Spain in 1518, 186
Torres, Antonio de: arrives at Isabela, 28; considered for quartermaster of Indies navigation, 32; death of, 241*n;* mentioned, 24; return to Spain in 1495, 28
Torres, Diego de: elected Franciscan provincial, 155; death of, 155
Towns: coats of arms on Española, 74; elections in on Española, 70
Trasierra, Juan de, 46
Treasury, 51–52, 67
Tribute, 29
Trinidad, Cuba, 119
Troche, García: marries Juana Ponce de León, 227–28; mentioned, 225
Troche, Gaspar: marries María Ponce de León, 227–28; mentioned, 225
Troche, Vasco, 225

Urbina, Duke of, 68
Ureña, Count of: mentioned, 67

Valladolid, Cortes of, 182, 197–98
Vallejo, Francisco de, 208
Vázquez de Ayllón, Lucas: *alcalde mayor* at Concepción, 68; appellate judge on Española, 138, 144; attempts to prevent conflict in New Spain, 218; departs for Spain in 1521, 215; elected *procurador general* of 1518 assembly, 182; last

years and death of, 230; marriage to Juan Becerra's daughter, 79–80; mentioned, 53, 190, 223; named *juez de residencia* of Puerto Rico, 215, 218; views on urbanizing Indians, 174
Vázquez de Mella, Pedro, 224, 229
Vega, Battle of the, 28–29, 238*n*
Vega, Hernando de: holds encomienda, 163; mentioned, 145
Velázquez, Antonio, 131, 164
Velázquez, Bernaldino, 178
Velázquez clan. *See* Velázquez, Diego
Velázquez, Diego: career summarized, 80–81; *criado* of Bartolomé Colón, 19, 137; departs Salvatierra de la Sabana for Cuba, 113, 251*n;* encomiendas on Española, 81; establishes Salvatierra de la Sabana, 63; establishes towns in Oriente province, 119; mentioned, 63, 80, 139, 161; mining contract with king, 127, 130; named *adelantado* of Yucatán, 211; property on Cuba, 228; resumes power as governor of Cuba, 213; selected to lead Cuban expedition, 113
Velázquez, Francisco, brother of Sancho, 215
Velázquez, Francisco, vecino of Española and Cuba, 71
Velázquez, Sancho: death of, 189; fiscal of the *audiencia,* 144; named *juez de residencia* on Puerto Rico, 147, 160; personality of, 188; takes *residencia* of Ponce de León, 129
Verapaz, 63
Vespucci, Amerigo, 94
Villafáfila, 90
Villalobos, Marcelo de: appellate judge on Española, 144; conducts investigation at Santiago de Cuba, 212
Villoria, Juan de: marriages of daughters, 229; mentioned, 79, 223
Visitador, 64
Vithern, Juan: at Cumaná, 196; returns to Cumaná in 1521, 208

Yucayeque, 162
Yaguana, Santa María del Puerto de, 162
Yáñez Pinzón, Vicente: contracts to settle Puerto Rico, 89; mentioned, 112

Zapata, Luis, 163
Zuazo, Alonso: arrives at Santo Domingo, 173; departs Spain for Española, 170; educational background, 170; *juez de residencia* for Española and Puerto Rico, 169–70, 175; mentioned, 159; named *juez de residencia* of Cuba, 211; *oidor* at Santo Domingo, 227; supports restoration of Diego Colón, 196–97

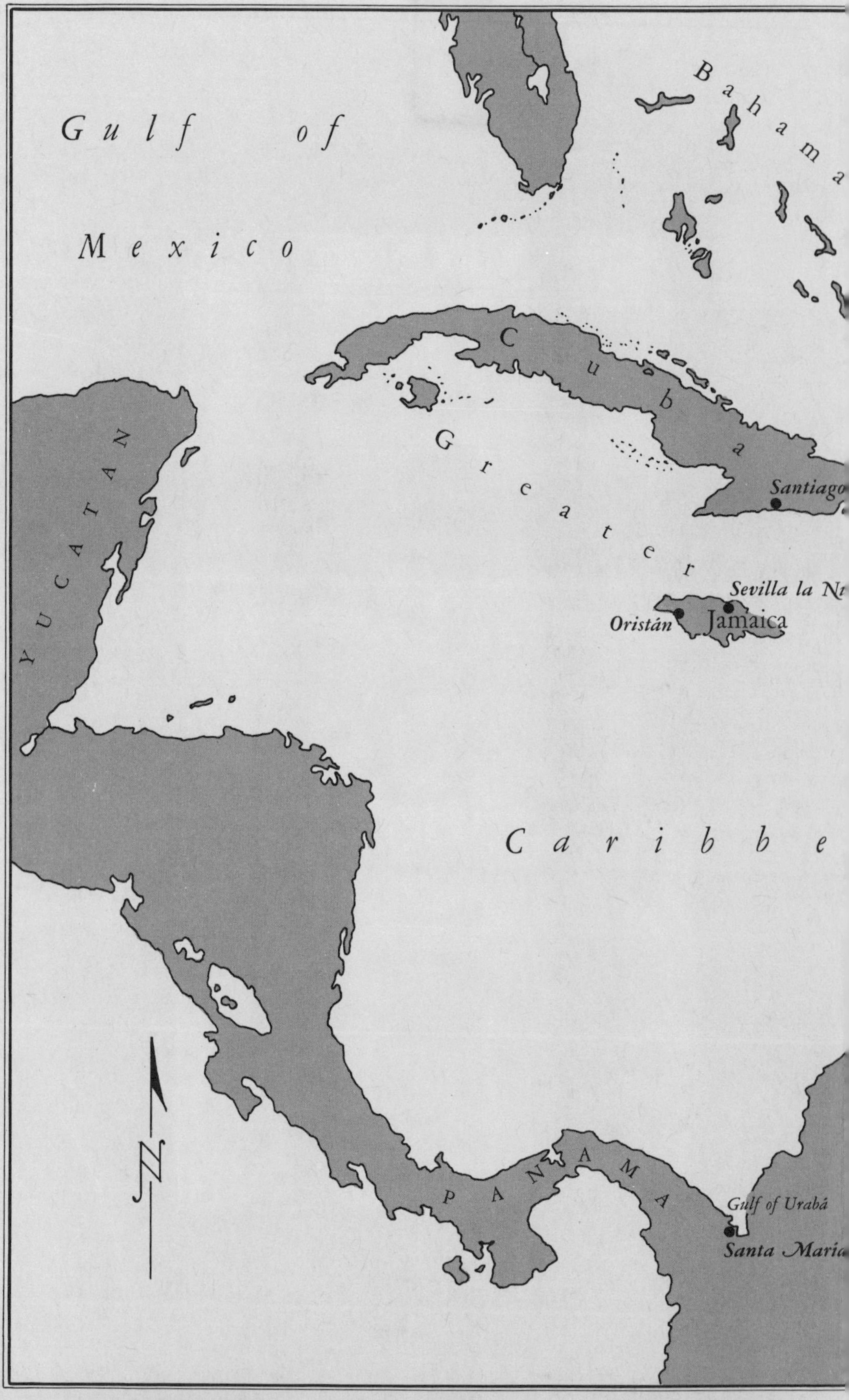

Gulf of

Mexico

Bahama

Cuba

Greater

YUCATAN

Santiago

Sevilla la N

Oristán

Jamaica

Caribbe

PANAMA

Gulf of Urabá

Santa Mari